T0338767

Multimedia and Sensory Input for Augmented, Mixed, and Virtual Reality

Amit Kumar Tyagi
Vellore Institute of Technolgy, Chennai, India

A volume in the Advances in Computational
Intelligence and Robotics (ACIR) Book Series

Published in the United States of America by
    IGI Global
    Engineering Science Reference (an imprint of IGI Global)
    701 E. Chocolate Avenue
    Hershey PA, USA 17033
    Tel: 717-533-8845
    Fax: 717-533-8661
    E-mail: cust@igi-global.com
    Web site: http://www.igi-global.com

Copyright © 2021 by IGI Global. All rights reserved. No part of this publication may be reproduced, stored or distributed in any form or by any means, electronic or mechanical, including photocopying, without written permission from the publisher. Product or company names used in this set are for identification purposes only. Inclusion of the names of the products or companies does not indicate a claim of ownership by IGI Global of the trademark or registered trademark.

Library of Congress Cataloging-in-Publication Data

Names: Tyagi, Amit, editor.
Title: Multimedia and sensory input for augmented, mixed, and virtual
  reality / Amit Tyagi, editor.
Description: Hershey, PA : Information Science Reference, an imprint of IGI
  Global, [2021] | Includes bibliographical references and index. |
  Summary: "This book touches on many possible use of augmented and
  virtual reality in many industries or sectors, and also discusses
  essential terms importance, challenges and opportunities for researchers
  or industry partners"-- Provided by publisher.
Identifiers: LCCN 2020035626 (print) | LCCN 2020035627 (ebook) | ISBN
  9781799847038 (hardcover) | ISBN 9781799870098 (paperback) | ISBN
  9781799847045 (ebook)
Subjects: LCSH: Multimedia systems. | Virtual reality. | Haptic devices.
Classification: LCC QA76.575 .M7765 2021 (print) | LCC QA76.575 (ebook) |
  DDC 006.7--dc23
LC record available at https://lccn.loc.gov/2020035626
LC ebook record available at https://lccn.loc.gov/2020035627

This book is published in the IGI Global book series Advances in Computational Intelligence and Robotics (ACIR) (ISSN: 2327-0411; eISSN: 2327-042X)

British Cataloguing in Publication Data
A Cataloguing in Publication record for this book is available from the British Library.

All work contributed to this book is new, previously-unpublished material. The views expressed in this book are those of the authors, but not necessarily of the publisher.

For electronic access to this publication, please contact: eresources@igi-global.com.

Advances in Computational Intelligence and Robotics (ACIR) Book Series

Ivan Giannoccaro
University of Salento, Italy

ISSN:2327-0411
EISSN:2327-042X

MISSION

While intelligence is traditionally a term applied to humans and human cognition, technology has progressed in such a way to allow for the development of intelligent systems able to simulate many human traits. With this new era of simulated and artificial intelligence, much research is needed in order to continue to advance the field and also to evaluate the ethical and societal concerns of the existence of artificial life and machine learning.

The **Advances in Computational Intelligence and Robotics (ACIR) Book Series** encourages scholarly discourse on all topics pertaining to evolutionary computing, artificial life, computational intelligence, machine learning, and robotics. ACIR presents the latest research being conducted on diverse topics in intelligence technologies with the goal of advancing knowledge and applications in this rapidly evolving field.

COVERAGE

- Natural Language Processing
- Adaptive and Complex Systems
- Agent technologies
- Computational Intelligence
- Computer Vision
- Machine Learning
- Cyborgs
- Neural Networks
- Synthetic Emotions
- Robotics

IGI Global is currently accepting manuscripts for publication within this series. To submit a proposal for a volume in this series, please contact our Acquisition Editors at Acquisitions@igi-global.com or visit: http://www.igi-global.com/publish/.

The Advances in Computational Intelligence and Robotics (ACIR) Book Series (ISSN 2327-0411) is published by IGI Global, 701 E. Chocolate Avenue, Hershey, PA 17033-1240, USA, www.igi-global.com. This series is composed of titles available for purchase individually; each title is edited to be contextually exclusive from any other title within the series. For pricing and ordering information please visit http://www.igi-global.com/book-series/advances-computational-intelligence-robotics/73674. Postmaster: Send all address changes to above address. Copyright © 2021 IGI Global. All rights, including translation in other languages reserved by the publisher. No part of this series may be reproduced or used in any form or by any means – graphics, electronic, or mechanical, including photocopying, recording, taping, or information and retrieval systems – without written permission from the publisher, except for non commercial, educational use, including classroom teaching purposes. The views expressed in this series are those of the authors, but not necessarily of IGI Global.

Titles in this Series

For a list of additional titles in this series, please visit: http://www.igi-global.com/book-series/advances-computational-intelligence-robotics/73674

Applications of Artificial Intelligence for Smart Technology
P. Swarnalatha (Vellore Institute of Technology, Vellore, India) and S. Prabu (Vellore Institute of Technology, Vellore, India)
Engineering Science Reference • © 2021 • 330pp • H/C (ISBN: 9781799833352) • US $215.00

Resource Optimization Using Swarm Intelligence and the IoT
Vicente García Díaz (University of Oviedo, Spain) Pramod Singh Rathore (ACERC, Delhi, India) Abhishek Kumar (ACERC, Delhi, India) and Rashmi Agrawal (Manav Rachna University, India)
Engineering Science Reference • © 2021 • 300pp • H/C (ISBN: 9781799850953) • US $225.00

Deep Learning Applications and Intelligent Decision Making in Engineering
Karthikrajan Senthilnathan (Revoltaxe India Pvt Ltd, Chennai, India) Balamurugan Shanmugam (Quants IS & CS, India) Dinesh Goyal (Poornima Institute of Engineering and Technology, India) Iyswarya Annapoorani (VIT University, India) and Ravi Samikannu (Botswana International University of Science and Technology, Botswana)
Engineering Science Reference • © 2021 • 332pp • H/C (ISBN: 9781799821083) • US $245.00

Handbook of Research on Natural Language Processing and Smart Service Systems
Rodolfo Abraham Pazos-Rangel (Tecnológico Nacional de México, Mexico & Instituto Tecnológico de Ciudad Madero, Mexico) Rogelio Florencia-Juarez (Universidad Autónoma de Ciudad Juárez, Mexico) Mario Andrés Paredes-Valverde (Tecnológico Nacional de México, Mexico & Instituto Tecnológico de Orizaba, Mexico) and Gilberto Rivera (Universidad Autónoma de Ciudad Juárez, Mexico)
Engineering Science Reference • © 2021 • 554pp • H/C (ISBN: 9781799847304) • US $295.00

Applications of Artificial Neural Networks for Nonlinear Data
Hiral Ashil Patel (Ganpat University, India) and A.V. Senthil Kumar (Hindusthan College of Arts and Science, India)
Engineering Science Reference • © 2021 • 315pp • H/C (ISBN: 9781799840428) • US $245.00

Analyzing Future Applications of AI, Sensors, and Robotics in Society
Thomas Heinrich Musiolik (Berlin University of the Arts, Germany) and Adrian David Cheok (iUniversity, Tokyo, Japan)
Engineering Science Reference • © 2021 • 335pp • H/C (ISBN: 9781799834991) • US $225.00

701 East Chocolate Avenue, Hershey, PA 17033, USA
Tel: 717-533-8845 x100 • Fax: 717-533-8661
E-Mail: cust@igi-global.com • www.igi-global.com

Editorial Advisory Board

Samaher Al Janabi, *University of Babylon, Iraq*

A. Amuthan, *Pondicherry Engineering College, Puducherry, India*

Abhishek Bhattacharya, *Whrrl, India*

Robertas Damasevicius, *Kaunas University of Technology, Lithuania*

Nebojša Bačanin Džakula, *Faculty of Informatics and Computing, Singidunum University, Serbia*

Richa Goyal, *J. L. N. Government College, Haryana, India*

R. Jagadeesh Kannan, *School of Computer Science and Engineering, Vellore Institute of Technology, Chennai, India*

Rajesh S. Karvande, *Ministry of Defence, Hyderabad, India*

Kailash Kumar, *College of Computing and Informatics (CCI), Saudi Electronic University, Riyadh, Saudi Arabia*

Magdy Mahmoud, *Computer Science and Information System, Ismailia, Egypt*

Shaveta Malik, *Terna Engineering College, Mumbai, India*

Sanjay Misra, *Covenant University, Nigeria*

Shalini Rajawat, *Poornima University, Rajasthan, India*

Ashraf Saad, *Department of Computer Science and Information Technology, Armstrong Atlantic State University, USA*

Niloy Sarkar, *The Neotia University, India*

Sobhan Sarkar, *Management Science Division, Business School, University of Edinburgh, UK*

Lalit Singh, *BARC, Department of Atomic Energy, Government of India, India*

Pooja Singh, *Department of Mathematics, VJTI, Mumbai, India*

N. Sreenath, *Pondicherry Engineering College, Puducherry, India*

Table of Contents

Preface xvi

Acknowledgment xxii

Chapter 1
An Useful Review on Optical Character Recognition for Smart Era Generation 1
    Abhishek Das, ITER, Siksha 'O' Anusandhan (Deemed), India
    Mihir Narayan Mohanty, ITER, Siksha 'O' Anusandhan (Deemed), India

Chapter 2
Using IoTs-Based Monitoring System in a Smart Ambulance for E-Healtcare Applications: A
Systematic Review 42
    Aswathy S. U., Jothy Engineering College, Kerala, India
    Ajesh F., Musaliar College of Engineering and Technology, India
    Felix M. Philip, Jain University (Deemed), Kochi, India

Chapter 3
Augmented and Virtual Reality and Its Applications 68
    S. Graceline Jasmine, Vellore Institute of Technology, Chennai, India
    L. Jani Anbarasi, Vellore Institute of Technology, Chennai, India
    Modigari Narendra, Vignan's Foundation for Science, Technology, and Research (Deemed),
        India
    Benson Edwin Raj, Higher College of Technology, Fujairah Women's Campus, Fujairah,
        UAE

Chapter 4
Comparison Analysis of Prediction Model for Respiratory Diseases 86
    Priya R. L., Noorul Islam Centre for Higher Education, India
    S. Vinila Jinny, Noorul Islam Centre for Higher Education, India

Chapter 5
Dynamic Data Mining Based on the Stability of Dynamic Models 99
    Hocine Chebi, Faculty of Electrical Engineering, Djillali Liabes University, Sidi Bel Abbes,
        Algeria

Chapter 6
Augmented Reality Application: AR Learning Platform for Primary Education............................ 118
    S. Geetha, Vellore Institute of Technology, Chennai, India
    L. Jani Anbarasi, Vellore Institute of Technology, Chennai, India
    Arya Vardhan Prasad, Vellore Institute of Technology, Chennai, India
    Aayush Gupta, Vellore Institute of Technology, Chennai, India
    Benson Edwin Raj, Higher College of Technology, Fujairah Women's Campus, Fujairah, UAE

Chapter 7
Analyzing Knowledge Representation of University Ontology Through Semantic Web:
Representation of University Ontology 134
    Juli Kumari, Indira Gandhi Delhi Technical University for Women (IGDTUW), India
    Deepak Kumar, Amity University, Noida, India
    Ela Kumar, Indira Gandhi Delhi Technical University for Women (IGDTUW), India

Chapter 8
Efficient Virtual Reality-Based Platform for Virtual Concerts 148
    Roshan Fernandes, NMAM Institute of Technology, India
    Arjun P. Gaonkar, NMAM Institute of Technology, India
    Pratheek J. Shenoy, NMAM Institute of Technology, India
    Anisha P. Rodrigues, NMAM Institute of Technology, India
    Mohan B. A., Nitte Meenakshi Institute of Technology, India
    Vijaya Padmanabha, Modern College of Business and Science, Oman

Chapter 9
Increasing Participation in Large-Scale Virtual Environments: Rethinking the Ecological
Cognition Frameworks for the Augmented, Mixed, and Virtual Reality 165
    Jonathan Bishop, Crocels Community Media Group, UK

Chapter 10
LIFI-Based Radiation-Free Monitoring and Transmission Device for Hospitals/Public Places 195
    T. Ananth kumar, IFET College of Engineering, India
    T. S. Arun Samuel, National Engineering College, Kovilpatti, India
    P. Praveen kumar, IFET College of Engineering, India
    M. Pavithra, IFET College of Engineering, India
    R. Raj Mohan, IFET College of Engineering, India

Chapter 11
The Gamification in Education, Healthcare, and Industry 206
    Puvvadi Baby Maruthi, Sri Venkateswara College of Engineering, Tirupathi, India

Chapter 12
Multimedia Data Transmission: Algorithm to Improve Reliability in Multimedia Data
Transmission 233
 Deepalakshmi Rajendran, Velammal College of Engineering and Technology, India
 Vijayalakshmi R., Velammal College of Engineering and Technology, India

Chapter 13
Optimal Camera Placement in a Virtual Environment 247
 Hocine Chebi, Université Sidi Bel Abbes, Algeria

Chapter 14
Scalable Data Analysis Application to Web Usage Data.. 261
 Hocine Chebi, Faculty of Electrical Engineering, Djillali Liabes University, Sidi Bel Abbes.
  Algeria

Chapter 15
Current Trends, Challenges, and Future Prospects for Augmented Reality and Virtual Reality........ 275
 Sathiya Narayanan, School of Electronics Engineering, Vellore Institute of Technology,
  Chennai, India
 Nikshith Narayan Ramesh, School of Electronics Engineering, Vellore Institute of
  Technology, Chennai, India
 Amit Kumar Tyagi, Research Division of Advanced Data Science, Vellore Institute of
  Technology, Chennai, India
 L. Jani Anbarasi, School of Computer Science and Engineering, Vellore Institute of
  Technology, Chennai, India
 Benson Edwin Raj, Higher Colleges of Technology, Fujairah, UAE

Compilation of References 282

About the Contributors 303

Index 309

Detailed Table of Contents

Preface xvi

Acknowledgment xxii

Chapter 1

An Useful Review on Optical Character Recognition for Smart Era Generation 1

Abhishek Das, ITER, Siksha 'O' Anusandhan (Deemed), India
Mihir Narayan Mohanty, ITER, Siksha 'O' Anusandhan (Deemed), India

In this chapter, the authors have reviewed on optical character recognition. The study belongs to both typed characters and handwritten character recognition. Online and offline character recognition are two modes of data acquisition in the field of OCR and are also studied. As deep learning is the emerging machine learning method in the field of image processing, the authors have described the method and its application of earlier works. From the study of the recurrent neural network (RNN), a special class of deep neural network is proposed for the recognition purpose. Further, convolutional neural network (CNN) is combined with RNN to check its performance. For this piece of work, Odia numerals and characters are taken as input and well recognized. The efficacy of the proposed method is explained in the result section.

Chapter 2

Using IoTs-Based Monitoring System in a Smart Ambulance for E-Healtcare Applications: A Systematic Review 42

Aswathy S. U., Jothy Engineering College, Kerala, India
Ajesh F., Musaliar College of Engineering and Technology, India
Felix M. Philip, Jain University (Deemed), Kochi, India

In today's world, traffic jams during rush hours are a major concern. During rush hours, emergency vehicles like ambulances get stuck in jams. The smart ambulance systems are most suitable to provide clearance to emergency vehicles during rush hours. Many systems are used to implement the smart ambulance systems. The primary objective is to identify the emergency vehicle and track its location so that wireless signals to the emergency vehicles can be provided. Conventional technologies use image processing systems to identify the emergency vehicle. But these systems have a drawback during bad weather conditions. Due to wind, rain, fog, etc., the image received by the camera is distorted by noise and it becomes difficult for the system to identify the desired vehicle. In this chapter, the authors discuss in detail the existing techniques on smart ambulance based on IoT using zig bee, GSM module, Adriano, Raspberry Pi, etc., its drawback, and its future scope.

Chapter 3
Augmented and Virtual Reality and Its Applications 68
    S. Graceline Jasmine, Vellore Institute of Technology, Chennai, India
    L. Jani Anbarasi, Vellore Institute of Technology, Chennai, India
    Modigari Narendra, Vignan's Foundation for Science, Technology, and Research (Deemed),
        India
    Benson Edwin Raj, Higher College of Technology, Fujairah Women's Campus, Fujairah,
        UAE

Augmented reality (AR) overlies manually made materials directly over the real-world materials. This chapter addresses the technological and design frameworks required to create realistic motion tracking environments, realistic audio, 3D graphical interactions, multimodal sensory integration, and user interfaces and games using virtual reality to augmented reality. Similarly, the portfolio required to build a personal VR or AR application is detailed. Virtual and augmented reality industry committed innovative technologies that can be explored in the field of entertainment, education, training, medical and industrial innovation, and the development are explored. Augmented reality (AR) allows the physical world to be enhanced by incorporating digital knowledge in real time created by virtual machine. Few applications that have used augmented and virtual reality in real-world applications are discussed.

Chapter 4
Comparison Analysis of Prediction Model for Respiratory Diseases.. 86
    Priya R. L., Noorul Islam Centre for Higher Education, India
    S. Vinila Jinny, Noorul Islam Centre for Higher Education, India

Millions of people around the world have one or many respiratory-related illnesses. Many chronic respiratory diseases like asthma, COPD, pneumonia, respiratory distress, etc. are considered to be a significant public health burden. To reduce the mortality rate, it is better to perform early prediction of respiratory disorders and treat them accordingly. To build an efficient prediction model for various types of respiratory diseases, machine learning approaches are used. The proposed methodology builds classifier model using supervised learning algorithms like random forest, decision tree, and multi-layer perceptron neural network (MLP-NN) for the detection of different respiratory diseases of ICU admitted patients. It achieves accuracy of nearly 99% by various machine learning approaches.

Chapter 5
Dynamic Data Mining Based on the Stability of Dynamic Models 99
    Hocine Chebi, Faculty of Electrical Engineering, Djillali Liabes University, Sidi Bel Abbes,
        Algeria

This work presents a new approach based on the use of stable dynamic models for dynamic data mining. Data mining is an essential technique in the process of extracting knowledge from data. This allows us to model the extracted knowledge using a formalism or a modeling technique. However, the data needed for knowledge extraction is collected in advance, and it can take a long time to collect. The objective is therefore to move towards a solution based on the modeling of systems using dynamic models and to study their stability. Stable dynamic models provide us with a basis for dynamic data mining. In order to achieve this objective, the authors propose an approach based on agent-based models, the concept of fixed points, and the Monte-Carlo method. Agent-based models can represent dynamic models that mirror or simulate a dynamic system, where such a model can be viewed as a source of data (data generators).

In this work, the concept of fixed points was used in order to represent the stable states of the agent-based model. Finally, the Monte-Carlo method, which is a probabilistic method, was used to estimate certain values, using a very large number of experiments or runs. As a case study, the authors chose the evacuation system of a supermarket (or building) in case of danger, such as a fire. This complex system mainly comprises the various constituent elements of the building, such as rows of shelves, entry and exit doors, fire extinguishers, etc. In addition, these buildings are often filled with people of different categories (age, health, etc.). The use of the Monte-Carlo method allowed the authors to experiment with several scenarios, which allowed them to have more data to study this system and extract some knowledge. This knowledge allows us to predict the future situation regarding the building's evacuation system and anticipate improvements to its structure in order to make these buildings safer and prevent the greatest number of victims.

Chapter 6

Augmented Reality Application: AR Learning Platform for Primary Education............................ 118

    S. Geetha, Vellore Institute of Technology, Chennai, India
    L. Jani Anbarasi, Vellore Institute of Technology, Chennai, India
    Arya Vardhan Prasad, Vellore Institute of Technology, Chennai, India
    Aayush Gupta, Vellore Institute of Technology, Chennai, India
    Benson Edwin Raj, Higher College of Technology, Fujairah Women's Campus, Fujairah,
        UAE

Augmented reality (AR) is an extension of extended reality that superimposes virtual images onto real world view. It has been implemented across a versatile range of fields including education, entertainment, military, and much more. Unlike virtual reality (VR), AR focuses on enhancing the real-world view and enriching people with a better way to display the learning content in an attractive way. AR provides content simulation and interaction which can display textual data in a more immersive way which can retain learner's concentration for longer periods of time. Technology has always helped people with disabilities. Mentally differently abled children require special attention right from their childhood. Many applications have analysed the challenges faced on a daily basis by the differently abled. Hence, AR-based learning would make their learning much more easier through the personalized and immersive platform. In the given context, this chapter analyses the use of AR in education and developed an AR-learning platform for mentally differently abled based on Unity3D and Vuforia.

Chapter 7

Analyzing Knowledge Representation of University Ontology Through Semantic Web:
Representation of University Ontology 134

    Juli Kumari, Indira Gandhi Delhi Technical University for Women (IGDTUW), India
    Deepak Kumar, Amity University, Noida, India
    Ela Kumar, Indira Gandhi Delhi Technical University for Women (IGDTUW), India

Nowadays, people are using lots of websites for searching and retrieving information. Most of the websites keep information in a simple format with all information simply linked with each other. Such type of information has less accuracy. So, there is utmost important to work on knowledge-based, information presentation. Hence, the advent of the semantic web called intelligent and meaningful web is a new trend in the area of web development. Ontology is a key term widely used in the development of the Semantic Web. It is an idea, which strongly focused on class, object, and relationship relatively than information. Protégé is a tool widely used for ontology development and customization. It has a user interface for ontology results visualization. It provides a view for a developer for a strong focus on creating knowledge rather than syntax. It provides the flexibility to add-on more additional features by the extendable plug-in. The purpose of this work is to develop a knowledge-based university system. Here, as an example of Indira Gandhi Delhi Technical University Delhi has been taken and created a university ontology using protégé tool. It also includes various aspects like classes, class hierarchy, superclass and subclass, and also created a subclass instance for designing class, class hierarchy, query searching, and retrieval process, and the result is demonstrated in graphical form.

Chapter 8
Efficient Virtual Reality-Based Platform for Virtual Concerts 148
    Roshan Fernandes, NMAM Institute of Technology, India
    Arjun P. Gaonkar, NMAM Institute of Technology, India
    Pratheek J. Shenoy, NMAM Institute of Technology, India
    Anisha P. Rodrigues, NMAM Institute of Technology, India
    Mohan B. A., Nitte Meenakshi Institute of Technology, India
    Vijaya Padmanabha, Modern College of Business and Science, Oman

Virtual reality is a computer-generated three-dimensional environment where seemingly real graphics are used to simulate an imaginary world. It is generally accessed by using a special VR helmet or spectacles which enable you to access this imaginary world. Virtual reality uses the concept of split-screen to project to different images to our eyes in a selected angle which makes our brain believe that we are viewing a three-dimensional image. This tricks the brain into thinking that the human is standing in a three-dimensional environment where they can move around. Over the years, virtual reality has been included in a lot of traditional fields to challenge the endless possibilities in those fields. It has been used in medical sciences to train doctors, the aerospace industry to train the pilots and astronauts, the architecture industry to obtain maximum efficiency in designing the structures, and many more fields. VR gaming is also becoming a huge market where people can interact with the game components to get a realistic experience of being in a game. VR is also being used by counselors and psychiatrists around the world to treat people with mental health problems. In this chapter, the authors use the concept of virtual reality in the live music industry to simulate realistic music concerts by designing and developing a platform to host virtual concerts using virtual reality.

Chapter 9
Increasing Participation in Large-Scale Virtual Environments: Rethinking the Ecological
Cognition Frameworks for the Augmented, Mixed, and Virtual Reality 165
    Jonathan Bishop, Crocels Community Media Group, UK

The proliferation of media-rich social networking services has changed the way people use information society and audio-visual media services. Existing theories of cognition in human-computer interaction have limitations in dealing with the unique problems that exist in contemporary virtual environments. The presence of significant numbers of people using these at the same time causes behavioural issues not previously envisaged at the time of multi-user domains (MUDs) or the first massively-multiplayer online role-playing games. To understand such large-scale virtual environments, this chapter makes use of data generated from questionnaires, usability testing, and social and web metrics to assess the relevance of ecological cognition theory for the current age. Through making use of a biometric measure called 'knol', the chapter suggests a new framework for measuring emotion and cognition in these and future environments.

Chapter 10

LIFI-Based Radiation-Free Monitoring and Transmission Device for Hospitals/Public Places 195

T. Ananth kumar, IFET College of Engineering, India

T. S. Arun Samuel, National Engineering College, Kovilpatti, India

P. Praveen kumar, IFET College of Engineering, India

M. Pavithra, IFET College of Engineering, India

R. Raj Mohan, IFET College of Engineering, India

A wireless patient monitoring system involves remote supervision of sensitive patients by wirelessly transmitting patient information to distant locations, especially in pandemic situations like COVID-19. Li-fi-based communication protocol is used in healthcare which helps in reducing the challenges faced by medical professionals in effectively monitoring multiple patients as well as average persons in public places. Due to COVID-19, doctors/healthcare workers are compelled to work with infected patients. This proposed technique lets them observe patients without being on their bedside, whether in the hospital or at home. This device can also be installed in public places to detect the abnormal and symptomatic persons who are affected by COVID-19. It is used to monitor patient health, ranging from heart rate, body temperature, ECG, breathing, non-invasive blood pressure, oxygen saturation, etc. Wireless patient monitoring using li-fi eliminates national therapy barriers. Thus, a li-fi-based patient monitoring system will lead to a significant role in Healthcare services. The radiation-free device shall be implemented in all the industries to find the COVID-19-affected persons easily.

Chapter 11

The Gamification in Education, Healthcare, and Industry.. 206

Puvvadi Baby Maruthi, Sri Venkateswara College of Engineering, Tirupathi, India

Wireless sensor networks (WSN) consist of large numbers of sensor nodes, which are limited in battery power and communication range and have multi-modal sensing capabilities. In this chapter, energy-efficient data aggregation technique is proposed to improve the lifetime of the sensor. Here, the author has used three layer architecture by deploying mobile element/node, which can periodically visit cluster heads (CHs) at which first level data aggregation has been applied to eliminate redundancy. After collecting data from all CHs, mobile element itself will perform second level of data aggregation to eliminate further redundancy. After collecting data from CHs, mobile element will move towards base station/ sink and transmits data to base station/sink in order to save energy of entire network. Here, the author has made an attempt to prove that in WSN during data gathering if mobile elements are used to collect the aggregated data from CHs, energy consumption of the entire network will be reduced. The proposed data aggregation with mobile node helps in improving the lifetime of the WSN.

Chapter 12

Multimedia Data Transmission: Algorithm to Improve Reliability in Multimedia Data
Transmission 233

Deepalakshmi Rajendran, Velammal College of Engineering and Technology, India

Vijayalakshmi R., Velammal College of Engineering and Technology, India

Investigating multimedia traffic over optical networks that provide extremely high data rates makes it a very attractive medium for multiservice transmission in building networks at low cost. Recently, there has been active research going on congestion control in optical networks to provide the communication reliability and bandwidth efficiency. The authors investigate the mutual diversity technique as a candidate solution for congestion control over multimedia traffic in optical network. This chapter proposes a new robust medium access control (MAC) protocol, called mutual diversity MAC (MD-MAC), where each terminal proactively selects a consort for mutual operation and lets it pass on concurrently so that this mitigates interference from nearby terminals and thus improves the reliability of network and its bandwidth efficiency. For meticulous evaluation, this study presents and uses a realistic reception by taking bit error rate (BER) and the corresponding frame error rate (FER) into consideration.

Chapter 13

Optimal Camera Placement in a Virtual Environment 247
Hocine Chebi, Université Sidi Bel Abbes, Algeria

Camera placement in a virtual environment consists of positioning and orienting a 3D virtual camera so as to respect a set of visual or cinematographic properties defined by the user. Carrying out this task is difficult in practice. Indeed, the user has a clear vision of the result he wants to obtain in terms of the arrangement of the objects in the image. In this chapter, the authors identify three areas of research that are relatively little covered by the literature dedicated to camera placement and which nevertheless appear essential. On the one hand, existing approaches offer little flexibility in both solving and describing a problem in terms of visual properties, especially when it has no solution. They propose a flexible solution method which computes the set of solutions, maximizing the satisfaction of the properties of the problem, whether it is over constrained or not. On the other hand, the existing methods calculate only one solution, even when the problem has several classes of equivalent solutions in terms of satisfaction of properties. They introduce the method of semantic volumes which computes the set of classes of semantically equivalent solutions and proposes a representative of each of them to the user. Finally, the problem of occlusion, although essential in the transmission of information, is little addressed by the community. Consequently, they present a new method of taking into account occlusion in dynamic real-time environments.

Chapter 14

Scalable Data Analysis Application to Web Usage Data 261
*Hocine Chebi, Faculty of Electrical Engineering, Djillali Liabes University, Sidi Bel Abbes.
Algeria*

The number of hits to web pages continues to grow. The web has become one of the most popular platforms for disseminating and retrieving information. Consequently, many website operators are encouraged to analyze the use of their sites in order to improve their response to the expectations of internet users. However, the way a website is visited can change depending on a variety of factors. Usage models must therefore be continuously updated in order to accurately reflect visitor behavior. This remains difficult when the time dimension is neglected or simply introduced as an additional numeric attribute in the description of the data. Data mining is defined as the application of data analysis and discovery algorithms on large databases with the goal of discovering non-trivial models. Several algorithms have been proposed in order to formalize the new models discovered, to build more efficient models, to process new types of data, and to measure the differences between the data sets. However, the most traditional algorithms of data mining assume that the models are static and do not take into account the possible evolution of these models over time. These considerations have motivated significant efforts in the analysis of temporal data as well as the adaptation of static data mining methods to data that evolves over time. The review of the main aspects of data mining dealt with in this thesis constitutes the body of this chapter, followed by a state of the art of current work in this field as well as a discussion of the major issues that exist there. Interest in temporal databases has increased considerably in recent years, for example in the fields of finance, telecommunications, surveillance, etc. A growing number of prototypes and systems are being implemented to take into account the time dimension of data explicitly, for example to study the variability over time of analysis results. To model an application, it is necessary to choose a common language, precise and known by all members of a team. UML (unified modeling language, in English, or unified modeling language, in French) is an object-oriented modeling language standardized by the OMG. This chapter aims to present the modeling with the diagrams of packages and classes built using UML. This chapter presents the conceptual model of the data, and finally, the authors specify the SQL queries used for the extraction of descriptive statistical variables of the navigations from a warehouse containing the preprocessed usage data.

Chapter 15
Current Trends, Challenges, and Future Prospects for Augmented Reality and Virtual Reality........ 275
> *Sathiya Narayanan, School of Electronics Engineering, Vellore Institute of Technology, Chennai, India*
> *Nikshith Narayan Ramesh, School of Electronics Engineering, Vellore Institute of Technology, Chennai, India*
> *Amit Kumar Tyagi, Research Division of Advanced Data Science, Vellore Institute of Technology, Chennai, India*
> *L. Jani Anbarasi, School of Computer Science and Engineering, Vellore Institute of Technology, Chennai, India*
> *Benson Edwin Raj, Higher Colleges of Technology, Fujairah, UAE*

In the recent years, innovations such as Augmented Reality (AR), Virtual Reality (VR), and internet of things have enhanced user experience dramatically. In general, AR is completely different from VR and provides real-time solutions to users by projecting layers of information on real-world environments. Advancements in computer-generated sensory have made the concept of believable virtual environments a reality. With the availability of such technologies, one can investigate "how these technologies can be applied beyond gaming or other useful applications" and "how further improvements can be made to allow for full digital immersion." This chapter provides a detailed description about AR and VR, followed by interesting real-world examples of AR applications. In addition, this chapter discusses the issues and challenges faced with AR/VR with a motivation of exploring the options for improvement.

Compilation of References 282

About the Contributors 303

Index 309

Preface

With the pace development in technology and reduce in price of Smart objects, today many great innovations have changed people life. These smart objects are using with several innovations and have made human life convenient to live, i.e., these innovations have made people life easier and longer to live. Notable among these innovations are Augmented Reality (AR), Virtual Reality (VR), and Internet of Things. In general, AR is completely differ from virtual reality, provides real-time solutions to users by projecting layers of information on real-world Environments. AR provide more meaningful user experiences than VR and have more possibility to use in many critical applications like manufacturing, e-healthcare, etc., to solve complex problems. Some low cost VR technologies like Oculus Rift, the HTC Vive and the Sony PlayStation VR are attracting attention of many youngsters and researchers, showing that it may be largest growth technology in near future (in technological innovation). AR is quickly becoming common place in our daily lives and in many information-sharing fields. Advancements in computer-generated sensory have made the concept of believable virtual environments a reality. With the availability of such technologies, new possibility are came out "how these technologies can be applied beyond gaming or other useful applications" and "how further improvements can be made to allow for full digital immersion".

Today's Augmented and Virtual Reality (AR and VR) offers exciting opportunities for Human Computer Interaction (HCI), the enhancement of places and new business cases. Augmented reality is technology that combines virtual reality with the real world in the form of live video imagery that is digitally enhanced with computer-generated graphics. Virtual reality means putting or feeling about things virtually. VR is most popular for video games, especially among young generation. AR and VR can be used in following applications like military AR use, Medical Personal use, Gaming AR use, Navigation AR use, Sightseeing in AR, Maintenance and Repair, Advertising and Promotion AR use. The Augmented Reality and Virtual Reality Conference organizers seek original, high-quality papers in all areas related to Augmented Reality (AR), Virtual Reality (VR), Mixed Reality (MR) and 3D user interfaces. This book aims to include many business case studies covering a variety of topics related to AR, VR, and MR including its use in possible applications. This book also try to touch every possible use of AR and VR in many industries or sectors, also discuss essential terms importance, challenges and opportunities for researchers or industry partners (for increasing the profit).

Hence, the overview of this book can be summarized as:

Summary of each chapter will be:

Chapter 1: A Useful Review on Optical Character Recognition for Smart Era Generation

In the new generation, different smart technologies are used for different image recognition purpose. In this chapter, we have reviewed the state-of-art for printed and handwritten character recognition like license plate recognition, TV scene text detection, and recognition, historical document restoration, meter reading recognition, mathematical expression recognition. This study is categorized into two groups i.e. Deep learning-based and other techniques. It is observed that the combined classifier is providing significant performance as compared to single models. So, combined models can be considered as suitable models in optical character recognition.

Chapter 2: Using IoT-Based Monitoring Systems in a Smart Ambulance for E-Healthcare Applications – A Systematic Review

In today's world, traffic jams during rush hours is one of the major concerns. During Rush hours, emergency vehicles like Ambulances get stuck in jams. The smart Ambulance systems are most suitable to provide clearance to emergency vehicles during rush hours .Many systems are used to implement the smart ambulance systems. The primary objective is to identify the emergency vehicle and track its location so that wireless signals to the emergency vehicles can be provided. Conventional technologies use image processing systems to identify the emergency vehicle. But these systems have a drawback during bad weather conditions. Due to wind, rain, fog, etc., the image received by the camera is distorted by noise and it becomes difficult for the system to identify the desired vehicle. In this paper we are trying to discuss in details about the existing techniques on smart ambulance based on IoT using zig bee, GSM module , Adriano , Rasberry pi etc., its draw back and its future scope.

Chapter 3: Augmented and Virtual Reality and Their Applications

Augmented Reality (AR) overlies manually made materials directly over the real world materials. This section addresses the technological and design frameworks required to create realistic motion tracking environments, realistic audio, 3D graphical interactions, multimodal sensory integration, and user interfaces and games using virtual reality to augmented reality. Similarly the portfolio required to build a personal VR or AR application is detailed. Virtual and Augmented Reality industry committed innovative technologies that can be explored in the field of entertainment, education, training, medical and industrial innovation, and the development are explored. Augmented Reality (AR) allows the physical world to be enhanced by incorporating digital knowledge in real time created by virtual machine. Few applications that have used augmented and virtual reality in real world applications are discussed.

Chapter 4: Comparison Analysis of Prediction Model for Respiratory Diseases

Millions of people around the world have one or many respiratory related illness. Many chronic respiratory diseases like asthma, COPD, pneumonia, respiratory distress etc. are considered to be most significant public health burden. To reduce the mortality rate, it is better to perform early prediction of respiratory disorders and treat them accordingly. To build an efficient prediction model for various types of respiratory diseases, machine learning approaches are used. The proposed methodology build classifier model using supervised learning algorithms like Random forest, decision tree and Multi-layer Perceptron Neural network (MLP-NN) for the detection of different respiratory diseases of ICU admitted patients. Note that it achieves accuracy of nearly 99 percent by various machine learning approaches. In summary, this chapter provides a useful comparison analysis of prediction model for respiratory diseases.

Chapter 5: Dynamic Data Mining Based on the Stability of Dynamic Models

This chapter presents a new approach based on the use of stable dynamic models for dynamic data mining. Data mining is an essential technique in the process of extracting knowledge from data. This allows us to model the extracted knowledge using a formalism or a modeling technique. However, the data needed for knowledge extraction is collected in advance and it can take a long time to collect. Our objective is therefore to move towards a solution based on the modeling of systems using dynamic models and to study their stability. Stable dynamic models provide us with a basis for dynamic data mining. In order to achieve this objective, we propose an approach based on agent-based models, the concept of fixed points and the Monte-Carlo method in this this chapter.

Chapter 6: Augmented Reality Application – AR Learning Platform for Mentally Differently Abled Kids

The purpose of this research was to develop an AR-based learning application primarily for the mentally differently abled children for their initial learning period. The developed application consists of alphabets, words associated with alphabets, recognition of various animals and animated rhymes as 3D objects which could be rotated and audio voiceovers. The developed learning platform is cost effective and would lead to an improvement in concentration, retention and understanding capabilities of a mentally differently abled child.

Chapter 7: Analyzing Knowledge Representation of University Ontology Through Semantic Web: Representation of University Ontology

Today's people are using lots of website for searching and retrieving information, most of the website keeps information in a simple format, all information simply linked with each other. It is of utmost importance to work on knowledge-based, information presentation, hence the advent of the semantic web called as intelligent and meaningful web, is a new trend in the area of web development. So, the development of the semantic web becomes a keystone in the real-world applications, it plays a vital crucial role in healthcare also. This chapter discusses several interesting concepts regarding analyzing knowledge representation of university ontology through semantic web.

Chapter 8: Efficient Virtual Reality-Based Platform for Virtual Concerts

The proposed chapter is all about a platform which is a 3D computer-generated environment that holds a live music arena consisting of a 3D stage, speakers, lights, console, and a virtually projected artist. We used traditional building information modeling software to create 3D structures of the stage, speakers, the console, and the whole arena which were then exported in the required graphic formats to the rendering engine. The rendering engine is where all the components came to life to generate a VR based application. The music generated by the artist was fed as an mp3 input to the speakers which would react accordingly with the user, it also had a 3D surround sound module implemented to give the user a complete experience of hearing the music at the highest quality. The lighting for the system was controlled through a third party lighting software which used Artnet UDP to communicate with the rendering engine and provide the lighting data at the exact times. The 3D stage had certain portions that were converted into LED screens to display the background visuals for the performance. The visuals were fed in as an mp4 input and programmed to play along with the music. The most challenging and exciting part was the projection of the artist in this 3D environment. We recorded a 2D video of the artist in a green screen studio, which was then programmed to be projected in a small holographic section on the stage, to convert it into a 3D projection. We also included other special effects like firecrackers, Co2 jets, Smoke, lasers, and pyro jets to simulate the whole experience of a real-life EDM concert. After developing the whole concert arena, we had to program some other light components like enabling it to interact along with the VR headset to give the user the complete experience. The chapter discuss about the results and conclusion.

Chapter 9: Increasing Participation in Large-Scale Virtual Environments – Rethinking the Ecological Cognition Frameworks for the Augmented, Mixed, and Virtual Reality

The proliferation of media rich social networking services, including Second Life, Amazon Prime Video, and services provided through Tobii Eye-Tracking, as well as Oculus, Google Glass and Microsoft HoloLens headsets, has changed the way people use information society and audio-visual media services. Existing theories of cognition in human-computer interaction have limitations in dealing with the unique problems that exist in contemporary virtual environments. To understand such large-scale virtual environments, this chapter makes use of data generated from questionnaires, usability testing and social and web metrics, to assess the relevance of ecological cognition theory for the current age.

Chapter 10: LIFI-Based Radiation Free Monitoring and Transmission Device for Hospitals/Public Places

A wireless surveillance system is required which includes remotely monitoring the public locations, particularly in pandemic circumstances like Covid-19. Li-Fi-based contact protocol is used in hospitals, and aims to minimize the barriers posed by medical practitioners to efficiently track various patients and ordinary users in public areas. It may also be mounted in public places to diagnose irregular and symptomatic individuals affected by COVID-19. It is used to monitor patient health, ranging from heart rate, body temperature, ECG, breathing, non-invasive blood pressure, oxygen saturation, etc. The proposed radiation-free surveillance system shall be implemented in all sectors to locate the infected persons effectively.

Chapter 11: The Gamification in Education, Healthcare, and Industry

The main goal of introducing this chapter is to enhance interest by adopting augmented reality and virtual reality technologies in the non-gaming applications. The most commonly devices used for augmented reality and virtual reality discussed briefly in this chapter. The importance of gamification can be viewed in the fields of industry, healthcare and education explained briefly by describing various instances in real life situations.

Chapter 12: Algorithm to Improve Reliability in Multimedia Data Transmission – Algorithm to Improve Reliability in Multimedia Data Transmission

Investigating Multimedia traffic over Optical Networks that provide extremely high data rates makes it a very attractive medium for multiservice transmission in building networks at low cost. Recently, there has been active research going on congestion control in optical networks to provide the communication reliability and bandwidth efficiency. We investigate the mutual diversity technique as a candidate solution for congestion control over multimedia traffic in Optical Network. This chapter proposes a new robust Medium Access Control (MAC) protocol, called Mutual Diversity MAC (MD-MAC), each terminal proactively selects a consort for mutual operation and lets it pass on concurrently so that this mitigates interference from nearby terminals and thus improves the reliability of network and its bandwidth efficiency. For meticulous evaluation, this study presents and uses a realistic reception by taking Bit Error Rate (BER), and the corresponding Frame Error Rate (FER) into consideration. When a communication link is unreliable, a sender transmits its signal together with its consort delivering the signal with greater reliability. In order to select a consort, each node sleuths its neighbors with respect to link quality by receiving periodic hello packets and overhearing ongoing communications. The proposed MD-MAC is designed based on the IEEE 802.3 network architecture without requiring any changes in frame formats. According to the system-level simulation results, MD-MAC significantly outperforms the conventional IEEE 802.3 standards, particularly in a harsh environment.

Chapter 13: Optimal Camera Placement in a Virtual Environment

In this chapter, author identifies three areas of research that are relatively little covered by the literature dedicated to camera placement and which nevertheless appear essential to us. On the one hand, existing approaches offer little flexibility in both solving and describing a problem in terms of visual properties, especially when it has no solution. The Author proposes a flexible solution method which computes the set of solutions, maximizing the satisfaction of the properties of the problem, whether it is over constrained or not.

Chapter 14: Scalable Data Analysis Application to Web Usage Data

Data Mining is defined as the application of data analysis and discovery algorithms on large databases with the goal of discovering non-trivial models. Several algorithms have been proposed in order to formalize the new models discovered, to build more efficient models, to process new types of data and to measure the differences between the data sets. However, the most traditional algorithms of data mining assume that the models are static and do not take into account the possible evolution of these models over time. These considerations have motivated significant efforts in the analysis of temporal data as well as the adaptation of static data mining methods to data that evolves over time. The review of the main aspects of data mining dealt with in this thesis constitutes the body of this chapter, followed by a state of the art of current work in this field as well as a discussion of the major issues that exist there.

Chapter 15: Current Trends, Challenges, and Future Prospects for Augmented Reality and Virtual Reality

This chapter provides a detailed description about AR and VR, differentiates AR and VR, followed by interesting real-world examples of AR applications. Also, this article also discuss AR's strengths (also future expected VR's capacities), weaknesses, and potential in near future with adding useful and possible AR/ VR project in the hope of offering a roadmap to other sectors/applications.

Acknowledgment

First of all, we would to extend our gratitude to our Family Members, Friends, Reviewers and Supervisors, which stood with us as an advisor in completing this book titled *Multimedia and Sensory Input for Augmented, Mixed, and Virtual Reality.* Also, we would like to thanks our almighty "God" who makes us to write this book. We also thank IGI Global Staff (who has provided their continuous support during this COVID-19 Pandemic) and our colleagues with whom we have work together inside the college/ university and others outside of the college/ university who have provided their support.

Also, we would like to thank my wife Ankita Tyagi (or Shabnam K Tyagi) our Respected Madam, Prof. G Aghila, and our Respected Sir Prof. N Sreenath for giving their valuable inputs and helping us in completing this book.

Amit Kumar Tyagi

Chapter 1
An Useful Review on Optical Character Recognition for Smart Era Generation

Abhishek Das
ITER, Siksha 'O' Anusandhan (Deemed), India

Mihir Narayan Mohanty
ITER, Siksha 'O' Anusandhan (Deemed), India

ABSTRACT

In this chapter, the authors have reviewed on optical character recognition. The study belongs to both typed characters and handwritten character recognition. Online and offline character recognition are two modes of data acquisition in the field of OCR and are also studied. As deep learning is the emerging machine learning method in the field of image processing, the authors have described the method and its application of earlier works. From the study of the recurrent neural network (RNN), a special class of deep neural network is proposed for the recognition purpose. Further, convolutional neural network (CNN) is combined with RNN to check its performance. For this piece of work, Odia numerals and characters are taken as input and well recognized. The efficacy of the proposed method is explained in the result section.

1. INTRODUCTION

Optical character recognition (OCR) is the process of extracting editable text from an image containing either typed or handwritten characters. It may be alphabets, numerals, or the combination of both the categories. Text location, feature extraction, and recognition are the three operations in OCR to detect the text/character. In recent decades, OCR has drawn extensive attention in the field of computer vision, health care applications, smart transport systems, historical manuscript restoration and image to speech translation, etc (Singh, Bacchuwar, Bhasin, & Computing, 2012). It has a major role in the banking sector where an optical reader is used to extract detailed information printed on any credit card, bank

DOI: 10.4018/978-1-7998-4703-8.ch001

Copyright © 2021, IGI Global. Copying or distributing in print or electronic forms without written permission of IGI Global is prohibited.

passbook, or scanned forms (Warthan & McMillan, 1983). Optical character recognition is categorized into two groups depending upon the method of inputting data i.e. online OCR and offline OCR as shown in Figure 1. When characters are written on a Smartphone screen or tablets using fingertip or stylus or pen etc and the corresponding characters are extracted. In the case of the offline form of OCR, data acquisition involves images of documents containing either handwritten or typed characters.

Figure 1. Classification of Optical Character Recognition in terms of data feeding

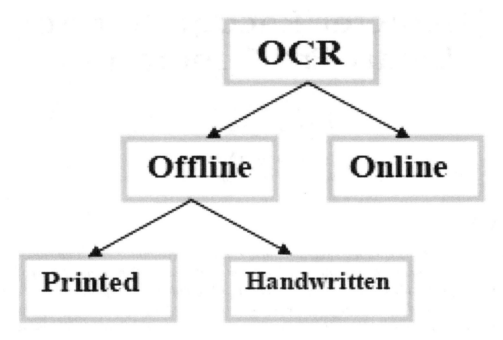

Optical character recognition involves various steps that are almost mandatory in any technique. The basic steps include: i) Data acquisition ii) Preprocessing iii) Feature extraction, and iv) Classification. The workflow diagram of OCR is shown in Figure 2.

Figure 2. Basic workflow diagram of OCR

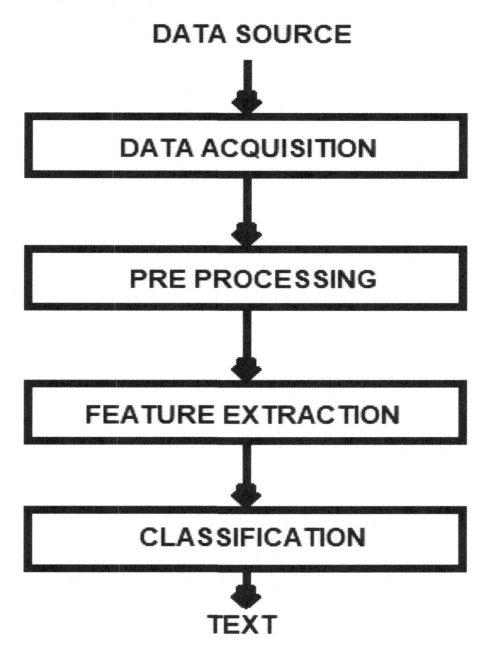

Different techniques are developed for data preprocessing i.e. binarization, normalization, morphological operation, skew error removal, etc. The way of feature extractions is also differently considered for getting a better result in recognition. Various single-handed or hybrid techniques are developed for training and classification. All these aspects of OCR are summarized in this paper in detail. Starting from software-based simulations to system on chip-based works for practical implementations is considered for detailed study in the field of Optical character recognition. Application of OCR in various fields is also taken care which includes handwritten historical document recognition, natural scene text recognition, multimedia communication, TV screen text recognition, license plate recognition for smart transportation, meter readings recognition, and shop hoardings text recognition. Deep learning-based approaches like Convolutional Neural Networks (CNNs), Recurrent Neural Networks (RNNs), Long Short Term Memory (LSTM) neural networks, Gated Recurrent Unit (GRU) based networks, and their hybrid structures are discussed with proper analysis. Other methods, without deep learning in OCR, are also discussed to highlight the improved characteristics of methods including Artificial Neural Network (ANN), Spiking Neural network (SNN), Support vector machine (SVM), k-Nearest Neighbors (k-NN) algorithm, Fuzzy logic, Zoning, Stroke features based approaches, and Linear discriminant analysis (LDA). Always, it is not suitable to extract features and classification by the same model. To verify this concept, certain hybrid models have been developed with one method for feature extraction and other classification methods. The combinations of models are of different possibilities, including both deep learning and classical models. A comparative table is provided for deep learning-based methods for easy analysis in terms of network structure; the dataset used, and obtained accuracy. In OCR, the segmentation of a captured image into individual characters is an important step. A few research works are also discussed which excludes segmentation step and recognized characters with comparative accuracy concerning the state of the art methods. Dynamic improvements in classical as well as deep learning-based methods are analyzed properly, so that, it will provide the correct direction to develop new and improved methodologies in the field of optical character recognition. Finally, for verification of handwritten OCR, authors have performed the work of Odia character recognition using Recurrent Neural Network as well as with a combined CNN-RNN model.

The rest of the part of this chapter is arranged in the following manner: Section 2 describes the general methods other than Deep learning. Methods based on Deep learning and combined structures are described in section 3. A comparison among deep learning-based methods is done with a comparison table in section 4. Application of Recurrent neural network and combined CNN-RNN on Odia handwritten numerals and characters are briefly described in section 5. The 6th section provides a summary of this chapter.

2. DIFFERENT TECHNIQUES OF OCR

Different pattern recognition algorithms like Support vector machine, K-nearest neighbor, and character recognition based on structural details, Hidden Markov models, Template matching, zoning, stroke extraction techniques are also used in the field of optical character recognition. A brief study of these techniques used in recent research works is studied in this section. The application of a specially arranged three-layered neural network named Spiking neural network is found in recent works.

2.1 Hidden Markov Model (HMM)

Hidden Markov Model has been used for Hindi and Tamil character recognition (Bharath, Madhvanath, & intelligence, 2011). The datasets have gone through a preprocessing step which includes re-sampling and normalization. The symbol writing order fed to HMM is termed as a lexicon-based approach whereas no prior knowledge of writing order based approach is named as lexicon free character recognition. Accuracy of 87.13% was achieved on Devanagari language when both approaches of lexicon-based and lexicon free were combined. On the Tamil language dataset, the lexicon-based approach resulted in 91.8% of accuracy.

For Chinese and Japanese handwritten string recognition a semi-Markov CRF model (Zhou et al., 2013) has been used. CRF stands for Conditional random fields. The authors have used posterior probability to get the labels of recognized string. The input data contains the character string which is passed through oversampling to get character lattice. Linguistic and geometry features were utilized for the string of characters in the MAP algorithm. For the Japanese language TUAT, the Kondate dataset has been used and the correct rate of 95.44% was achieved in character level. For the Chinese language, CASIA-OLHWDB has been used and the correct rate of 95.20% in character level was obtained.

Handwritten dataset collection and developing different strategies for detection is the basic way of research in optical character recognition. A new approach that is based on writing the characters on any surface using a pressure sensor and its recognition (Blumrosen, Sakuma, Rice, & Knickerbocker, 2020) has been emerged as a new aspect of improved research. In this work, the authors have used a pressure sensor on the fingernail to write characters on any surface. The movement of the finger and the pressure data from the sensor have been used to recognize the characters written by users. The Hidden Markov Model-based strategy has been used to recognize the words or sentences written using the pressure sensor. An accuracy of more than 80% was achieved by writing letters and near 70% on word detection. The test has been done by writing with a fingertip on a table.

2.2 Gaussian Mixture Models

A similarity and dissimilarity index based Gaussian mixture model (Khan, Khelifi, Tahir, Bouridane, & Security, 2018) has been developed for offline handwritten writer identification. The weighted histogram of the GMM score was calculated to evaluate the system. Similarity Gaussian mixture model (SGMM) has been used to measure the similarity among handwritten texts of the same writer. The dissimilar GMM has been used to find the dissimilarity present among the writers writing with different hands. The proposed algorithm was then verified using three English datasets, two Arabic, and one hybrid dataset of both languages. 97.28% of accuracy has been obtained in this text-independent GMM based approach.

2.3 Template Matching

A segmentation and recognition based system (Q.-F. Wang, Yin, Liu, & intelligence, 2011) has been proposed to recognize Chinese characters from text line images. The Bayesian decision-making system was used for path evaluation. Then the outputs were used for calculation of posterior probability. Text line images were further segmented for character extraction and recognition. Different models like a geometric model, the language model have been integrated for this purpose. The CASIA-HWDB has been used for testing. 90.75% and 91.39% of character recognition accuracy and correct accuracy obtained in this multiple context algorithms.

For automatic number plate detection, three methods have been designed using zoning, vector crossing and the third one was the combination of both the methods mentioned earlier for feature extraction and template matching for recognition (Farhat et al., 2018). Hardware was also designed which consumed only 36W and provided the recognition result in 0.63ms. Xilinx zynq-7000 based system on chip (SoC) has been developed with an ARM processor and suitable programmable logic. This hardware with small size in comparison to present systems provided the recognition accuracy of 99.5% which would be help full for automatic number plate recognition.

In general, for monetary transactions in mobile phones users have to put a pin or password to enable the money transfer. But a segmentation based signature verification (Y. Ren, Wang, Chen, Chuah, & Yang, 2019) approach has been provided for mobile transactions. The steps followed to complete and accurately recognize the signatures are signature normalization, then interpolation, and segment extraction followed by feature extraction. The quality and geographical information of signatures were also used to determine the behavioral characteristics of the user to verify the authenticity. The true positive rate for the proposed algorithm resulted in 95% whereas the false-positive rate of 10%.

Template matching using Siamese Convolutional neural network (Li, Xiao, Wu, Jin, & Lu, 2020) has been used to recognize Chinese handwritten characters. The Siamese neural network is a kind of neural network that consists of two sub-networks working parallel to each other. The two sub-networks receive two inputs and share the same weights and other properties. The handwritten characters were matched with preloaded templates to recognize correctly where the trained Siamese network has been treated as a binary classifier. The proposed Siamese network was trained with CASIA-HWDB1.0 and CASIA HWDB1.1 datasets and the performance was evaluated using the ICDAR-13 dataset. 92.31% accuracy has been achieved by this method on the ICDAR-13 dataset. The accuracy found on the MNIST dataset when trained with Chinese characters was 75.44% and after fine-tuning the network the accuracy increased to 99.10%.

As the PIN and pattern for unlocking a digital system can be forgotten a Fuzzy vault based template generation (Ponce-Hernandez, Blanco-Gonzalo, Liu-Jimenez, & Sanchez-Reillo, 2020) and the matching scheme has been proposed for signature verification with higher protection. 15 important features have been extracted in a different way of calculations to generate the template for a particular user. Then during verification, the new features were matched with a previously stored set of features. The following novel features set was considered in their work,

- The ratio of initial-stroke to total signature length.
- The ratio of end-stroke to total signature length.
- The ratio of the total shift to X in pen down to total signature length.
- The ratio of initial-stroke to total signature time.
- The ratio of end-stroke to total signature time
- The ratio of pen-down to total signature time.
- The ratio of pen-up to total signature time.
- The ratio of pen-down to total signature time.
- The ratio of pen down to top pen down time^2
- The ratio of total signature to top total signature time^2
- The total number of strokes.
- The ratio of the initial stroke to the total signature area.
- The ratio of end stroke to the total signature area.
- The ratio of initial stroke dots to total dots recovered.
- The ratio of end stroke dots to total dots recovered.
- The ratio of the difference between X(1st pen down) and min(X) to the total shift of X

2.4 Stroke Features Based Techniques

For scene text recognition a mid-level character representation and recognition scheme have been developed which was termed as Strokelets(X. Bai, Yao, & Liu, 2016). Strokelets are the set of strokes present in a character. First, the text area has been determined by the voting algorithm. Using the Hough map scheme the characters were then bounded by a box that separates each character. Then detected characters were replaced by most similar text from a dictionary. The classifier used in this approach is the Random forest classifier which was trained in the set of Strokelets for recognition and classification.

Stroke based parameters have been used to restore and recognize video scene text. Contour restoration was the main step used in this approach to extract the text area from complicated video scene images with a hedgy background (Y. Wu et al., 2016). Using the Laplacian form of any image the zero-crossing points have been detected. Probable stroke pairs were formed using the Fourier phase-angle and gradient magnitude. ICDAR dataset, SVT, and MSRA datasets were used to verify the workability of the proposed method. OCR, PSNR, MSE, and SSIM values obtained in the proposed model are 0.55, 6.19, 15620, and 0.28 respectively on the ICDAR-13 dataset.

For handwritten digit recognition, an optimum path forest algorithm has been developed using signature features (Lopes, da Silva, Rodrigues, & Reboucas Filho, 2016). The proposed method has been verified using MNIST data that resulted in 99.53% of accuracy and 99.91% of F-score. The training and testing times using this method were smaller in comparison to the state of the art methods which was the result of utilizing optimum path forest algorithm with signature features.

The writer identification method based on features like the n-tuple direction of contour (Ghanbarian, Ghiasi, Safabakhsh, & Arastouie, 2019) has been proposed in Farsi and English language. The contours from connected components were extracted, then n+1 number of points were taken on the extracted contours with some instant of gaps. These points were moved on the contour and histograms in a different direction were utilized as features for writer identification. The proposed work resulted in 92.2% writer identification accuracy in the English language where 900 persons were under observation. For Farsi language writer identification the authors have considered 600 numbers of people that resulted in 97.7% accuracy.

Basic deep learning algorithms require a huge amount of datasets for training purposes. To overcome this problem a concept learning algorithm (Xu, Wang, Li, & Pan, 2019) has been developed for Chinese character recognition. The Chinese characters were first processed to get the strokes from its skeleton image. The sequence of strokes was utilized as an important feature for training purposes. Monte Carlo Markov chain based sampling model has been used for character recognition. An accuracy of 98.20% was achieved in the proposed stroke-based concept learning approach. The basic example of stroke extraction is shown in Fig.3.

Figure 3. Strokes defined in Chinese Characters

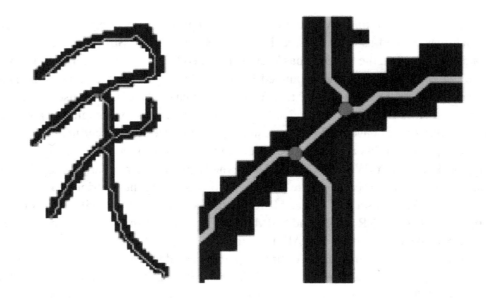

Lower case English handwritten alphabets based human behavior analysis (Ghosh, Shivakumara, Roy, Pal, & Lu, 2020) system has been developed using structural features like several loops, straight lines, slants, the thickness of strokes, shape or contour, cursiveness in writing style, aspect ratio, and other properties. In this approach, the graphical features were used to generate a hypothesis that have been used to analyze the sociological positive aspects or negativity of a person. This experiment was done upon 5300 persons and the accuracy in recognizing the personality from lower case handwritten characters has been found to be 86.70%.

For the recognition of handwritten mathematical expressions a stroke extraction based model has been developed (Chan, 2020). The components of the mathematical expressions were first processed to extract the junctions and strokes. The strokes have been recovered sequentially as appear in the expression from the binarized skeleton of the document provided to recognize the characters or symbols. Salt and pepper noise were removed from the binarized image for proper preprocessing. The stroke tracing has been used as the next step to it.

2.5 Linear Discriminate Analysis Algorithms

Considering different techniques for feature generation is the new approach of the present generation of research. For Arabic handwritten character recognition, a hybrid model has been developed using neighborhood rough sets and binary whale optimization (Sahlol, Abd Elaziz, Al-Qaness, & Kim, 2020) for feature extraction and Linear discriminate analysis (LDA) has been used as a classifier. The CEN-PARMI dataset was used for extracting features and training. The accuracy obtained in this approach was found to be higher than previously developed models like VGGNet, Resnet, Inception, etc. In that approach, 96% of accuracy was obtained.

2.6 Histogram of Gradients based models

For industrial applications, an illumination fusion-based metal stamping enhancement and recognition system has been proposed (Xiang et al., 2018). In this method the metal stamping was passed through different stages like illumination from a different angle, then image acquisition in grayscale, binarization, and morphological operation to locate and segment the character string present on the metal bars. Histogram of gradient (HOG) based feature was used to detect the string boundaries which differentiate the character from the metal surface. Then these features were used in three layers of a backpropagation-based neural network to recognize the characters. 99.6% accuracy has been achieved which shows the high effectiveness of the proposed algorithm.

2.7 K-Nearest Neighbor (KNN)

Handwritten characters are recognized not only for digitization purpose but it has vast application in medical applications. One of them is predicting the emotional condition of people like happy, sad, or stress. Online handwriting and signatures (Ayzeren, Erbilek, & Çelebi, 2019) has been considered for this purpose so that the number of features will be more in comparison to offline data collection. The data collection has been done using electronic tablets and pen because of which features like velocity, acceleration, azimuth, altitude, pressure, and several times the pen moves in the middle of signatures and handwriting were possible to collect. Then all the features were fed to KNN, JRIP, and Random forest networks for classification. The highest accuracy was achieved using the Random forest network i.e. 58% for handwriting and 50% for signature inputs.

For character recognition from Quranic images a similarity matching approach has been used (Alotaibi et al., 2017). Quranic images contain diacritics and characters. The diacritics were first extracted and then labels were assigned manually to form a dataset. This dataset has been used to train a K-Nearest Neighbor (KNN) network for training. Using the baseline method the characters were separated from the diacritics and using similarity matching concerning Arabic characters the Quranic characters were recognized. 96.4286% and 92.3077% of accuracies were obtained for diacritics and character recognition.

A structural and graph-based approach (Sahare & Dhok, 2018) have been utilized for character segmentation in the case of single and connected characters respectively. The structural features were fed to support vector machine for segmentation and using k-nearest neighbor characters were classified. The accuracy using SVM and KNN were found to be 98.86% and 99.84% respectively for segmentation and recognition. Datasets containing both typed and handwritten characters in Latin as well as Devanagari characters have been used to verify the performance of the proposed technique.

2.8 Fuzzy Zoning

A fuzzy membership function based zone dependent features have been developed and used for the classification of handwritten characters (Pirlo & Impedovo, 2011). In this work, the authors have used a genetic algorithm to improve the recognition performance by combining optimal zoning and fuzzy membership function. Buffalo NY, CEDAR, ETL, and Tsukuba, Japan datasets were used to verify the workability of the proposed method. Voronoi Tessellation method has been used to represent the optimal zoning which influences the highest order accuracy. The result of recognition in this approach was 93%, which has been found to be higher than other methods available i.e. zoning based on measurement level, ranked level, and abstract level.

2.9 Artificial Neural Network

A combined framework of the Genetic algorithm and multi-layer perceptron (MLP) (Katiyar & Mehfuz, 2016) has been used for English handwritten character recognition. A genetic algorithm has been used to optimize the features considered to train the model whereas MLP was used for character classification. CEDAR dataset was used in this piece of work to check the performance of the proposed hybrid model. Seven numbers of features were considered which were given as follows: box features, mean, gradient operation, diagonal distance, standard deviation, a center of gravity, and edge detection.

A segmentation free approach has been adopted using ligature details as a benchmark for character recognition in Urdu printed text (Din, Siddiqi, Khalid, Azam, & Processing, 2017). 1525 numbers of ligatures containing datasets were used in this work to train the Hidden Markov Model as a classifier. The Urdu text data was divided into two groups of data. The first one was the set containing the main body and the second containing the diacritics and dots. Ligatures having similar characteristics were grouped into clusters using a sequential cluster algorithm. The proposed algorithm has been verified using the UPTI Urdu database which results in 92% accuracy.

First binarization and then text line extraction approach (Ahn, Ryu, Koo, Cho, & Processing, 2017) have been used on historical documents affected by noise and skew errors. Binarization was then applied to the document to highlight text line separating from noisy background i.e. only focusing on a region of interest (ROI). First Otsu's binarization have been applied and then to remove the unwanted connected components morphological operation was applied. To remove the skew errors Global skew estimation was used. The text line was detected using a connected component re-grouping. The proposed algorithm resulted in 69.53% of recognition accuracy on ICDAR-2015 which was better than the state of the art methods.

Recognition of handwritten digits is not limited to software-based implementation. Its practical application is the major work in research where a device is to be developed which will detect and recognize the characters and numerals with higher accuracy. The electro-optical neural network (Zang, Chen, Yang, & Chen, 2019) has been designed which is based on a three-layer feed-forward neural network for training but the device designed for practical application is based on photon energy based pulse widening algorithm termed as the time stretch method. An N-1 loop of N layered neural network has been designed using a fiber optic-based digital signal processing platform. The accuracy achieved on the MNIST dataset in this practical approach was found to be 88%.

Hardware implementation using cellular automata (Morán, Frasser, Roca, & Rosselló, 2019) has been proposed to overcome the high-cost complexity of implementing deep learning algorithms for practical use. In this approach, a linear regression method has been applied to train the model. The reservoir computing scheme with one input layer, four hidden layers, and one output layer is designed which is shown in Fig.4. The proposed scheme was applied on the MNIST dataset that resulted in 97.10% accuracy without data augmentation and 98.08% with data augmentation and consumed 15% less energy in comparison to CNN based FPGA models.

Figure 4. Architecture of Reservoir Computation scheme

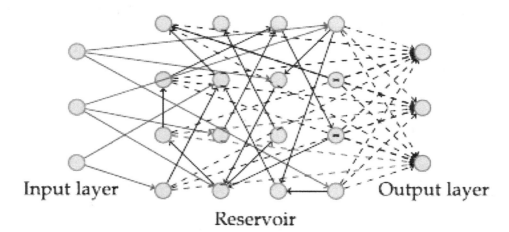

Optical interference to a feed-forward artificial neural network (ANN) (Williamson et al., 2019) has been found as a new approach in the hardware implementation of handwritten digit classification. In this approach, a nonlinear activation function derived from a small portion of an optical signal has been designed which was used after each hidden layer of ANN. The speed of operation has been found to be maintained as before the application of nonlinear activation function. The proposed nonlinear activation function was utilized in the multi-input XOR learning algorithm and MNIST classification. The accuracy found using this activation function was 94% for MNIST handwritten numeral classification.

For visual analysis like character recognition, a positive and unlabeled (PU) learning (Gong, Shi, Yang, Yang, & Technology, 2019) approach has been developed. The dataset comprised of some labeled data and more unlabeled data. To classify the unlabeled data to their corresponding class a data manifold method has been adopted. Data belonging to different categories have generated different manifold so it could be used as a feature to classify the dataset. The English numerals having a similar appearance like 2 & 7, 6 & 9 have been considered for verification of the proposed multi-manifold PU learning method.

For ligature segmentation in Urdu nastalique language a scale and rotation oriented method along with a feed-forward neural network has been utilized (Rehman & Khan, 2019). The ligatures were formed due to high cursive writing styles. Scale and rotation based features were used to feed a neural network that classified the Urdu nastalique after proper training. The feed-forward neural network with backpropagation has been used in this piece of work. The steps in this proposal involve image acquisition, pre-processing like text line extraction, and ligature segmentation. After this step, the labeled ligatures have been fed to previously describe the deep neural network. An accuracy of 96.113% has been obtained in the proposed model.

2.10 Spiking Neural Networks

The compression technique to get less circuitry complexity in the Spiking Neural Network (SNN) based chip (Liu et al., 2019) has been developed with the aim to reduce the number of SRAMs in the chip while maintaining the accuracy. The reduction in components resulted in less area of development and less consumption of power. The proposed SNN based model has been used to classify MNIST handwritten digits. Deep compression have been achieved by using sparsity and weight sharing techniques. The designed SNN chip consisted of 6 numbers of cores and each core had 32 neurons and 1024 synapses. The basic structure of each SNN network is shown in Fig. 5.

Figure 5. Basic SNN topology

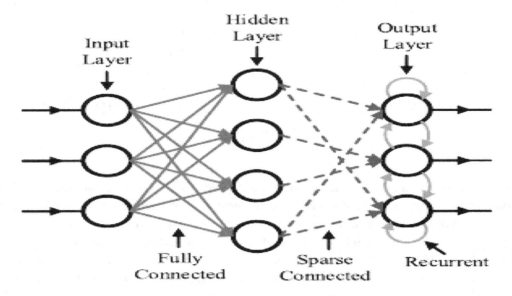

The accuracy achieved in this proposed deep compressed SNN based chip resulted in 91.2% accuracy on the MNIST dataset.

Designing circuits with less area, low power consumption and quick response is the present topic of interest in the field of the practical application of optical character recognition. Application of a Spiking neural network (SNN) (Pagliarini et al., 2019) has been found in classifying handwritten MNIST dataset. The proposed algorithm was implemented in a CMOS28-nm processor. To improve the performance, magnetic tunnel junction (MTJ) devices along with transistors were used as memory onboard components. The SNN model was developed by integrating probabilistic synapse with basic digital neurons. The area covered by the proposed synapse was found to be 3.64μm²/unit. The power and energy required were 675 pW and 8.87fJ respectively to transmit the spikes when firing.

Research in image processing is not only limited to developing algorithms, different processors for implementing the proposed methods are also developed. The factors in designing processors are energy consumption, time for executing the programs, and showing the results, cost of manufacturing, and others. A recent development of neuromorphic processor (Park, Lee, & Jeon, 2019) with a very small size of 65-nm for image processing has been found that resulted in 97.83% of classification accuracy on the MNIST dataset. A segregated dendrite based algorithm using the information of spikes (single bit precision only) has been developed and installed in a 65-nm LP CMOS chip for end-user applications. Apical, basal, and somatic dendrites were the three basic components of the network used in the proposed SD algorithm. The Apical dendrites were used to collect the spikes multiplied by feedback weights from the output layers. The basal dendrites performed just opposite to that of apical ones i.e.

to collect the spikes multiplied by feed-forward weights. Finally, in the somatic dendrites, the signals were converted into spikes with the application of sigmoid function acted as firing probability. This procedure was followed to train the network and during the testing section the apical dendrites were removed and the teaching signal has been applied to get the classification result. A basic block diagram of this algorithm is shown in Fig. 6.

Figure 6. Training and Testing phases in Segregated Dendrite Algorithm

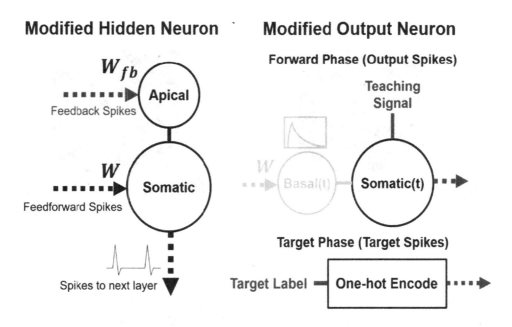

A modified spiking neural network (SNN) named SpikeProp learning algorithm (Hong et al., 2019) has been developed for a better learning scheme during training with robust structure and coding. The authors in this work have tried to overcome the gradient exploding problem by assigning a threshold in a spike gradient. Some graphical features such as connectivity of characters, synaptic dynamics, and sparse connections in layers are focused to control the training performance. A balance weight initialization along with homeostatic regulation have been found in this piece of work.

2.11 Support Vector Machine (SVM)

For handwritten English digit recognition Support vector machine (SVM) has been used that was fed by the combined features including offline (static) and online (dynamic) features (Sharma, 2015). The offline features were developed by considering the number of white pixels in vertical, horizontal, diagonal, and square areas formed in a binarized image of input. The dynamic features included the writing order of each digit extracted from the boundary as well as skeleton images of binarized input. The proposed combined feature based SVM classifier resulted in 99.27% accuracy on the MNIST dataset. The error rate was 0.73, which was also smaller than that of state of the art methods. Samples of static feature selection from handwritten digits were shown in Fig.7and 8 represents the way of dynamic feature extraction.

Figure 7. Static Feature Extraction

a)Vertical   b)Horizontal   c)Left-Diagonal   d) Right-Diagonal   e) Square

Figure 8. Dynamic Feature Extraction

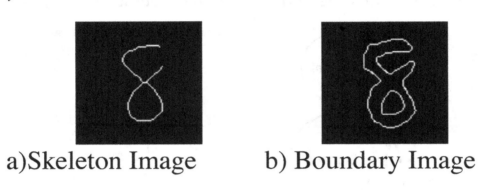

a)Skeleton Image   b) Boundary Image

Signatures are always handwritten to increase the security parameters of any documents. Signature verification systems have previously-stored signature samples in memory so that these samples can be used for verification. But an automatic signature verification scheme has been developed with no reference signatures (Diaz, Ferrer, Ramalingam, Guest, & Security, 2019) to determine whether considered signatures belong to the same person or not. Three methods were adopted in this work. The first method was based on similarity square matrix calculation and classification using the least square-Support vector machine (LS-SVM). In the second method, the feature distance was calculated for a different set of signatures and fed to LS-SVM to decide whether all the signatures belong to one writer or not. The third method included the extension of the second method by adding a pre-classification set of signatures. The error was quantified in terms of equal error rate (EER) and AreaUnder Curve (AUC). For method_3 the EER and AUC obtained were 34% and 75.33% that were considered as a remarkable result in the field of automatic signature verification approach.

For the recognition of handwritten digits string, a segmentation based algorithm has been developed by combining the principal component analysis model with the SVM classifier (Aly & Mohamed, 2019). The proposed model was trained with various groups of isolated and touching digits. The whole model was the cascade connection of PCA-SVM networks. The first PCA-SVM network has been used to process isolated strings whereas the next level of PCA-SVM was used to extract and label two touching digits and so on. In this way, a length free segmentation based handwritten digit recognition has been designed. The touching pair dataset and NIST SD19 dataset were used to validate the proposed method. 95.05% and 96.12% of accuracy were obtained in the TP dataset and NIST SD19 dataset respectively.

Researches on Mid-air handwriting are increasing as this provides the user with writing surface free experience. The 3D space gesture-based handwritten characters may be affected by mirror imaging and rotation angles. Authors in (Y. Zhang et al., 2020) have reduced the dimension from 3D to 2D and developed the algorithm to remove the mirror imaging effect and angle of rotation. The 3D bounding box was formed with the help of 3D coordinates, and then trajectory points were taken into consideration to get the trajectory surface. From this surface, the written characters have been processed to remove the angle of rotation and mirror imaging effect to obtain a simple 2D image. The proposed method performed better in comparison to PCA, KPCA, Isomap, and MDS to obtain better images of characters. After obtaining the mirror imaging and rotation-free 2D character images it was then ready for image processing for recognition. Three methods have been used for the classification of characters i.e. SVM, KNN, and Naïve Bayes with an accuracy of 91.5%, 89.9%, and 86.9% respectively.

Writer identification from an individual handwritten style is another application of optical character recognition. An adaptive sparse network has been developed (Venugopal & Sundaram, 2020) to identify the writer through online handwritten data inputs. The proposed method has been divided into two components. The first approach was to extract the features based on sub-strokes from the handwritten characters and the second component has been based on similarity score calculation for writer identification. The saliency features obtained by applying average pooling operation on sparse code were given as the input to the Radial basis function (RBF) kernel for training and SVM for classification. IAM and IBM-UB1databases were used in this approach for training purposes and the accuracy obtained were 99.69% and 97.44% respectively in paragraph extraction.

2.12 Deep Learning Techniques

The artificial neural network is the first step in artificial intelligence that is developed to mimic the human brain (Chen, Lin, Kung, Chung, & Yen, 2019). The number of layers in a basic ANN is three i.e. one input layer, one hidden layer, and one output layer with limited nodes. Deep learning is the subset of machine learning which has more hidden layers with activation functions and limited nodes (Deng & Yu, 2014). Deep learning includes deep neural networks, deep belief networks, Convolutional neural networks (CNN), and recurrent neural networks (RNN). In the field of image processing, CNN models are mostly used as different filters in CNN models are capable of generating a large number of features. Recurrent neural networks are having applications in sequential data. To overcome the vanishing gradient and exploding gradients like problems long shirt term memory (LSTM) and Gated recurrent unit (G. Wu, Tang, Wang, Zhang, & Wang) models were developed. In this section, these deep learning methods are analyzed with various applications in image processing, especially in character recognition.

2.12.1 Deep Neural Network Models

Power efficiency, scalability, and speed of computation in Optical neural networks (ONN) have been combined with electronic neural networks(Mengu, Luo, Rivenson, & Ozcan, 2019) for recognition of fashion products and handwritten digits. A modified diffractive deep neural network (D^2NN) has been advised with a changed loss function. The vanishing gradient problem in backpropagation has also been minimized in this piece of work. The combined Optical-Electronic neural network outperformed the state-of-art models in designing practical applicable devices for recognition. By combining five-layer D^2NN with a fully connected layer the accuracy obtained in recognition of handwritten digits and fashion object dataset were 98.71% and 90.04% respectively.

2.12.2 Convolutional Neural N Models

For scene text detection and Chinese character recognition a combined feature extractor model has been designed using structural data and by using the residual network (X. Ren et al., 2017). The text detection and recognition are spontaneous in humans. This concept has been applied in this work where the detection of text was done during training for recognition of texts. Both structural feature extractors and residual networks were specially arranged, convolutional models. ReLU activation function has been used. The basic TSCD (text structure component detector) is shown in Figure 9.

Figure 9. Basic TSCD block

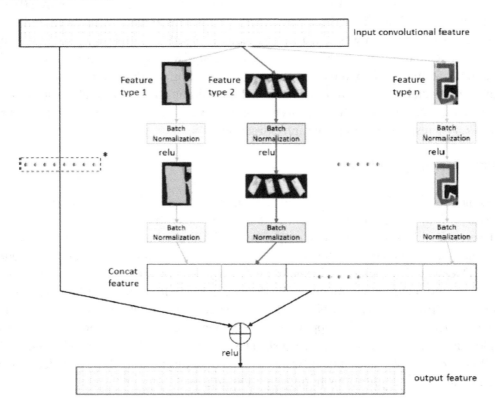

The whole model comprised of two convolutional layers followed by a TCSD layer which acted simultaneously for text detection and recognition. The precision, recall, and f-measure resulted from this combined architecture were 0.87, 0.82, and 0.84 respectively on Ren's dataset.

License plate recognition helps in finding the owner details for road assistance. A combined CNN and kernel dependent Extreme learning machine algorithm (Y. Yang, Li, & Duan, 2017) has been developed for Chinese license plate recognition. The convolutional layers were used for feature extraction whereas for classification a kernel-based ELM layer was used. The proposed model has been trained with license plate datasets. Testing accuracy of 96.38% has been achieved in less time interval.

Another approach for license plate localization has been found where the authors have used a sparse network using a winnows classifier and CNN (Bulan, Kozitsky, Ramesh, & Shreve, 2017). The captured image of a vehicle was first processed for license plate location detection and then the characters present in the plate were recognized using the Hidden Markov Model (HMM) based on probabilistic inference.

Text information present in videos can be extracted for data transfer in for of text with proper optical character techniques. In this context, a combined system of corner response based features and deep CNN has been proposed (Lu, Sun, Chu, Huang, & Yu, 2018). The corner response approach was useful in extracting the text region from the whole image. Then CNN architecture has been used for character recognition. A fuzzy c means clustering algorithm has also been used to get the text lines from hedgy background. The CNN model used in this approach is based on transferred-VGG16 architecture. Recall, precision, and F1- measure obtained in the proposed TVGG model on TV news test dataset were 0.89, 0.96, and 0.92 respectively.

Scene text recognition is having importance when we want to share the information from the TV scene to someone via mobile phone in the form of text. It demonstrates the application of optical character recognition in multimedia applications. A combined model has been developed in (Tang & Wu, 2018), where handcrafted features and deep learning-based features were considered and classification was done by using a fully convolutional network. The handcrafted features included the color of characters, geometry, and strokes area. Convolutional layers have also been used for deep features. Both models of feature extractors were then merged to a fully connected CNN model for region extraction and recognition.

Reconstruction of handwritten trajectory and its recognition using an inertial measuring unit (IMU) (Pan, Kuo, Liu, & Hu, 2018) has been designed in smartphones so that no extra sensor would be used to reduce the computation complexity. The flowchart of the proposed process is given in Figure 10. The smartphone has been directly used as a pen. So writing through the phone will affect the IMU sensor directly. The signal processing has been done by calibrating the sensor and then converting digital to an analog signal. A smoothing filter was used to remove the white noise present in the IMU signal. Then features like acceleration, angular velocity, and coordinates were considered for reconstruction. The characters were recognized using the Hidden Markov model, dynamic time wrapping, and Convolutional Neural Network with 71.47%, 88.53%, and 92.74% of accuracy.

Figure 10. Workflow of trajectory reconstruction and recognition

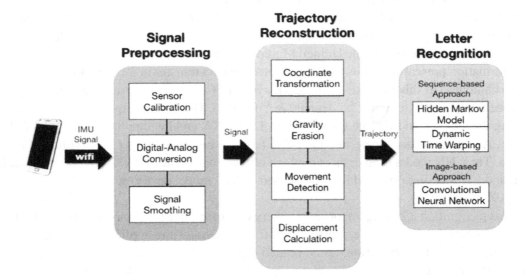

An intelligent system is designed for automatic mathematical expression detection and check whether the answer given by the students is correct or not (Shao, Li, Yuan, & Gui, 2019). To locate the position of mathematical expressions in the scanned image Yolo-v3 network is used. Once the location is detected a bounding box is formed around the mathematical expressions. Then all detected numerals along with symbols are sent for recognition through the YOLO-v3 network and calculation of the actual answer. Template matching is used to check whether the student's answer is correct or not. The wrong answers are bounded by red-colored boxes. The proposed algorithm is developed to help teachers in correcting the answer sheets. The proposed method results in 97.15% of recognition accuracy on the arithmetic expression dataset.

For Chinese handwritten character recognition, a smart handwriting system (Jian Zhang et al., 2019) has been developed using a smartwatch. In this approach, the hand movements like handwriting and wrist gestures have been considered as important features. Data over-fitting was avoided by using a data augmentation approach for Chinese characters which were large in number. The accelerometer and gyroscope were used in the wristwatch to measure the acceleration of hand movement and the angular velocity. The features were then fed to a Deep Convolutional neural network for proper recognition. The accuracy obtained in this approach was 96%.

Clinical named entity recognition was an emerging research topic in clinical and health care facilities. A combined architecture of residually dilated (Diaz et al.) Convolutional neural network (CNN) and conditional random field (CRF) (Qiu, Zhou, Wang, Ruan, & Gao, 2019) were developed to recognize the clinical named entities which outperform n comparison to the recurrent neural network. Both residually dilated convolutional layers and basic convolutional layers using a dictionary were used to extract the features in parallel and combined to CRF which tags the sequences correctly to form the sentence. The proposed model works properly with precision, recall, and F_1 score values 90.63%, 92.02%, and 91.32% respectively on the CCKS-2017 dataset.

A text length independent writer identification system (Sulaiman, Omar, Nasrudin, & Arram, 2019) is proposed by utilizing the combined features of the handcrafted network like Local Binary Pattern

(LBP) and deep learning-based features extracted using the CNN model. This work aims to identify the writer from texts ranging from a single word to a long sentence. Different patches are formed depending on the characters and features are extracted from these patches. The two types of features are then combined using a Vector of Locally Aggregated Descriptor (VLAD) encoding algorithm. IAM, CVL, and Khatt datasets are used to check the validity of the proposed algorithm, and accuracy obtained is 80.81%, 89.32%, and 97.10% respectively in the patch-based method and 78.36%, 86.1%, and 94.21% in the image-based deep neural network model.

A fully convolutional network-based sequence recognition system (F. Yang, Jin, Lai, Gao, & Li, 2019) has been developed for water meter reading recognition. The authors have developed a dataset containing 6000 numbers of water meter readings. The images containing the reading were fed to convolutional layers for feature extraction. The two-dimensional feature matrices were converted to single dimensional form by a temporal mapper to make a data sequence. In the end, a transcription layer has been used to recognize the meter reading. Augmented loss was designed to evaluate the model. Data augmentation has also been used to increase training performance. The accuracy achieved in recognizing the characters is 97.82%.

Recent work in handwritten character recognition has been based on the combination of a Convolutional neural network with an extreme gradient (XG) boosting classifier (Weldegebriel, Liu, Haq, Bugingo, & Zhang, 2019). The CNN model has been used to extract the features and the XGBoosting was used as a classifier. XGBoost classifier was developed by modifying a simple gradient boosting algorithm. The traditional gradient boosting was based on activating one tree at a time to minimize errors of other trees. But in this piece of work, the authors have changed the way of performance of the traditional gradient boosting technique to get better accuracy and less time of operation. To achieve this goal multiple cores have been used for each tree. The proposed model was applied to handwritten Ethiopian characters. The training and testing error rates for the CNN-XGBoost model were found to be 0.1334 and 0.1612 that was far better than that of CNN with fully-connected last layer i.e. 0.2188 and 0.4010 respectively. Due to the addition of the XGBoosting layer at the end of CNN, the complexity has been slightly increased in comparison to the basic CNN model with a fully-connected layer.

Whenever we think about Mid-air handwriting, many parameters come to mind that affects the recognition process like distance of the writer, orientation, shape of the hand, hand size, speed of hand movement, or sensor arrangements. To overcome these basic interferences in recognizing Mid-air handwriting a new approach has been developed where the gesture of the hand in Mid-air was converted to images and then processed in a basic convolutional neural network (Leem, Khan, Cho, & Measurement, 2019) for higher accuracy. In this work, authors have used a set of three radar sensors present in three different locations to track the X and Y coordinates of hand gestures. All points in the air were correlated to form the image of the written digit and then it was passed through the CNN model containing convolutional layers followed by max-pooling, then fully connected layer and the last Softmax activated fully-connected layer, that was a general structure. The authors have used single beam based radars which operate only on 2D space processing on single digits only.

An adversarial network-based convolutional neural network (Zhao, Chu, Zhang, & Jia, 2020) with a different optimization technique has been used to recognize handwritten Shui characters. The optimization in CNN used was based on the clustering distance (d_c). The Adversarial network has been designed to generate high-resolution Sui characters which were based on the Laplacian pyramid structure. The annotation of data was done by calculating Mahalanobis distance. The Peak Signal to noise ratio (PSNR) was calculated to evaluate the quality of the generated images. The maximum PSNR value obtained in this work was 27. The generated Shui characters were fed to the CNN model for training that increased the number of training samples and the recognition accuracy also increased.

Symbol recognition in the handwritten formula is another aspect of optical character recognition. A modified structure of CNN with multi-feature input (Fang & Zhang, 2020) has been developed for symbol recognition in the handwritten formula. The model included the convolutional layers followed by batch normalization and SEDB units. The SEDB units were comprised of a squeeze-expansion network and full connections. The deep features and the SEDB features have been concatenated to improve the training procedure and to classify the symbols with more accuracy.

Digitization of historical Tibetan documents is proposed in terms of segmentation and recognition (Ma et al., 2020). The authors of this work have passed the documents through pre-processing steps in which the noise, tilt, and unwanted illuminations were removed after which the document was binarized. The layout segmentation was done by block projection method. Connected components were recognized using the 8 neighborhood seed filling method. To extract the corner details for connected portions, the Harris corner point detection method has been utilized. A graph model method has been proposed to extract the text lines. After this step, the text was extracted using LeNet-5 CNN architecture. The proposed method of segmentation and recognition of Tibetan characters from historical document resulted in a 97.14% of accuracy.

Bangla and Devanagari handwritten word segmentation and classification (Pramanik & Bag, 2020) have been done using convolutional neural network-based transfer learning. The authors have used the basic characteristics of water that water flows from top to bottom and fills the rifts to extract the segmentation area. The workflow of this approach included binarization, noise normalization, skew removal, headline estimation, upper modified segmentation, constituent character segmentation, feature extraction, classification, and recognition. In Bangla and Devanagari character recognition the authors achieved 94.01% and 93.32% accuracy respectively.

To improve the quality of the handwritten character a Smart-GE device has been developed (Bi, Zhang, & Chen, 2020) which was based on identifying correct hand gestures in terms of pen holding. The authors have used an accelerometer and gyroscope to get information about the acceleration of hand movement and angular velocity. These factors were used as feature matrix which was fed to a deep convolutional neural network (DCNN) model to recognize whether the features were indicating a correct pen holding gesture or not. The DCNN model comprised an input layer, two convolutional layers with the ReLU activation function, two max-pooling layers, one fully connected layer after which another fully connected layer with Softmax function have been used in which the correctness of the gesture has been determined. The extracted features were also verified with other classifiers like the random forest, SVM, and KNN where the highest accuracy was found in the DCNN model with an accuracy of 98.3%.

A two-step convolutional neural network-based identity card OCR (Chernyshova, Sheshkus, & Arlazarov, 2020) has been proposed in which the text line segmentation was treated as a language-independent operation whereas character recognition was considered as a language-dependent one. The method was the combination of two sub-models named SEGMENTER designed with a fully connected network (FCN) and the second one was a CLASSIFIER designed with a language-dependent Convolutional neural network (CNN). Another importance of this work was that the number of parameters for training purposes has beenn found to be 3.4×10^4 which was very small in comparison to the state of the art methods. For classification, the CNN model was trained with synthetic datasets but evaluated using MNIST, MINDV-500, and 1961 England and Wales census dataset.

Figure 11. Architecture of Bidirectional LSTM for handwritten password detection

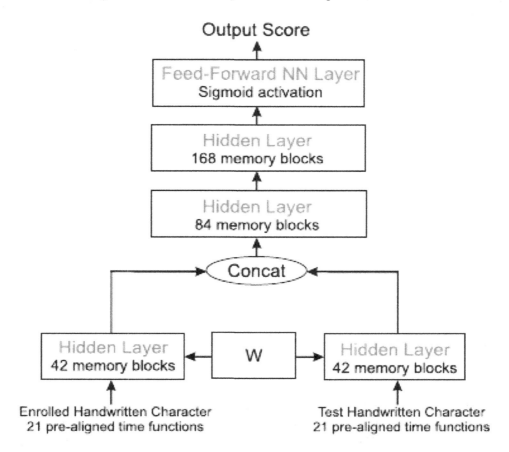

2.12.3 RNN models

Font detection from documents is also another application of optical character recognition. Once the characters are recognized their font can be recognized with the proper methodology. A recurrent network like a 2-dimensional LSTM network has been combined with a principal component-based Convolutional network for Chinese character font detection (Tao, Lin, Jin, & Li, 2015). The architecture has been used for feature extraction from stroke information using the PC-convolutional network then converted to sequential data for training and classification through the LSTM network. 97.77% of accuracy has been achieved in the proposed model.

A multidimensional Long Short Term (MDLSTM) network with CTC has been used to extract the sequential features from Urdu Nastalique characters (Naz et al., 2016) and also for classification. 98% accuracy has been achieved in this method. Openly available UPTI dataset has been used to train the LSTM model.

Chinese character drawing and recognition have been proposed with Recurrent units like bidirectional LSTMs and GRUs (X.-Y. Zhang et al., 2017). No trajectory information has been captured. The structure of the characters was used to form sequential features directly using the recurrent models. Recurrent units along with batch normalization and fully connected layers worked as both generative and discriminative models so that human-readable Chinese characters were drawn with higher accuracy and successfully recognized. 98.15% of accuracy has been obtained when the system was trained with the ICDAR-2013 dataset.

Figure 12. Samples of Arithmetic operation dataset

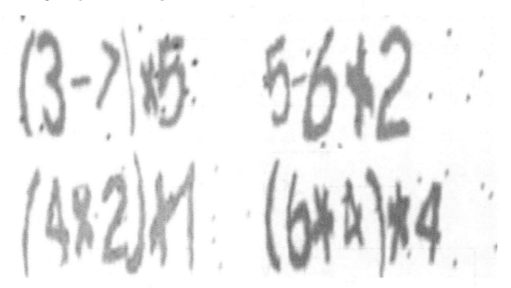

For online recognition of handwritten mathematical equations, a neural network-based approach has been developed named Trap, attend, and parse network (Jianshu Zhang, Du, & Dai, 2018). The bidirectional Gated recurrent unit (G. Wu et al.) has been used to extract the online features from the input data termed as a tracker. A watch operation based system was combined with a tracker so that the portions marked as individual objects were connected to create an image for more feature extraction using the FCN network. The parser was also designed for GRU with hybrid attention based network which generates the Latex notations representing the labels of mathematical expression and was the final result.

An attention technique oriented Bidirectional Long short term memory (LSTM) with Conditional random field (CRF) (G. Wu et al., 2019) has been proposed for Chinese clinical report analysis. The self-attention technique has been used to interlink the characters throughout a long sentence. To learn the semantic information a Part-of-Speech (POS) operation has been added. The proposed algorithm was implemented using the CCKS-2017 Task-2 dataset. Precision, recall, and F1-measure obtained in this method are found to be 92.04, 90.68, and 91.35 respectively.

Updating weights of all the layers in a network may be time-consuming. To overcome this reservoir computing has been developed in which the last layer weights were only optimized for better accuracy. A feed-forward network followed by a Recurrent neural network (RNN) (Antonik, Marsal, & Rontani, 2019) approach has been developed for handwritten digit classification. This method has been implemented on a spatiotemporal based reservoir computer for faster practical application. Zoning, Gabor filters, and histograms of gradient (HOG) methods were used for features generation in the feed-forward portion of the network which has been fed to the recurrent unit for classification.

Figure 13. DCNN architecture for air writing recognition

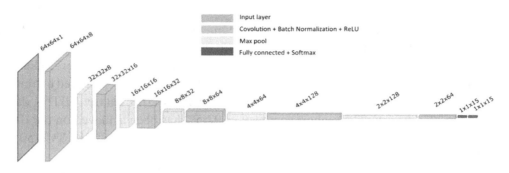

A different level application of character recognition and generation have been found in (Shao, Liang, et al., 2019) developing an intelligent system. The work involves the recognition of printed characters and their removal by the use of attention GAN and in the place of removed printed characters the handwritten characters were generated. The area of interest contains only the printed characters which were detected with the help of attention map based recurrent neural network (RNN). The characters were recognized using you only look once architecture (YOLO-v3). The generated characters were having a structural similarity of 0.89 and recognition accuracy obtained in this approach was 91.34%.

A new application of handwritten characters and their recognition has been found in (Tolosana, Vera-Rodriguez, Fierrez, Ortega-Garcia, & Security, 2020) where the authors have proposed the use of handwritten character typing as the password for unlocking mobile phones. The concept of dynamic time warping (DTW) and Recurrent Neural Network (RNN) have been mutually used for instant recognition of a handwritten password. '*MobiletouchDB*' dataset has been used to train the network which consists of 64000 numbers of online character entries collected from 217 users. The recurrent network used in approach was a Bi-directional Long Short Term Memory (BLSTM) unit with Siamese architecture. The architecture of used BLSTM is shown in Figure 11.

Figure 14. Sequence data extraction by CNN-RNN

2.13 Hybrid Models

Scene text conversion to text without character level segmentation has been done in (F. Wang, Guo, Lei, & Zhang, 2017) using a combined architecture of Convolutional layers and recurrent layers. The dataset used in this work was not having any label for the characters. The whole procedure has been lexicon data-driven instead of a label. A Gaussian Hidden Markov Model has been used to train the CNN model. The proposed algorithm has been verified with the ICDAR-2011 dataset, IIIT5K dataset, and Street View Text (STV) dataset. The highest accuracy of 92.5% has been achieved on the IIIT5K-50K dataset whereas 86.7%, 90.2%, 91.6%, and 86.9% were achieved on IIIT5K-100K, SVT-50, IC11-50, and IC-11 Full datasets.

Arithmetic operations with different sizes have been recognized using the Deep CNN model and combined CNN-RNN with CTC loss (Jiang, Dong, & El Saddik, 2018). The dataset contains different colored arithmetic operation images with the corresponding labeling. The two models have been verified and the accuracy of 99.985% was achieved in the DCNN model and 98.087% in the C-RNN model. A sample of the dataset used in this approach is shown in Figure 12.

For Japanese handwritten historical document character recognition (Le, Clanuwat, & Kitamoto, 2019) a human reading style inspired system has been proposed. Human reads from a text starting point and change the text line after the end of a line. This concept of reading style was applied by combining CNN and attention-based LSTM. The CNN module has been used for feature extraction termed as the encoder and the attention-based LSTM system has been used for recognition of pre-modern Kuzushiji characters from historical documents. To maximize the probability of recognized characters cross-entropy was used. AdaDelta optimization with gradient clipping has been applied to optimize the system for better performance. The proposed algorithm achieved 15.2% and 60.3% of the sequence error rate in levels 2 and 3 respectively which was a better result in comparison to the winner of the 2017 PRMU Kuzushiji competition.

Air writing recognition is a sophisticated application of optical character recognition. Radars with a specification of a 60-GHz millimeter-wave (Arsalan & Santra, 2019) have been used to collect the hand movement details for feature generation. The features were then fed to a convolutional neural network followed by LSTM layers for recognition of air written characters. Connectionist temporal classification (CTC) loss has been used as a metric evaluation of the system. The two-dimensional projection of the characters written has also been fed to a deep CNN (DCNN) model for feature extraction and recognition which resulted in almost the same accuracy of 98.33% as the CNN-LSTM-CTC combination. The proposed DCNN architecture is shown in Figure 13.

A transfer learning-based hybrid neural network (Ahmed, Hameed, Naz, Razzak, & Yusof, 2019) for Urdu text recognition has been developed which incorporates the weights achieved by CNN from MNIST dataset training. CNN was then connected to a multi-dimensional LSTM network with connectionist temporal classification loss (CTC loss) which has been used as a classifier of Urdu text. It was possible to get a remarkable result in training with the MNIST dataset and classifying the UNHD Urdu dataset because of the stroke similarity in handwritten English numerals with Urdu numerals. 93% of accuracy has been obtained in recognizing Urdu numerals in this approach.

For recognition of unconstrained handwritten words in offline mode, a combined network of Residual networks and Bidirectional-LSTM (X. Wu, Chen, You, & Xiao, 2019) has been proposed. The images of words with some missing characters or small portions were fed to the ResNets with 101 layers for feature extraction. Then to get the location data of characters position embeddings were added. Both the character and location features have been fed to the Bidirectional LSTM network for recognition. RIMES dataset was provided in the ICDAR-2011 competition used for both training and testing. The character error rate in this proposed methodology obtained in the RIMES dataset was 1.79 and on the ESPOSALLES dataset was 0.49 which were found to be less in comparison to sate of the art methods.

Figure 15. Architecture of Hybrid-DNN

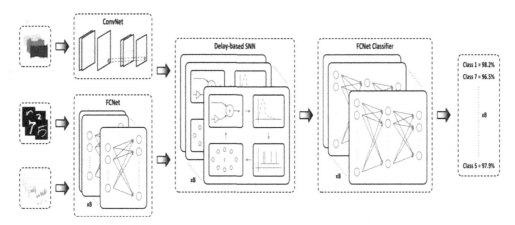

A combination of CNN and RNN has been designed for license plate localization in Chinese as well as other languages (Jingjing Zhang, Li, Li, Xun, & Shan, 2019). Authors have considered CNN for feature extraction from unconstrained images of license plates. The extracted features were then converted to sequential data for further processing in the recurrent network. In this piece of work bi-directional long shirt term memory layers have been used as the recurrent model. A sample of sequence data generated from the license plate is shown in Figure 14.

An average precision of 97.11% has been achieved on a multi-language dataset. Whereas on the Chinese language the precision and recall values obtained were 99.10% and 98.68% respectively.

A combination of CNN and bi-directional LSTM networks have been proposed for text recognition in the natural scene (Zuo, Sun, Mao, Qi, & Jia, 2019). The proposed model was termed as encoder-decoder as the CNN and bi-directional networks have been used to extract the features i.e. encoding and CTC and attention method was used to form the words from the recognized characters i.e. decoder. Synth90k dataset has been used to train the model whereas ICDAR 2003, ICDAR 2013, SVT, and IIIT5K datasets have been used for the testing operation. Depending upon the number of layers in LSTM the recognition accuracy also varied. The highest accuracy obtained in this approach was 97.5%.

Table 1. Comparison of Deep learning models.

References	Model	Dataset	Handwritten/ Printed	Accuracy (in %age) or F1-score(in decimal)
(Mengu et al., 2019)	D²NN	MNIST	Handwritten	98.71%
(Weldegebriel et al., 2019)	CNN-XGBoost	MNIST	Handwritten	86.66%
(Leem et al., 2019)	CNN	MNIST	Handwritten	97%
(Zhao et al., 2020)	Clustering-CNN	Shui Character dataset	Handwritten	93%
(Fang & Zhang, 2020)	SE-MCNN	CHROME	Handwritten	92.96%
(Ma et al., 2020)	LeNet-5 CNN	Tibetan Historical dataset	Handwritten	97.14%
(Pramanik & Bag, 2020)	CNN-Transfer Learning	Cmaterdb(Bangla)	Handwritten	94.01%
		Cmaterdb(Devanagari)		93.32%
(Jian Zhang et al., 2019)	DCNN	Chinese Characters Dataset	Handwritten	96%
(Bi et al., 2020)	DCNN	Chinese Characters Dataset	Handwritten	98.3%
(Chernyshova et al., 2020)	FCN-CNN	MIDV-500 and Census 1961 Project datasets	Printed	96.69%
(Shao, Li, et al., 2019)	YOLO-3	Arithmetic Problem Dataset	Printed	97.15%
(Sulaiman et al., 2019)	LBP-CNN	IAM	Handwritten	78.36%
		CVL		86.15%
		KHATT		94.21%
(Diaz et al., 2019)	CNN-CRF	CCKS-2017 Dataset	Printed	92.02%
(Y. Yang et al., 2017)	CNN-ELM	CLPR Dataset	Printed	96.38%
(F. Yang et al., 2019)	CNN	Water meter image dataset	Printed	97.82%
(Tang & Wu, 2018)	Fully Connected CNN	ICDAR2011	Printed	0.8776
		ICDAR2013		0.885
		SVT		0.631
(Lu et al., 2018)	Fuzzy-CNN	TV frame dataset	Printed	0.92
(Tolosana et al., 2020)	DTW-BiLSTM	MobileTouchDB and e-BioDigitDB databases.	Handwritten	97.62%
(Antonik et al., 2019)	HOG-RNN	MNIST	Handwritten	98.7%
(Shao, Liang, et al., 2019)	RNN-YOLOv3	Mathematical Expression Image dataset	Handwritten	91.34%
(Jianshu Zhang et al., 2018)	Bi-GRU	CHROME-2014	Handwritten	61.16%
		CHROME-2016		57.02%
(X.-Y. Zhang et al., 2017)	LSTM-GRU	ICDAR-2013	Handwritten	98.15%
(G. Wu et al., 2019)	LSTM-CRF	CCKS-2017	Printed	91.35
(Naz et al., 2016)	MD-LSTM	UPTI	Handwritten	98%
(Tao et al., 2015)	CNN-BiLSTM	CCFR	Printed	97.77%
(Arsalan & Santra, 2019)	CNN-LSTM	Air writing trajectory Dataset	Handwritten	98.33%
(Ahmed et al., 2019)	CNN-LSTM	MNIST & UNHD	Handwritten	93%
(X. Wu et al., 2019)	ResNets-BiLSTM	RIMES	Handwritten	98.21%
(Jiang et al., 2018)	DCNN	CAPTCHA-style	Handwritten	99.985%
	CNN-GRU			98.087%
(F. Wang et al., 2017)	HMM-CNN	IIIT5K-50K Dataset	Printed	92.5%
(Jingjing Zhang et al., 2019)	CNN-BDLSTM	License Plate Dataset	Printed	98.89
(Zuo et al., 2019)	CNN-BDLSTM	Synth90K	Printed	97.5%

2.13.1 Combined CNN-SVM Model

Handwriting quality and gesture of hands are controlled by the mutual understanding of muscles and the nervous system of the human being. So, the analysis of handwriting is now a point attraction in medical applications to detect the behavioral and health condition of a person. An online handwriting analysis based system has been developed for the detection of Alzheimer's disease (AD) as well as Parkinson's disease (PD) (Impedovo & Pirlo, 2018). PaHaW, NewHandPD,ParkinsonHW, ISUNIBA, EMOTHAW datasets have been used. The features used to detect the presence of AD and PD were divided into two categories, one that depends on time stamp termed as function features and others which were independent of time, termed as parameter features. Different classifiers as SVM with radial basis function, discriminate analysis, CNN, Naïve Bayes have been utilized to classify the patient categories. A CAD system can have been developed using all the characteristics of the end-user application.

The Bengali handwritten scripts have been used for writer verification (Adak, Chaudhuri, & Blumenstein, 2019) with the help of features extracted by support vector machine (SVM) termed as handcrafted features and by Convolutional Neural Networks termed as automated features. The dataset of Bengali handwriting has been formed by collecting data from 100 people and then by applying data augmentation the dataset was enlarged. The macro and micro features were derived as handcrafted features. The macro features include gray level entropy and threshold, count of total black pixels, and so on as described in (Srihari, Cha, Arora, & Lee, 2002). The micro-features include the aspect ratio of the page containing the handwritten details, the width of margins, upper zone, and lower zone ratio, and its length. The automated features have been generated by passing the images of pages to the CNN model which involved feature generation and writer identification.

2.13.2 Combined CNN-SNN Models

A hybrid model that combined basic Deep Neural Network (DNN) and memristive synapses (reconfigurable) along with delay-based Spiking neural network (SNN) (K. Bai, An, Liu, & Yi, 2019) has been used to classify handwritten digits and recognition of spoken digits. The DNN portion in the model consisted of CNN and FCNet for feature extraction. The extracted features were then passed to the SNN layer for spike generation and the last layer was an FCNet classifier. The proposed hybrid DNN model resulted in 99.03% and 99.63% accuracy on MNIST digit classification and recognition of spoken digits respectively. The architecture of hybrid-DNN is shown in Figure 15.

Due to similarity in terms of function, in this section, a comparison table (Table 1) is provided representing different deep learning-based models.

3. METHOD FOR ODIA HANDWRITTEN CHARACTERS RECOGNITION

Odia is the official language of Odisha, a state of India. Different documents are written in Odia, different news channels show information on the TV screen in Odia. So, Odia character recognition in multimedia applications is an essential requirement to share the information in the form of text. To achieve this requirement, the authors have tested Odia handwritten characters for recognition using recurrent neural networks.

Figure 16. Architecture of Proposed RNN model

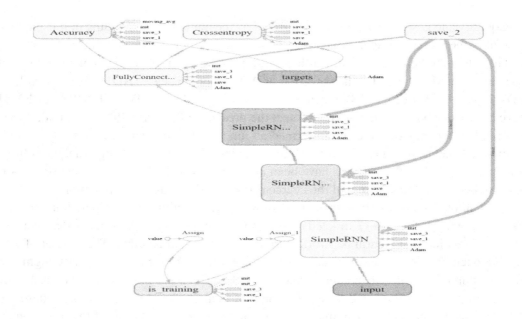

3.1 Various Approaches in Odia Character Recognition

Various researches are performed for Odia printed and handwritten character recognition. In this section, different methods developed for Odia character recognition are discussed.

In recent decades, Deep learning is gaining its importance in pattern recognition problems due to its human-like performance. Convolutional Neural Networks have a greater impact on image classification that extracts features using different filters with proper kernels. This concept has been used in Odia handwritten recognition. Convolutional filters have been used to generate features from handwritten images. Three datasets developed on Odia handwritten characters and numerals were used in this work. IIT-BBS Odia numeral dataset and ISI-Kolkata Odia numeral dataset were used to verify the method that results in 98.6% and 99.3% accuracy respectively. Recent work has been developed based on a deep learning-based LSTM network for Odia handwritten numeral recognition (A. Das, Patra, & Mohanty, 2020). Long short term memory-based models are usually applied for time series prediction. But in this piece of work authors have used LSTM for the recognition of two-dimensional images by converting the pixels of images into time-dependent sequences and obtained 97.93% accuracy. Transfer learning plays a significant function in pattern recognition problems as it is possible to recognize one set of data when the model is trained with another type of data with even little similarity. This algorithm has been used for Odia character recognition (S. Sahoo & Lakshmi, 2020), where the pre-trained model has been formed with Convolutional neural networks. VGG16 model has been used for feature extraction and classification. The model has been trained with features extracted from COCO and ImageNet datasets. The same pre-trained model has been used for the classification of Odia handwritten characters and obtained an accuracy of 89.92% with proper fine-tuning.

Figure 17. Architecture of Proposed Combined CNN-RNN Model

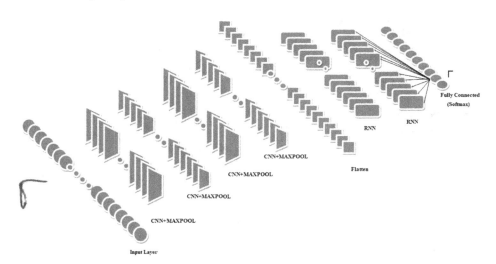

Use of Rectangle Histogram-Oriented Gradient (R-HOG) along with PCA has been done for feature extraction, whereas SVM and Quadratic Classifier (QC) have been used for classification based on extracted features. In this approach, SVM performed better than QC (Sethy & Patra, 2020). The accuracy obtained in SVM has been found to be 98.85% whereas QC resulted in 96.8%. Spatio-spectral decomposition for feature representation plays an important role in handwritten character recognition. In this perspective, a sparse concept code based Terolets have been used for image representation (Kalyan S Dash, Puhan, & Panda, 2020). Tetrolets were formed with different sized blocks for different characters. The features extracted in this approach from Odia characters and numerals were fed to different classifiers like SVM, Random forest, modified quadratic discriminant function (MQDF), and Nearest Neighbor. The accuracy obtained for IITBBS numeral dataset were 98.36%, 95.79%, 97.14%, and 98.725 respectively for previously mentioned classifiers. The same classifiers resulted 89.75%, 90.06%, 91.18%, and 93.24% respectively on the IIT BBS Odia characters dataset. Optical printed character recognition is also a challenging task when different font styles are used. Application of Discrete Wavelet Transform (DWT) for feature extraction and SVM for classification have provided 99% accuracy when used for printed complex symbols in Odia characters(Pattanayak, Pradhan, & Mallik, 2020). As features play important role in pattern recognition problems different algorithms have been developed to optimize the feature selection process. To achieve better-optimized features authors have used a multi-objective Jaya optimizer (MJO) to update weights derived by convolution and multiplication filters(D. Das, Nayak, Dash, Majhi, & Applications, 2020). The optimized features have then been fed to SVM, Random Forest, Backpropagation Neural network, and K-nearest neighbor for classification of Odia handwritten numerals and achieved an accuracy of 97.70%, 97.20%, 95.10%, and 96.50% respectively. Another approach in Odia printed character recognition has been developed using a self-organizing map (SOM) network(Jena, Pradhan, Biswal, & Nayak, 2020). The height, width, circle, circle start, circle end, cross-section, and other structural characteristics were used as features to train the SOM model that results in 97.55% accuracy. Storing and recalling for recognizing Odia handwritten characters has been performed using a Hopfield neural network(R. C. Sahoo & Pradhan). The network has been trained with features extracted using HOG features. Before extracting the features, the NIT Rourkela handwritten Odia character dataset was passed through differ-

Figure 18. Odia handwritten Numerals

Figure 19. Odia handwritten Vowels

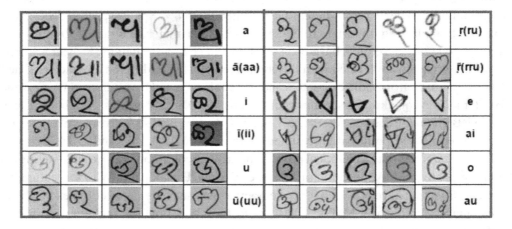

ent pre-processing steps such as resizing, application of Gaussian filters to remove noise present in the images, binarization, and normalization. 94.66% of pattern recall efficiency has been achieved in this approach. For printed Odia character recognition, authors have used Hopfield neural network trained with features generated by different zoning algorithm(Jena, Pradhan, Biswal, Tripathy, & Engineering, 2019). The number of zones considered in this approach were three such as upper, middle, and lower zones. Some pre-processing steps such as image binarization, normalization, thinning, skew detection and removal, line segmentation, word segmentation, and character segmentation were performed before extracting the features using zoning based algorithm. The backpropagation neural network havs shown a significant result in handwritten character recognition(Sethy, Patra, & Nayak, 2018). In this approach the authors have utilized PCA for getting optimized features from the total features obtained using dis-

Figure 20. Recognition result of Odia Numerals

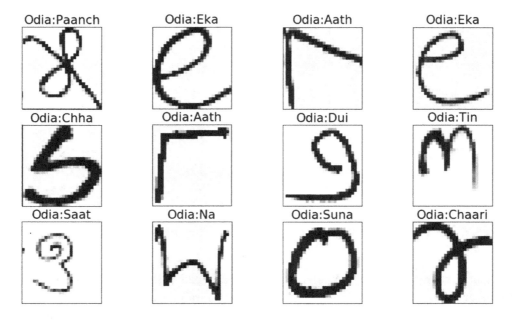

Figure 21. Recognition result of Odia Vowels

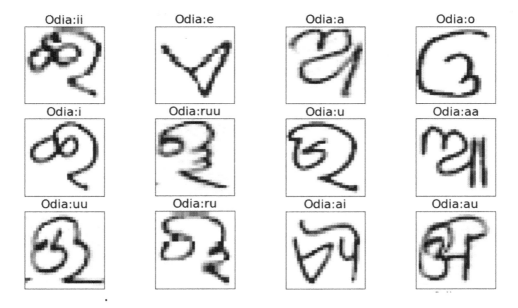

crete wavelet transform. In this method the authors have achieved 94.8% accuracy on Odia handwritten character recognition. For printed character recognition, a four layered back propagation neural network has been used(Nayak, Nayak, & Robotics, 2017). Features were extracted in two different ways. One way follows the structural features and the authors have proposed binary features in this work. The images of

Figure 22. Accuracy plot for Numerals in RNN model

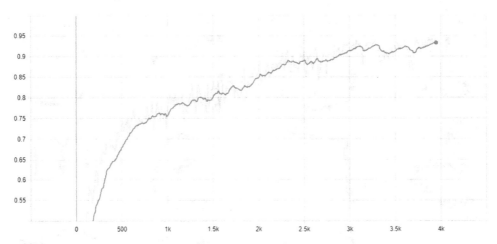

15x15 segmented characters were converted to one row and 225 column matrix. Then these data have been fed as binary features to the backpropagation network for training and testing steps. A non-redundant Stockwell transform approach has been considered for handwritten Odia character recognition (Kalyan Sourav Dash, Puhan, & Panda, 2015). The proposed model has been trained with the features generated using optimal zoning based algorithm. To train the model from the errors, a bio-inspired optimization technique has been followed in an adaptive manner. Accuracy of 99.1% has been achieved from this method on the ISI Kolkata database and 98.6% accuracy from the IIT, Bhubaneswar database.

Figure 23. Accuracy plot for Vowels in RNN model

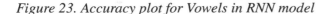

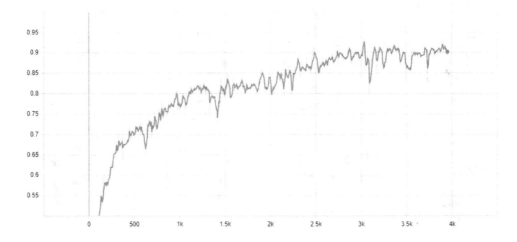

Figure 24. Accuracy plot for numerals in combined CNN-RNN Model

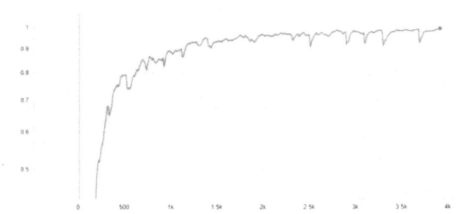

3.2 Proposed Method

The proposed recurrent neural network consists of a total of 5 layers. The first layer is an input layer, then three recurrent layers are used for feature extraction, then a fully connected layer with 12 neurons is used for the classification of 12 vowels of Odia characters. The same architecture is also used for the recognition of Odia numerals. The architecture of the proposed RNN is shown in Figure 16.

From the literature study, it is found that the combined structures are performing better in comparison to single methods. So a combined CNN-RNN is also designed for recognition of Odia handwritten numerals and characters. In this approach, the Convolutional filters are used first to generate different features from the input images, and then the corresponding results are then converted to time-dependent sequences to train the part of the RNN model. So training in this approach is passing through two stages. Both the stages are graphically mentioned in Figure 17.

Figure 25. Accuracy plot for vowels in combined CNN-RNN Model

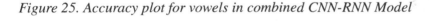

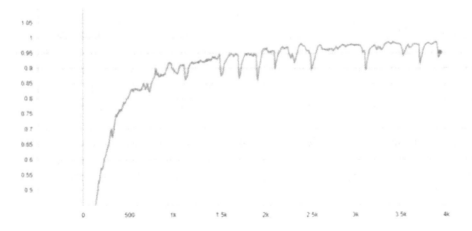

The results obtained in both methods are shown in sub-section 3.4.

3.3 Dataset

The proposed architectures of RNN and combined CNN-RNN are verified using two datasets. One dataset consists of Odia handwritten numerals and another dataset consists of Odia handwritten Vowels. The IIT Bhubaneswar numeral dataset consists of 5164 numbers of numeral images of 10 categories i.e. from 0 to 9 (in Odia, it is from Suna to Na). The ITER, Bhubaneswar Odia Vowels dataset consists of 5160 numbers of images of 12 categories. The samples of Odia numerals and vowels are shown in Figures 18 and 19 respectively.

3.4 Results and Discussion

The proposed RNN model is verified using the previously mentioned two datasets in the Python environment. The recognition results for numerals and vowels are sown in figures 20 and 21 respectively.

Due to more complexity in Odia vowels in comparison to numerals, a slight variation among accuracy values is also observed. The corresponding accuracy plots are given in Figures 22 and 23.

An accuracy of 92.96% is achieved in recognition of Odia numerals whereas 89.27% is achieved for vowels.

The proposed combined CNN-RNN is also verified with above mentioned two datasets and the result obtained is better in comparison to the single RNN model. The accuracy plots for numerals and character recognition are shown in Figures 24 and 25.

Accuracy of 99.99% is achieved for numerals recognition and 95.96% is achieved for vowel recognition using a combined CNN-RNN model that is showing the improved performance in comparison to a single RNN model. The above study on all the models whether single or combined architectures are summarized in the next section.

4. CONCLUDING REMARKS

In new generation, different smart technologies are used for different image recognition purpose. In this chapter, we have reviewed the state-of-art for printed and handwritten character recognition like license plate recognition, TV scene text detection, and recognition, historical document restoration, meter reading recognition, mathematical expression recognition. This study is categorized into two groups i.e. Deep learning-based and other techniques. It is studied that a particular method may not be good in both feature extraction and recognition. So, in recent decades, the application of hybrid networks are developed to get better features and to classify them with higher accuracy with corresponding suitable networks. Development in algorithms for designing systems on chips is also increased to provide end-user applications. It is observed that combined classifier is providing significant performance as compared to single models. So, combined models can be considered as suitable model in optical character recognition.

REFERENCES

Adak, C., Chaudhuri, B. B., & Blumenstein, M. J. I. A. (2019). *An empirical study on writer identification and verification from intra-variable individual handwriting*. Academic Press.

Ahmed, S. B., Hameed, I. A., Naz, S., Razzak, M. I., & Yusof, R. J. I. a. (2019). *Evaluation of handwritten Urdu text by integration of MNIST dataset learning experience*. Academic Press.

Ahn, B., Ryu, J., Koo, H. I., Cho, N. I. J. E. J. o. I., & Processing, V. (2017). *Textline detection in degraded historical document images*. Academic Press.

Alotaibi, F., Abdullah, M. T., Abdullah, R. B. H., Rahmat, R. W. B. O., Hashem, I. A. T., & Sangaiah, A. K. J. I. A. (2017). *Optical character recognition for quranic image similarity matching*. Academic Press.

Aly, S., & Mohamed, A. J. I. A. (2019). *Unknown-length handwritten numeral string recognition using cascade of PCA-SVMNet classifiers*. Academic Press.

Antonik, P., Marsal, N., & Rontani, D. J. I. J. o. S. T. i. Q. E. (2019). *Large-scale spatiotemporal photonic reservoir computer for image classification*. Academic Press.

Arsalan, M., & Santra, A. J. I. S. J. (2019). *Character recognition in air-writing based on network of radars for human-machine interface*. Academic Press.

Ayzeren, Y. B., Erbilek, M., & Çelebi, E. J. I. A. (2019). *Emotional state prediction from online handwriting and signature biometrics*. Academic Press.

Bai, K., An, Q., Liu, L., & Yi, Y. J. I. T. o. V. L. S. I. S. (2019). *A training-efficient hybrid-structured deep neural network with reconfigurable memristive synapses*. Academic Press.

Bai, X., Yao, C., & Liu, W. J. I. T. o. I. P. (2016). *Strokelets: A learned multi-scale mid-level representation for scene text recognition*. Academic Press.

Bharath, A., Madhvanath, S. J. I. t. o. p. a., & Intelligence, m. (2011). *HMM-based lexicon-driven and lexicon-free word recognition for online handwritten Indic scripts*. Academic Press.

Bi, H., Zhang, J., & Chen, Y. J. I. A. (2020). SmartGe. *Identifying Pen-Holding Gesture With Smartwatch.*, 8, 28820–28830.

Blumrosen, G., Sakuma, K., Rice, J. J., & Knickerbocker, J. J. I. A. (2020). Back to Finger-Writing. *Fingertip Writing Technology Based on Pressure Sensing.*, 8, 35455–35468.

Bulan, O., Kozitsky, V., Ramesh, P., & Shreve, M. J. I. T. o. I. T. S. (2017). *Segmentation-and annotation-free license plate recognition with deep localization and failure identification*. Academic Press.

Chan, C. J. I. A. (2020). *Stroke extraction for offline handwritten mathematical expression recognition*. Academic Press.

Chen, Y.-Y., Lin, Y.-H., Kung, C.-C., Chung, M.-H., & Yen, I. J. S. (2019). *Design and implementation of cloud analytics-assisted smart power meters considering advanced artificial intelligence as edge analytics in demand-side management for smart homes*. Academic Press.

Chernyshova, Y. S., Sheshkus, A. V., & Arlazarov, V. V. J. I. A. (2020). *Two-Step CNN Framework for Text Line Recognition in Camera-Captured Images.* Academic Press.

Das, A., Patra, G. R., & Mohanty, M. N. (2020). *LSTM based Odia Handwritten Numeral Recognition.* Paper presented at the 2020 International Conference on Communication and Signal Processing (ICCSP). 10.1109/ICCSP48568.2020.9182218

Das, D., Nayak, D. R., Dash, R., Majhi, B. J. M. T., & Applications. (2020). *MJCN: Multi-objective Jaya Convolutional Network for handwritten optical character recognition.* Academic Press.

Dash, K. S., Puhan, N. B., & Panda, G. J. a. p. a. (2020). Sparse Concept Coded Tetrolet Transform for Unconstrained Odia Character Recognition. Academic Press.

Dash, K. S., Puhan, N. B., & Panda, G. J. I. I. p. (2015). *Handwritten numeral recognition using non-redundant Stockwell transform and bio-inspired optimal zoning.* Academic Press.

Deng, L., & Yu, D. (2014). Deep learning: Methods and applications. *Found Trends Signal Process, 7*(3–4), 197–387. doi:10.1561/2000000039

Diaz, M., Ferrer, M. A., Ramalingam, S., Guest, R. J. I. T. o. I. F., & Security. (2019). *Investigating the Common Authorship of Signatures by Off-line Automatic Signature Verification without the Use of Reference Signatures.* Academic Press.

Din, I. U., Siddiqi, I., Khalid, S., Azam, T. J. E. J. o. I., & Processing, V. (2017). *Segmentation-free optical character recognition for printed Urdu text.* Academic Press.

Fang, D., & Zhang, C. J. I. A. (2020). *Multi-Feature Learning by Joint Training for Handwritten Formula Symbol Recognition.* Academic Press.

Farhat, A., Hommos, O., Al-Zawqari, A., Al-Qahtani, A., Bensaali, F., Amira, A., . . . Processing, V. (2018). *Optical character recognition on heterogeneous SoC for HD automatic number plate recognition system.* Academic Press.

Ghanbarian, A., Ghiasi, G., Safabakhsh, R., & Arastouie, N. J. I. I. P. (2019). *Writer identification with n-tuple direction feature from contour.* Academic Press.

Ghosh, S., Shivakumara, P., Roy, P., Pal, U., & Lu, T. J. C. T. o. I. T. (2020). *Graphology based handwritten character analysis for human behaviour identification.* Academic Press.

Gong, C., Shi, H., Yang, J., Yang, J. J. I. T. o. C., & Technology, S. f. V. (2019). *Multi-manifold positive and unlabeled learning for visual analysis.* Academic Press.

Hong, C., Wei, X., Wang, J., Deng, B., Yu, H., Che, Y. J. I. t. o. n. n., & Systems, L. (2019). *Training spiking neural networks for cognitive tasks: A versatile framework compatible with various temporal codes.* Academic Press.

Impedovo, D., & Pirlo, G. J. I. r. i. b. e. (2018). *Dynamic handwriting analysis for the assessment of neurodegenerative diseases: a pattern recognition perspective.* Academic Press.

Jena, O. P., Pradhan, S. K., Biswal, P. K., & Nayak, S. (2020). *Recognition of Printed Odia Characters and Digits using Optimized Self-Organizing Map Network*. Paper presented at the 2020 International Conference on Computer Science, Engineering and Applications (ICCSEA). 10.1109/ICCSEA49143.2020.9132915

Jena, O. P., Pradhan, S. K., Biswal, P. K., Tripathy, A. R. J. I. J. o. R. T., & Engineering. (2019). *Odia Characters and Numerals Recognition using Hopfield Neural Network based on Zoning Features*. Academic Press.

Jiang, Y., Dong, H., & El Saddik, A. J. I. A. (2018). *Baidu Meizu deep learning competition: Arithmetic operation recognition using end-to-end learning OCR technologies*. Academic Press.

Katiyar, G., & Mehfuz, S. J. s. (2016). *A hybrid recognition system for off-line handwritten characters*. Academic Press.

Khan, F. A., Khelifi, F., Tahir, M. A., Bouridane, A. J. I. T. o. I. F., & Security. (2018). *Dissimilarity Gaussian mixture models for efficient offline handwritten text-independent identification using SIFT and RootSIFT descriptors*. Academic Press.

Le, A. D., Clanuwat, T., & Kitamoto, A. J. I. A. (2019). *A human-inspired recognition system for pre-modern Japanese historical documents*. Academic Press.

Leem, S. K., Khan, F., Cho, S. H. J. I. T. o. I., & Measurement. (2019). *Detecting mid-air gestures for digit writing with radio sensors and a CNN*. Academic Press.

Li, Z., Xiao, Y., Wu, Q., Jin, M., & Lu, H. J. T. J. o. E. (2020). *Deep template matching for offline handwritten Chinese character recognition*. Academic Press.

Liu, Y., Qian, K., Hu, S., An, K., Xu, S., Zhan, X., & ... Systems. (2019). *Application of Deep Compression Technique in Spiking Neural Network Chip*. Academic Press.

Lopes, G. S., da Silva, D. C., Rodrigues, A. W. O., & Reboucas Filho, P. P. J. I. L. A. T. (2016). *Recognition of handwritten digits using the signature features and Optimum-Path Forest Classifier*. Academic Press.

Lu, W., Sun, H., Chu, J., Huang, X., & Yu, J. J. I. A. (2018). *A novel approach for video text detection and recognition based on a corner response feature map and transferred deep convolutional neural network*. Academic Press.

Ma, L., Long, C., Duan, L., Zhang, X., Li, Y., & Zhao, Q. J. I. A. (2020). *Segmentation and Recognition for Historical Tibetan Document Images*. Academic Press.

Mengu, D., Luo, Y., Rivenson, Y., & Ozcan, A. J. I. J. o. S. T. i. Q. E. (2019). *Analysis of diffractive optical neural networks and their integration with electronic neural networks*. Academic Press.

Morán, A., Frasser, C. F., Roca, M., & Rosselló, J. L. J. I. T. C. (2019). *Energy-Efficient Pattern Recognition Hardware With Elementary Cellular Automata*. Academic Press.

Nayak, M., Nayak, A. K. J. I. J. o. C. V., & Robotics. (2017). *Odia character recognition using back-propagation network with binary features*. Academic Press.

Naz, S., Umar, A. I., Ahmed, R., Razzak, M. I., Rashid, S. F., & Shafait, F. J. S. (2016). *Urdu Nasta'liq text recognition using implicit segmentation based on multi-dimensional long short term memory neural networks*. Academic Press.

Pagliarini, S. N., Bhuin, S., Isgenc, M. M., Biswas, A. K., Pileggi, L. J. I. T. o. N. N., & Systems, L. (2019). *A Probabilistic Synapse With Strained MTJs for Spiking Neural Networks*. Academic Press.

Pan, T.-Y., Kuo, C.-H., Liu, H.-T., & Hu, M.-C. J. I. T. o. E. T. i. C. I. (2018). *Handwriting trajectory reconstruction using low-cost imu*. Academic Press.

Park, J., Lee, J., & Jeon, D. J. I. J. o. S.-S. C. (2019). *A 65-nm Neuromorphic Image Classification Processor With Energy-Efficient Training Through Direct Spike-Only Feedback*. Academic Press.

Pattanayak, S. S., Pradhan, S. K., & Mallik, R. C. (2020). Printed Odia Symbols for Character Recognition: A Database Study. In Advanced Computing and Intelligent Engineering (pp. 297-307). Springer. doi:10.1007/978-981-15-1081-6_25

Pirlo, G., & Impedovo, D. J. I. T. o. F. S. (2011). *Fuzzy-zoning-based classification for handwritten characters*. Academic Press.

Ponce-Hernandez, W., Blanco-Gonzalo, R., Liu-Jimenez, J., & Sanchez-Reillo, R. J. I. A. (2020). *Fuzzy Vault Scheme Based on Fixed-Length Templates Applied to Dynamic Signature Verification*. Academic Press.

Pramanik, R., & Bag, S. J. I. I. P. (2020). *Segmentation-based recognition system for handwritten Bangla and Devanagari words using conventional classification and transfer learning*. Academic Press.

Qiu, J., Zhou, Y., Wang, Q., Ruan, T., & Gao, J. J. I. T. o. N. (2019). *Chinese clinical named entity recognition using residual dilated convolutional neural network with conditional random field*. Academic Press.

Rehman, K. U. U., & Khan, Y. D. J. I. A. (2019). *A Scale and Rotation Invariant Urdu Nastalique Ligature Recognition Using Cascade Forward Backpropagation Neural Network*. Academic Press.

Ren, X., Zhou, Y., Huang, Z., Sun, J., Yang, X., & Chen, K. J. I. A. (2017). *A novel text structure feature extractor for Chinese scene text detection and recognition*. Academic Press.

Ren, Y., Wang, C., Chen, Y., Chuah, M. C., & Yang, J. J. I. T. o. M. C. (2019). *Signature verification using critical segments for securing mobile transactions*. Academic Press.

Sahare, P., & Dhok, S. B. J. I. a. (2018). Multilingual character segmentation and recognition schemes for Indian document images. *6*, 10603-10617.

Sahlol, A. T., Abd Elaziz, M., Al-Qaness, M. A., & Kim, S. J. I. A. (2020). *Handwritten Arabic Optical Character Recognition Approach Based on Hybrid Whale Optimization Algorithm With Neighborhood Rough Set*. Academic Press.

Sahoo, R. C., & Pradhan, S. K. Pattern Storage and Recalling Analysis of Hopfield Network for Handwritten Odia Characters Using HOG. In *Advances in Machine Learning and Computational Intelligence* (pp. 467–476). Springer.

Sahoo, S., & Lakshmi, R. (2020). *Offline handwritten character classification of the same scriptural family languages by using transfer learning techniques.* Paper presented at the 2020 3rd International Conference on Emerging Technologies in Computer Engineering: Machine Learning and Internet of Things (ICETCE).

Sethy, A., & Patra, P. K. (2020). R-HOG Feature-Based Off-Line Odia Handwritten Character Recognition. In *Examining Fractal Image Processing and Analysis* (pp. 196–210). IGI Global. doi:10.4018/978-1-7998-0066-8.ch010

Sethy, A., Patra, P. K., & Nayak, D. R. (2018). Off-line handwritten Odia character recognition using DWT and PCA. In *Progress in Advanced Computing and Intelligent Engineering* (pp. 187–195). Springer. doi:10.1007/978-981-10-6872-0_18

Shao, L., Li, M., Yuan, L., & Gui, G. J. I. A. (2019). *InMAS: Deep learning for designing intelligent making system.* Academic Press.

Shao, L., Liang, C., Wang, K., Cao, W., Zhang, W., Gui, G., & Sari, H. J. I. A. (2019). *Attention GAN-based method for designing intelligent making system.* Academic Press.

Sharma, A. J. V. J. o. C. S. (2015). *A combined static and dynamic feature extraction technique to recognize handwritten digits.* Academic Press.

Singh, A., Bacchuwar, K., Bhasin, A. J. I. J. o. M. L., & Computing. (2012). *A survey of OCR applications.* Academic Press.

Srihari, S. N., Cha, S.-H., Arora, H., & Lee, S. J. J. o. f. s. (2002). *Individuality of handwriting.* Academic Press.

Sulaiman, A., Omar, K., Nasrudin, M. F., & Arram, A. J. I. A. (2019). *Length Independent Writer Identification Based on the Fusion of Deep and Hand-Crafted Descriptors.* Academic Press.

Tang, Y., & Wu, X. J. I. T. o. M. (2018). *Scene text detection using superpixel-based stroke feature transform and deep learning based region classification.* Academic Press.

Tao, D., Lin, X., Jin, L., & Li, X. J. I. t. o. c. (2015). *Principal component 2-D long short-term memory for font recognition on single Chinese characters.* Academic Press.

Tolosana, R., Vera-Rodriguez, R., Fierrez, J., & Ortega-Garcia, J. J. I. T. o. I. F., & Security. (2020). BioTouchPass2. *Touchscreen Password Biometrics Using Time-Aligned Recurrent Neural Networks, 15,* 2616–2628.

Venugopal, V., & Sundaram, S. J. I. B. (2020). *Online writer identification system using adaptive sparse representation framework.* Academic Press.

Wang, F., Guo, Q., Lei, J., & Zhang, J. J. I. C. V. (2017). *Convolutional recurrent neural networks with hidden Markov model bootstrap for scene text recognition.* Academic Press.

Wang, Q.-F., Yin, F., Liu, C.-L. J. I. t. o. p. a., & Intelligence, M. (2011). *Handwritten Chinese text recognition by integrating multiple contexts.* Academic Press.

Warthan, J. G., & McMillan, R. M. (1983). OCR/Variable head slot reader. Google Patents.

Weldegebriel, H. T., Liu, H., Haq, A. U., Bugingo, E., & Zhang, D. J. I. A. (2019). *A New Hybrid Convolutional Neural Network and eXtreme Gradient Boosting Classifier for Recognizing Handwritten Ethiopian Characters.* Academic Press.

Williamson, I. A., Hughes, T. W., Minkov, M., Bartlett, B., Pai, S., & Fan, S. J. I. J. o. S. T. i. Q. E. (2019). *Reprogrammable electro-optic nonlinear activation functions for optical neural networks.* Academic Press.

Wu, G., Tang, G., Wang, Z., Zhang, Z., & Wang, Z. J. I. A. (2019). *An Attention-Based BiLSTM-CRF Model for Chinese Clinic Named Entity Recognition.* Academic Press.

Wu, X., Chen, Q., You, J., & Xiao, Y. J. I. S. P. L. (2019). *Unconstrained Offline Handwritten Word Recognition by Position Embedding Integrated ResNets Model.* Academic Press.

Wu, Y., Shivakumara, P., Lu, T., Tan, C. L., Blumenstein, M., & Kumar, G. H. J. I. T. o. I. P. (2016). *Contour restoration of text components for recognition in video/scene images.* Academic Press.

Xiang, Z., You, Z., Qian, M., Zhang, J., Hu, X. J. E. J. o. I., & Processing, V. (2018). *Metal stamping character recognition algorithm based on multi-directional illumination image fusion enhancement technology.* Academic Press.

Xu, L., Wang, Y., Li, X., & Pan, M. J. I. A. (2019). *Recognition of Handwritten Chinese Characters Based on Concept Learning.* Academic Press.

Yang, F., Jin, L., Lai, S., Gao, X., & Li, Z. J. I. A. (2019). *Fully convolutional sequence recognition network for water meter number reading.* Academic Press.

Yang, Y., Li, D., & Duan, Z. J. I. I. T. S. (2017). *Chinese vehicle license plate recognition using kernel-based extreme learning machine with deep convolutional features.* Academic Press.

Zang, Y., Chen, M., Yang, S., & Chen, H. J. I. J. o. S. T. i. Q. E. (2019). *Electro-optical neural networks based on time-stretch method.* Academic Press.

Zhang, J., Bi, H., Chen, Y., Wang, M., Han, L., & Cai, L. J. I. I. T. J. (2019). SmartHandwriting. *Handwritten Chinese Character Recognition With Smartwatch.*, *7*(2), 960–970.

Zhang, J., Du, J., & Dai, L. J. I. T. o. M. (2018). *Track, attend, and parse (tap): An end-to-end framework for online handwritten mathematical expression recognition.* Academic Press.

Zhang, J., Li, Y., Li, T., Xun, L., & Shan, C. J. I. S. J. (2019). *License plate localization in unconstrained scenes using a two-stage CNN-RNN.* Academic Press.

Zhang, X.-Y., Yin, F., Zhang, Y.-M., Liu, C.-L., Bengio, Y. J. I. t. o. p. a., & Intelligence, M. (2017). *Drawing and recognizing chinese characters with recurrent neural network.* Academic Press.

Zhang, Y., Lu, J., Wang, K., Zhao, J., Cui, G., & Gao, X. J. I. A. (2020). *Dimensionality Reduction Method for 3D-Handwritten Characters Based on Oriented Bounding Boxes.* Academic Press.

Zhao, H., Chu, H., Zhang, Y., & Jia, Y. J. I. A. (2020). *Improvement of Ancient Shui Character Recognition Model Based on Convolutional Neural Network.* Academic Press.

Zhou, X.-D., Wang, D.-H., Tian, F., Liu, C.-L., Nakagawa, M. J. I. T. o. P. A., & Intelligence, M. (2013). *Handwritten Chinese/Japanese text recognition using semi-Markov conditional random fields*. Academic Press.

Zuo, L.-Q., Sun, H.-M., Mao, Q.-C., Qi, R., & Jia, R.-S. J. I. A. (2019). *Natural scene text recognition based on encoder-decoder framework*. Academic Press.

Chapter 2
Using IoTs-Based Monitoring System in a Smart Ambulance for E-Healtcare Applications:
A Systematic Review

Aswathy S. U.
Jothy Engineering College, Kerala, India

Ajesh F.
Musaliar College of Engineering and Technology, India

Felix M. Philip
Jain University (Deemed), Kochi, India

ABSTRACT

In today's world, traffic jams during rush hours are a major concern. During rush hours, emergency vehicles like ambulances get stuck in jams. The smart ambulance systems are most suitable to provide clearance to emergency vehicles during rush hours. Many systems are used to implement the smart ambulance systems. The primary objective is to identify the emergency vehicle and track its location so that wireless signals to the emergency vehicles can be provided. Conventional technologies use image processing systems to identify the emergency vehicle. But these systems have a drawback during bad weather conditions. Due to wind, rain, fog, etc., the image received by the camera is distorted by noise and it becomes difficult for the system to identify the desired vehicle. In this chapter, the authors discuss in detail the existing techniques on smart ambulance based on IoT using zig bee, GSM module, Adriano, Raspberry Pi, etc., its drawback, and its future scope.

DOI: 10.4018/978-1-7998-4703-8.ch002

Copyright © 2021, IGI Global. Copying or distributing in print or electronic forms without written permission of IGI Global is prohibited.

INTRODUCTION

India, one of the world's most populous nations, is an issue of road pollution and delayed medical treatment. Ambulatory health care is a form of remote patient surveillance that enables a healthcare facility to utilise the diagnostic equipment for the regular examination in the ambulance and to provide a healthcare specialist with the test results in real time. While there are different strategies for tracking the patient's wellbeing at home and in the hospital, the requirement for urgent action in case of an emergency is not yet met. One of the most dynamic and interesting advances in information and communications technologies is the introduction of the Internet of Things. Real-time parameter for patients' wellbeing is communicated to the cloud by internet access in the patient tracking framework centred on the Internet of Things. These criteria are sent to a distant place on the Internet. When the individual spontaneously becomes sick and admitted, the specialist can hear about the disorder or trigger only after diagnosing the patient, which will take longer.

In ambulances, tracking equipment is needed because in case of an accident a lot of time is spent in transporting and diagnosing patients to the hospital. Immediate treatment for seriously injured people and crash victims includes a mechanism for sharing information on the status of cars. A centralized control system needed in hospitals that provide car and emergency records on the crash victims. The practitioner wants to consider the clinical and physiological state of the patient so that the proper judgement can be made regarding medication administration and travel destinations. Communication between the emergency personnel and the monitoring station is also important. This can be accomplished through the application of an ambulance device which transmits the patient's current condition exclusively through parameters such as cardiac beat rate and temperature. The machine transmits details on the position of the ambulance to the traffic control rooms where appropriate arrangements can be made in the traffic island.

Literature Review

A description of the literature or a narrative analysis is a form of review article. Literature reviews are reference documents that may not report existing or original findings. These publications are often linked to scientific research in academic journals and should not be confused with book reviews, which may also be found in the same publication. Literature reviews are the basis for almost every academic field of research. As part of a peer-reviewed journal paper presenting a fresh study, the thesis must be included in the associated literature and history for the reader, a narrow-scope literature review may also be included.

Monitoring Patients Health with Smart Ambulance Using IoT

India is one of the most populous nations in the world. Ignorance of health remains a big concern in India due to overpopulation. Death swoops every minute because of a heart attack. The saving of a life is both auspicious and spiritual. The goal is to provide an integrated smart health system with some sensors and microcontrollers, to feel the body and to upload the data to the collaborative hospital website. If the condition is critical, an ambulance is dispatched to the patient's immediate premises. To reach the destination on time, the driver uses Google Maps utilizing the website and avoids crashes, obstacles, built-in hardware and sensors. In simple words, IOTs are nothing but those machines that link and interact with each other via the Internet. The innovations embedded in them make it possible for them to communicate with internal states or external environments, which in turn affect decisions. A variety of peoples describe the Internet of Things. If devices / objects can be digitally mirrored, they can be controlled from anywhere (Saha et. Al 2017).

Smart Health and Smart Ambulance System

Life is quite precious. People are losing their lives because of a heart attack and unequal body temperature. In India, every minute of death is triggered by a heart attack. So, in order to diagnose a heart attack, a computer must be built utilizing the new technology, here we are using the IOT definition. Here, with the aid of numerous sensors and microcontrollers, we have proposed a system that can monitor both heart attack and body temperature. For the past few decades, traffic control is a critical concern in major cities. Traffic performance can be increased with the aid of the Internet of Things (IoT). Here, it explains items that utilize Internet of Things technology to monitor traffic so that the ambulance can enter a patient position on time via Google Maps. Integrated technology is built to eliminate accidents / obstacles if the driver is not warning.

Smart Architecture

The proposed system is to design a device in which the heart beat sensor will sense the heart beat and temperature sensor will sense the body temperature. After sensing, sensors will send respective data to the microcontroller. After that microcontroller will send it to raspberry-piwhich will connect with the internet or IOT cloud. In the collaborating hospital the patient's heart rate and body temperature data will be sent through the internet. In the hospital the respective doctor will continuously monitor the patient's health system. If that patient will be in critical condition then an alert message will alert the doctor and then he will allot an ambulance. If the condition is critical, an ambulance is allotted to that particular location where the patient lives. To reach the destination on time the driver will use Google map with the help of the website but somehow if the driver is not alert while driving the ambulance, there is a chance of accident so as to avoid accident or obstacles, a hardware is made using Arduino UNO, ultrasonic sensors, buzzer, resistors, leds, buzzer, connecting wires, breadboard. The work here is if any obstacle comes in front of the ambulance within some specific range the buzzer will blow, the red led will be blinking so the driver will come to know and so he/she could prevent the accident.

Figure 1. Block Diagram of Smart System

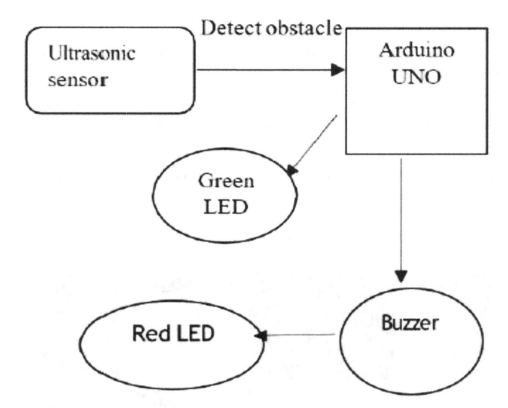

Here, in Fig 2.1.2 it depicts the block diagram of a smart ambulance system.It mainly consist of a.) Ultrasonic sensor b.)Arduino UNO c.) Green LED d.) Red LED e.) Buzzer .With the help of Internet of things (IoT) technologies, we can control the traffic so that the ambulance will reach apatient location on time using Google Maps (Reddy et al 2017).

A. Smart Device

Once the hardware is purchased by the user, the patient's name and patient's address must be provided to the collaborated hospital website. Through the website it will monitor patient's condition live [6]. The pulse rate sensor and body temperature sensor will start continuously sensing the condition once it receives the power supply. After sensing the data from the patient, it will send the data to the micro-controller and with the help of raspberry pi it will upload the data live with the help of the internet and if the condition is critical it will alert the hospital to allot an ambulance. Another website is made for ambulance monitoring i.e. when an ambulance is allotted by the hospital, the ambulance driver will get the patient's name and address. To reach on time is another hurdle so here we are connecting the website with Google map. Another separate click on button is provided in the website i.e. Reach patient, by clicking on Reach patient it will open Google map with destination fetch in it

B. Accident Avoidance

In India, on daily basis more than 400 people died because of road accidents which results in huge traffic jam. Here, the primary aim is to reach the patient locations on time so as to reach the destination on time, a hardware is made using an Arduino, Ultrasonic sensor which will avoid accidents and obstacles so that the ambulance can reach the destination on time. If the distance between one vehicle and another vehicle is less than (1m) it will alert the driver to slow down. The proposed system comprises an idea of having safety while reversing a vehicle, detects any object within the following distance then red led will blink and a buzzer will blow to alert the driver to prevent the ambulance from accident.

Circuit Description: The full circuit has been constructed into two parts: a) Circuit diagram for heart rate and body temperature monitoring.

Figure 2. A circuit diagram of heart beat & body temperature monitoring

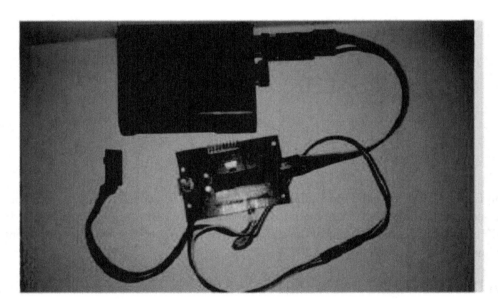

From Fig 2.1.2 A. Pulse rate sensor and temperature sensor is connected with Analog pins (A0 and A1) of Arduino. Arduino is connected with raspberry pi using serial to USB converter. Writing code in Arduino software then uploading the sketch in Arduino. With the help of Raspberry pi the hardware will be connected with the internet so that the monitoring of patient's will be shown live on the hospital monitoring website.

Circuit diagram for Accident Avoidance

In the Fig 2.1.2 B, given below The Ultrasonic sensor is connected with Arduino through a breadboard. The 2 LEDs i.e. RED, GREEN is connected with a 500E resistor so that it will give notification to the driver and a buzzer is also there. When the distance between the ambulance and vehicles is more than

2m GREEN LEDs will be continuously glowing else RED and Buzzer will also blow so that the driver will come to know about the danger.

Figure 3. Circuit diagram

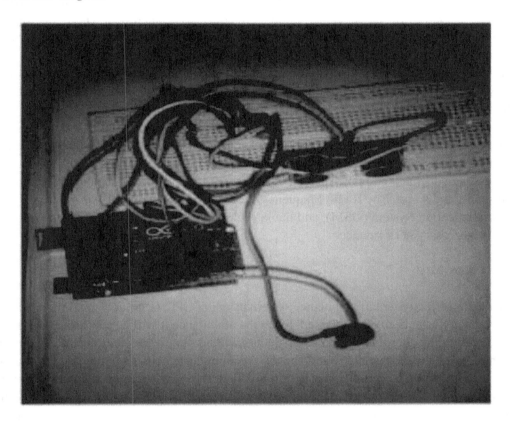

Summary

Here, existing IOT-based live monitoring system for patients with the risk of heart attack and uneven body temperature. If the condition is critical an alert notification will be sent to the hospital monitoring website. We also implemented a live trafficking system using Google map so that the ambulance will reach on time. To avoid accident, integrated hardware is made so that the ambulance will reach the patient's location on time

A Smart Ambulance System

Traffic jams in peak hours are one of the significant challenges confronting the world today. At rush hours, jams are trapped in rescue vehicles like ambulances. Consequently, these emergency programs frequently arrive on schedule, culminating in a loss of human life. Smart ambulance devices are best suited for emergency vehicle clearance during early hours. Many devices are used to incorporate intelligent ambulance systems. Consequently, Zigbee Technology, the Global Mobile Messaging Infrastructure, and the Global Positioning System (GPS) and modern high-speed microcontrollers have developed a cost-effective system to achieve these results. The primary goal is to identify and monitor an emergency vehicle so that radio signals can be sent to emergency vehicles. Conventional systems allow the use of emergency vehicle image recognition equipment. However, in poor weather, these systems have a drawback.

The image received by the camera is obscured by the noise associated with wind, rain, fog, etc., and it is difficult for the computer to identify the target vehicle. Therefore, we have fitted our equipment with ZigBee transponders and receivers (Bhushananantramani & Amuthajeyakumar,2018). The advantage of ZigBee is that it is a cost-effective approach that guarantees continuous access to our network, including in bad weather conditions. Recently, portable sensors and sensor networks have become a critical topic in the scientific and technological world of analysis. While sensor networks have been in service for several decades, a whole new sensor technology area has been opened up in the wireless domain. Green Bay systems may have emergency response clearance during rush hours. Many technologies are needed to integrate a green-wave framework. Wireless devices and sensor networks differ from traditional wireless networks and computer networks and face further obstacles such as electricity scarcity, shorter lifespans, and so on. The Radio Frequency Identification System (RFID) program, the Global Mobile Communication System (GSM), and the latest high-speed microcontroller have been designed to achieve the necessary performance.

System Architecture

For this system, an effective smart ambulance system by using GPS, GSM and smart mobile along with ZigBee Technology have been implemented. From the ambulance it will be capturing the patient's parameters along with the coordinates; these two details will be sent to the control center. Control center will be going to send the nearest hospital details to the ambulance, then the ambulance will choose the path to the hospital and the traffic signal within this direction will be green light and this route will be considered as green bay. Along with this every few minutes patient' parameter's will be sent to the hospital to get suggestions to monitor the patient's condition. This project is targeted to design and develop a real time smart ambulance system. To implement the proposed system, the ARM Cortex-M3 is interfaced with the traffic signal and ambulance section. The ARM Cortex-M3 (LPC 1768) The ARM Cortex-M3 is a next generation core that offers system enhancements such as enhanced debug features and a higher level of support block integration.

2.2.1.1 System Features

Categories: The system has three predefined sections Ambulance, Control Center and Traffic signal along with the hospital.
Patient Parameters: There are three parameters of patient's Bp, Temperature and Heart Beat the pulse of the patient will be sent to the control center with actual ambulance location coordinates.
Control Center: Based on the details sent from the smart mobile it will decide the nearest hospital to the ambulance and hospital details will be sent to the ambulance.
Traffic Signal: Once ambulances get response from the control center with hospital details, the ambulance traffic signal will be controlled and given as green light.

2.2.1.2 System Structure and Block Diagram

The basic block diagram of the system is illustrated in Fig 2.2. The system comprises a Zigbee Transmitter and Zigbee Receiver or transponder. Here, a high frequency reader which will provide long range to the system will be used. During the manufacturing of vehicles, ZIGBEE or transponders are embedded inside the dashboard of the vehicle such that it is not easily visible to human eyes. For this system, an effective smart ambulance system by using GPS, GSM and smart mobile along with ZigBee Technology have been implemented. From the ambulance it will be capture ng the patient "parameters along with the coordinates; these two details will be sent to the control center. Control center will be going to send the nearest hospital details to the ambulance, then the ambulance will choose the path to the hospital and the traffic signal within this direction will be green light and this route will be A REVIEW – Using IOT based Monitoring system in a Smart Ambulance with Patients.

Zig-bee: Zig-bee is a framework for a series of high-level networking protocols utilizing lightweight, low-power digital radios based on IEEE 802.15.4,2006 standard for wireless personal area networks (WPANs), such as wireless headsets connected to mobile phones via short-range radio. The Zig-bee specification technology is meant to be easier and less costly than other WPANs, such as Bluetooth. Zig-bee is aimed at applications with low data speeds, good battery life and safe networking.

GPS (Global Positioning System): The GPS is a U.S.-based space radio navigation system that includes precise positioning, navigation, and timing facilities for civilian users worldwide — widely available to anyone. The unit provides location and time for anyone with a GPS receiver. GPS gives a specific location and period for an unlimited number of people everywhere in the world, day and night. GPS is made up of three components:

- Control and monitoring stations on Earth
- Satellites orbiting the Earth
- The GPS receivers owned by users

GPS satellites broadcast signals from space that are picked up and identified by GPS receivers. Each GPS receiver then provides three-dimensional location (latitude, longitude, and altitude) plus the time.

Figure 4. Transmitter

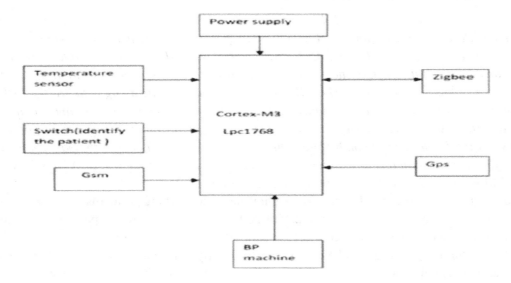

GSM Modem : The "Mobile Station" (MS) or "Mobile Appliances" (ME) language is used for mobile terminals delivering GSM installs. A GSM cell phone call to the PSTN is referred to as a 'mobile source call' (MOC) or 'outgoing call,' A fixed network call to the GSM mobile phone is called a 'mobile end call.'

Blood Pressure machine: Blood pressure and pulse control are seen onboard for external projects to produce and show integrated circuits. Plays systolic, diastolic, and pulse readings. Compact design is like a watch on your hand. The easy-to-use style of the wrist avoids pumping.

Blood Pressure machine: The LM35 series of sensors is precision-integrated-circuit temperature sensors whose output voltage is linearly proportional to the Celsius (Centigrade) temperature. The LM35 series is a precision integrated-circuit temperature sensor of LM35, the output voltage of which is linearly proportional to the temperature of Celsius (Centigrade). As a result, the LM35 sensor profits from linear temperature sensors calibrated at ° Kelvin. The user does not need to eliminate a large constant voltage from its output to achieve convenient Centigrade scaling.

Summary

Here, in this project "A Smart Ambulance System" has been successfully designed and tested. In this implementation we have used advanced technology components GPS and GSM along with ZigBee Technology. Integrating features of all the hardware components used have developed it. Presence of every module has been reasoned out and placed carefully thus contributing to the best working of the unit. Secondly, using highly advanced IC"s and with the help of growing technology the project has been successfully implemented.

2.3 Smart Ambulance System

Vehicle traffic in cities has been exponentially enhanced due to the vast number of vehicles on the road. As a result of this heavy traffic, severe traffic delays also occur due to which emergency vehicles, such as ambulances and fire vehicles, are stuck in traffic, which may contribute to a loss of human life. The present traffic control systems are a static situation in which cars have to wait for a predefined amount of time until the microcontroller switches the green signal to the route. When a traffic light delays the ambulance, the traffic police can prioritize the ambulance by giving the necessary signals or signs to the driver to move out of the traffic as quickly as possible. In comparison, if the emergency workers are stuck in a lane far from the traffic signal, the ambulance siren might not be able to enter the traffic police, in which case the rescue vehicles would have to wait until the road is open, so we will have to depend on other vehicles to move away, which is not an easy task in terms of traffic situations. The initiative incorporates a system through which the emergency driver tracks the traffic signal using the web interface. The emergency driver may ask the traffic light to turn the green lights on the lane in which it is located. This way, the ambulance could conveniently avoid traffic and reach the goal as soon as possible.

2.3.1 System Architecture

Previous systems have used RFID tags to detect ambulances; the problem is that the ambulance must be next to the RFID detectors. The ambulance driver also uses Android apps. The downside is that it only runs on Android devices or that the software has to be installed on other platforms. The text points out the process in which the ambulance driver uses the online program to request that the traffic controller make a green signal for the lane where the ambulance is positioned. As the web is accessible on any computer, this device is useful in an emergency.

Figure 5. Block diagram of Smart Ambulance System

be useful in emergency situations.

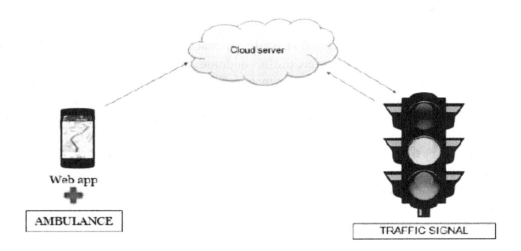

As shown in Fig 2.3 the whole system is divided into three parts. Their description is as follows:

Web Application: The online programmed is designed for the emergency driver. The benefits of a mobile app over an Android app would be as follows: Can be used on any network, e.g. Android, iOS, Blackberry, Windows, well. Any device that is open to the consumer can be utilized for emergency purposes. The software provides an emergency driver user experience to pick the route and man oeuvre the ambulance properly (Udawant et al,2017). The positional details of the ambulance shall be tracked by GPS and sent to the server. As the ambulance is entering the traffic signal, the ambulance driver will make a request to switch the required lane into amber. The data is sent to the server from which the traffic signal transforms the lane to green for the ambulance to pass.

Cloud Server: The central server is used to coordinate the traffic signal and the ambulance. The server will have input about what the ambulance driver requested. This information is used by the traffic signal to rise the appropriate path. API and authorization server was provided through the Google Cloud application platform.

Traffic Signal: The Arduino Uno board interfaced to the Esp 8266 Wi-Fi module is used as a traffic signal. The Arduino module is designed to retrieve server info. The traffic signal watches for a server interrupt, i.e. an ambulance order to transform a certain lane green. When an appeal is made, the lane is switched off before the ambulance exits. The traffic light then continues where it left off.

2.3.2 Summary

When an ambulance requests a certain lane to be switched on using the app, the traffic light transforms the lane to green, and also switches back to its original list. The web application that was created will show a google map and a form to upload the information. The ambulance driver will click the direction in which he or she travels and step forward. The data shall be processed in the form of the initials of the specific path. Traffic signals normally operate until the ambulance driver asks that a certain lane be green.

2.4 Smart Ambulance System using IoT

In emergencies such as body part transplantation, road crashes and so on, emergency services are strongly impacted when considering the existing severe traffic conditions in India. People suffer when they do not get adequate and prompt care, which is a serious matter. Time is a very critical element in emergency circumstances, so we have proposed a method to cope with this issue. Here, the device, i.e. 'Green Corridor,' for the ambulance, offers a special route along which all the red signals can be made green for the ambulance, which allows the ambulance to meet its destination in time. Generally, the ambulances pick up the patients and carry them to the hospital. Once they enter the hospital, the real procedure begins. So much time is lost in this, and the patient might risk his life. The machine constantly analyses the patient's critical health metrics, such as blood pressure, pulse rate, body temperature in the ambulance itself, and reports them to the medical database before approaching the hospital, so that the hospital officials can realize what form of care should be provided to the patient, saving so much time to save the patient's life. In wireless sensor networks, data obtained by installed sensor nodes is transmitted hop-by-hop across sensor nodes present at separate hops. When data is transmitted in wireless sensor networks, latency can occur, which can be minimized by utilizing various protocols. Packet retransmission in wireless sensor networks can be minimized by transferring data hop to hop using an exponential routing algorithm to mitigate network congestion. In order to prevent congestion, latency times and priority-based intervals may be used in packet routing.

2.4.1 Working of Wireless Sensor Network

Fig 2.4 shows the working of wireless sensor networks. Is a network made of sensor nodes which are deployed in the environment for sensing the physical parameters? Sensor senses physical parameters like humidity, temperature, pressure, direction, moisture etc. Nodes which sense the data or collect the data those nodes are called as source nodes. Source nodes send data to the destination node which is also called a sink node. Wireless sensor networks are used in many applications like home automation, forest fire detection, robotics, healthcare monitoring systems etc. In WSN data from source node is sent hop by hop to destination node. Single hop or multi hop transmission of data is done in WSN.

Figure 6. Working of wireless sensor network

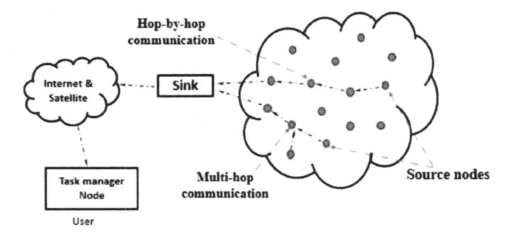

2.4.2 Analysis

In the Green corridor SMART AMBULANCE system, a number of 11 sensor nodes are deployed in the sensor area. Rate of data transmission from one node to another node is 0.1 i.e. 10 packets per seconds with 100 packet size in bytes. Nodes are deployed in 100m*100m area for data dissemination using chain topology, AODV (Ad-hoc on demand DistanceVector),CSMA (Carrier Sense Multiple Access), TDMA (Time Division Multiple Access), 802.15.4 (Zig-Bee), and SMAC (Sensor Medium Access Control protocol).

2.4.3 Summary

Various issues in ambulance service in the case of an injury have been studied here. Various variants of MAC protocols are being studied for the dissemination of data for SMART ambulance networks. The performance of the CSMA MAC protocol is substantially higher for PDR, PLR, End to End delays and network production. It offers 30 to 60 per cent better results for PDR, 40 to 60 per cent better results for average PLR, 15 to 35 per cent better overall, 20 to 50 per cent better results for average end-to - end latency than for TDMA, SMAC and 802.15.4 MAC protocols. The performance of SMAC, TDMA and

802.15.4 MAC protocols is very poor for latency, packet transfer, packet loss ratio and network output. CSMA Collision Protocol-Avoidance Solutions greatly increase the efficient performance of the network.

2.5 Smart Ambulance System

Nowadays, there are a number of neighbourhoods centred on becoming smart cities. If the region is to be called Smart City, all future developments in the area of smart technology could take place. Improving the standard of health care is one of the most challenging and daunting jobs. It refers to different aspects, such as getting an ambulance within a minimum amount of time, presenting the patient with the required treatment to maximise the probability of life. Traffic congestion is one of the main challenges in urban centres that have caused a variety of emergency shocks. In addition, traffic collisions in the city have increased and it is even more necessary to prevent loss of life as a consequence of accidents. These vulnerabilities can be resolved by upcoming technologies such as IoTi.e, the Internet of Things. The tools and software systems for wired and wireless networking can connect various hardware devices. Using separate REST APIs, the server-client end added in this project can connect (HimadriNathSaha et.al, 2017). REST APIs are designed to dramatically minimise time burden by exchanging only the required data with the server to minimize traffic and data packet loss during the transaction. Using state-of-the-art technology and bearing in mind the aim of developing this application. It also seeks to effectively participate in the move to a smart city and to make substantial services more accessible.

Figure 7. A Module1: Finding Ambulance & Hospital

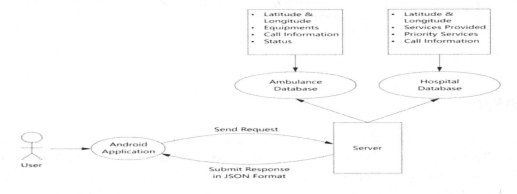

2.5.1 About Smart Ambulance System Overview

The system is classified into two modules depending on their functional and behavioral. implementation. Both modules use the IoT concept with the aid of the REST APIs. The first module is used to identify the position of the ambulance within a distance of 5 km from the patient's site. The same module is also used to classify hospitals and their services within a radius of 10 km from the client's current location. Here, the position of the user is tracked using a GPS hardware system. In the sense of a double value of latitude and longitude, the location is recovered. For eg, 19.54526, 73.87099. This is the format of latitude and longitude. This location is communicated to the server via the execution of POST requests. Depending on the customer 's position, the server processes the data and matches the data in the database. The output of the user's query is submitted back to the user in JSON format after those results have been analyzed. The Smartphone application reads the server 's response and retrieves the related data and places it on the Google Map client of the smartphone device or displays it in the specified format, depending on the user 's preferences.

2.5.2 Architecture

Here, Fig.2.5.A, suggests user sends requested to server regarding the required service i.e. either hospital information or ambulance details.

Figure 8. B Module Two: Sending Patient's information's to the Hospital

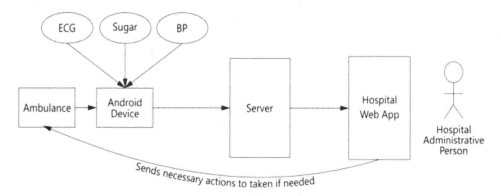

The second module is used to pass patient health information live to the client hospital (Fig.2.5.B). The readings are reported by an ambulance-accessible machine with various smart devices enabling triggered hardware components. The application may submit live data in such a way that the medical administration would have the necessary specifications before the patient enters the hospital. Treatment is reported to be especially important in the case of heart-related problems and emergencies when taking people from the source to the hospital. The administrative person in the hospital would then guide what steps should be taken when the patient reaches the hospital (HoomanSamani et.al., 2016).

2.5.3 Summary

Here's an idea to save a patient's life in a faster way. It is useful to customers in disaster times because it saves resources. This system allows the ambulance to reach the patients as they are located in the app and to include the necessary patient safety equipment. The specifics of the services that have been provided provide for the provision of an adequate hospital for the treatment of patients. The transfer of clinical knowledge to hospitals allows medical workers to achieve the appropriate criteria for the care of the patient. The future reach of this project can be developed by using some similar concepts found in this project. In order to preserve lives, even other factors can be taken into account. Traffic is one of the most serious problems in everyday life. This would render the ambulance sluggish to enter the facility. The traffic police can help if they recognize the current emergency location in advance. For the same cause, a traffic police application will be issued that displays the current location of the ambulances via GPS. The traffic officers will now be forced to clear the traffic so that the ambulance can take action.

2.6 Call Ambulance Smart Elderly Monitoring System with Nearest Ambulance Detection using Android and Bluetooth

In the real world, the patient must be monitored by the client at home or by the helpers. There is no automatic alerting device in operation so far. The patient is entirely monitored by the Micro-Electro Mechanical System (MEMS), Heart Rate, Temperature and Vibration Sensors related by wireless communication. These sensors recognise the various parameters of the patient, and these parameters are monitored using a Bluetooth-linked android phone. Mobile GPS is automatically triggered in case of an emergency and the alarm is sent to the server via mobile GSM. The server decides the nearest path to the hospital and sends an SMS alert to the relatives. The Wireless Sensor Network (WSN) is an enticing field for research and scientific and technological development. The creation of wireless network sensor technologies, such as battlefield control, was influenced by military applications. Today, such networks are used in a wide range of industrial and environmental applications, such as industrial process management and tracking, health surveillance equipment, plant monitoring, forest fire detection, groundwater monitoring, welfare monitoring, etc. Wearable sensors are placed on or beside the person on the surface of the human body. The human body is inserted with implantable medical devices.

2.6.1 System Architecture

In the medical industry, new developments and proposals for automated patient monitoring networks, such as the Wireless Sensor network and Android, are developing that exploit the versatility of technologies such as Bluetooth, Wi-Fi and Radio Frequency. This raises the ability to rescue people. The proposed system consists of a few sensors, such as the temperature, pulse, vibration and MEMS sensors of the patient. Ses Instruments note the important parameters of the patient, such as temperature and pulse. The complete system block diagram as seen in Fig 2.6.1 below.

Figure 9. Block diagram of proposed system

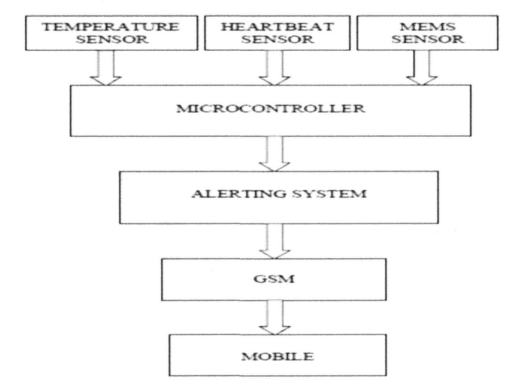

2.6.2 Hardware Components:

Temperature Sensor: Various temperature sensors are available. In this device, LM35 is used to calculate the patient's body temperature. LM35 is a built-in circuit temperature sensor able to calculate temperature with a more precise electrical output, equal to degree Celsius temperature.

Heart Beat Sensor: When the finger is placed on the beat sensor, the digital output of the heat beat is produced. The heart beat detector acts on the principle of light amplification by pushing blood through the finger with each pulse.

RFID: In the proposed method, Radio Frequency Identification (RFID) is used to immediately collect diagnostic details regarding the patient in critical condition. At first, specific information about the patient is processed on the registry and the associated RFID tag is created. The RFID reader is used to query the tag by sending encoded radio signals.

2.6.3 Summary

WSN is projected to play an important role in wireless technology and networking in the future. The purpose of this paper is mainly to set up a wireless sensor network to form the patient monitoring system and to take effective action under critical conditions. This application can have a great deal of scope in the future by incorporating more sensors. Other frameworks, such as intrusion detection or target discovery, can also be integrated with this structure. The core idea of developing this module is to give timely help to patients and elderly people in emergency scenarios. The patient's warning of sickness shall be given to the caregiver for immediate assistance. The system prototype was developed and effectively tested with the same.

Figure 10. The system Architecture

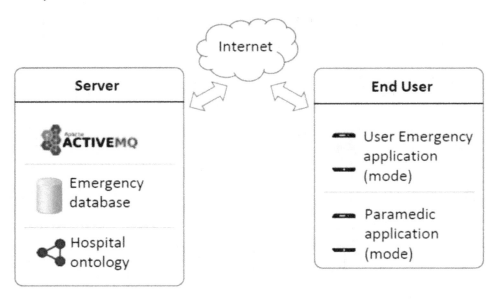

2.7 Smart Ambulance System for Highlighting Emergency-Routes

An ambulance is a truck carrying medical equipment to guarantee that patients are transported to care services, such as specialist hospitals and general hospitals. It is planned to provide easy access to paramedics, provide adequate medication and medical services during patient transfer. In a life-threatening scenario, paramedics must act quickly to rescue patients, even though there is traffic. In fact, traffic and emissions are a big obstacle to the movement of the ambulance. Drivers who are near to the ambulance should take timely steps to make space for the ambulance. And the drivers who are far from the ambulance will not take any action until they see the ambulance behind them. In other words, those drivers are not aware of the successful emergency route chosen by the ambulance. Several solutions have been introduced to improve the responsiveness of ambulances in order to render transportation to patients and hospitals more effective. However, these techniques do not resolve the emergency route chosen by ambulances resulting in responsiveness discrepancies. Here, a smart ambulance system has been proposed that takes into consideration the emphasis on emergency roads. The response is in the area of Smart Health Emergency Software built to advance the ambulance infrastructure. The goal is to keep drivers mindful of the emergency routes selected by the ambulances. The platform contains a cloud software, an end-user emergency user application and a paramedical end-user device. The server is responsible for managing interactions between end-user applications. The Consumer Emergency Software is clearly designed to show the condition of the patient and the location of the ambulance. And the paramedical application is structured to locate the patient and find the closest hospital. Based on the initial review of the questionnaire, the system proposed could improve the duration of patient travel.

2.7.1 System Architecture

Here, a smart ambulance system that is capable of marking a route as emergency-route has been proposed. It helps paramedics to drive patients faster to hospitals. The system is composed of two android applications including (1) user emergency: Users make an emergency request to call for an ambulance by showing the location of the patient. The application enables them to see also emergency-routes and the location of the ambulance. And (2) paramedic application: it enables the paramedics to locate the patient and locate the appropriate hospital. Drivers who are driving onthesamerouteoftheambulancewillgetnotificationaboutthecomingambulance.

Mobile Application Operation: The aim of the mobile app is to link to the server to read emergency routes, emergency accidents and ambulance sites. Loads the contents of the user interface, based on the setup state, where: (a) User emergency mode: presents a map showing emergency routes and ambulances. (b)Paramedical mode: presents a map indicating the status of the patient.

Real-time Communication: In order to have real-time communication to end-user apps, a message broker, ActiveMQ, is built to manage StoMP communications. There are two forms of texts, including:

Category of emergency: involves the status of the patient, the amount of ambulances requested, and an emergency description.

Multi-Cast Path Type: This is a notification that displays users the preferred emergency route. The location of the patient may be automatically sensed or manually adjusted by the operator.

Hospital ontology: An ontology has been developed to store semantic hospital information. The ontology with Protege has been established. Open-source framework for editing ontologies and knowledge acquisition systems. The system promotes the development of ontologies and retains the api for the application of knowledge-based constructs.

Emergency-route: Both paramedics will be informed that patient transport must be carried out after an emergency case request has been given. Once an emergency call has been accepted by one or more ambulances, an emergency path is formed from the ambulance location to the patient site, taking into consideration the shortest route. Therefore, before an ambulance appears at the patient, an escape route will be established from the patient's location to the nearest hospital.

2.7.2 Summary

Intelligent ambulance technology has been proposed to bring people closer to hospitals. It determines the direction of ambulances as a route of evacuation for alert drivers, although the ambulance is not obvious to the pilot. The emergency path is selected on the shortest route between the point of departure and the destination. The system proposed is a type of intelligent emergency medical application designed to advance the ambulance infrastructure. This is the first solution, based on the literature attested, that allows users to see the emergency route in real time. Based on initial questionnaire studies, paramedics suggested that the proposed device would improve the time for patients to drive to hospitals. Technology is currently in development with the goal of evaluating its usability in real-life conditions for paramedics and drivers.

2.8 Smart Ambulance Approach Alarm System Using Smartphone

Traffic disruptions are often exacerbated by high population densities in Japan 's metropolitan environment. Many cars also close the window and run due to high temperatures and humid weather, particularly in summer. There are some times, then, where the warning siren can not register. This leads to the emergency waiting period. In order to overcome this problem, a smart ambulance alert device has been created that can be used to open the ambulance position information. The purpose of this unit is to make an IoT ambulance only to position a mobile device on a dashboard. This computer can just send the positioning information of the ambulance to the cars on the ambulance side. In addition, this unit does not include medical position information while the ambulance does not travel on major roads due to safety issues. Thanks to these characteristics, a low-speed smart ambulance approach warning system can be mounted (ArifShaik et.al.2018)

2.8.1 Proposed System: Smart Ambulance Approach Alarm System

System Flow

This device comprises of emergency and general-vehicle smartphones and a cloud service as seen in Fig 2.8.1. The ambulance mobile programmed is used to transmit details on the location of the ambulance to the cloud server. The sound system between the ambulance and the mobile has been built to be mounted on the ambulance dashboard. When the siren blasts, the emergency mobile device transmits details on the status of the ambulance to the cloud server

Figure 11. System flow of Smart Ambulance Approach Alarm System

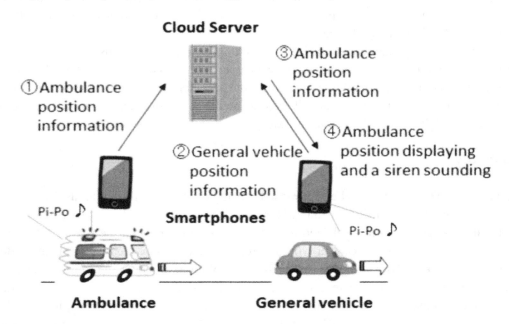

The Cloud Service programme distributes details on the location of the ambulance to other general vehicles thus fulfilling the next requirement. The ambulance is on a big highway. The general car and emergency span is less than 500 m. Come next to the general car and hospital. The general automobile mobile application transmits the location details of the vehicle to the cloud service application to determine these circumstances. If a requirement has been met, the ambulance location details was passed to the smartphone application of the general automobile. The ambulance position is shown on the general smartphone application of the vehicle and the siren is heard by the general smartphone vehicle.

The Ambulance Smartphone Application

This software acquires the sound of a mobile microphone and determines if the sensitivity of the particular frequency exceeds a specific volume. If this is met, the positioning information of the ambulance will be submitted to the cloud server. The Japanese warning sirens are 960Hz and 770Hz.

The General Vehicle Smartphone Application

This software is built as a web server here. After user verification, the location of the ambulance near the vehicle itself is displayed on a map based on guidance from the cloud service. In addition, the ambulance siren feature is also introduced.

The Cloud Server Application

From the details on the direction of the ambulance and the road chart, this application maps the place of the ambulance with respect to the street. It even forecasts the evacuation line. Upon receipt of the request from the general vehicle, the general vehicle in the ambulance role shall respond when the necessity referred to in A (System Flow) is met.

2.8.2 Summary

The smart ambulance approach alert system was installed here, which can be used to open the ambulance position records. In this way, the reliability of emergency activities will be done without unnecessary costs or with reference to the rights of privacy. The basic functionality of this system has been tested by a public road test.

2.9 IOT Based Traffic Signal Control For Reducing Time Delay of an Emergency Vehicle Using GPS

Human life is a very important thing for any world. Accidents and medical emergencies, such as burning, road accidents, medical emergencies, etc., are common. It is really necessary that emergency services hit the spot on order to prevent critical human casualties. Thus, hospitals and fire departments in the city minimise reaction time in the event of such emergencies. Traffic is a crucial element that adds to the pause in accessing the destination. This delay may be a question of life and death in the case of emergency services such as Ambulance, Fire Department, etc. Nearly all traffic signals are automatic now, when an emergency truck goes into an intersection without a green signal, there is a risk to traffic that is entering the signal from other roads on which the signal is green. Thus, in order to prevent significant collisions, the emergency driver must wait before the whole traffic light period is finished and generates an approved green signal. This is an important explanation for the reduction in response time of the emergency car. As a consequence, the requirement for a traffic light has been hourly, in big areas where traffic conditions are a significant reason for delay. Effective traffic signal Preemption can serve to minimise the pause and improve the reaction time and can be really beneficial in preserving a significant number of human life that will also give public protection to all traffic at a minimum cost. Here, it introduces an approach that monitors traffic signals such that the emergency car is on its way to a certain location. The location of the car is monitored using the GPS. This location is submitted to the request. The programme uses this data and the Google Map to execute the algorithm.

2.9.1 System Architecture

The new approaches to speeding up the visibility of emergency vehicles are measures such as sirens, warning lights and other advanced tactics, such as RFID stickers, etc. The use of the IOT GPS device and the Android app is more applicable to the proposed framework. Using all of these combined to resolve the traffic problem in such a manner that the emergency car moves across the signal traffic without further delay (C. Kotronis,2017). The diagram of the proposed method is seen in Fig 2.9.1.

GPS System: The GPS device used to chart the position of the Android mobile is used to monitor

Figure 12. Diagrammatic representation of the system

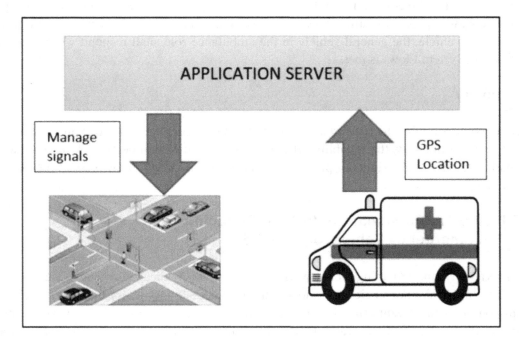

the vehicle's emergency location. The GPS system offers the shortest route to the goal. The latest functionality of the system that shows traffic on the road and the resulting delay. The driver will enter the destination on the Google Maps, which will return all travel options along with the approximate time of travel. Then the driver can choose one of the best paths.

Android Application: Android is a handheld device interface that comprises the operating system, the middleware and the core programs. The APIs used by the main applications. The architecture is structured to simplify the re-use of materials. Both programs have the right to allow use of the functionality of other apps. The Android SDK provides a complete package of Android system APIs. GPS is a satellite navigation system that offers location and time details both under environmental circumstances and elsewhere on Earth. This road is primarily used by those places where there is an unobstructed line of sight.

They are:

- Location Manager
- Location Provider
- Geocoding.
- Google Maps.

The proposed model will use an android application which will be used on a smartphone or tablet installed in every ambulance.

Application Server: In this process, the server plays an extremely important role. It recognizes the location of the ambulance or other emergency vehicle on the GPS of the Android customer. The server sends the warning to the closest emergency traffic signal. Both signals are controlled by Raspberry Pi.

Microcotroller (Raspberry Pi /Arduino): A Raspberry Pi is a micro-computer credit card that was originally designed for the purpose of knowledge and was inspired by the BBC Micro in 1981. The Raspberry Pi is an open hardware computer, with the exception of the Raspberry Pi main processor. This chip is named BroadcommSoC (a chip system). This chip is responsible for operating different components on Raspberry Pi boards such as Processor, graphics, memory, USB controller, etc.

2.9.2 Summary

The proposed approach is very useful in this regard, as it makes the almost very productive use of data sent by role providers. Android app not only works on traffic signal control, it also sends messages to the hospital and the doctor in question to get arrangements ready. The hospital will priorities the patient and provide attention to the information gathered by the medical personnel. The theory of Blue Light should be taken into consideration in the confusion that can be created by a shift in light between the heads of people waiting for the signal. This approach improves the state of the art of emergency routing by introducing complex path planning in combination with the prevention of traffic signals. As the results indicate, the complicated path planning has demonstrated that the travel time of the emergency response is reduced.

2.10 Smart Traffic Management System Using IOT

A city is a dynamic structure composed of several interdependent subsystems where a traffic system is one of the most significant subsystems. A report says it is the central pillar of the global economy. It is also declared to be one of the main dimensions of the intelligent region. With the exponential increase of the world's population, the amount of cars on the highways is therefore rising, with traffic jams still expanding in the same direction. Traffic delays not only consume resources, but in certain situations, illegal acts, such as cell snatching, often take place in metropolitan cities.

The successful traffic management system is therefore defined as a necessity. The traffic management system is perceived to be one of the key dimensions of an intelligent community. The exponential increase in people and urban mobility in urban areas also contributes to congestion of traffic on highways. To solve multiple traffic management problems and assist authorities in careful preparation, a smart traffic management framework utilising the Internet of Things (IoT) is suggested here. Such systems can crash in the event of networking problems. Furthermore, there is fewer reliance on traffic volatility. The proposed framework therefore handles local and unified server traffic by jointly leveraging the principles IoT and Artificial Intelligence. The mathematical depiction of traffic data may also be useful for authorities to monitor and handle traffic in real time. In addition, it may also be beneficial in future planning.

2.10.1 System Architecture

The system functions in a distributed manner, handles node level sensor data and video data on the local server, calculates the combined intensity to monitor the density of traffic. It also applies to emergency services, such as ambulances, fire brigades. It also helps users to estimate the congestion on the road. There are three stages to the unit. (a.) The data acquisition and selection sheet. (b) Data Processing and Decision Making Layer (C.) The proposed structure, as seen in Fig. 2.10.1 is intended to monitor road flow, sensor transmitters, surveillance cameras and route-embedded RFIDs

Figure 13. The System Model

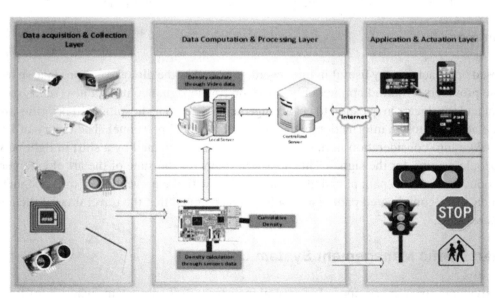

Data Acquisition and Collection Layer

The state-of-the-art specialists have used a range of different types of traffic monitoring, including ultrasonic sensors, RFIDs, camera monitoring and light beams. Many of these sources have benefits as well as demerits; safety detectors, ultrasonic sensors, RFIDs and smoke sensors are the appropriate sources for the proposed system.

The security camera is the most popular source of traffic monitoring in this field, due to its reliability and ease of maintenance. In addition to mirrors, ultrasonic devices are used to improve sensitivity. Sensors are a major part of the traffic volume found in various implementations for traffic control systems.

Data Processing and Decision-Making Layer

Several ways of traffic control have been utilised by cutting edge experts, including ultrasonic monitors, RFIDs, detectors and light beams. Many of these sources have advantages as well as demerits; fire alarms, ultrasonic sensors, RFIDs and smoke sensors are the appropriate sources for the proposed device (Jalali et al, 2015). Due to its reliability and ease of maintenance, the security camera is the most common source of traffic monitoring in this region. In addition to the mirrors, ultrasound systems are used to enhance sensitivity. Sensors are a significant part of the amount of traffic contained in different applications for traffic control systems.

Application and Actuation Layer

In this layer there are two types of details provided: the duration of the green signal from the node to the traffic signal; and (ii.) daily, weekly, monthly and annual traffic management framework administering data through the centralised portal web application. Second, when a hurry period is observed, the local server intimates the respective microcontroller with road I d. After the intimation of the rush period has been received, the decision-making module adjusts the duration of the green signal to the respective traffic signal.

2.10.2 Summary

It presents an effective solution for the rapid growth of traffic, especially in large cities, and traditional solutions have certain limitations because they are not efficient in managing existing traffic. In view of the state-of-the-art system for traffic control strategies, an integrated traffic management system is introduced for more efficient and productive regulation of road conditions. It intelligently changes signal timing by roadside traffic strength and monitors traffic by communicating more effectively than ever with local servers. The distributed approach optimises and lets it run as the mechanism runs even when a local server or centralised server fails. In the event of an incident, the centralised registry shall connect to the nearest emergency service to guarantee timely human safety. In addition, a commuter can ask about future traffic standards on a particular road in order to avoid wasting traffic jam time. The system also provides higher authorities with useful information that can be utilised in road planning to enhance the usage of services.

CONCLUSION

IoT is a fast-growing sector for applications and has been used successfully in an ambulance. In addition, there are accidents in so many places; there is a risk of survival leading to a break in the ambulance response and a gap in healing. The new facility is designed to avoid side-by - side hospital configurations. The victim's body status was automatically transmitted to the cloud and admin server through the sensor and the GPS location. The biometric system extracts details from the central database. The occurrence of the incident diagnosis will be confirmed to the hospital and the relatives of the wounded. Our potential endeavour will be to acquire information on the aadhar card by utilising the victim's fingerprint sensor in real time, using the injured person's fingerprint, so that we can gather the particulars of the injured person and send them to their families without the patient's prior knowledge.

REFERENCES

Bhushananantramani & Amuthajeyakumar. (2018). *Smart ambulance guidance system*. Academic Press.

Bhushananantramani & Amuthajeyakumar. (2016). Smart Ambulance System. *International Journal of Computer Applications*.

Building an intelligent transport system using internet of things (IOT). (n.d.). intelligent-transport-systemblueprint.pdf

Jalali, R., El-Khatib, K., & McGregor, C. (2015). Smart city architecture for community level services through the Internet of Things. *Proc. IEEE 18th Int. Conf. Intell. Next Generat. New. (ICIN)*, 108–113.

Khan, A., Pohl, M., Bosse, S., Hart, S., & Turowski, K. (2017). A Holistic View of the IoT Process from Sensors to the Business Value. *Proceedings of the 2nd International Conference on IoTBDS*, 392-399. 10.5220/0006362503920399

Kotronis, C. (2017). *Managing Criticalities of e-Health IoT systems. IEEE Wireless Broadband*.

Li, X., Zhao, Z., Zhu, X., & Wyatt, T. (2011). Covering models and optimization techniquesfor emergency response facility location and planning: A review. *Mathematical Methods of Operations Research*, *74*(3), 281–310. doi:10.100700186-011-0363-4

Reddy & Khare. (2017). *A Smart Ambulance System*. Academic Press.

Saha Raun, & Saha. (2017). *Monitoring Patient's Health with Smart Ambulance system using Internet of Things (IOTs)*. IEEE.

Saha, Raun, & Saha. (2017). Monitoring Patient"s Health with Smart Ambulance system using Internet of Things (IOTs). *8th Annual Industrial Automation and Electromechanical Engineering Conference (IEMECON)*.

Samani & Zhu. (2016). Robotic Automatetd External Defibrillator Ambulance for Emergency Medical Service in Smart Cities. *IEEE Access, 4*.

Shaik, Bowen, Bole, Kunzi, Bruce, Abdelgawad, & Yelamarthi. (2018). Smart Car: An IoT Based Accident Detection System. *2018 IEEE Global Conference on Internet of Things (GCIoT).*

Udawant, Thombare, Chauhan, Hadke, & Waghole. (2017). Smart Ambulance System using IoT. In *2017 International Conference on Big Data, IoT and Data Science (BID).* Vishwakarma Institute of Technology.

Chapter 3
Augmented and Virtual Reality and Its Applications

S. Graceline Jasmine
Vellore Institute of Technology, Chennai, India

L. Jani Anbarasi
Vellore Institute of Technology, Chennai, India

Modigari Narendra
Vignan's Foundation for Science, Technology, and Research (Deemed), India

Benson Edwin Raj
Higher College of Technology, Fujairah Women's Campus, Fujairah, UAE

ABSTRACT

Augmented reality (AR) overlies manually made materials directly over the real-world materials. This chapter addresses the technological and design frameworks required to create realistic motion tracking environments, realistic audio, 3D graphical interactions, multimodal sensory integration, and user interfaces and games using virtual reality to augmented reality. Similarly, the portfolio required to build a personal VR or AR application is detailed. Virtual and augmented reality industry committed innovative technologies that can be explored in the field of entertainment, education, training, medical and industrial innovation, and the development are explored. Augmented reality (AR) allows the physical world to be enhanced by incorporating digital knowledge in real time created by virtual machine. Few applications that have used augmented and virtual reality in real-world applications are discussed.

1. INTRODUCTION

Augmented Reality (AR) enables digital knowledge to be overlaid directly over the physical world (Azuma, 1997). Technology can be used to perform the Knowledge relevant to real world entities to assist the user in carrying out a particular task. AR has penetrated almost all fields of healthcare, gaming, entertainment, retail, digital marketing, education, services and so forth. Augmented reality (AR) allows

DOI: 10.4018/978-1-7998-4703-8.ch003

Copyright © 2021, IGI Global. Copying or distributing in print or electronic forms without written permission of IGI Global is prohibited.

the physical world to be improved by incorporating digital knowledge generated by virtual computers in real time. This helps advertisers to reach and connect with consumers with previously unimagined choices. With the capacity to deliver (virtual) goods to the consumer, the user may communicate with the brand, the services and products.

Microsoft Holo-lens:

Microsoft HoloLens is a pair of smart glasses designed and manufactured by Microsoft, known as the Baraboo project under development. HoloLens was the first Windows Mixed Reality device head-mounted monitor on the Windows 10 machine. Figure 1 shows the Microsoft HoloLens.

Figure 1. Microsoft HoloLens (Microsoft, n.d.)

HTC Vive:

The HTC Vive has been developed by HTC and Valve which is a virtual reality headset. The Headset uses room-scale tracking technology to allow the user to move into 3D space and to interact with the environment with motion-tracked handheld controllers (figure 2).

Figure 2. Room-Scale VR (Vive, n.d.)

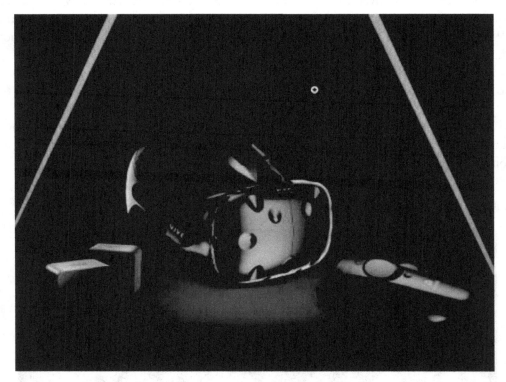

Intel Vaunt: Intel Vaunt is smart glasses appearing as traditional glasses with retinal projection displays. No camera can be used to move people out, no pushbutton, no swipe-motion field, no flashing LCD screen, no strange neck, no speaker and no microphone. Vaunt lenses look like normal eye lenses from the outside. You see a variety of details about what appears like a mirror when you wear them — but it's actually projected on the retina (Verge, n.d.). In December, the prototypes used were almost indistinguishable from regular glasses. These are available in various styles, function with prescriptions and are easy to wear all day. Aside from the tiny red lens that is often shown on the right eye, you may not even be aware of the fact that you wear intelligent lenses (figure 3).

Figure 3. Intel Vaunt (Verge, n.d.)

2. AUGMENTED AND VIRTUAL REALITY IN GAMING

Gaming using hand Gestures: Augmented reality application that can make use of hand detection can be performed using Machine Learning techniques. Most AR application uses a physical controller to give user input. Instead hand detection can be performed to let the user interact with the surrounding AR virtual world without the usage of a physical controller. POSENET can be implementing for performing hand detection. AR based VR based video games are growing in popularity and are likely to dominate the gaming market in the future. This will help the individuals to interact with these types of video games through gesture-based controls. JS and Tensor flow are used to implement to enable gesture recognition.

Air Motion (By LG): Air motion helps to access the LG G8 Mobile phone using hand gestures. Eventually, you can accept or reject calls and alarms from within the control calls and alarms tab, by keeping the hand in a clav shape above the Z camera and wiggling right or left when the manual appears. The main feature of Air Motion is to quickly leap into the application shortcuts. **Hovering Controls (XDA Developer):** Created by an XDA Senior International Member, Hovering Controls uses your device's proximity sensor to record simple motions. Pre-defined applications can be started by floating, swiping once or twice over the sensor. The XDA Forum framework allowed users to monitor and touch their computers. Three approved gestures were already in place: hover hold, swipe once, and swipe twice. These settings can be assigned to start any application selected by the user.

Wave Control: Wave Control is an application in mobile that helps us to control the music and video playback, using hand gestures over phone. No need to touch to change the applications, this can be performed even when the screen is off. Wave Control helps to work with the any of user favorite music and video applications. **Just a line (by Google):** Just a line is an AR experiment, which lets you draw simple images in virtual and augmented reality and then allows to share it in the form of a short video .

Figure 4. AR Stickers (Celsoazevedo, n.d.)

Pokémon GO: In collaboration with the Pokémon group, Pokémon Go is an Augmented Reality game developed and released by Niantic for iOS and Android devices. The game is the result of a partnership between Niantic, Nintendo and The Pokémon Company as part of Pokémon's Company. It uses GPS for finding, capturing, battling and training virtual creatures, called Pokémon, that seem to be in the real world of the player. The game is free to play; it uses a free business model and encourages purchasing in-app for extra things in the game. The game began with approximately 150 Pokémon species, which had risen to approximately 600 by 2020.

Google AR Stickers: Playground is a new camera mode to help you build and play around the world. Playmohi, characters interacting with you and to each other, bring to life your images and videos. Put sticks around you, and funny subtleties, where words are used. Playground understands your world and gives you insightful ideas to help you articulate yourself and add life to your plot. The new version of ARCore will first be installed (https:/goo.gl/77tPbU) (figure 4).

AR Foundation: The AR Framework allows you to work several platforms within Unity with enhanced technology platforms. AR Framework is a compilation of MonoBehaviors and APIs that support concepts for apps. Tracking the location and orientation of the unit in physical space, detection of the plane: detection horizontal and vertical surfaces, clouds of points, often know as characteristic points, point of reference: the location and the orientation of the object; Samples of the environment: a way of creating a cube map for a certain area of the physical environment; Face tracking: detects and monitors human face; image tracking: 2D pictures detect and monitor and object tracking: detects 3D objects. Light estimate: estimates of average color temperature and brightness in physical space;

3. AUGMENTED AND VIRTUAL REALITY IN ONLINE SHOPPING

It helps advertisers to connect and communicate with an unimagined ways to their customers. AR creates a potential to place (virtual) products in the hands of the people in real time, where the users are getting an opportunities to engage with products so that decisions can be made accurately. The Augmented reality is a technology that overlays a picture created by a computer and offers a composite view of the reality for a consumer. This product intends to bridge the gap between online shopping platforms and traditional methods of shopping. It provides the consumers a functionality to try-on their desired items thus increasing a sense of reliability on online platforms. Hence, it addresses one of the most prevalent disadvantages of online shopping methods subsequently leading to a wider customer base. Increased retail reality, Wikitude reports that 32% of consumers are frequent users of AR and 73% are extremely pleased with experience. These rising statistics on retail reality demonstrate how the consumer embraces and exponentially increases the technology. Issues like Travelling, Compartmentalization, Insufficient items with traditional retail marketing can be overcome through AR.

4. AUGMENTED AND VIRTUAL REALITY IN HEALTHCARE

AR has an outstanding role in the development of medical and medical devices. This technology provides healthcare practitioners, medical students and others a broad set of incentives and advantages for a healthier experience. Augmented diagnosis, Augmented Surgery, Augmented Training and Practice are the few areas where Augmented Reality really helps. This technique, for the reconstruction of patients with serious lesions, is being used in various hospitals including Imperial College and St. Mary's Hospital in London. AccuVein helps nurses and medical professionals to assess location of their veins by projecting a handheld scanner onto the skin of the patient. This reduces the time for the treatment, makes the operation easier and increases the patient satisfaction rate (Appinventiv, n.d.b).

5. AUGMENTED AND VIRTUAL REALITY REAL ESTATE

The technology has certainly paved the way for higher performance in recognizing the advantages of the growing realities in real estate. It enabled entrepreneurs to overcome the limits of current resources in their real estate activities. IKEA Place and Curate are the two best examples of inclusion of Augmented Reality in the Real estate domain. In this case, Augmented Reality allows users to display and interact with a 3D image of the house. In other words, they can switch items from one corner to another to allow them to appear in their homes. The system also makes it easy to calculate the apartment / land measurements in real time.

6. AUGMENTED AND VIRTUAL REALITY MOBILE APPS

The application is introduced, which provides consumers with a creative shopping experience. Regardless of the shift in e-commerce patterns and the vast rise in the usage of smartphones and tablets, many consumers are accepted because of their new apps. We can infer from this paper that increased reality is yet another step into digital times, because soon we can see complex changes in our environments, whether through a smartphone, glasses, windshields and even windshields, to display enhanced content and media directly to our customers. This has incredible applications that allow us to live our lives in a more efficient, healthy and insightful manner. (Tilty et al., 2017). Digital shopping and the Consumer loyalty can be assessed by mobile apps through augmented reality (McLean & Wilson, 2019). Whilst AR is at its infancy in consumers' markets, several creative retailers have used mobile AR technology. The research identifies the variables that affect the brand's participation through retail mobile apps and the outcome of the AR brand engagement through a Web-based survey of 441 consumers. Tobias et al (Richter & Raška, n.d.) research explored whether and how interactions with the AR shopping application would affect the purpose of the consumer. Following the AR-Application, the experimental methodology had a more beneficial impact on customers' buying intention within the study community than in the control community who saw a screenshot of the conventional ecommerce website. Therefore, the findings indicate that a committing AR program may not be a fun jigsaw but that it actually influences the purchase intention of users and can potentially turn them into paying customers.

7. AUGMENTED REALITY APPLICATIONS IN CULTURAL HERITAGE

Over the past few years, numerous cultural activities and museums have concentrated its attention on the fields of digital visualization and interactive technology, with the goal of better facilitating the dissemination of art, music, literature and learning between the tourists of various ages and culturally diverse backgrounds (Ott & Pozzi, 2011). Indeed, in order to recreate completely simulated artifacts or dynamically increase a actual one with simulated content, the 3D-display systems are very popular in museums. In museums interactive chat guides have been increasingly used to allow effective access and understandable culture content overview (Fatta, 2015; Gaia et al., 2019; Gonizzi Barsanti et al., 2015a; Terlikkas & Poullis, 2014). However, many current applications aim to enhance visitors' cultures by enhancing their interest through a personalized experience through single technology that focuses on visualisation, movement or verbal interplay. To address this limit, an integrating state-of-the-art technology is proposed using holograms and artificial intelligence (AI) to provide an enhanced room for museums capable of laying new interaction forms which can improve and strengthen their engagements (Caggianese et al., 2020). The device consists of a semi-transparent glass that allows users to imagine floating 3D holograms, an interface to control virtual objects and an interface to communicate in a colloquial language with tourists while maintaining the context of communication. It was created as a design prototype capable of reproducing holograms of realistic 3D models of Leonardo' machines and answering questions about these artifacts, their contex tual details and, more generally, about Leonardo life. The system has been widely installed and used for the shows in Genoa, Milan's and Naples. In order to achieve the holographic effect, the device uses Peppers Ghost's illusory technique (Sprott, 2006). The Gesture module extracts the information from the optical hand tracking sensor and map visitor hand movements for communicating with the system. The hand, fingers and body posture detection performs the detection and recognition of hand posture. Thus tracks the hand movements. If detected, visual feedback will be provided to the user on a virtual replica of the user's hand. The search strategy used a wait-to-click metaphor implementation technique. When the model has been chosen, which means that the module for visualization is in the visualization state, two other movements are allowed to control the model. The visitors can pick a Leonardo da Vinci's machine, turn it and zoom in with a virtual magnifying glass. The gesture module performs a rotating motion when the visitor moves his hand on the right or on the left of the model. This movement helps users to continuously rotate in virtual model in the appropriate direction and is shown in fig 1. The Visualization Module analyses and manipulates gesture module inputs. The conversation module interprets visitor's queries in order to suit the visually to the system's response. The conversational module evaluates the user language; estimate its intent; create and maintain a communication with the user using Natural Language (NL) dialogs; request the missing information which not able to infer from the dialog; derive correct answers to user questions from an organized knowledge base; to generate the NL speech to provide the user with understandable answers and to enable multimodal interaction to the Visualization module. Attention module is used to tell whether the visitor talks to a machine or if he or she concentrates on something else. In the Evaluate user attention state, the module decides if a customer is available and is viewing at the holographic projection as shown in Fig. 5.

Figure 5. The rotation (a) and zooming (b) interaction techniques (Caggianese et al., 2020).

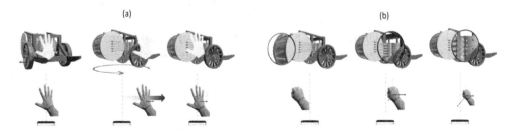

Figure 6a. Data overview, filtering and visualisation (Caggianese et al., 2019).

Figure 6b. Accessing and visualisation of the situated information details using gaze (Caggianese et al., 2019).

Table 1. Configuration Used in AR Models

Ref	Augmentation and Reality Tool	Operating System	Cameras	Dataset
Caggianese, G. et al (2019)	Microsoft HoloLens (Microsoft Corp., Redmond, USA) (Microsoft, microsoft hololens, n.d.)	Windows 10	depth camera, an HD video camera 2 MP photo camera, four microphones	
Caggianese, G.et al (2020)			Leap Motion controller	One-hundred-and-sixty-four subjects (93 male, 71 female) Age 6 to 72

Over the last few years, Augmented Reality (AR) systems have progressed to a close link between the representation of information and the actual world, which is often the source of the data. Look at the example from Internet of Things (IoT) and ubiquitous computing where real-world entities may generate the data, a Contextualized visualisation might help to expose the semantics OD the generated data. The ability to access and discover knowledge relating to the environment through computer-based access representation of spatial and semantic context is labelled as "situated visualization" by White and Feiner (White & Feiner, 2009b). This description does not take into account the knowledge type seen, which means there's no difference between Data types and, in particular, it can be abstract data (White & Feiner, 2009a) or Physical data (Tatzgern, 2015) when placed can be visualized. In addition, Definition just talks about visualization and not about the system to visualise the data. Any solution for registration of Actual real world data can be sufficient, which means that the mere fact that the visualization uses an AR-Technology does not mean that the visualization is automatically situated. In order to be situated, the visualisation must be connected to an entity in the real world (Tatzgern, 2015). In the visualization-physical relationship, the situated visualization is an 'embedded' referent when the data correspond spatially with the visualization and data referents, ensures a visualisation can be either or not embedded (Caggianese et al., 2020). The new AR applications, Microsoft HoloLens HMD (Microsoft, microsoft hololens, n.d.) provide a fine real-world environmental awareness by a collection of meshes that reflect the environment geometry. In this research, an issues related to knowledge exploration related to situated knowledge is analysed using technologies of AR. Strategies are proposed to reduce the technical constraint of an ego-centric viewpoint and a real-world spatial perception (Caggianese et al., 2019). The proposed study helps to ● get an outline of the knowledge concerning its relation with and therefore semantics in the real world; ● the user's information are used for filtering the data ● Acquisition of data information without moving in the real world (figure 6 a, b).

Figure 7. Visualization of information related to the user experience. (Caggianese et al., 2018)

Pilot study was performed to evaluate the perceived performance. Usage of the strategies suggested to get a summary the details and the location to search and retrieve the extract information is obtained through an AR system. Tools and OS used in different environments are given in table 1.

Cultural fields like Museums, art exhibition, archaeological and historical centre parks have been growing the rate of digitized Cultural Heritage (CH) content in almost all developed countries (UNESCO, 2005). Digital technology applications have been used to connect the cultural spaces and the tourist to promote the enjoyment of the visitor thereby improving the awareness of CH purpose. CH began to use immersive, enhanced- technologies including virtual and mixed reality for Training, development of exhibits, discovery, reconstruction and virtual museum presentation. Such tools make the digital representation of a cultural object available even though access is restricted to physical ones. In that way, consumers can perceive cultural assets in a whole new way and take advantage of a physical experience with several composites of digital and real content (Caggianese & Gallo, 2016; Styliani et al., 2009). Virtual Reality (VR) is the most promising immersive technologies to enable these compositions. In this sense, researchers began to utilize both VR and digital content to convey to non-CH specialists the importance of historical objects (Gonizzi Barsanti et al., 2015b). The authors (Caggianese et al., 2018) inspired by the evolution of GUI in gaming industry, diegetic and non-diegetic interfaces has been analysed for their sustainability in the Cultural Heritage (CH) domain. To achieve a more natural and interactive experience for the user a new graphical user interfaces should be developed. Diegetic approach opportunities will be presented and its significance to the cultural sector is evaluated. The problems related to the implementation of diegetic user interfaces to an interactive virtual exhibition by analysing the different types of cultural data that can be suggested and the fictional incorporation into the visitors is performed. The 3D reconstructions of structures (Andreoli et al., 2005), (Deggim et al.,

2017) or artworks (Apollonio et al., 2012), (Ebner et al., 2017) with antique and aesthetic value having strong traditional and cultural background have been focused. To enrich the visitor's view, the communication between the users and the virtual objects had immersive effects (Bekele et al., 2018). The contextualization of the artwork therefore includes the exposure to certain types of details via the user interfaces. Tangible and intangible aspects related to multimedia resources associated with the virtual reproductions to enrich the visitor experience are improved. These authors presented this information using the majority of completely immersive VR systems using a head mounted devices (HMD) resulting in that producing constant disturbances of user experience interfaces. In the context of archaeological studies, a CAVE system is implemented to create an immersive virtual environment (VE) (Acevedo et al., 2001). The research in (Rua & Alvito, 2011) demonstrates how architectural history is learned by VR. The 3D models along with UI displays avatar data such as 2D objects projected at the screen for the point of view. GUI elements and diegetic approach is proposed for Cultural Heritage (CH) and Diegetic experiences in video games allows players to experience immersive feel allowing players to use hands to interact with the environment (Figure 7).

Figure 8. Crash Accident Training (Dudeja et al., 2019)

Figure 9. Branching Story Path

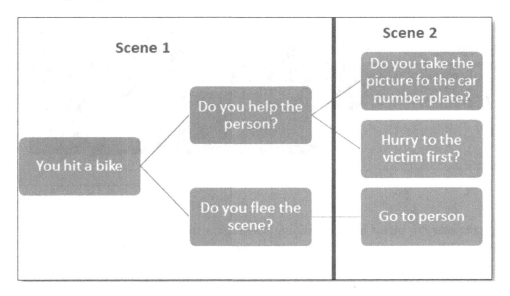

8. VIRTUAL REALITY (VR) ENABLED FIRST AID TRAINING PROGRAMS TO HANDLE EMERGENCY

The aim of this project is to conducts first aid training programs through VR and Filming. In order to test the user's knowledge on road safety, first aid knowledge, important emergency helpline numbers, Basic Life Support Guidelines and how to approach victims in emergency situations. The plan is to recreate the environment and the soundscape of an accident scene in virtual reality, so as to give the user the immersive experience of the scene at a crash accident while we conduct an interactive questionnaire with him. The capacity of the lay person to provide early treatment in emergency situations and assistance for basic life (BLS) is important for life survival and sequelae prevention. The simulation of virtual reality involves using 3D objects and environments to construct realistic and engaging experiences of learning. The idea of e-learning is to connect, practice and test user know-how through interactive simulations and environments to mimic circumstances of real life (Dudeja et al., 2019) (figure 8).

Figure 10. Augmented Reality view of the training kit using OculusGo & Unreal

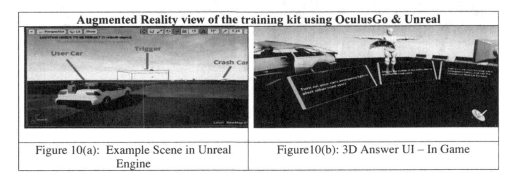

Figure 11. Controller Setup

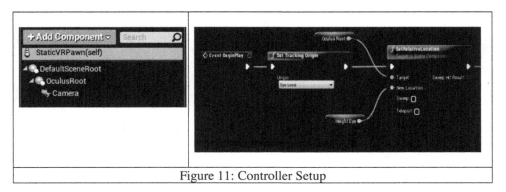

Figure 11: Controller Setup

It is also necessary to invest in BLS training courses for the lay population, since, although it is a reality, there are still large gaps for the start of basic manoeuvres, due to the lack of awareness and also the fear of social reproach for a possible failure. The main objectives included

Ø Conduct questionnaire on the Basic Life Support Guidelines and First Aid Knowledge
Ø Create an atmosphere that simulates a real accident scene
Ø Create a smooth and interactive experience

This work presents two non-immersive virtual reality first aid systems. The first is a testing system and the second is a narrative guided experience on the correct responses for the first responders. Both the systems follow the DRSABC Action Plan, which is a set of guidelines a first responder must follow when administering first aid to a victim in an emergency situation.

Figure 12. a) In – game screenshot: Color coded answers, DRSABC guidance, Audio and Visual Feedback, b) Remove obstacles button (action) in the scene is placed closed to the lying obstacles

Fig12 (a) : In – game screenshot: Color coded answers, DRSABC guidance, Audio and Visual Feedback	Fig 12 (b): Remove obstacles button (action) in the scene is placed closed to the lying obstacles

Table 2. Adreno 530 Graphics Processor Unit specification

Name	Adreno 530
Manufacturer	Qualcomm
Type	Mobile GPU
Manufacturing Process	14nm FinFET
Used In	Snapdragon 820/821
Clock Rate	510/624/650 MHz
GFLOPS	407/498/519
Direct3D	12
Vulkan Support	Yes, 1.0
OpenGL	3.2
DirectX Version	11.2

Table 3. Specification of the Oculus Go Processor

CPU	Kyro 64-bit Quad-core 2.4 GHz (14nm process technology)
GPU	Adreno 530
Memory Support (RAM)	LPDDR4 1866MHz dual-channel RAM
Display & Video	1080p, 4k Ultra on Output and 4k Ultra HD capture and playback
Storage	UFS 2.0, eMMC 5.1, SD 3.0 (UHS-I)
Camera	Up to 25 Megapixel, Qualcomm Spectra Image Sensor Processor (14-bit dual-ISP)
Sound	Qualcomm Hexagon 680 DSP
Modem	X12 LTE with 600Mbps download speed
Wi-Fi	Qualcomm VIVE 802.11ac, Tri-band Wi-Fi
USB	USB 3.0 / 2.0
NFC	Yes
Bluetooth	Bluetooth 4.2
Charging	Quick Charge 3.0, Wireless Charging

Table 4 Performance Analysis

S. No.	Name	FPS
1	Enabling Compute Static Lights + Mobile HDR	25 - 35
2	Disabling Compute Static Lights + Mobile HDR	35 - 45
3	Rendering UI	35
4	No UI	45

D – Look for Danger and remove potential hazards
R – Check for the Victims Response
S – Send for help
A – Check and open the airway
B – Check for Breathing
C – Do CPR

Since, VR devices are now more accessible we intend to put the user in a virtually created computer generated environment that simulates the scene and soundscape at a scene of an accident and test his knowledge through an interactive questionnaire. After the questionnaire round, the user is shown an interactive film in which the viewer will make the decisions for the main character. The users will have 5-10 seconds to make a choice. With the interactive film, we aim to replicate the human dilemma between binary choices in timed crucial situations where wrong decisions could mean incorrect safety procedure of attending crash victims. This training program aims at qualifying staff and investing in people.

To put the user in a head-on-car-to-bike collision simulation, the trainee chooses how the simulation is to be played out. At the initial scene, does the car-hitter help the victim or not? On this decision, this affects in the next scene when you will be pedestrian running to the crash site(Shukla et al., 2019), can you take the picture of his number if he were there or not? If you choose initially to flee the scene, you won't see the car in the next scene figure 9,10.

Ø VR Camera and Controller

Setting up the camera and the controller from the Oculus Go SDK was necessary to let the user view the virtually built world. How this Camera is setup is on Begin Play, we set the tracking origin to the eye level, which is set to X:0 Y:0 Z:180, where 1 Unreal Unit = 1cm. Then set the relative location of the OculusRoot to these new coordinates. With the integration of the SDK and that small code, we can view the world in VR (figure 11).

Now for the controller, we would like to spawn the Motion Controller Class with the parent set to this Camera and attach it to the camera, or our viewpoint. This gives us the ability to use the Motion Controller Oculus Go Remote. We then have to give the ability to the user to receive input from the user. For that, we change a default class setting, let the user become the Player 0 in the game as detailed in figure 12.

Specification of the Adreno 530 Graphics Processor Unit in the Oculus Go, Specification of the Oculus Go Processor and the performance evaluation isgiven in the table 2, 3 and 4.

It was noted that the prolonged inactivity in the VR Questionnaire broke the immersiveness and users specifically requested for a "repeat question" button and to add some movement in the scene. This blending of interactivity with 3D objects over 2D backgrounds will go a long way in making viable but immersive user experiences.

9. CONCLUSION

Augmented Reality (AR) allows an overlaying of synthetic information directly on top of the real world. Various real world scenarios' that used virtual reality and augmented reality are detailed in this chapter. Augmented and virtual reality in gaming, real estate, education, cultural heritage, training aid were described along with its application and use.

REFERENCES

Acevedo, D., Vote, E., Laidlaw, D. H., & Joukowsky, M. S. (2001). Archaeological data visualization in vr: Analysis of lamp finds at the great temple of petra, a case study. *Proceedings of the conference on Visualization'01*, 493–496. 10.1109/VISUAL.2001.964560

Andreoli, R., De Chiara, R., Erra, U., Scarano, V., Pontrandolfo, A., Rizzo, L., & Santoriello, A. (2005). An interactive 3d reconstruction of a funeral in andriuolos necropolis in paestum. CAA 2005-Computer Applications and Quantitative Methods in Archaeology, 1.

Apollonio, F. I., Gaiani, M., & Benedetti, B. (2012). 3d realitybased artefact models for the management of archaeological sites using 3d gis: A framework starting from the case study of the pompeii archaeological area. *Journal of Archaeological Science*, *39*(5), 1271–1287. doi:10.1016/j.jas.2011.12.034

Appinventiv. (n.d.a). https://appinventiv.com/blog/augmented-reality-in-retail/

Appinventiv. (n.d.b). https://appinventiv.com/blog/augmented-reality-benefits-for-businesses/

Azuma, R. T. (1997). A survey of augmented reality. *Presence (Cambridge, Mass.)*, *6*(4), 355–385. doi:10.1162/pres.1997.6.4.355

Bekele, M. K., Pierdicca, R., Frontoni, E., Malinverni, E. S., & Gain, J. (2018). A survey of augmented, virtual, and mixed reality for cultural heritage *Journal on Computing and Cultural Heritage*, *11*(2), 7. doi:10.1145/3145534

Caggianese, G., Colonnese, V., & Gallo, L. (2019). Situated Visualization in Augmented Reality: Exploring Information Seeking Strategies. *2019 15th International Conference on Signal-Image Technology & Internet-Based Systems (SITIS)*. 10.1109/SITIS.2019.00069

Caggianese, G., De Pietro, G., Esposito, M., Gallo, L., Minutolo, A., & Neroni, P. (2020). Discovering Leonardo with artificial intelligence and holograms: A user study. *Pattern Recognition Letters*, *131*, 361–367. doi:10.1016/j.patrec.2020.01.006

Caggianese, G., & Gallo, L. (2016). Smart underground: Enhancing cultural heritage information access and management through proximity-based interaction. *International Conference on P2P, Parallel, Grid, Cloud and Internet Computing*, 105–114.

Caggianese, G., Gallo, L., & Neroni, P. (2018). Exploring the feasibility of diegetic user interfaces in immersive virtual exhibitions within the cultural heritage. *2018 14th International Conference on Signal-Image Technology & Internet-Based Systems (SITIS)*. 10.1109/SITIS.2018.00101

Celsoazevedo. (n.d.). https://www.celsoazevedo.com/files/android/google-camera/ar/

Deggim, S., Kersten, T. P., Tschirschwitz, F., & Hinrichsen, N. (2017). Segeberg 1600–reconstructing a historic town for virtual reality visualisation as an immersive experience. *The International Archives of the Photogrammetry, Remote Sensing and Spatial Information Sciences*, *42*(W8), 87–94. doi:10.5194/isprs-archives-XLII-2-W8-87-2017

Dudeja, K., Baidya, S., & Gupta, S. S. (2019). Low-Cost 3DOF Virtual Reality First Aid Training Programs. *International Journal of Engineering and Advanced Technology, 8*(5).

Ebner, T., Feldmann, I., Renault, S., Schreer, O., & Eisert, P. (2017). Multi-view reconstruction of dynamic real-world objects and their integration in augmented and virtual reality applications. *Journal of the Society for Information Display*, *25*(3), 151–157. doi:10.1002/jsid.538

Fatta, F. (2015). Communication, technology, and digital culture for the conservation and enhancement of the architectural heritage. In *Handbook of Research on Emerging Digital Tools for Architectural Surveying, Modeling, and Representation* (pp. 446–475). IGI Global. doi:10.4018/978-1-4666-8379-2.ch016

Gaia, G., Boiano, S., & Borda, A. (2019). Engaging museum visitors with ai: the case of chatbots. In *Museums and Digital Culture* (pp. 309–329). Springer. doi:10.1007/978-3-319-97457-6_15

Gonizzi Barsanti, S., Caruso, G., Micoli, L., Covarrubias Rodriguez, M., & Guidi, G. (2015a). 3d visualization of cultural heritage artefacts with virtual reality devices. *25th International CIPA Symposium 2015, Copernicus Gesellschaft mbH*, 165–172.

Gonizzi Barsanti, S., Caruso, G., Micoli, L., Covarrubias Rodriguez, M., & Guidi, G. (2015b). 3d visualization of cultural heritage artefacts with virtual reality devices. *The International Archives of the Photogrammetry, Remote Sensing and Spatial Information Sciences*, *XL-5*(W7), 165–172. doi:10.5194/isprsarchives-XL-5-W7-165-2015

Grasset, R., Langlotz, T., Kalkofen, D., Tatzgern, M., & Schmalstieg, D. (2012). Image-driven view management for augmented reality browsers. *2012 IEEE International Symposium on Mixed and Augmented Reality (ISMAR)*, 177–186. 10.1109/ISMAR.2012.6402555

McLean, G., & Wilson, A. (2019). Shopping in the digital world: Examining customer engagement through augmented reality mobile applications. *Computers in Human Behavior*, *101*, 210–224. doi:10.1016/j.chb.2019.07.002

Microsoft. (n.d.). https://www.microsoft.com/en-us/hololens

Microsoft, microsoft hololens. (n.d.). Available: https://www.microsoft.com/it-it/hololens

Ott, M., & Pozzi, F. (2011). Towards a new era for cultural heritage education: Discussing the role of ict. *Computers in Human Behavior*, *27*(4), 1365–1371. doi:10.1016/j.chb.2010.07.031

Richter & Raška. (n.d.). Influence of Augmented Reality on Purchase Intention", Master Thesis in International Marketing, http://hj.diva-portal.org/smash/get/diva2:1115470/FULLTEXT01.pdf

Rua, H., & Alvito, P. (2011). Living the past: 3d models, virtual reality and game engines as tools for supporting archaeology and the reconstruction of cultural heritage–the casestudy of the roman villa of casal de freiria. *Journal of Archaeological Science, 38*(12), 3296–3308. doi:10.1016/j.jas.2011.07.015

Shukla, U., Mishra, A., Jasmine, S. G., Vaidehi, V., & Ganesan, S. (2019, January 1). A Deep Neural Network Framework for Road Side Analysis and Lane Detection. *Procedia Computer Science, 165*, 252–258. doi:10.1016/j.procs.2020.01.081

Sprott, J. C. (2006). *Physics Demonstrations: A sourcebook for teachers of physics*. Univ of Wisconsin Press.

Styliani, S., Fotis, L., Kostas, K., & Petros, P. (2009). Virtual museums, a survey and some issues for consideration. *Journal of Cultural Heritage, 10*(4), 520–528. doi:10.1016/j.culher.2009.03.003

Tatzgern, M. (2015). *Situated visualization in augmented reality* (Ph.D. dissertation). Graz University of Technology.

Terlikkas, C., & Poullis, C. (2014). Towards a more effective way of presenting virtual re- ality museums exhibits. *2014 International Conference on Computer Vision Theory and Applications (VISAPP)*, 237–241.

Tilty, Mary, & Baspin. (2017). Shopping Application using Augmented Reality. *International Journal of Interdisciplinary Research, 3*(3).

Toumanidis, L., Karapetros, P., Giannousis, C., Kogias, D. G., & Feidakis, M. (2019). Developing the museum-monumental experience from linear to inter- active using chatbots. In *Strategic Innovative Marketing and Tourism* (pp. 1159–1167). Springer. doi:10.1007/978-3-030-12453-3_133

UNESCO. (2005). *Information and communication technologies in schools - a handbook for teachers*. UNESCO.

Verge. (n.d.). https://www.theverge.com/2018/2/5/16966530/intel-vaunt-smart-glasses-announced-ar-video

Vive. (n.d.). https://www.vive.com/sea/product/#vive

White, S., & Feiner, S. (2009a). Sitelens: situated visualization techniques for urban site visits. *Proceedings of the SIGCHI conference on human factors in computing systems*, 1117–1120. 10.1145/1518701.1518871

White, S., & Feiner, S. (2009b). *Interaction and presentation techniques for situated visualization*. Columbia University.

Chapter 4
Comparison Analysis of Prediction Model for Respiratory Diseases

Priya R. L.
Noorul Islam Centre for Higher Education, India

S. Vinila Jinny
Noorul Islam Centre for Higher Education, India

ABSTRACT

Millions of people around the world have one or many respiratory-related illnesses. Many chronic respiratory diseases like asthma, COPD, pneumonia, respiratory distress, etc. are considered to be a significant public health burden. To reduce the mortality rate, it is better to perform early prediction of respiratory disorders and treat them accordingly. To build an efficient prediction model for various types of respiratory diseases, machine learning approaches are used. The proposed methodology builds classifier model using supervised learning algorithms like random forest, decision tree, and multi-layer perceptron neural network (MLP-NN) for the detection of different respiratory diseases of ICU admitted patients. It achieves accuracy of nearly 99% by various machine learning approaches.

1. INTRODUCTION

Respiratory illness become a common problem and causes an immense health burden in all age groups of people. It may include chronic obstructive pulmonary disease (COPD), Emphysema, Asthma, Chronic Bronchitis, pneumonia, lung cancer, and pulmonary hypertension and so on. In addition to hereditary effects, environmental exposures could also play a major role in causing respiratory diseases (GBD, 2018; Mayo Foundation for Medical Education and Research, 2017). The evolution of chronic epidemics is usually slow in nature and it provides greater opportunities for disease prevention. Still millions of people in every corner of the world suffer from such preventable chronic respiratory diseases. Hence,

DOI: 10.4018/978-1-7998-4703-8.ch004

Copyright © 2021, IGI Global. Copying or distributing in print or electronic forms without written permission of IGI Global is prohibited.

the care for patients of chronic respiratory illness is very essential and should define as an integral part of health care management services.

Chronic respiratory diseases are defined as a group of various chronic diseases that affects airflow in the lungs. Latest survey in the Lancet Global Health (India State-Level Disease Burden Initiative CRD Collaborators, 2018) says that there were nearly 10 million deaths and 486 million DALYs in 2017, especially in India. It is also estimated that one of the major DALYs rate arose in rural and urban areas are for chronic respiratory diseases and other respiratory infections. The major risk factors associated with preventable chronic respiratory diseases are Asthma and respiratory allergies, COPD, occupational lung diseases, sleep apnea syndrome and pulmonary hypertension.

The severity of asthma is measured with respect to hospitalization of asthma patients. In few countries, mortality due to asthma is high due to shortage of drugs availability (India State-Level Disease Burden Initiative CRD Collaborators, 2018). COPD is a heterogeneous and a kind of lung disease, that causes difficulty in breathing. Recent survey says that chronic bronchitis and emphysema are not considered as a part of COPD. COPD (Global Initiative for Chronic Obstructive Lung Disease, n.d.) is defined as a ratio between forced expiratory volume in one second (FEV1) and to the forced vital capacity (FVC). It is estimated that COPD would be fourth cause of mortality by the year 2030(Global Initiative for Chronic Obstructive Lung Disease, n.d.). Since 40 years, the prevalence of asthma patients has increased a lot in all countries as population adopts towards modern lifestyles and become urbanized. Several other risk factors have been identified for morbidity chronic disorders. In order to attain Sustainable Development Goals (SDGs) (India State-Level Disease Burden Initiative CRD Collaborators, 2018), the progress rate on many health-related indicators is required to speed up substantially between 2017 and 2030.

One of the rapid expansions of machine learning and big data analytics is chronic respiratory disease management. At times, chronic health conditions may result in hospitalization or emergency visit and is common in children and adult of age groups > 40(Global Initiative for Chronic Obstructive Lung Disease, n.d.). Such risky conditions may be prevented if it is diagnosed in advance and provides timely need to handle the health conditions getting worsen. Hence there is an urgent need to develop efficient approaches for better care in patients of respiratory diseases .

The main focus of this paper is to build an efficient predictive model for the admitted patients in hospitals. The model will classify the patients of all ages, who suffer from diseases related to various chronic respiratory disorders.

The structure of the paper is as follows. Section 2 provides some background information of the study and a review about few machine learning applications in health care of respiratory disease management. Section 3 explains the proposed methodology of the system. Section 3.1 describes the data collection and parameters included for the study. Section 3.2 discusses about the conceptual architecture of the proposed system and section 3.3 gives the descriptive detail about the prediction model designed using various machine learning approaches. Section 4 describes the results obtained with experiments and its analysis. Finally, section 5 gives the conclusion of the paper.

2. BACKGROUND

Huge amount of admitted patients specific information are being managed by various health centers. These patients health information are scattered at different places based on their visit to nearby hospitals or clinics. Such information usually includes disease specific symptoms either reported by patients or their kins and other health parameters obtained from either spirometry or automated systems (Mayo Foundation for Medical Education and Research, 2017). Automated systems consist of wearable devices, sensors or other devices like home based tele-monitoring systems located in the surrounding environment.

High prevalence of chronic respiratory illness is mostly found in urban cities due to increase in air pollution and effect of deforestation. Among various respiratory illness, COPD, Bronchitis and Asthma are having major contribution towards mortality and morbidity rates in Indian states. (India State-Level Disease Burden Initiative CRD Collaborators, 2018)

Of the total global Disability-adjusted life years (DALYs) (GBD, 2018; Global Initiative for Chronic Obstructive Lung Disease, n.d.), chronic respiratory diseases are contributed a lot, which ranges from 4.5% in 1990 to 6.4% in 2016. According to the survey report (GBD, 2018), it is projected that more than one billion deaths every year around the world happens due to lower respiratory infections, COPD and other few communicable and non-communicable diseases. Especially in India, 75.6% people are suffering from COPD and nearly 20% population is asthma patients.

Chronic bronchitis is a kind of COPD, caused by repeated irritation and damage to the lung tissue. Bronchitis is characterized by coughing, low fever, wheezing, chest tightening and shortness of breath (Mayo Foundation for Medical Education and Research, 2017). The severity of disease (Global Initiative for Chronic Obstructive Lung Disease, n.d.) can be sub-classified as mild, moderate and severe stages based on post-bronchodilator, FEV_1 (FEV1 $\geqslant$80% pred, 50–<80% pred, and <50% pred). But the prevalence of chronic bronchitis symptoms varies across different studies. In respiratory diseases like pneumonia and other lower respiratory track illness, respiratory rate is considered as another major indicator (Groeneveld et al., 2019; Richard et al., 2019). Also studies says that (Himes, 2009), several other disorders such as Acute bronchitis, pneumonia, shortness of breath, respiratory distress and diabetes are dependent factors on COPD. It is very challenging task to diagnose and differentiate between asthma, bronchitis or emphysema among COPD patients, particularly in the age group of 40-70. It is very important to provide an efficient and optimal health care management for respiratory disease patients. Such optimality in health care can be achieved by applying appropriate approaches to different cases.

Machine learning is a set of algorithms and predictive models helps to learn from experiences in order to extract useful patterns. Various classification methods are used in the research of health domain. For the risk prediction and diagnosis of asthma patients (Ullah et al., n.d.), algorithms such as Support Vector Machine (SVM), Random Forest and ANN were used. The study was carried out using Raman spectral variations to differentiate between healthy and asthmatic patients. Based on observable characteristics (Deliu et al., 2016), distinct subtypes of asthma are examined using different unsupervised clustering hierarchical and non-hierarchical algorithms. The risk prediction to COPD among asthma patients was examined using Electronic Medical Records (EMR) (Himes, 2009). The model was predicted using Bayesian network, which helps to obtain the accuracy of 83.3%, which was computed using area under the Receiver Operating Characteristic curve (AUROC). Especially for children, respiratory illness (Porter et al., 2019) was considered as a multi-class classification prediction problem. Triage predicative model (Garmendia, 2017) was built from physiological features (heart rate, temperature, respiratory frequency, blood oxygen saturation etc.) using various supervised algorithms and achieves accuracy of 85%. Recent study (Porter et al., 2019) discuss about the high-level diagnostic technology for respiratory illness based on sound analysis using acoustic engineering and artificial intelligence.

Pneumonia is a type of respiratory illness (Groeneveld et al., 2019; Tse, 2018) and is a great challenging factor to diagnose the presence in patients of acute respiratory infection. The model (Richard et al., 2019) was designed to determine risk factors of pneumonia using uni-variate and multi-variate analysis based on clinical variables and biomarkers.

The presence or absence of chronic bronchitis was calculated based on various potential risk parameters such as patients demographic data (age, education, family history, occupational details and their environmental factors), and other co-morbidity conditions (Mejza et al., 2017). The examination was carried out using ML approaches like Linear Regression model, Logistic Regression model and other statistical models. Acute respiratory distress syndrome is another crucial disorder especially among elderly population (Taoum et al., 2019). Hence the real time model was designed to provide alerts at severe stage of illness using various classifier models. The predictive model (Hernandez-Pereira et al., 2015) estimates the best respiratory pattern classifier model along with the involvement of five missing data imputation techniques. Such classification model was created to carry out the comparison study of various linear and non-linear machine learning algorithms for the unknown imputed data. Among various data imputation techniques, machine learning algorithms may yield better result compared to statistical models as ML algorithms helps to improvise accuracy of prediction model. The results of the study (Hernandez-Pereira et al., 2015) shown as that the non-linear classification methods are more appropriate for the respiratory pattern classification task. It does not conclude that such prediction model is a generalized structure for any datasets.

3. AN OVERVIEW – MACHINE LEARNING

With tremendous increase in amount of data available either in structured or unstructured form, an efficient automated intelligent system for knowledge extraction is needed. Machine Learning plays a major role in optimizing the performance criterion through its computer programming algorithms with the help of sample data or past experience. The main aim of machine learning (Marsland, n.d.) is to automatically discover an interesting patterns from available sources and to predict the future data or helps in decision making process. It uses the tools of Probabilistic theory to make the machines to learn from data. Machine Learning is also closely related to data mining, statistics, neural network and deep learning.

3.1 Related fields of Machine Learning

Machine Learning is related to many other fields, which aims to make machines learn from available data (doctor prescriptions, various lab reports, Electronic health Record (EHR) or any other form of clinical data). It also helps in predicting machine behavior depends on available data. The related fields identified among the papers reviewed are summarized in Fig. 1 as depicted below. It clearly indicates that among total number of reviewed papers more papers uses algorithms of machine learning for various disease prediction, which helps in assisting diagnosis of healthcare professionals.

Figure 1. Machine Learning and its Related Fields

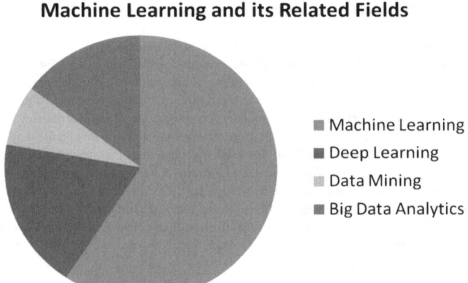

Machine Learning and its Related Fields

- Machine Learning
- Deep Learning
- Data Mining
- Big Data Analytics

3.2 *Model Description in Machine Learning*

In general, machine learning models are mainly classified as supervised learning model, unsupervised learning model and Reinforcement learning model. Though there are dozens of machine learning algorithms available, choosing an algorithm for any given problem statement is a challenging task. It is impossible to determine if a particular machine learning algorithm is the best method that fits for all. The various approaches of machine learning models are identified among the reviewed papers and summarized in Fig. 2. It clearly indicates that the Structured Prediction models or supervised learning models are widely applied in the healthcare industry.

Figure 2. Different Machine Learning Approaches

Machine Learning Approaches

- ■ Supervised
- ■ UnSupervised
- ▒ Reinforcement Learning

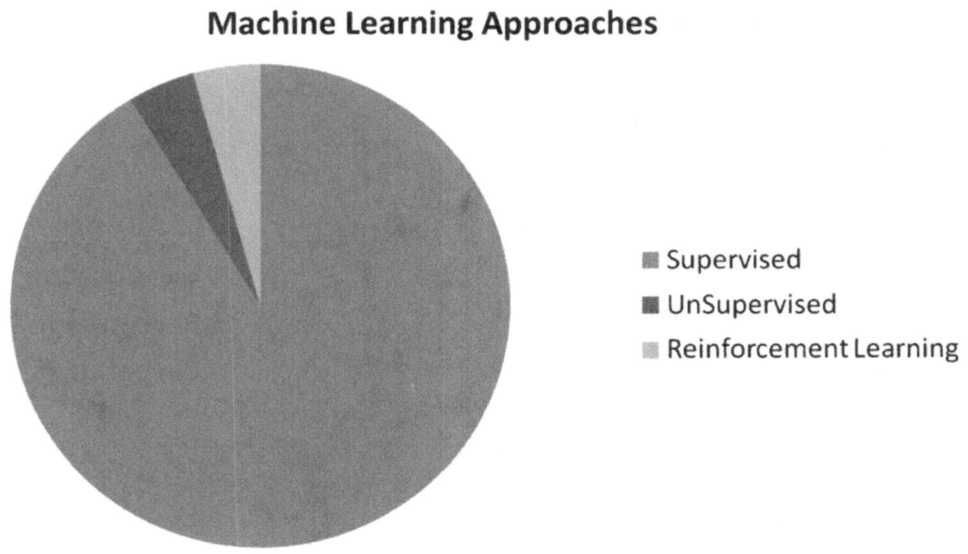

3.3 *Machine Learning Techniques*

Various classification and Regression techniques such as Naïve Bayes, K-Nearest Neighbor, Neural Networks, Support Vector Machine (SVM), Linear Regression, Ensemble methods etc. are used in supervised model (Chen et al., 2017; Lee et al., 2014). In unsupervised model, clustering and association methods such as K-means, Hidden Markov models, Market basket analysis etc. are often used (Chen et al., 2017; Fernández-Caballero et al., 2016). Few machine learning algorithms such as Q-Learning, Temporal Difference (TD) Learning, Deep Adversarial Networks etc. are used in Reinforcement Learning (Fernández-Caballero et al., 2016). The following Fig. 3 shows the various techniques of Machine Learning derived from the reviewed papers. The Fig. 3 entries depicts that supervised learning algorithms such as Regression and then followed by classification techniques are most commonly used in elderly healthcare domain for disease prediction.

Figure 3. Major Techniques of Machine Learning

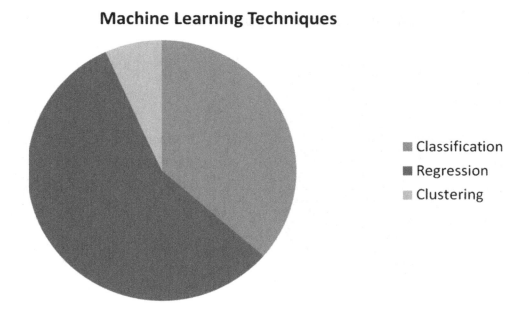

4. THE PROPOSED METHODOLOGY

The model proposes a predictive system for respiratory illness of admitted patients in hospitals based on the clinical symptoms. The comparison of efficiency of various machine learning approaches to classify respiratory diseases are analyzed and discussed.

4.1 Dataset Collection

To build prediction model MIMIC III dataset (Goldberger et al., 2000; Johnson et al., 2016), which was released in September 2016 is used. MIMIC III is a clinical database (Goldberger et al., 2000; Johnson et al., 2016) of admitted patients, which contains Protected Health Information (PHI) based on HIPAA definitions. The dataset comprise of nearly sixty one thousand patients, who admitted in Intensive Care Unit during the period of June 2001to October 2012. The clinical dataset consists of patient's demographic information and their associated clinical stay and symptoms.

4.2 Conceptual Architecture

Accuracy is an important aspect in the prediction model of any healthcare system. Accuracy cannot be compromised a lot especially in medical field for healthcare management. To achieve and improve the better accuracy of prediction system, traditional machine learning and advanced machine learning methods are widely used. Some research work discuss about the combination of statistical methods and machine learning methods to predict. There are few researchers adopt some optimization techniques into machine learning approach. Some studies describes about the combination of artificial intelligence with hybrid system.

The below fig. 4 depicts the conceptual architecture of respiratory illness prediction model. In the proposed work, respiratory disease prediction from the admitted patient's datasets is implemented using ML algorithms. The prediction task involves Data Preparation, building classifier models using different ML algorithms such as Random Forest, Decision Tree and Multi-layer Perceptron Neuron Network through training and testing the efficiency of each classifier models with unknown samples.

Figure 4. Conceptual diagram of Respiratory Disease Prediction Model

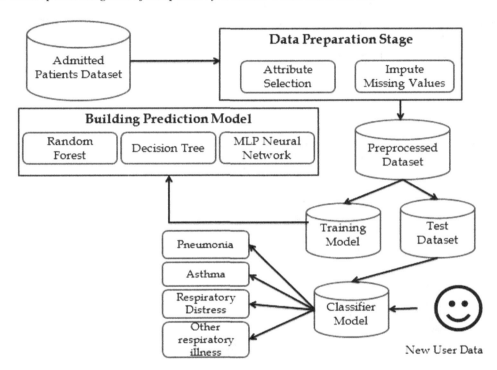

Table 1. Major Classification of Respiratory diseases and number of patients diagnosed

Sr. No.	Respiratory Disease	#No. of Patients diagnosed
1	Respiratory Distress & Failure	25,500
2	Pneumonia	23,319
3	Asthma / COPD	7,194
4	Bronchitis	1,440
5	Tuberculosis	296

4.3 Prediction Model

The model uses the primary and clinical symptoms of admitted patients in ICU and their stay at hospital. The early prediction of the chronic respiratory illness is developed in mainly three stages by providing admitted patients dataset as input. In the first stage, the system builds the preprocessed dataset by applying imputation of missing values and attributes selection method. During data preparation, we identify the missing values and fill them with suitable values using cluster based imputation techniques. Next step in data preparation stage is to generate the subset of attributes which plays crucial role in disease development. Wrapper Methods like forward selection, backward selection and recursive feature elimination and filter methods (ANOVA, Chi-Square) were applied on input dataset.

In the second stage of prediction model, the preprocessed dataset is provided as input to the training dataset. The prediction model is trained using machine learning algorithms such as Random Forest, Decision Tree and Multi-Layer Perceptron Neural Network independently and its performances are evaluated and compared using the classifier model. The importance of the final stage is to predict the disease for a new patient by choosing the best technique.

Figure 5. Comparison of different machine learning algorithms

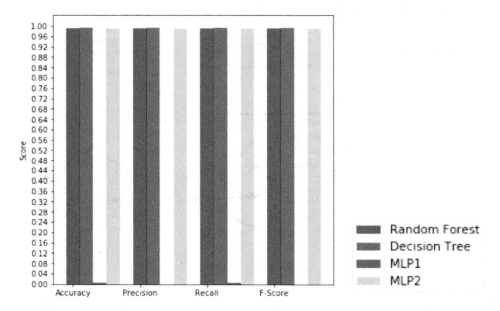

5. EXPLORATORY ANALYSIS OF DATA

The proposed system built a prediction model based on the data given under MIMIC III dataset to identify and classify them into various respiratory diseases. There were total 15,693 distinct diagnoses for 58,976 hospital admissions. These diagnoses are either in the form of informative like Asthma or its vague information. It provided with the following categories of chronic respiratory illness such as Respiratory distress, Pneumonia, Asthma, COPD, tuberculosis etc.

The following table 1 describes the total number of admitted patients are diagnosed with different classification of chronic respiratory diseases.

The experiment was conducted using python on ICU admitted patients dataset. After preprocessing, Scikit-Learn library is used to implement Random Forest, Decision Tree and MLP neural Network algorithm in python. MLP Neural network is implemented with NumPy library using sigmoid activation function.

5.1 Performance Measures

Next major step after implementation is to evaluate the model based on dataset using various performance metrics such as accuracy, recall, precision and F-score. In Classification algorithms, accuracy is defined as the ratio between numbers of correct predictions to the total number of samples considered. The Prediction accuracy obtained by the system using Random forest, Decision Tree and MLP NN are 99.21%, 99.41% and 99.18% respectively. Precision is measured using number of correctly identified positive results divided by total number of positive results predicted by the classifier. Recall is defined as the ratio between the number of correctly identified positive results and number of all samples considered. F-Score is used to measure the classifier model's accuracy. These performance measures obtained by various machine learning algorithms are shown in fig. 5.

DISCUSSION

The survey found that major population of elderly people suffer from one or more chronic diseases with substantial amount of elders having physical and functional disability. Among older adults, few illness like diabetes, arthritis, hypertension, bronchitis were found to be the most common chronic diseases.

The healthcare monitoring and assistance system is a major key contributor for the improvement of elderly people. The great challenge is to use an efficient smart cutting end technology with correctly chosen machine learning or deep learning algorithms for the prediction of one or more chronic diseases based on real time and available health records. Moreover, health care prediction results are very much sensitive, if it does not provide either true positive or true negative results.

Health care system results varies based on the volume of data sets, choosing an appropriate prediction model and selection of features present in the datasets. Certain studies uses statistical methods and data mining methods for the selection of features in predicting any chronic disease. In such proposed system accuracy and performance levels are only at an acceptable criteria. Few other survey results clearly indicates that various ML algorithms such as linear SVM, Apriori, C4.5, CART, Random forest etc. provides better performance for feature selection process as compared to other techniques. Such methods yield better accuracy due to its simplicity, ability to use it on numerical as well as nominal attributes even with the presence of an overfitting issue.

In addition, disease-rule generation (IF-THEN rules) are also applied to the training dataset to obtain better disease prediction and detection.

Based on the discussion and review, the computational complexity of machine learning algorithms are particularly important as it deals with very large datasets. It is better to choose algorithms with low computational lost. It would add benefits of adding disease-domain knowledge into the classifier model to avoid using huge number of attributes at an initial stage of training set. Few papers also suggested that the improvement in such type of predictive models can be attained through deep learning or other computational intelligence techniques like hybrid systems. Such papers demonstrated clearly that Multi-modal Deep Learning Model (MMDL) perform better as when compared to other approaches, especially with more number of data points. Any parametric and non-parametric statistical test like rank-based non-parametric results indicates that deep learning model is statistically better than the SuperLearner algorithm for classification tasks. It is clearly understood as per the review process that the machine learning and deep learning algorithms performance are better as compared to other related techniques in many aspects.

Furthermore, diverse smart environment techniques using any wearable device are likely to incorporate with machine learning / deep learning mechanism such as Recurrent Neural Network (RNN) based multimodal system for building more sophisticated prediction and feature extraction models. Also to facilitate better computational speed, GPU are utilized along with smart edging technologies like IoT, Cloud-of-Things etc

CONCLUSION

Respiratory diseases are reported as the most commonly found health issues in the world. It may affect any part of the body, which is associated with human breathing process. Machine learning models help to assist the doctors in diseases diagnosis and detection at early stage. The work proposes classifier model to predict the probability of getting respiratory illness based on clinical symptoms and patient's demographical information. Hence the threat about the respiratory related problems can be significantly reduced by taking proper medications as per doctor's advice.

REFERENCES

21Chen, M., Hao, Y., Hwang, K., Wang, L., & Wang, L. (2017). Disease Prediction by Machine Learning Over Big Data From Healthcare Communities. *IEEE Access: Practical Innovations, Open Solutions*, 5, 8869–8879. doi:10.1109/ACCESS.2017.2694446

8Deliu, M., Sperrin, M., Belgrave, D., & Custovic, A. (2016). Identification of Asthma Subtypes Using Clustering Methodologies. *Pulmonary Therapy*, 2(1), 19–41. doi:10.100741030-016-0017-z PMID:27512723

22Fernández-Caballero, A., Martínez-Rodrigo, A., Pastor, J. M., Castillo, J. C., Lozano-Monasor, E., López, M. T., Zangróniz, R., Latorre, J. M., & Fernández-Sotos, A. (2016). Smart environment architecture for emotion detection and regulation. *Journal of Biomedical Informatics*, 64, 55–73. doi:10.1016/j.jbi.2016.09.015 PMID:27678301

12Garmendia, A. (2017). Triage prediction in pediatric patients with respiratory problems. *Neurocomputing*. Advance online publication. doi:10.1016/j.neucom.2017.01.122

2GBD. (2018). *Institute for Health Metrics and Evaluation (IHME). In Findings from the Global Burden of Disease Study 2017*. IHME.

3Global Initiative for Chronic Obstructive Lung Disease. (n.d.). *Global Strategy for the Diagnosis, Management, and Prevention of COPD*. https://goldcopd.org/gold-2017-global-strategy-diagnosis-management-prevention-copd

14Goldberger, A. LAmaral, L. A. NGlass, LHausdorff, J. MIvanov, PMark, R. GMietus, J. EMoody, G. BPeng, CStanley, H. E. (2000). Physiobank, physiotoolkit, and physionet components of a new research resource for complex physiologic signals. *Circulation, 101*(23), pe215–e220.

11Groeneveld, G. H., van 't Wout, J. W., Aarts, N. J., van Rooden, C. J., Verheij, T. J. M., Cobbaert, C. M., Kuijper, E. J., de Vries, J. J. C., & van Dissel, J. T. (2019). Prediction model for pneumonia in primary care patients with an acute respiratory tract infection: Role of symptoms, signs, and biomarkers. *BMC Infectious Diseases, 19*(1), 976. doi:10.118612879-019-4611-1 PMID:31747890

6Hernandez-Pereira, Alvarez-Estevez, & Moret-Bonillo. (2015). Automatic classification of respiratory patterns involving missing data imputation techniques. *Journal of Innovations in Medicine and Healthcare.* DOI: doi:10.1016/j.biosystemseng.2015.06.011

7Himes, B. E. (2009). Prediction of Chronic Obstructive Pulmonary Disease (COPD) in Asthma Patients Using Electronic Medical Records. *Journal of the American Medical Informatics Association, 16*(3), 371-379.

1India State-Level Disease Burden Initiative CRD Collaborators. (2018). The burden of chronic respiratory diseases and their heterogeneity across the states of India: The global burden of disease study 1990-2016. *Lancet Glob Health.*

15Johnson, A. E. W., Pollard, T. J., Shen, L., Lehman, L., Feng, M., Ghassemi, M., Moody, B., Szolovits, P., Celi, L. A., & Mark, R. G. (2016). MIMIC-III: a freely accessible critical care database. Available at: http:// www.nature.com/articles/sdata201635

20Lee, S.-K., Son, Y.-J., Kim, J., Kim, H.-G., Lee, J.-I., Kang, B.-Y., Cho, H.-S., & Lee, S. (2014). Prediction Model for Health-Related Quality of Life of Elderly with Chronic Diseases using Machine Learning Techniques. *Healthcare Informatics Research, 20*(April), 125. Advance online publication. doi:10.4258/hir.2014.20.2.125 PMID:24872911

19Marsland. (n.d.). *Machine Learning – An Algorithmic Perspective* (2nd ed.). Chapman & Hall, CRC Press.

18Mayo Foundation for Medical Education and Research. (2017). *Mayo Clinic: COPD and Asthma Definition.* http://www.mayoclinic.com/health/

5Mejza, F., Gnatiuc, L., Buist, A. S., Vollmer, W. M., Lamprecht, B., Obaseki, D. O., Nastalek, P., Nizankowska-Mogilnicka, E., & Burney, P. G. J. (2017). Prevalence and burden of chronic bronchitis symptoms: Results from the BOLD study. *The European Respiratory Journal, 50*(5), 1700621. doi:10.1183/13993003.00621-2017 PMID:29167298

16Porter, Abeyratne, U., Swarnkar, V., Tan, J., Ng, T., Brisbane, J. M., Speldewinde, D., Choveaux, J., Sharan, R., Kosasih, K., & Della, P. (2019). A prospective multicentre study testing the diagnostic accuracy of an automated cough sound centred analytic system for the identification of common respiratory disorders in children. *Respiratory Research, 20*(1), 81. doi:10.118612931-019-1046-6 PMID:31167662

13Richard, G., Bachur, M. D., Kenneth, A., & Michelson, M. D. (2019). Temperature-Adjusted Respiratory Rate for the Prediction of Childhood Pneumonia. *Academic Pediatrics.* Advance online publication. doi:10.1016/j.acap.2018.11.015

9Taoum, A., Mourad-Chehade, F., & Amoud, H. (2019). Evidence-based model for real-time surveillance of ARDS. *Biomedical Signal Processing and Control, 50*, 83–91. doi:10.1016/j.bspc.2019.01.016

10Tse. (2018). *Clinical prediction rule to predict pneumonia in adult presented with acute febrile respiratory illness.* Yajem. doi:10.1016/j.ajem.2018.10.039

4Ullah, Khan, Ali, Chaudhary, Bilal, & Ahmad. (n.d.). A comparative study of machine learning classifiers for risk prediction of asthma disease. Journal of Photo diagnosis and Photodynamic Therapy. DOI: doi:10.1016/j.pdpdt.2019.10.011

17Ulukaya, S., Serbes, G., & Kahya, Y. P. (2017). Over complete discrete wavelet transform based respiratory sound discrimination with feature and decision level fusion Sezer. *Journal of Biomedical Signal Processing and Control, 38*, 322–336. doi:10.1016/j.bspc.2017.06.018

Chapter 5
Dynamic Data Mining Based on the Stability of Dynamic Models

Hocine Chebi

Faculty of Electrical Engineering, Djillali Liabes University, Sidi Bel Abbes, Algeria

ABSTRACT

This work presents a new approach based on the use of stable dynamic models for dynamic data mining. Data mining is an essential technique in the process of extracting knowledge from data. This allows us to model the extracted knowledge using a formalism or a modeling technique. However, the data needed for knowledge extraction is collected in advance, and it can take a long time to collect. The objective is therefore to move towards a solution based on the modeling of systems using dynamic models and to study their stability. Stable dynamic models provide us with a basis for dynamic data mining. In order to achieve this objective, the authors propose an approach based on agent-based models, the concept of fixed points, and the Monte-Carlo method. Agent-based models can represent dynamic models that mirror or simulate a dynamic system, where such a model can be viewed as a source of data (data generators). In this work, the concept of fixed points was used in order to represent the stable states of the agent-based model. Finally, the Monte-Carlo method, which is a probabilistic method, was used to estimate certain values, using a very large number of experiments or runs. As a case study, the authors chose the evacuation system of a supermarket (or building) in case of danger, such as a fire. This complex system mainly comprises the various constituent elements of the building, such as rows of shelves, entry and exit doors, fire extinguishers, etc. In addition, these buildings are often filled with people of different categories (age, health, etc.). The use of the Monte-Carlo method allowed the authors to experiment with several scenarios, which allowed them to have more data to study this system and extract some knowledge. This knowledge allows us to predict the future situation regarding the building's evacuation system and anticipate improvements to its structure in order to make these buildings safer and prevent the greatest number of victims.

DOI: 10.4018/978-1-7998-4703-8.ch005

Copyright © 2021, IGI Global. Copying or distributing in print or electronic forms without written permission of IGI Global is prohibited.

INTRODUCTION

In recent years, the use of Data Mining techniques has expanded very rapidly, where it has become ubiquitous in the practices of businesses and individuals. The information explosion that is emerging in the world due to the size, sensitivity and complexity of the set of data collected; plays a leading role in the emergence of the field of data mining, where the use of data mining greatly improves the performance of data analysis techniques, in order to provide useful, understandable and up-to-date models or information. Additionally, data mining techniques and methods allow organizations to derive more information through understandable models that are constructed using homogeneous or heterogeneous data sets collected from various data sources (such as databases). distributed, web, data warehouses and satellite images).

Generally, data mining can be used in any field, where there is a need to analyze a large collection of data or to predict the evolution of a given process or system. Some fields of application for data mining include e-commerce, marketing, medicine, biology, information security, education and telecommunications.

The data mining process is based on data collections recorded in centralized or distributed storage media, where these collections are static and do not undergo any change. However, in real life, the analyzed data becomes more and more complicated and dynamic (continually changing), such as time series, real-time data, satellite data and the behaviors of individuals. In addition, the need to speed up the data mining process and to have up-to-date or real-time knowledge for, for example, security or competitiveness needs lead to the search for new tools to generate data collections., taking into account the characteristics of the system studied. The challenges mentioned above are mainly involved in the emergence of new trends in data mining, namely dynamic data mining, which consists of processing dynamic data, using dynamic models. Some of the techniques used in dynamic data mining include dynamic Bayesian networks, dynamic neural networks and dynamic clustering.

Data mining can have several trends depending on the types of data processed, such as text mining, web mining, and medical data mining. However, users of installed data mining systems are also interested in their associated technologies, and will be all the more so as most of these installations will have to be updated in the future as and when changes occur. can appear at the level of the systems studied, or in databases or data warehouses that are constantly changing over time.

Time series mining or data stream mining can be used by many applications such as e-commerce, intrusion detection, and ubiquitous data mining, which requires dynamic data mining models. For example, time series mining can be used to study cyclical trends, seasonal trends, random events or processes, relating to weather phenomena and stock market changes. On the other hand, in the mining of spatial, environmental or geographic data (which can have several aspects, such as distance, topology and aspect of time), the construction of data mining models which turns from synchronous with the studied system, greatly improves the quality and reliability of the information obtained.

Indeed, for each data mining technique used, we can find corresponding dynamic methods. For example, for Bayesian networks, there are dynamic Bayesian networks, for clustering, there is dynamic clustering and for classification, there is dynamic classification.

In addition, the data used for the data mining process is collected beforehand, and the collection time may be long. Since the main objective of data mining is to make the right decisions in order to gain in the operation of a system, leaving the system running for a long time in order to collect this data can lead to losses. . Therefore, there appears to be a need to speed up the data collection process.

Usually, the data gathered represents the history of a given system. However, to obtain these data more quickly, simulation tools can provide appropriate mechanisms and means. To achieve this goal, it is necessary to first build a simulator (a dynamic model) which properly represents the studied system, before exploiting the data generated by this alternative model.

To solve the above problems of obtaining the data set necessary for a data mining study through a dynamic model, we propose a solution based on the modeling of systems using models based on social agents (Naili et al., 2018). Agent-based modeling is adopted to model many complex dynamic systems, especially those that include autonomous individuals such as partnerships, animal societies, collaborative robots, and insect societies. Among the systems that can be modeled by agent-based social simulation are the evacuation systems of buildings or buildings, such as supermarkets, hospitals and factories.

The evacuation of supermarkets mainly takes place in buildings with different constraints such as the locations of rows of shelves, the locations of people and those of exit doors. In the event of a disaster like fire, studying such a system using a dynamic model is of great importance in order to avoid maximum losses. So, the model that represents this type of system has to take into account several factors such as weather, characteristics of the supermarket and characteristics of people. In this study, a social agent-based model was designed to visualize the dynamic behavior of this system through these internal entities and their interactions. To assess the behavioral stability of this model, we use the Monte Carlo method and the concept of stable state, which provides us with a stable database for dynamic data mining.

Since obtaining the dataset is a significant challenge for a data mining study, especially in the case where the data is not complete or not yet collected, it is necessary to have methods appropriate to solve such problems. The proposed solution is to use a dynamic model which can generate this dataset. This type of dynamic model is an agent-based social simulation model.

One of the main challenges of social simulation is the study of the emergence of macroproperties from micro-interactions or interactions at a lower level (Davidsson, 2002; Shingo et al., 2007); That is, to clarify the link between social phenomena considered at the level of a given society and local phenomena considered at the level of individuals in that society. Another major challenge is to present the dynamic aspect of simulation, ie to study the importance of the evolution of the system as a dynamic system and the role of time in the social phenomena studied.

To overcome these challenges, we can use social agent-based simulation to build a dynamic social simulation model that can reflect very well the behaviors of a given society in relation to those of its individuals. In addition, the application of the Monte-Carlo method to the agent-based social simulation model for experimental and analytical purposes can help to better understand the systems studied.

COMPUTER SIMULATION

According to Shannon (Shannon, 1976), computer simulation is the process of designing a computer model that simulates a system and then performs experiments using that model to understand the behavior of the real system and evaluate different operating strategies. Computer simulation generally includes the following tasks (Fishwick, 1997):

- Identify the system to be studied.
- Build a computer model (operational model) that simulates this system.
- Carry out experiments using the operating model.
- Analyze the results of experiments carried out in order to gain a better understanding of the modeled system.

SOCIAL SIMULATION

Social systems generally refer to organizations of individuals divided into groups or structures with different functions, characteristics, origins or status. Social sciences are a category of academic disciplines concerned with society and the relationships between individuals within a society. The social sciences as a whole have many branches, each of which is considered a social science, and they include, but are not limited to, anthropology, archeology, economics, history, human geography, linguistics, political science, psychology and public health (Kuper, 2005).

With the growing popularity of social software and increased academic interest in social media analysis, social computing has gained increasing attention in recent years. Social computing takes a computational approach to the study and modeling of social interactions (Wang et al., 2007; Zeng et al., 2007). As a research area of social informatics, computer simulation of social phenomena is a promising area of research located at the intersection of social sciences, mathematical sciences, and computer science (Conte et al., 1998). So, we can consider that social simulation is the simulation of phenomena or social objects (society, organizations, markets, human beings) which are produced by computer.

Indeed, the social and natural sciences make great use of computer simulation to explain, predict and study certain phenomena (Shingo et al., 2007), as well as the validation of scientific theories or the study of a real system (Fishwick, 1997). To do this, it is necessary to establish models that work on a computer, but respecting the descriptions and especially the constraints of the systems studied.

In addition, simulation is a great way to model and understand social processes, as well as to predict the future, that is, develop a model that faithfully reproduces the dynamic side of a given behavior, and then simulate the passage of time, in order to obtain information that was not previously available. Social simulation in general brings several advantages to research in the social fields, because it makes it possible to:

- Simulate and study the phenomena that could result from social analysis.
- Design models based on phenomena observed in nature, where a given society can be modeled explicitly with independent entities.
- Study properties that are difficult to observe in nature.
- Predict certain situations which cannot be calculated directly.
- Compare two or more systems.
- Evaluate real or virtual systems.

AGENT-BASED MODELING

Agent Based Modeling (ABM) is used to model many dynamic and complex systems, especially those that include autonomous individuals, such as human societies, animal societies, robots, insect societies . It allows us to represent the evolution of a set of agents in an environment where the organization and the interaction between agents are essential.

The structure of an agent-based model

Primarily, an agent-based model consists of an organized set of agents interacting in a common environment. This system also has a clearly defined border with well defined entrances and exits. To develop an agent-based model, it is necessary to identify, model and program its elements. An agent-based model generally has three elements (Taylor, 2014):

- A set of agents, their attributes and their behaviors.
- The set of relationships and methods of interaction between agents, which define the underlying topology of connectivity, that is, define how and with whom agents interact.
- The environment of the agents where they are located. Also, agents interact with their environment in addition to other agents.

After identifying the conceptual model, it is necessary to build and run the operational model that simulates the behaviors and interactions of agents, using an agent-based modeling platform or programming language.

To run an agent-based model, agents must repeatedly execute their behaviors and interactions. This process often operates on a time counter basis as in discrete event simulation structures.

The structure of an agent-based model is illustrated in Figure 1, each component of which is discussed in this section.

Figure 1. Structure of an agent-based model (Taylor, 2014).

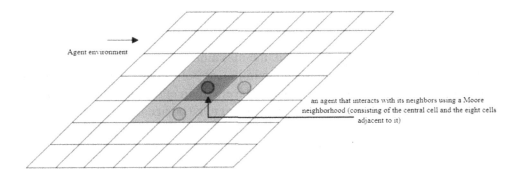

1)   A set of autonomous agents

An agent can be considered as a computer system located in a given environment, and which is able to act autonomously in this environment, in order to achieve the objectives which have been delegated to it (Jennings & Wooldridge, 1998). According to another definition, an agent is considered to be a software or hardware entity located in a virtual or real environment, and which has certain characteristics, for example, the agent can act in his environment and be managed by own individual objectives, goals, motivations or functions of satisfaction (Ferber, 2001).

Each agent has a set of attributes that describe its state and a set of specific behaviors (rules governing its behavior) that define how an agent behaves in response to changes in its environment and, possibly, to a set of goals or objectives. 'Goals.

For example, in a scenario of evacuating a building, we might want to understand how people might evacuate that building. So we can model these individuals as agents with several attributes, such as speed of movement, position in the building, and degree of disturbance. The behaviors of individuals include the different rules of action or reaction, such as the rules of movement or the rules of interaction with the environment or with other individuals. The objectives include, for example, the different strategies used by these individuals to avoid danger and reach the exit door.

2)   A set of relationships between agents

Each relationship defines how an agent interacts with other agents or with its environment. It also involves the way each agent is connected to other agents, that is, an "underlying connection topology", for example, the way people interact with each other when they try to leave. building.

Relationships and boundaries between agents must be clearly specified. The reason is that the agents must be autonomous. That is, the agent must be able to make decisions based on his own state and that of his environment. Relationships or interactions between agents can be simple or extremely complex.

Some general modularity rules and factors such as coupling and cohesion that exist in software engineering can be used. For example, if two types of agents have an extremely complex and tightly coupled relationship in which their functional boundaries are difficult to define, then the two types of agents might be better conceptualized as a single agent.

Not all agents should interact with all other agents. If an agent needs to make a decision based on the state of another agent, it must interact with that agent to find out.

3)   The agent environment

It is the "world" in which the agents exist, i.e. the minimum set of variables or "global" structures necessary to define how the agents react to their environment (for example, the fire alarm, the building where the people are and the capacity of each lane). The environment is the element of the system with which the agents interact and it is not generally considered to be an agent in its own right, that is to say it is passive and global (it does not actively assert behavior and it potentially affects all agents). It can have a simple or complex limit, depending on the modeled system.

ANALYSIS AND DESIGN OF AGENT-BASED MODELS

As agent-based simulation is a complex process that requires careful study before starting to collect and analyze the results, a well-designed model for such a process would be more than necessary. Among the analysis and design methods that allow us to describe models based on individuals IBM (Individuals Based Model) or models based on agents ABM (Agents Based Model) is the method (Grimm et al., 2006). This method is based on a standard three-block protocol, denoted by ODD (Overview Design Details).

In the method mentioned above, based first on the overview of the model, then on the design concepts (Design) and finally on the details. In such a protocol, the first block "View" aims to give the objective and the overall structure of the agent-based model. The concepts of Model Design in this protocol, as the name suggests, serve to clarify general concepts of the model. After specifying the design view and concepts of the model, the initialization data, input data and sub-models of the overall model are gathered in the Details part of this protocol.

In article (Helbing, 2012), the author discusses the principles of agent-based modeling. According to the author, it is essential to have a clear picture of the modeling process, i.e. describing, explaining and justifying the purpose, mechanisms, agents and their behaviors in the system. In order to validate the designed model, its results must be rigorously compared to empirical evidence.

The design of agent-based models has always been an active area of research, where it is very important to follow the best standards, in order to help design good agent-based models for socio-environmental projects. . Since modeling involves creating an abstraction of a real world system; Doran J.E (Doran, 2006) considers that defining the best level of abstraction and aggregation is very important in order to be able to focus only on the objective of the model. In addition, the author expressed the same point of view as (Helbing, 2012) on defining the agents of the model which must be among the first things to do, where the author emphasizes that the cognition and the architecture of the agent must be taken into account.

In their work, García-Magariño et al. (García-Magariño et al., 2015) have proposed an iterative process (requirements specification, development, evaluation and deployment) called PEABS (Process for developing Efficient Agent-Based Simulators) to assist in the development of agent-based simulators in which they focus on efficiency.

Nikolic and Ghorbani (Nikolic & Ghorbani, 2011) worked on socio-technical systems, where they proposed a method to develop such systems. Their method is broken down into a set of steps, namely analysis (identification and conceptualization of the goal and the system), the design of models which includes the identification of agents and their behavior, the implementation of software and evaluation of models.

In their article (García-Magariño et al., 2017), García-Magariño et al. propose a new approach for the development of simulators based on agents ABS (Agent-Based Simulators). The proposed technique could guide modelers in the design and implementation of agent decision-making processes in non-deterministic scenarios. These ABS are deployed as both mobile applications and online tools. The proposed approach is explained with two case studies in the fields of health and tourism.

In fact, the design of agent-based simulation software has been at the heart of several works in recent years (Abar et al., 2017; García-Magariño & Lacuesta, 2017; Hooshangi & Alesheikh, 2018; Lamy et al., 2015; Nascimento et al., 2015). In order to help the agent-based simulation community to perform efficient experiments, a significant number of agent-based simulators have already been proposed and put into service. We will see some of them in the following.

The agent-based simulator driven by self-organizing maps, denoted by SOM (Self-Organizing Maps), proposed by Resta et al. (Resta, 2015). According to the authors, in this simulator, agents can learn and interact, where the impact of their interactions on the overall behavior and evolution of the economic system, as well as the impact of modeled spatial connections between agents on individual decision, could also be noticed. These features would help to detect and study some interesting patterns.

In addition, the agent-based simulator for tourist urban routes ABSTUR (Agent-based Simulator for Tourist Urban Routes) by Garcia-Maganrino (García-Magariño, 2015) has been designed to help choose the best tourist routes, based on information of routes and different types of tourists. This system simulates the number of people who can choose certain routes based on their characteristics, which could help to avoid overloaded routes and save time and money.

AGENT-BASED SOCIAL SIMULATION

Simulation in sociology makes it possible to model certain phenomena observed in a given society. The application of agent-based modeling for the simulation of social phenomena is generally associated with the sociological tendency of individualism, which considers the individual as the basic unit (Bae et al., 2016). In addition, the expressiveness of the agent-based model facilitates dialogue with non-social scientists, and allows for the explicit inclusion of models of individuals in the sociological sense in the modeled system.

The application of agent-based modeling in social simulation is called agent-based social simulation (ABSS) (Davidsson, 2002; Li et al., 2008; Phan & Amblard, 2007). Therefore, as shown in Figure 2, this type of simulation represents an area of intersection of computer simulation, agent-based modeling, and social science.

Figure 2. The three domains constituting ABSS (Davidsson, 2002).

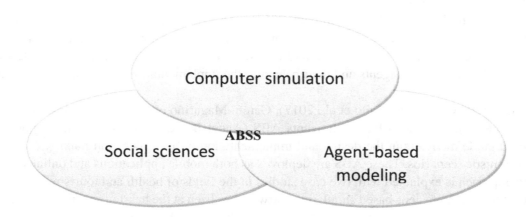

For example, evacuation systems resulting from disasters like fires, earthquakes and floods, are types of social systems that include people with different behaviors, and who are in the same place, at the same time. time and at the start of a disaster. In evacuation operations, people tend to navigate as quickly as possible to a safe area and avoid sources of danger and collisions. The places where an evacuation operation takes place are diverse, for example, stations, stadiums, boats, planes, tunnels, etc.

Indeed, the analysis of drainage systems has enormous advantages such as:

- Assist in the preparation of effective and efficient rescue plans.
- Construct secure buildings to avoid as many victims as possible in the event of a disaster.
- Anticipate situations which may occur, but which are unknown (they have not been part of the prior knowledge or have not occurred before).

To perform such an analysis, it is important to use a relevant model to represent this type of systems. This model could be a physical model, an analytical model or a simulation model (Law, 2015). However, the physical model and the analytical model might be impossible to build due to the cost, time or effort required to do so, so the simulation model may be preferred. In addition, it might be very difficult and sometimes impossible to rely solely on analytical models to analyze and evaluate systems made up of different components with varying states over time. So, to solve this problem, agent-based modeling denoted by ABM (Agent Based Modeling) might be one of the best solutions.

Indeed, the social sciences are part of a wide range of fields that benefit from agent-based modeling, where researchers widely use computer simulation to explain, analyze and predict social phenomena (Aschwanden et al., 2012; Caplat et al., 2008; Ch'ng, 2010; Hughes et al., 2012; Kvasnička, 2014; Lorig & Timm, 2014; Niazi & Hussain, 2009; Stefan & Atman, 2015; Vanhaverbeke & Macharis, 2011; Wirth et al., 2016).

After having introduced agent-based social simulation, we discuss in the following sections the integration of the concept of steady state and Monte-Carlo analysis in ABSS models. Such integration is very important to efficiently analyze the results of experiments performed using simulation by an ABSS model.

The concept of steady state in agent-based social simulation

According to the theory of dynamical systems, a system is in a stable state if the variables that define its behavior do not change over time.

When we talk about stability, we say that a stable state of a given system is approached asymptotically, if the system is in a stable state and its recently observed behavior will continue. However, in stochastic systems, the probabilities that various states are repeated will remain constant (Gagniuc, 2017).

Let x be the vector of state variables of a dynamic system, and f the function that indicates how this system changes. Under special circumstances, this system does not change and it may be stuck in a special state. These states are called fixed points of the dynamic system (Scheinerman, 1995).

In continuous time, this means that for each property p of the system, the partial derivative with respect to time is zero, as the following equation shows.:

$$\frac{\partial p}{\partial t} = 0 \tag{1}$$

In discrete time, this means that the variation of each property is zero, as the following equation shows.:

$$p'_t - p'_{t-1} = 0; \textit{ for all } t \tag{2}$$

A fixed point $\tilde{x}$ is called stable, if for all the starting values x_0 near, $\tilde{x}$ the system does not only stay close to $\tilde{x}$ but also x (t) → $(x)\tilde{}$ when t → ∞.

b. A fixed point $\tilde{x}$ is called marginally stable or neutral, if for all the starting values x_0 near, $(x)\tilde{}$ the system stays near $\tilde{x}$ but does not converge towards $\tilde{x}$.

vs. A fixed point $\tilde{x}$ is called unstable if it is neither stable nor marginally stable, ie there are starting values x_0 very close to $\tilde{x}$ so that the system moves away from $\tilde{x}$.

Figure 3 illustrates each of these possibilities:

- The fixed point on the left of the figure is stable. All the trajectories which are close to $\tilde{x}$ remain close and converge towards $\tilde{x}$.

- The fixed point in the center of the figure is marginally stable (neutral). Trajectories that start near $\tilde{x}$ stay close, but never converge to $\tilde{x}$.
- The fixed point to the right of the figure is unstable. There are trajectories that start near $\tilde{x}$ and move away from $\tilde{x}$.

Figure 3. Examples of fixed points with three different types of stability. The fixed point on the left is stable, the fixed point in the center is marginally stable and the fixed point on the right is unstable (Scheinerman, 1995).

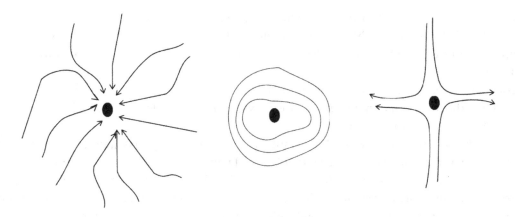

With regard to the ABSS models, they can be considered as variants of the discrete event simulation models (Law, 2013). It should also be mentioned that for each experiment on the simulation model, the input parameter values must be identified. Then, after performing this experiment, we obtain output parameter values which also represent the state parameter values of the dynamic model (simulation result). In addition, these output parameter values can change over time, so they can be viewed as random variables that reach stable values after a certain time. These stable values of the output parameters are also considered as the end result of this experiment.

Let Y_t be an output parameter of the ABSS model. When t is large enough, Y_t often tends to a stable value Y_s (s is the moment when Y_t holds its stable state Y_s), therefore:

$$Y_{t+1} - Y_t = 0, \forall t \geq s \tag{3}$$

Often the value of Y_s is unique and related to a single experiment on the ABSS model.

The application of the Monte-Carlo method in the ABS

The Monte-Carlo method is a heuristic technique in which a large number of the randomly generated values are analyzed using a probabilistic model to find an approximate solution to a numerical problem that would be difficult to solve using other methods (Metropolis & Ulam, 1949; Metropolis, 1987).

In order to have a good knowledge of the behavior of social systems which are simulated by ABSS models, it is necessary to obtain stable simulation results. This is why our proposal takes advantage of the Monte-Carlo method in the ABSS process, in order to draw more stable and general conclusions. This approach is based on performing a large number of experiments using random samples of the input parameters. This set of experiments provides information about the final results of the simulation, for example, the estimate and standard deviation of an output parameter. In what follows, we will give more details on this approach.

Let $X = (X\_1, X\_2 \ldots \ldots X\_r)$ be a set of random variables which represent r input parameters of a given ABSS model, $Y = (Y\_1, Y\_2 \ldots \ldots Y\_s)$ the set of random variables which represent s output parameters and n is the number of experiments to be performed.

The following steps generally describe what to do when using the Monte Carlo method:

- Identify the probability distribution of each input parameter.
- Perform n sampling operations of the random variables X according to their distributions.
- Perform n experiments using the values of X, in order to reach the values of Y.
- Analyze the values of Y, in order to have certain information such as the estimate and the standard deviation.

As an example, considering $z\_1, z\_2 \ldots \ldots z\_n$ the values of an output variable Z for n experiments. In this case, Z can be considered to be a random variable, where its estimate μ, its standard deviation $\mathsf{+}$ and its probability distribution are unknown.

The mean and the standard deviation of Z for n experiments are defined respectively by the following equations:

$$\hat{\mu}_n = \frac{1}{n} \sum_{i=1}^{n} Z_i \tag{4}$$

$$\hat{\sigma}_n = \sqrt{\frac{1}{n} \sum_{i=1}^{n} (Z_i - \hat{\mu}_n)^2} \tag{5}$$

Moreover, if Δ a comparison operator $(=, =, \geq, \leq, <, >)$ and $\overset{\smile}{}$ a given value of Z, then to estimate the value of the mean μ, the standard deviation σ and the probability $P(Z \Delta z)$ we can use the following formulas (Thomas & Luk, 2008):

$$\mu \approx \hat{\mu}_n \tag{6}$$

$$\sigma \approx \sqrt{\frac{1}{n} \sum_{i=1}^{n} (z_i - \hat{\mu}_n)^2} \tag{7}$$

$$P\left(Z \Delta z\right) \approx \frac{1}{n} \sum_{i=1}^{n} I_i \tag{8}$$

Such that I a random variable defined as follows:

$$I_k = \begin{cases} 1, \textit{if } Z\Delta z \textit{ In the kth } \exp \textit{eriment} \\ \quad\quad 0 \textit{ If not} \end{cases}, k = 1, 2, \ldots, n \tag{9}$$

The values calculated above are only estimates, but by the law of large numbers their convergence to the exact values μ and σ is ensured when the sample size n tends to infinity, so that:

$$P\left(\lim_{n\to\infty} \hat{\mu}_n = \mu\right) = 1 \tag{10}$$

$$P\left(\lim_{n\to\infty} \hat{\sigma}_n = \sigma\right) = 1 \tag{11}$$

In the same context, when the value of n is large enough and on the basis of the central limit theorem (Agresti et al., 2016a), we can estimate an approximate normal distribution N ($\hat{\mu}$_n, $\hat{\sigma}$_n / $\sqrt{n}$) of the mean value μ .

In addition, the difference between the estimated value $\hat{\mu}$_n and the required value μ can be controlled by means of a confidence interval (Agresti et al., 2016b). For example, for the probability α = 0.95, we can be sure with a confidence α (95%), that the real value of μ is between μ_inf = $\hat{\mu}$_n-1.96 $\hat{\sigma}$_n / $\sqrt{n}$ and μ_sup = $\hat{\mu}$_n + 1.96 $\hat{\sigma}$_n / $\sqrt{n}$ that is to say P (μ_inf$\leq\mu\leq\mu$_sup) = 0.95. Note also that the size of the confidence interval I μ_sup, μ_inf I, which represents the uncertainty of the estimate μ, is proportional to $\sqrt{n}$.

ANALYSIS OF THE VALUES OF THE OUTPUT PARAMETERS

After performing these experiments using the NetLogo and R environments, we analyze their results by applying the Monte-Carlo method to, for example, estimate the values of the number of deaths and the number of injured, as well as the distribution of probability of each of these output parameters.

Table 1 shows some statistical parameters of the output variables. These parameters are calculated on the basis of the experiments carried out and the application of the Monte-Carlo method shown.

Table 1. Statistical parameters of the output variables obtained using the Monte-Carlo method.

Output parameter	Estimate	Standard deviation
Total number of deaths	46.42	37.60
Total number of injured	78.03	19.91
Total number of survivors	174.94	32.11
Number of adults dead	6.225	8.34
Number of dead children	20.24	16.14
Number of elderly people who died	19.97	15.94
Number of adults injured	8.38	7.31
Number of injured children	63.58	15.08
Number of elderly people injured	6.06	7.47

In what follows, figures 5.6, 5.7, 5.8 and 5.9 show the evolution of the parameters (estimate and standard deviation) of the number of deaths and the number of injured, compared to the number of experiments carried out. In these figures, the intersection between the horizontal dashed line colored in red and the Y coordinate axis gives the stable value of the statistical parameter. Whereas, the intersection between the vertical dashed line colored in blue and the coordinate axis, gives the minimum number of experiments to reach this stable value.

Figure 4 shows the evolution of the average number of deaths compared to the number of experiments carried out. According to this figure, we see that after about 520 experiments, the average number of deaths tends towards the stable value 46.42.

Figure 4. Evolution of the average number of deaths compared to the number of experiments carried out.

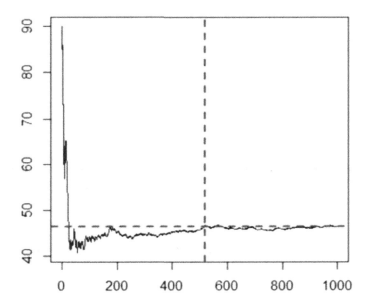

Figure 5 shows the standard deviation of the number of deaths versus the number of experiments performed. From this figure, it can be seen that this standard deviation tends to a stable value of 37.60 after about more than 350 experiments.

Figure 5. Evolution of the standard deviation of the number of deaths compared to the number of experiments performed.

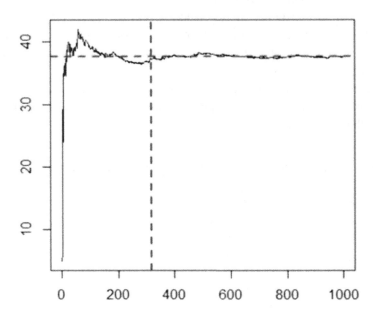

In Figure 6, we present the evolution of the average number of injured compared to the number of experiments performed. From this figure, we can see that this variable tends to a stable value of 78.03 after about more than 550 experiments.

Figure 6. Evolution of the average number of injured compared to the number of experiments carried out.

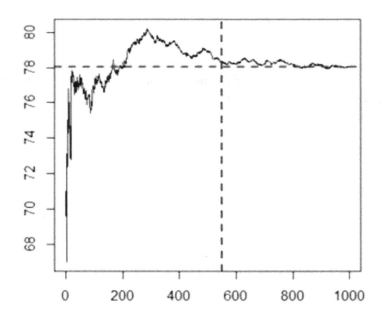

Figure 7 shows the variation of the standard deviation of the number of injured compared to the number of experiments performed. According to this figure, it can be seen that this variable also tends to a stable value of 19.91 after about 700 experiments.

Figure 7. Evolution of the standard deviation of the number of injured compared to the number of experiments performed.

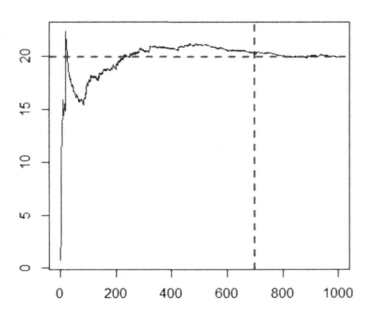

THE GENERAL RESULTS DRAWN FROM THE EXPERIMENTS CARRIED OUT

On the basis of Table 1 and Figures 4 to 7, we can deduce several useful results, among these we quote:

- The estimates and standard deviations of the output parameters tend to stable values when the number of experiments is large enough.
- In most cases, the average number of injured is higher than the number of deaths.
- The common number of experiments required to achieve stable values of the means and standard deviations of the output parameters is at least 700 experiments.
- The average number of victims of 46 dead and 78 injured is less than 50% of the average number of people before the fire started (300 people).
- As it was shown in section 4.7, the approximate normal distribution of the mean value of the number of deaths is (46.42, 1.19), while that of the number of injured is 78.03, 0.63).

CONCLUSION

The Monte Carlo method can be used to give more reliability to agent-based social simulation. Applying this method to the results of a large number of experiments performed using random samples of input parameters allows us to estimate some characteristics of the state parameters of this model, such as the mean value and the standard deviation. These stationary values make it possible to deduce more reliable information on the system studied. Therefore, the application of this approach to the study of a building drainage system is the subject of the next chapter. This approach is based on the development of an agent-based model representing as closely as possible the behavior of individuals in a supermarket in the event of a fire disaster.

Agent-based social simulation offers a great advantage to study, analyze and model complex social phenomena like disposal systems in supermarkets, which allows to design supermarkets with a more secure structure, for example, by choosing appropriate locations for exit doors, rows of shelves, and fire extinguishers to avoid large numbers of casualties. This model can also be applied to other types of buildings such as stadiums, theaters and hospitals. Given the multiplicity and variety of parameters that can be included in the simulation model, it is very useful to take advantage of the Monte-Carlo simulation and the concept of the steady state, thus obtaining results. more reliable and more stable.

REFERENCES

Abar, S., Theodoropoulos, G. K., Lemarinier, P., & O'Hare, G. M. P. (2017). Agent Based Modelling and Simulation tools: A review of the state-of-art software. *Computer Science Review*, *24*, 13–33. doi:10.1016/j.cosrev.2017.03.001

Agresti, A., Franklin, C. A., & Klingenberg, B. (2016a). *How Sample Means Vary Around the Population Mean. In Statistics: The Art and Science of Learning from Data, Global Edition* (4th ed.). Pearson.

Agresti, A., Franklin, C. A., & Klingenberg, B. (2016b). Constructing a Confidence Interval to Estimate a Population Mean. In Statistics: The Art and Science of Learning From Data. Pearson.

Aschwanden, G. D. P. A., Wullschleger, T., Müller, H., & Schmitt, G. (2012). Agent based evaluation of dynamic city models. *Automation in Construction*, *22*, 81–89. doi:10.1016/j.autcon.2011.07.001

Bae, J. W., Paik, E., Kim, K., Singh, K., & Sajjad, M. (2016). Combining Microsimulation and Agentbased Model for Micro-level Population Dynamics. *Procedia Computer Science*, *80*, 507–517. doi:10.1016/j.procs.2016.05.331

Caplat, P., Anand, M., & Bauch, C. (2008). Symmetric competition causes population oscillations in an individual-based model of forest dynamics. *Ecological Modelling*, *211*(3-4), 491–500. doi:10.1016/j.ecolmodel.2007.10.002

Ch'ng, E. (2010). An Artificial Life-Based Vegetation Modelling Approach for Biodiversity Research. In Nature-Inspired Informatics for Intelligent Applications and Knowledge Discovery: Implications in Business, Science, and Engineering. IGI Global. doi:10.4018/978-1-60566-705-8.ch004

Conte, R., Gilbert, N., & Sichman, J. S. (1998). MAS and Social Simulation: A Suitable Commitment. Academic Press.

Davidsson. (2002). Agent Based Social Simulation: A Computer Science View. *Journal of Artificial Societies and Social Simulation, 5*.

Doran, J. (2006). Agent Design for Agent-Based Modelling. In Agent-Based Computational Modelling Applications in Demography, Social, Economic and Environmental Sciences. doi:10.1007/3-7908-1721-X_11

Ferber, J. (2001). Multi-Agent System: An Introduction to Distributed Artificial Intelligence. Academic Press.

Fishwick, P. A. (1997). Computer simulation: Growth through extension. Transactions of the Society for Computer Simulation, 14, 13-23.

Gagniuc, P. A. (2017). *The Steady State of a Markov Chain. In Markov Chains: From Theory to Implementation and Experimentation* (1st ed.). Wiley. doi:10.1002/9781119387596

García-Magariño, I. (2015). ABSTUR: An Agent-based Simulator for Tourist Urban Routes. *Expert Systems with Applications, 42*(12), 5287–5302. doi:10.1016/j.eswa.2015.02.023

García-Magariño, I., Gómez-Rodríguez, A., González-Moreno, J. C., & Palacios-Navarro, G. (2015). PEABS: A Process for developing Efficient Agent-Based Simulators. *Engineering Applications of Artificial Intelligence, 46*, 104–112. doi:10.1016/j.engappai.2015.09.003

García-Magariño, I., & Lacuesta, R. (2017). ABS-SmartPriority: An Agent-Based Simulator of Strategies for Managing Self-Reported Priorities in Smart Cities. *Wireless Communications and Mobile Computing, 2017*, 1–9. doi:10.1155/2017/7254181

García-Magariño, I., Palacios-Navarro, G., & Lacuesta, R. (2017). TABSAOND: A technique for developing agent-based simulation apps and online tools with nondeterministic decisions. *Simulation Modelling Practice and Theory, 77*, 84–107. doi:10.1016/j.simpat.2017.05.006

Grimm, V., Berger, U., Bastiansen, F., Eliassen, S., Ginot, V., Giske, J., Goss-Custard, J., Grand, T., Heinz, S. K., Huse, G., Huth, A., Jepsen, J. U., Jørgensen, C., Mooij, W. M., Müller, B., Pe'er, G., Piou, C., Railsback, S. F., Robbins, A. M., ... DeAngelis, D. L. (2006). A standard protocol for describing individual-based and agent-based models. *Ecological Modelling, 198*(1-2), 115–126. doi:10.1016/j.ecolmodel.2006.04.023

Helbing, D. (2012). Agent-Based Modeling. In Social Self-Organization. Springer-Verlag Berlin.

Hooshangi, N., & Alesheikh, A. (2018). Developing an Agent-Based Simulation System for PostEarthquake Operations in Uncertainty Conditions: A Proposed Method for Collaboratio among Agents. *ISPRS International Journal of Geo-Information, 7*(1), 27. doi:10.3390/ijgi7010027

Hughes, H. P. N., Clegg, C. W., Robinson, M. A., & Crowder, R. M. (2012). Agent-based modeling and simulation: The potential contribution to organizational psychology. *Journal of Occupational and Organizational Psychology, 85*(3), 487–502. doi:10.1111/j.2044-8325.2012.02053.x

Jennings, N. R., & Wooldridge, M. J. (1998). Agent Technology Foundations, Applications, and Markets, 1. Academic Press.

Kuper, A. (2005). The Social Science Encyclopedia (Vol. 31). Academic Press.

Kvasnička, M. (2014). Viral Video Diffusion in a Fixed Social Network: An Agent-based Model. *Procedia Economics and Finance*, *12*, 334–342. doi:10.1016/S2212-5671(14)00353-0

Lamy, F., Bossomaier, T., & Perez, P. (2015). An ontologic agent-based model of recreational polydrug use: SimUse. *International Journal of Simulation and Process Modelling*, *10*(3), 207. doi:10.1504/IJSPM.2015.071378

Law. (2015). Systems, Models, and Simulation. In *Simulation Modeling and Analysis* (5th ed.). New York: McGraw-Hill Education.

Law, A. M. (2013). *Agent-Based Simulation and System Dynamics. In Simulation Modeling and Analysis* (5th ed.). McGraw-Hill.

Li, X., Mao, W., Zeng, D., & Wang, F.-Y. (2008). Agent-Based Social Simulation and Modeling in Social Computing. Presented at the *International Conference on Intelligence and Security Informatics*, Taipei, Taiwan. 10.1007/978-3-540-69304-8_41

Lorig, F., & Timm, I. J. (2014). How to model the "human factor" for agent-based simulation in social media analysis? work in progress paper. In Agent Directed Simulation, Tampa, FL.

Metropolis & Ulam. (1949). The Monte Carlo Method. *Journal of the American Statistical Association*, *44*, 335-341.

Metropolis, N. (1987). The Beginning of the Monte Carlo Method. *Los Alamos Science*.

Naili, Bourahla, & Naili. (2018). Stability-based model for evacuation system using agent-based social simulation and Monte Carlo method. *International Journal of Simulation and Process Modelling*.

Nascimento, V., Viamonte, M. J., Canito, A., & Silva, N. (2015). An agent-based electronic market simulator enhanced with ontology matching services and emergent social networks. *International Journal of Simulation and Process Modelling*, *10*(3), 265. doi:10.1504/IJSPM.2015.071376

Niazi, M., & Hussain, A. (2009). Agent-based tools for modeling and simulation of selforganization in peer-to-peer, ad hoc, and other complex networks. *IEEE Communications Magazine*, *47*(3), 166–173. doi:10.1109/MCOM.2009.4804403

Nikolic, I., & Ghorbani, A. (2011). A method for developing agent-based models of socio-technical systems. Presented at the *International Conference on Networking, Sensing and Control*, Delft, Netherlands. 10.1109/ICNSC.2011.5874914

Phan, D., & Amblard, F. (2007). *Agent-based Modelling and Simulation in the Social and Human Sciences*. The Bardwell Press.

Resta, M. (2015). An agent-based simulator driven by variants of Self-Organizing Maps. *Neurocomputing*, *147*, 207–224. doi:10.1016/j.neucom.2014.02.062

Scheinerman, E. R. (1995). *Invitation to Dynamical Systems* (1st ed.). Prentice Hall.

Shannon, R. E. (1976). Simulation modeling and methodology. *Winter Simulation Conference*, 9-15.

Shingo, T., David, S., & Juliette, R. (2007). Advancing Social Simulation. In *The First World Congress. Springer*.

Stefan, F. M., & Atman, A. P. F. (2015). Is there any connection between the network morphology and the fluctuations of the stock market index? *Physica A*, *419*, 630–641. doi:10.1016/j.physa.2014.10.026

Taylor. (2014). *Agent-based Modeling and Simulation*. Palgrave Macmillan.

Thomas, D. B., & Luk, W. (2008). Estimation of Sample Mean and Variance for Monte-Carlo Simulations. *Int. Conf. on Field-Programmable Technology*. 10.1109/FPT.2008.4762370

Vanhaverbeke, L., & Macharis, C. (2011). An agent-based model of consumer mobility in a retail environment. *Procedia: Social and Behavioral Sciences*, *20*, 186–196. doi:10.1016/j.sbspro.2011.08.024

Wang, F., Carley, K. M., Zeng, D., & Mao, W. (2007). Social Computing: From Social Informatics to Social Intelligence. *IEEE Intelligent Systems*, *22*(2), 79–83. doi:10.1109/MIS.2007.41

Wirth, E., Szabó, G., & Czinkóczky, A. (2016). Measure of Landscape Heterogeneity by AgentBased Methodology. *ISPRS Annals of Photogrammetry, Remote Sensing and Spatial Information Sciences*, *III-8*, 145–151. doi:10.5194/isprsannals-III-8-145-2016

Zeng, D., Wang, F., & Carley, K. M. (2007). Guest Editors' Introduction: Social Computing. *IEEE Intelligent Systems*, *22*(5), 20–22. doi:10.1109/MIS.2007.4338490

Chapter 6
Augmented Reality Application:
AR Learning Platform for Primary Education

S. Geetha
Vellore Institute of Technology, Chennai, India

L. Jani Anbarasi
Vellore Institute of Technology, Chennai, India

Arya Vardhan Prasad
Vellore Institute of Technology, Chennai, India

Aayush Gupta
Vellore Institute of Technology, Chennai, India

Benson Edwin Raj
Higher College of Technology, Fujairah Women's Campus, Fujairah, UAE

ABSTRACT

Augmented reality (AR) is an extension of extended reality that superimposes virtual images onto real world view. It has been implemented across a versatile range of fields including education, entertainment, military, and much more. Unlike virtual reality (VR), AR focuses on enhancing the real-world view and enriching people with a better way to display the learning content in an attractive way. AR provides content simulation and interaction which can display textual data in a more immersive way which can retain learner's concentration for longer periods of time. Technology has always helped people with disabilities. Mentally differently abled children require special attention right from their childhood. Many applications have analysed the challenges faced on a daily basis by the differently abled. Hence, AR-based learning would make their learning much more easier through the personalized and immersive platform. In the given context, this chapter analyses the use of AR in education and developed an AR-learning platform for mentally differently abled based on Unity3D and Vuforia.

DOI: 10.4018/978-1-7998-4703-8.ch006

Copyright © 2021, IGI Global. Copying or distributing in print or electronic forms without written permission of IGI Global is prohibited.

1. INTRODUCTION:

According to Azuma et al. (1998), Augmented Reality is a technology which is interactive, incorporates virtual images onto the real world view and is capable of supporting 3D features. Augmented reality makes the user interaction much more like in real life by diminishing the need of physical interfaces. Incorporating needs of each student in a classroom with a plain textual content is the greatest challenge for the educator. However AR allows for effective demonstration and visualization of difficult concepts allowing the children to understand effectively (Billinghurst, 2002).

AR can also be used remotely as it ensures collaboration by allowing multiple uses to observe the same 3D content from their location. It has been researched that learning disabilities can affect a child's self-esteem and self-confidence. In the initial 1-2 years, learning is less. However once schooling starts, facing fellow students and teachers could be difficult for mentally differently abled children. There have been multiple cases of such children being belittled, bullied and demeaned cause of their learning incapacity which leaves some life-long scars. They struggle to comprehend what is being taught and slowly lose their confidence. Thus, there is a need to provide such exceptional children with some unconventional learning techniques right from their childhood which can help them develop a healthy learning habit and caters to their needs as they grow older. Adoption of digital learning could make the entire learning process much more simple. According to a study, India has about 12 million children living with some kind of mental disability and out of these children only 1% of them have access to educational facilities focused on them. As a result these children as always dependant on someone for their entire life. It is crucial to provide them with proper resources and training so that the mentally differently abled children grow up as self-dependant individuals.

Thus, this research aims to develop an application for primary differently abled children so that they get an exposure to digital technology from an early age which could be later extended for further studies. This application would ensure a hassle free learning for differently abled children so that they don't feel left out. It would ensure that they learn through an engaging platform which would spark a sense of curiosity and increase the concentration levels of the students. This would also be their first introduction towards technology and would spark their imaginative minds with interactive visualizations and 3D images.

2. LITERATURE REVIEW

Several analysis and study has been performed for successful evaluation of AR based learning for mentally disabled children. Few related works that has contributed towards education through augmented reality, technologies required for developing a platform are detailed in this section.

2.1 Augmented Reality

Augmented reality is rapidly finding its presence in many fields. It engages the audience and help them connect more with an enhanced-real world. Studies have proved that a non-AR application has less audience base than an AR incorporated application. A study compared the experience of people playing an AR-enabled location based game with people playing the same game using different mobile interfaces (A. Morrison et al., 2009). It was observed that AR-app users found it fairly easy to navigate with an augmented map than the others. Thus AR provides a better engaging platform for users whether an outdoor location based game or indoor AR museum (D. Wagner et al., 2006).

2.2 Augmented Reality in Education

Designing, implementing and integration of AR in formal as well as informal learning environments are closely linked to the value of AR in Education (H. Wu et al., 2013). The most relevant thing to be considered is the less cost of AR integration in meaningful learning. If AR is considered as a concept rather than a technology, it would be much more productive for the educators. Discussions with the educators is important to increase the potential of AR in education as it helps to understand the needs of the children (X. Wei et al., 2015). It also helps in planning the way a mentally differently abled child should be taught. AR applications have been developed across many different areas of education.

Gopalan et al. (2016) researched on the impact of AR based science textbooks on a group of school students from Malaysia. It was observed that the students with AR-enabled textbooks scored higher than children without them. Akçayır et al. (2016) developed an AR enhanced laboratory manuals for college students and the study proved that the learning motivation of students increased significantly after using the AR laboratory manuals. Ibanez and Delgado-kloos (2018) presented a research based on the incorporation of AR in order to support the learning of STEM. It showed that with the inclusion of AR there us a growth in the concentration levels and students and they are much more motivated towards studies. Hannes Kaufmann et al. (2007) developed a 3D AR enabled geometric tool for geometrical and mathematical education. The tool enabled experimentations with geometric constructions to help the students understand. The tool showcased that with the help of AR students are able to improve their spatial skills and found the subject easy to learn.

2.3 Augmented Reality for Mentally Differently Abled Children

Mentally Differently abled Children find it difficult to accommodate in an educational setting as they find it very unfamiliar and are not able to cope up with the pace of the school education. The main reason behind this being the fact that the existing schooling system does not possesses the essential features needed for such children (Bauminger N., 2007). Visual approach of learning has found to be most effective for mentally differently abled children (Loring W. et al., 2011). It demonstrates improvement in attention, memorization, understanding and thinking capabilities of these children(Ministry of Education Special Programs Branch, 2000).

Differently-abled children have shown an affinity towards education incorporated with technology. Bacca et al. (2015) developed an application called 'Paint-cAR' for students with varied educational needs.

This application helped students to work on their logical competencies by following the long procedures of re-painting a car and also increased their level of concentration. Tobar-Muñoz et al. (2014) designed an AR game called 'Gremlings' which focused on developing mathematical skills in children with Autism. ADHD, Down Syndrome, and others.

3. TECHNOLOGIES USED FOR AR

Unity is a cross-platform game engine which supports the development of 2D, 3D games and interactive content (Unity Blog, 2020). It supports 20 target platforms for deploying, PC, Android and iOS being the most popular ones. Unity Program consists of multiple scenes, each containing many different models whose behaviour is controlled by scripts(JavaScript, C#, etc). The scene view is presented and controlled with the help of ARcamera. Figure 1 shows the hierarchy of Different Image Targets (Objects) under AR Camera. Unity was chosen as the main platform in this research for development of the application as it supports both 2D as well as 3D objects rendering. It also uses C# scripts for implementing various functionalities. Also, there are enough resources for understanding the working of Unity Editor which makes it easy to understand and quick to customize accordingly. Vuforia (Vuforia, 2020) is an Augmented Reality free-to-use library. It is integrated with Unity. There are several other AR libraries such as ARKit for iOS and ARCore for android. However, Vuforia supports both android and iOS. Hence, Vuforia was chosen for this application as an AR library. It supports image as well as video rendering using targets. It also possesses interaction capabilities in form of virtual buttons. An overview of the library architecture is presented in the following figure 2.

Figure 1. Hierarchy of Different Image Targets (Objects) under AR Camera

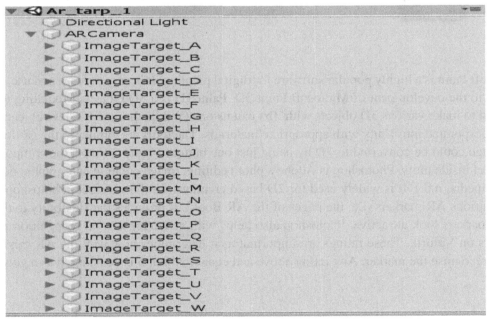

Figure 2. Vuforia AR SDK's Architecture (Fuguo Peng et a. 2017)

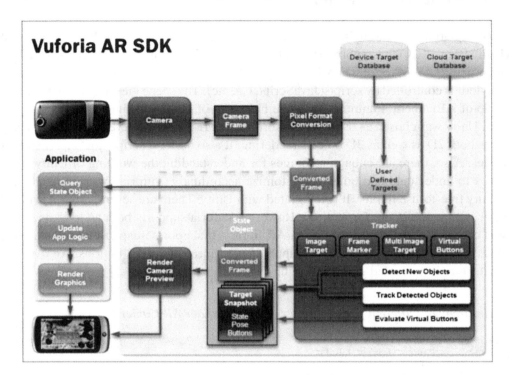

Microsoft Paint is a highly popular software for digital painting. It is easy to learn and use. The latest update led to the development of Microsoft Paint 3D. Paint 3D is a 3D Objects Modelling tool which can be used to make various 3D objects with .fbx extensions (Wikipedia, n.d.). These objects could be directly incorporated into Unity with appropriate materials. The tools are similar to the earlier versions and an image could be converted to 3D by using just one button. Figure 3 shows the components of a queen object inside unity. Photoshop is Adobe's photo editing, image creation and graphic design software (Wikipedia, n.d.). It is widely used for 2D based creations. In this research, Photoshop was used to create various AR markers (i.e. the pages of the AR Book). It provides the flexibility to design and make the markers look attractive. Photoshop also helps with achieving a good recognition ratings for the markers on Vuforia. These ratings are important as it determines how well the AR camera would be able to recognise the marker. Any rating above and equal to 3 out 5 is considered as a good rating.

Figure 3. Components of A Queen Object inside Unity

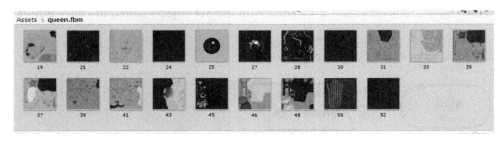

4. PROPOSED METHODOLOGY

4.1 AR Learning Platform for Mentally Differently Abled Kids

In previous works, the AR applications were restricted to a particular subject. However, the AR mobile application proposed in this work aims to cater the mentally differently abled children and enrich their education at a primary stage. In this paper, an Augmented-Reality application is developed which consists of various AR Markers, each serving as an interactive platform for the primary students. "Primary Playbook" consisting of various alphabets, related words, animals and some nursery rhymes is proposed. 3D models are used to make it interactive as well as engaging. There would be audios, animations and various attractive figures and colors to induce the habit of a happy learning. The mentally differently abled children would be able to engage in such platform without losing interest also it will fuel their imagination and make their every-day learning as an easy and holistic process. Unity 3D is used as the mainframe and Vuforia's AR SDK library is used. Paint 3D is used for modelling 3D objects and photoshop tool for designing AR markers. Figure 4 shows the proposed flow diagram for enhanced learning for mentally differently abled children.

The development of the application has been divided into given modules:

4.1.1 Design and Acquisition of AR Markers

The first step towards an AR application is the successful designing of AR Markers so that the AR camera can successfully identify the features and superimpose the 3D objects. The most preferable way is to achieve a Vuforia Image Rating>=3. Thus, Photoshop tool is used to design the AR Markers. The next step was Image acquisition where a local acquisition method is adopted. Firstly, the identification image is processed followed by matching it with the local data and return the result accordingly. Figure 5 shows the Image Targets' Ratings on Vuforia.

4.1.2 Building 3D Objects and Their Materials

The next step is the building 3D models according to the requirement of the proposed application. Thus, firstly the Paint 3D tool is used to create basic 3D models. The next step included the incorporation of material on the 3D Models to make them look more attractive and distinguishable. The materials of the 3D objects are stored separated(materials provide colour and texture to the object). Then, these materials are incorporated onto the 3D objects in the Unity Editor. Figure 6 shows the 3D model in Paint 3D and Figure 7 denotes the various materials associated with the 3D objects stored in Unity Editor.

Figure 4. Block Diagram of the Proposed Model

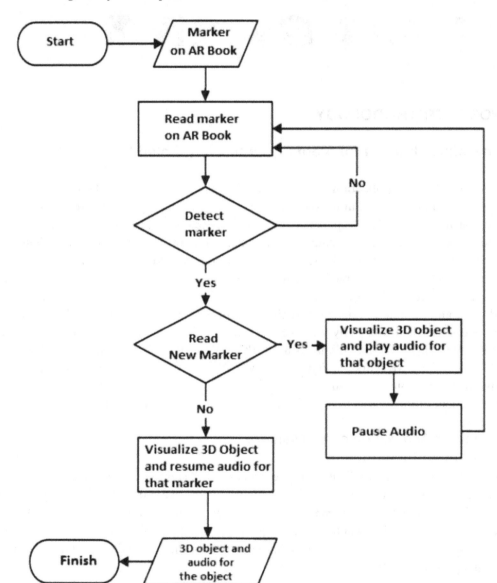

4.1.3 Superimposition of 3D Models in Real World

Using Unity the axes coordinates of the objects was monitored and then superimposed them onto the respective AR Markers. The figure 9 below depicts the same.

Figure 5. Image Targets' Ratings

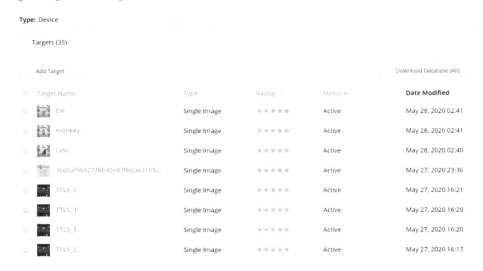

Figure 6. 3D Model of a Queen built on Paint3D

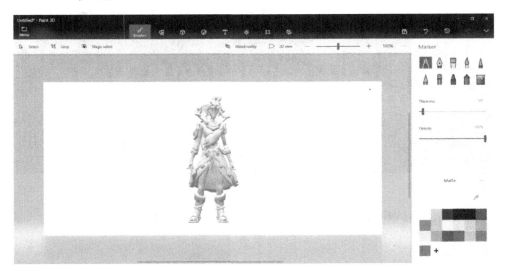

Figure 7. Incorporation of Materials of the above Object

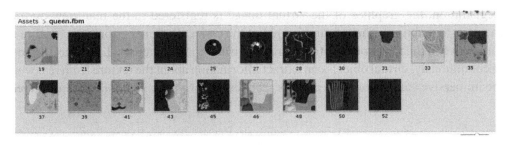

Figure 8. 3D Model of Queen built on Paint3D

Figure 9. Axes coordinates of Objects and AR Markers

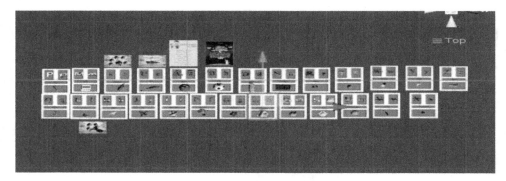

There are three aspects of superimposing virtual objects onto real world view:

i)   3D Registration
ii)   Object Posture
iii) Light Stripe

In 3D registration, the graphics of the virtual image is registered in the real view by tracking the camera behaviour in real time. The information about the Object Posture is stored by 'feature matching' the similarity between the real world features and the virtual model features. Lastly, as the environment is changing continuously, virtual objects can extract information about the texture from real world images and enhance immersive value in order to process seamless incorporation of both virtual and real objects.

4.1.4 Real-Life Incorporation of the Project

Marker is a kind of 2D matrix code, which is usually used in image recognition technology, and image symbol recognition is carried out by a special template matching algorithm. Firstly, the system saves the information of the Marker image and calculates the position of the virtual object in the camera according to the information. Then, the processor identified the Marker image in the real world view and finally incorporated the virtual image in the real world view.

Here's how the AR Camera identifies the various feature points present on an AR marker. Figure 10 shows the highlighted feature points on an AR Marker.

Figure 10. Highlighted feature points on an AR Marker

5. RESULTS AND DISCUSSIONS

In this research an AR based application developed while considering the need of the mentally differently abled children. It made use of Vuforia SDK along with Unity 3D to develop the AR-based application. The application developed comprised of all the alphabets[A-Z] along with their respective words. A 3D image of each word was added as well which could be touched and rotated. It also considered of multiple animals which would help the students learn the spellings as well the appearance of a particular animal. Further, it included a rhymes section which consisted of rhymes playing in the background and animations related to the particular rhyme. The multimedia data in each of these comprised of text, audio, animation, sound and 3D models. A key factor considered while developing this application was the expense. Thus, the aim was to develop an efficient application for low cost. When compared to the varied AR educational contents currently available for retail in USA, this AR based application would cost about 1/80th of the price.

Alphabets are basic foundation of learning. They are an important part of curriculum. However, the textbooks are not much of a help to the mentally differently abled children as they find it hard to absorb content from a sheet of paper. However, with AR incorporation the children are able to see the 3D models coming out of the sheets of paper which helps them in visualizing and learning. Thus, this application has AR objects of both the lowercase as well as uppercase of objects as well as a 3D model representing the word which starts from that alphabet. Figure 11 depicts the augmented letter 'A'.

Figure 11. Augmented alphabet 'A' in uppercase & lower with its corresponding object Apple

Our senses work as the greatest teachers. Hence, a multisensory approach with AR could help mentally differently abled children in recognising that particular object while also learning how the objects would look in real life. Hence, the 3D objects could be touch and rotated through the application. The figure 12 depicts touching and rotating the 'apple' object.

Figure 12. Touch to Rotate the Augmented Object: Apple

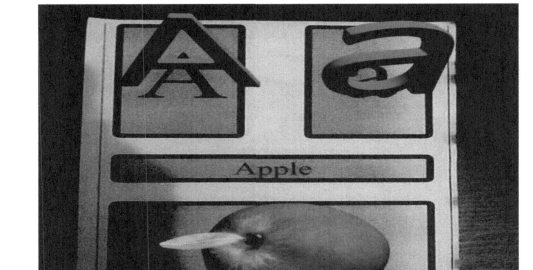

Rhymes are an important part of any primary education. However, studying rhymes from textual content could be difficult for the mentally differently abled children as. It is also difficult as memorizing rhymes becomes a mundane task. The incorporation of AR converts this mundane task to something new and engaging by the introduction of 3D objects, animations and voiceovers. Figure 13 depicts one such rhyme 'Twinkle Twinkle' with various animations of stars revolving and a voiceover of the rhyme plays in the background.

(Rhyme music playing in the background)

Primary children are taught about various outside world elements like animals with the help of the textbooks. They are taught about how they look and to identify one such animal. Thus, this application is incorporated with various real-life like 3D objects of various animals which could be touched and rotated to help in identification and recognition. Instead of the animated 3D objects, this application has been incorporated with real-life like 3D objects of animals. Figure 14 depicts the normal textbook page of lion and figure 15 depicts the augmented lion 3D image.

Figure 13. Rhymes: Relevant Objects being Augmented on the AR Marker – Rhyme

Figure 14. The way 'Lion' is depicted in an normal primary textbook

Figure 15. Augmented Lion on Lion AR Marker

6. CONCLUSION:

The targeted audience i.e. the Mentally Differently Abled students would be able to learn and visualize from a primary stage. This platform which consists of various AR Markers i.e. alphabets, rhymes, different animals etc. The end user would be able to see and visualize various objects and also interact through 'rotate' options. Whenever the user opens the AR Rhymes marker, the designated rhyme would play in the back ground. Although, this application has brought fresh outlook on the inclusion of AR for mentally differently abled children, there is still a need to polish this application to accommodate the mentally differently abled children universally of all ages and needs. As, this application is currently limited alphabets, rhymes and animals, it could be extended in many different ways.This research paper would lead to new ventures in this field of enhancing teaching and learning techniques for the differently abled children.

The future prospects of this research could be:

1) Elaborating this technology to other forms (numbers, daily activities {including tying shoe laces, recognizing the currency and its amount}).
2) Using the AR technology to develop not just educational but also vocational help for the differently abled children.
3) Developing a sensation technology using AR as the baseline which provides artificial sensation especially for students with autism and ADHD to help them in expression of emotions.
4) Games and Quizzes specifically designed for mentally differently abled children.
5) Adding a language based module to help them learn a particular language as well as the proper pronunciation of the words.

With our developed application, we have shown how AR could be successfully used primarily for the mentally differently abled children of primary classes. This application solves many issues such as lack of concentration, not able to visualize content and many others which mentally differently abled children face in their learning. It could also be developed for a very cost at a larger scale. In the future, we would collect sample data across various primary schools and conduct studies to add more personalized information for the mentally differently abled children in our application, so that this application could cater a much wider range of students.

REFERENCES

Adobe Photoshop. (n.d.). Retrieved from https://en.wikipedia.org/wiki/Adobe_Photoshop

Akçayır, M., Akçayır, G., Pektaş, H. M., & Ocak, M. A. (2016). AR in science laboratories: The effects of AR on university students' laboratory skills and attitudes toward science laboratories. *Computers in Human Behavior*, *57*, 334–342. doi:10.1016/j.chb.2015.12.054

Azuma, R. T. (1997). A survey of augmented reality. *Presence (Cambridge, Mass.)*, *6*(4), 355–385. doi:10.1162/pres.1997.6.4.355

Bacca, J., Baldiris, S., Fabregat, R., Kinshuk, & Graf, S. (2015). Mobile AR in vocational education and training. *Procedia Computer Science*, *75*, 49–58. doi:10.1016/j.procs.2015.12.203

Bauminger, N. (2007). Brief report: Group social-multimodal intervention for HFASD. *Journal of Autism and Developmental Disorders*, *37*(8), 1605–1615. doi:10.100710803-006-0246-3 PMID:17072752

Billinghurst, M. (2002). Augmented reality in education. *New Horizons for Learning*, *12*(5), 1-5.

Blog, U. (2020). *Add Unity Powered Features To Your App Using Unity As A Library*. Retrieved from https://blogs.unity3d.com/2020/09/16/add-unity-powered-features-to-your-app-using-unity-as-a-library/

Gopalan, V., Zulkifli, A. N., & Abubakar, J. A. A. (2016). A study of students' motivation using the AR science textbook. *AIP Conference Proceedings*, *1761*, 27–35. doi:10.1063/1.4960880

Ibáñez, M., & Delgado-kloos, C. (2018). AR for STEM learning: A systematic review. *Computers & Education*, *123*, 109–123. doi:10.1016/j.compedu.2018.05.002

Kaufmann & Schmalstieg. (2002). Mathematics and geometry education with collaborative augmented reality. In *ACM SIGGRAPH 2002 conference abstracts and applications (SIGGRAPH '02)* (pp. 37–41). Association for Computing Machinery.

Loring, W., & Hamilton, M. (2011). *Visual Supports and Autism Spectrum Disorder*. Academic Press.

Ministry of Education Special Programs Branch. (2000). *Teaching Student with Autism: A Resources Guide for Schools*.

Morrison, A. (2009). Like Bees Around the Hive: A Comparative Study of a Mobile Augmented Reality Map, *Proc. 27th Int'l Conf. Human Factors in Computing Systems*, 1889-1898. 10.1145/1518701.1518991

Paint 3D. (n.d.). Retrieved from https://en.wikipedia.org/wiki/Paint_3D

Peng, F., & Zhai, J. (2017). A mobile augmented reality system for exhibition hall based on Vuforia. *2nd International Conference on Image, Vision and Computing (ICIVC)*, 1049-1052.

Tobar-Muñoz, H., Fabregat, R., & Baldiris, S. (2014). Using a videogame with AR for an inclusive logical skill learning session. *2014 International Symposium on Computers in Education (SIIE)*, 189–194. 10.1109/SIIE.2014.7017728

Vuforia. (2020). *About Vuforia*. Retrieved from https://developer.vuforia.com/

Wagner, D., Schmalstieg, D., & Billinghurst, M. (2006). Handheld AR for Collaborative Edutainment. *Proc. 16th Int'l Conf. Artificial Reality and Telexistence (ICAT 06)*, 85-96.

Wei, X., Weng, D., Liu, Y., & Wang, Y. (2015). Teaching based on AR for a technical creative design course. *Computers & Education*, *81*, 221–234. doi:10.1016/j.compedu.2014.10.017

Wu, H., Lee, S. W., Chang, H., & Liang, J. (2013). Current status, opportunities and challenges of AR in education. *Computers & Education*, *62*, 41–49. doi:10.1016/j.compedu.2012.10.024

Chapter 7
Analyzing Knowledge Representation of University Ontology Through Semantic Web:
Representation of University Ontology

Juli Kumari
Indira Gandhi Delhi Technical University for Women (IGDTUW), India

Deepak Kumar
iD https://orcid.org/0000-0003-4487-7755
Amity University, Noida, India

Ela Kumar
Indira Gandhi Delhi Technical University for Women (IGDTUW), India

ABSTRACT

Nowadays, people are using lots of websites for searching and retrieving information. Most of the websites keep information in a simple format with all information simply linked with each other. Such type of information has less accuracy. So, there is utmost important to work on knowledge-based, information presentation. Hence, the advent of the semantic web called intelligent and meaningful web is a new trend in the area of web development. Ontology is a key term widely used in the development of the Semantic Web. It is an idea, which strongly focused on class, object, and relationship relatively than information. Protégé is a tool widely used for ontology development and customization. It has a user interface for ontology results visualization. It provides a view for a developer for a strong focus on creating knowledge rather than syntax. It provides the flexibility to add-on more additional features by the extendable plug-in. The purpose of this work is to develop a knowledge-based university system. Here, as an example of Indira Gandhi Delhi Technical University Delhi has been taken and created a university ontology using protégé tool. It also includes various aspects like classes, class hierarchy, superclass and subclass, and also created a subclass instance for designing class, class hierarchy, query searching, and retrieval process, and the result is demonstrated in graphical form.

DOI: 10.4018/978-1-7998-4703-8.ch007

Copyright © 2021, IGI Global. Copying or distributing in print or electronic forms without written permission of IGI Global is prohibited.

1. INTRODUCTION

Ontology is the main term in the semantic web (TIM BERNERS-LEE, 2001). Protégé tool is the most popular and widely used tool for ontology development. Here, this tool is used for developing university ontology emphases on different object concepts, which is used in the university system. In this paper, we have focused on the concept of semantic web, ontology and used languages and protégé tools and its attributes for analysis of different object used in the university system in details (Horridge et al., 2004).

1.2 Semantic Web

As the significance of web search engine, use of web data rises fastly. So there is a very big problem to arrange data in a web-database precisely(Bechhofer, 2009). Hence, for fine data management and representation of this, the semantic web comes in a scenario and the semantic web is an advanced form of simple form web form because it provides information in a well-defined form. So, the development of the semantic web becomes a keystone in real-world, it plays a vital crucial role to make web data meaningful and well representation of data on the web (Cardoso, 2007).

It makes data web understandable and integrates such a manner that, it will be helpful in actual detection, general accepting and also reusable for particular knowledge across various purposes (Vishal Jain, 2013). Also, it is perceived an important development of standards as advances and novelties support the transferring of more difficult, cultured and more extensive semantic applications.

1.3 Ontology

Ontology is a growing trend in the direction of modelling of knowledge, knowledge management and its application services. Its focus on developing a tool for result representation of ontologies and encouraging towards its assessment and analysis. It is a conceptualization are used for developing a machine-understandable format (Nicola Guarino, 1995)(Mike Uschold, 1996). So it has gained huge popularity in knowledge modelling in a specialized area and also a keystone of the semantic web. It also used for many other purposes like enterprise integration, database design, information retrieval and its representation and information interchange on the World Wide Web. For the representation of ontology in the semantic web, OWL language is used.

§   **OWL**-OWL stands for Web Ontology Language. It has many advanced features rather than other languages of ontology like RDF, RDFs. It has also an advanced version of DAML+Oil (Atzeni, 2007). It describes more vocabulary and the effective relationship of any particular domain. The OWL) language is divided into three syntax classes (Pilapitiya, 2017)(Asunción Gómez-Pérez and Oscar Corcho, 2002):

§   **OWL-Lite** – It deals with web data taxonomy view and basic restraints. It also maintenances cardinality controls, and allows only cardinality values 0 and 1. Also, provides a rapid migration path for vocabularies and classifications. It has lower complexity than OWL DL.

§   **OWL-DL** – It is used for the determined articulacy while retaining computational correctness and pre-defined. It allows all OWL language to create, with some limitation [16]. It is used with defined logics and it encouraging more for analysis of the basic logical form of ontology web language.

§ **OWL-Full** - OWL Full is applied in the extreme articulateness and the syntactic choice of RDF and not computational grantees. As an, for OWL Full a class is processed treated concurrently as a group of individuals. It also supports for ontology to extend the meaning already predefined (RDF or OWL) vocabulary.

§ The goal of this paper is to build university ontology in machine-readable format *i.e.* web ontology language. The method is explained with the help of University system based on university, academic, admission, examination and student life and its relationship by owl visualization and DL query retrieval (Vas, 2006).

1.4 Protégé Tool

Protégé is an ontology and knowledge base editor, especially used for the modelling of knowledge (Bechhofer, 2009). It allows the creation of ontologies domain and personalized data entry forms to enter data. For adding new, features and services in the tool can be added by the plug-in facility. It provides some more plugin for extra features such as extra ontology management, multimedia, query and reasoning engines and some problem-solving methods etc. It also defines the classes, class hierarchies, variables, attributes values and relationship between class and its attributes within the ontology. Protégé is an open-source and available on protégé home site(Horridge et al., 2004). It has also a visualization packages such as OntoViz; it graphically helps for visualization of ontologies. Today, ontology development becomes a more attractive field for building knowledge in the machine-readable form ("How to Improve Medical Diagnosis Using Machine Learning," 2017)(Ferndndez, Gmez-p, & Juristo, 1997).

2. METHODOLOGY

Demonstrating ontology development using protégé 4.3 beta versions, **Indira Gandhi Delhi Technical University for Women, Delhi,** India is used as an example for illustration the university ontology(Ding, 2009) .

A. **STEP- I**

Classes and class hierarchy

It illustrates the classes or its concepts used in building the university ontology. All the classes or concepts are mainly focused on Academic, Admission, Department, and Examination, Facilities, Research and Student life based as shown in *fig1.*

B. **STEP-II**

Object properties

Object property describes the relationship between each individual's classes used in ontology. It is added between every class, after defining the class as showed in *Fig3.*

C. STEP-III

Data properties

It is used to describe the relationship between individual to data literal in university ontology as shown in *Fig4.*

D.   STEP -IV

Property and relationship

In ontology, simply classes is not sufficient for describing property and relation of all the classes. so it require connection inside or among all classes. It also uses property, which show relationship each classes. Here, we have also defined object Properties Domain & ranges for example shown in Relational graph and Ontology Ring form.

```
<owl: ObjectProperty rdf:about="http://www.semanticweb.org/julikumari/ontolo-
gies/2018/4/untitled-ontology-47#IGDTUW">
<rdfs:range untitled-ontology-47 #ACADMIC"/>
<rdfs:domain untitled-ontology-47#ACADMIC"/>
<rdfs:domain untitled-ontology-47#ADMISSION"/>
<rdfs:range  untitled-ontology-47#ADMISSION"/>
<rdfs: range  untitled-ontology-47#DEPARTMENT"/>
<rdfs:domain untitled-ontology-47#DEPARTMENT"/>
<rdfs:range  untitled-ontology-47#EXAMINATION"/>
<rdfs:domain untitled-ontology-47#EXAMINATION"/>
<rdfs:domain untitled-ontology-47#FACILITIES"/>
<rdfs:range  untitled-ontology-47#FACILITIES"/>
<rdfs:range  untitled-ontology-47#RESEARCH"/>
<rdfs:domain untitled-ontology-47#RESEARCH"/>
<rdfs:range  untitled-ontology-47#STUDENT_LIFE"/>
<rdfs:domain untitled-ontology-47#STUDENT_LIFE"/>
</owl:ObjectProperty>
```

Figure 1. Relation graph of class, object and data property.

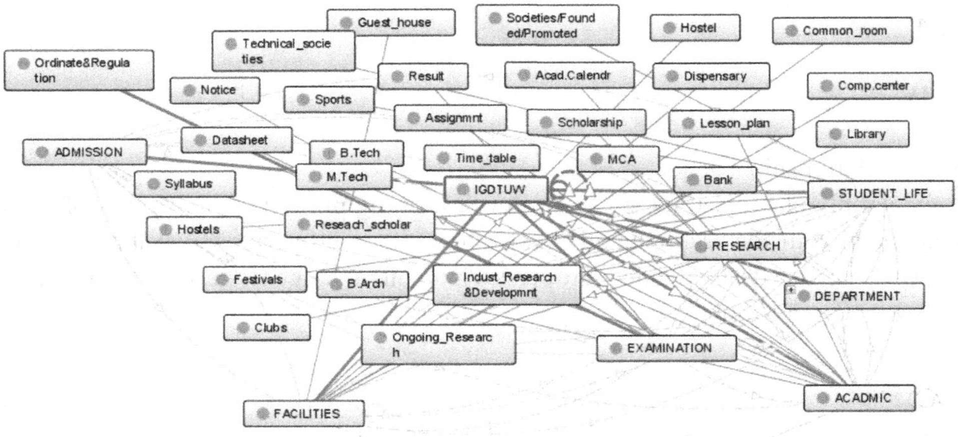

E.   STEP –V

The axioms of an ontology
The axioms for classes
Axioms define the relationship between classes, property and instances. It is divided into four types i.e. classes, the existence of class, subclass and equivalent class. The disjoint of all these classes defined by language such as RDF: id, rdfs: subclass, owl: equivalent class and owl: disjoint (Venugopal, 2015).

F.   The attributes of axioms

The axioms for attributes describe the links among attributes and it can be divided into the relation of Inclusion, Equivalent, Inverse, the limit function, inverse function, the relation of symmetry and transitive.

G.   The instances of axioms

In ontology web language, two types of instance exist among the axioms. First, classify the information, then define the structure of all class with the value of its attributes. In the Second type, instances can be defined into two types, either both are equivalent and related to each other, represented as OWL: same as, OWL: different form as and OWL: all different etc. (Xue, 2008). Mostly, an axiom is used to find better accurate results of Query search. It is also applied to describe the characteristic functional property of object property (Smith, Systems, Welty, & Mcguinness, 2009).

H.   STEP –VI

The instances for ontology

The instance of an ontology describing instances, initially choose the one class and define its instances for the class. rdf: type is used to define its class, and one instance may belong to many classes or more class belong to the same instance.

I.   STEP VII

The reasoning for ontology

Mostly, the reasoning of ontology is used to create correct and consistence ontology. In this reasoner check consistency and to get a logic contraction in the definition. This test consists detection of existing reflexive, transmission and redundancy of knowledge (Mizoguchi, 2016).

Figure 2. University classes hierarchy

Figure 3. Object property of University ontology

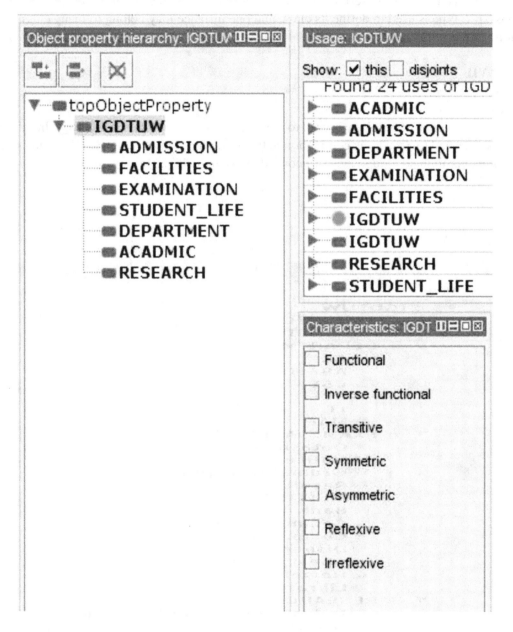

Figure 4. The data property of University ontology

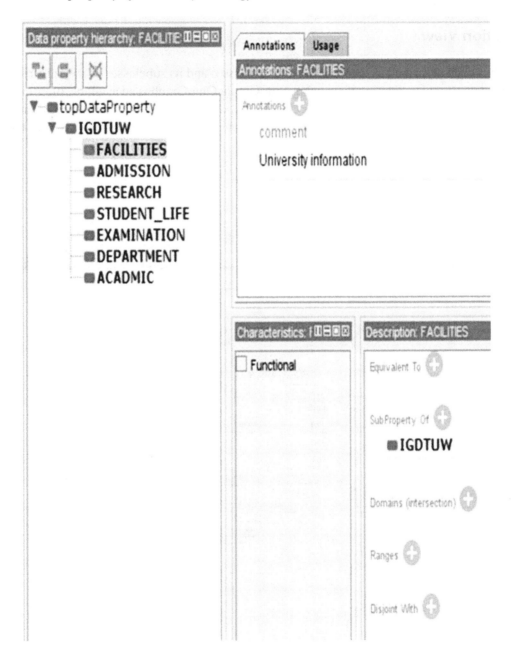

3. RESULT AND ANALYSIS

Visualization View

This work has been described as the main concept of classes and its subclasses of the university system, which is displayed by visualization view using OntoGraph. OntoGraph is an available plug-in of protégé tool. It shows classes, superclasses, ancestor classes etc., which is defined in the ontology and after reasoned tool to give the results corresponding to its relationship (Heflin, 2000). Ring form of OntoGraph concepts shown in below.

Figure 5. Ring form of OntoGraph concepts

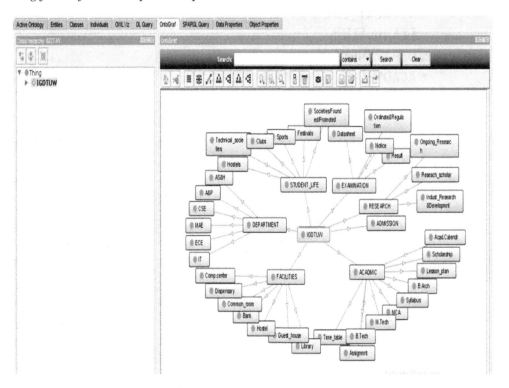

A. DEPARTMENT SYSTEM:

Figure 6. OntoGrap representation of Department system.

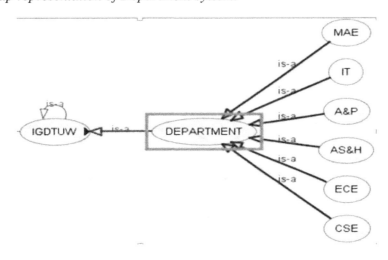

B. ACADEMIC SYSTEM

Figure 7. OntoGrap representation of Academic system.

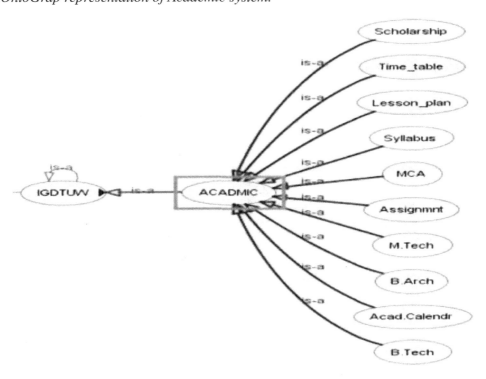

C.   STUDENT LIFE SYSTEM

Figure 8. OntoGrap representation of Student life system.

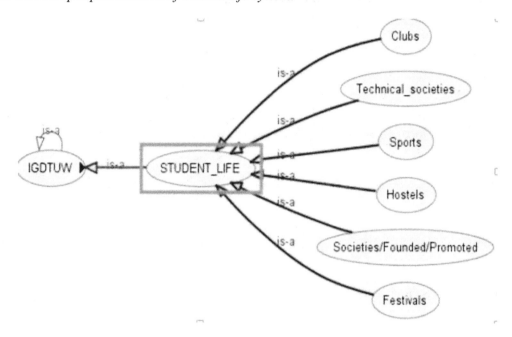

D.   RESEARCH

Figure 9. OntoGrap representation of Research system.

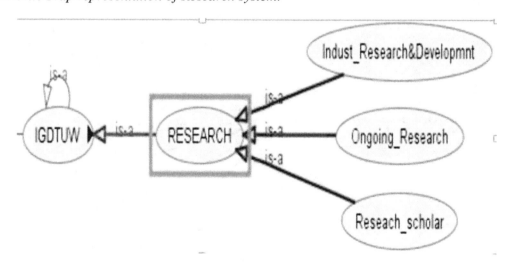

E.   EXAMINATION

Figure 10. OntoGraph representation of Examination system.

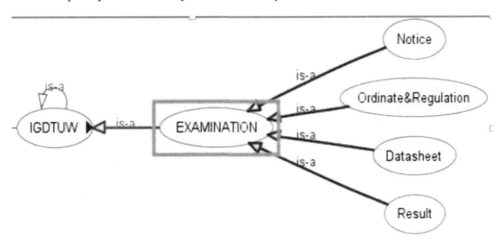

3.1 Query Retrieval Process

DL query retrieval process is used to retrieve information about any class, superclass, ancestor class, and equivalent class etc. of the university system. For this, first, start reasoner, then type a Class name or Object property name or data property name as a query keyword and execute the task. After that, reasoner displays related information about particular classes or property. It also provides the add class or property in the existing class or property. As an example, if we want to get the information of running Department, Academic, and Admission etc. under this university then enter Department, Academic, Admission as a query, it is not case sensitive as written in the ontology (Heflin, 2000).

A.   Department based DL query:

Figure 11. DL query retrieval and processing of the Department system.

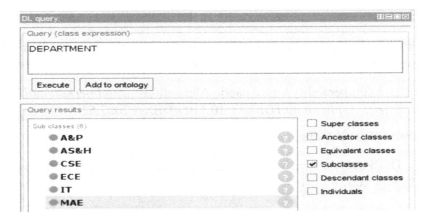

B.   Examination based DL query:

Figure 12. DL query retrieval and processing of the Department system.

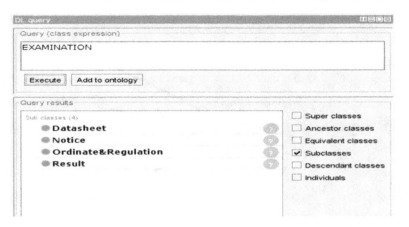

4. CONCLUSION

In this paper, the main objective to emphases the steps to describe information, more understandable for human as well as machine-readable form. It also focused to arrange information and represent web information in graphical form. It describes the class of information and refers to its relationship and constraint. This work will help to add new features in the semantic web so that the present web can understand more particular information and try to produce information intelligently. Hence, ontology is a crucial vision for performing this task. Protege tool has been used for creating and editing ontology and some basic term, languages and steps have been also described. The latest version of protégé tool has been used to make attractiveness in presentation view of information and also used some available plug-in tool in it. This work will use for sharing a general understanding of information regarding university system among people. Apart from this, the future plan is to use the university database and process query on it also try to make knowledge-based smart-university system.

REFERENCES

Gómez-Pérez & Corcho. (2002, February). Ontology languages for the Semantic Web. *IEEE Intelligent Systems*. Advance online publication. doi:10.1109/5254.988453

Atzeni, S. P. P. (2007). Interoperability for Semantic Annotations. *18th International Workshop on Database and Expert Systems Applications (DEXA)*. 10.1109/DEXA.2007.52

Bechhofer, S. (2009). *OWL: Web Ontology Language*. Academic Press.

Cardoso, J. (2007). The Semantic Web Vision : Where are We? *IEEE Intelligent Systems*, *22*(October), 22–26. doi:10.1109/MIS.2007.4338499

Ding, L. Z. (2009). Study on Construction of University Course Ontology : *Content. International Conference on Computational Intelligence and Software Engineering*. 10.1109/CISE.2009.5363158

Ferndndez, M., Gmez-p, A., & Juristo, N. (1997). Methontology: From Ontological Art Towards Ontological Engineering. *AAAI Technical Report*, 33–40.

Heflin, J. (2000). *University Ontology* (Vol. 0). Academic Press.

Horridge, M., Knublauch, H., Rector, A., Stevens, R., & Wroe, C. (2004). A Practical Guide To Building OWL Ontologies Using The Prot'eg'e-OWL Plugin and CO-ODE Tools Edition 1.0 Matthew. World. Academic Press.

How to Improve Medical Diagnosis Using Machine Learning. (2017). Academic Press.

Kalfoglou, Y., & Schorlemmer, M. (2003). Ontology mapping: The state of the art. *The Knowledge Engineering Review*, *18*(1), 1–31. doi:10.1017/S0269888903000651

Kumar Malik, S., Prakash, N., & Rizvi, S. A. M. (2010). Developing an University Ontology in Education Domain using Protégé for Semantic Web. *International Journal of Engineering Science and Technology*, *2*(9), 4673–4681.

Mike Uschold, M. G. (1996). Ontologies : Principles, Methods and Applications. *The Knowledge Engineering Review*, *11*(February).

Mizoguchi, R. (2016). Ontology development, tools and languages. *IEEE Intelligent Systems*, *2*, 1–27.

Nicola Guarino, P. G. (1995). *Ontologies and knowledge bases : towards a terminological clarification Ontologies and Knowledge Bases*. IOS Press.

Pilapitiya, S. U. (2017). Appropriate Ontology Matching Algorithm. IEEE.

Smith, M. K., Systems, E. D., Welty, C., & Mcguinness, D. L. (2009). OWL Web Ontology Language Guide. *W3C Recommendation*, 1–40.

Berners-Lee. (2001). The Semantic Web. *Scientific American*. doi:10.5209/CLAC.59071

Vas, G. K. R. (2006). Ontology based adaptive examination system in E-learning environment. *28th International Conference on Information Technology Interfaces*. 10.1109/ITI.2006.1708455

Venugopal, D. G. R. A. (2015). A Study On Verbalization Of OWL Axioms Using Controlled Natural Language Cite this Research Publication. *International Journal of Applied Engineering Research*, *10*(7), 16953–16960.

Vishal Jain, M. S. (2013). Ontology Development and Query Retrieval using Protégé Tool. *International Journal of Intelligent Systems and Applications*, *9*(9), 67–75. doi:10.5815/ijisa.2013.09.08

Xue, H. G. (2008). Research on the Building and Reasoning of Travel Ontology. In *International Symposium on Intelligent Information Technology Application Workshops* (pp. 1–2). 10.1109/IITA. Workshops.2008.162

Chapter 8
Efficient Virtual Reality–Based Platform for Virtual Concerts

Roshan Fernandes
NMAM Institute of Technology, India

Arjun P. Gaonkar
NMAM Institute of Technology, India

Pratheek J. Shenoy
NMAM Institute of Technology, India

Anisha P. Rodrigues

(iD) https://orcid.org/0000-0002-3050-4555
NMAM Institute of Technology, India

Mohan B. A.
(iD) https://orcid.org/0000-0002-0711-1550
Nitte Meenakshi Institute of Technology, India

Vijaya Padmanabha
Modern College of Business and Science, Oman

ABSTRACT

Virtual reality is a computer-generated three-dimensional environment where seemingly real graphics are used to simulate an imaginary world. It is generally accessed by using a special VR helmet or spectacles which enable you to access this imaginary world. Virtual reality uses the concept of split-screen to project to different images to our eyes in a selected angle which makes our brain believe that we are viewing a three-dimensional image. This tricks the brain into thinking that the human is standing in a three-dimensional environment where they can move around. Over the years, virtual reality has been included in a lot of traditional fields to challenge the endless possibilities in those fields. It has been used in medical sciences to train doctors, the aerospace industry to train the pilots and astronauts, the architecture industry to obtain maximum efficiency in designing the structures, and many more fields. VR gaming is also becoming a huge market where people can interact with the game components to get a realistic experience of being in a game. VR is also being used by counselors and psychiatrists around the world to treat people with mental health problems. In this chapter, the authors use the concept of virtual reality in the live music industry to simulate realistic music concerts by designing and developing a platform to host virtual concerts using virtual reality.

DOI: 10.4018/978-1-7998-4703-8.ch008

Copyright © 2021, IGI Global. Copying or distributing in print or electronic forms without written permission of IGI Global is prohibited.

INTRODUCTION

Virtual Reality is a computer-generated 3-dimensional environment where seemingly real graphics to simulate an imaginary world. It is generally accessed by using a special VR helmet or spectacles which enables you to access this imaginary world. Virtual Reality uses the concept of split-screen to project two different images to your 2 eyes in a selected angle which makes your brain believe that you are viewing a 3-dimensional image. This tricks the brain into thinking that the human is standing in a 3-dimensional environment where they can move around. Over the years, Virtual Reality has been included in a lot of traditional fields to challenge the endless possibilities in those fields. It has been used in Medical sciences to train doctors, the aerospace industry to train the pilots and astronauts, the architecture industry to obtain maximum efficiency in designing the structures, and many more fields. VR gaming is also becoming a huge market, where people can interact with the game components to get a realistic experience of being in a game. VR is also being used by counselors and psychiatrists around the world to treat people with mental health problems. In this article, we will be proposing to use the concept of Virtual Reality in the live music industry to simulate realistic music concerts.

The live music industry is a $26 Billion industry with more than 10,000 shows being held throughout the world with a total audience of 30M+ annually. Due to the ongoing Covid-19 pandemic, this industry has been affected the most. With no mass gatherings of more than 100 people, it has been very difficult for the artists and production houses to host concerts or live shows. In the work carried out by the authors, they were able to re-create a 3-dimmenssional environment of a concert arena which was then programmed to simulate an EDM concert. In every concert, the lighting and the SFX plays an important role in how a viewer experiences a concert differently than streaming music on a smart device. The authors were able to re-create these features to produce a realistic experience of a real-life concert. The performing artist or DJ, was projected onto this 3D arena using chromakey, a post processing technique used in many fields to eliminate the background.

Virtual Reality is a growing field in computer graphics and taking over the world with the limitless possibilities to create a virtual simulation of a real-life scenario. It is being used to train doctors, pilots and professionals who work in highly sensitive conditions to improve their skills. It is also being used in recreation and therapy to help people get over their fears and traumatic experiences. With Virtual Reality headsets, getting cheaper by the year, there are a lot more users coming into this field. It is reported that an estimated 171 million users presently exist in this growing industry which is estimated to reach a $34B in 2023.

Virtual Reality paired with Augmented Reality has been a significant approach for a lot of high-risk industries to perfect their products and human resources. It is also being used to train military officials to perfect their reflexes in high combat situations, to train astronauts to feel the outer space and get their bodies used to it. It is also being very instrumental in the field of education to teach young kinds better. AR/VR can be used to bring out the content from a book into the touch of your hands, which makes it easier for the students to imagine the world. Complex algebraic equations can be picturized in 3-dimensional space which makes learning much easier. There are products in the market, which enable streaming live videos through VR to simulate the environment of a Virtual Theatre. In the proposed work, the authors have made an attempt in using Virtual Reality to experience Virtual concerts.

Augmented Reality (AR), on the other hand, is something that alters certain things in our real world. People can get in imaginary characters, elements into the real world and experience it through the cameras in their devices. Augmented reality is a field that possesses massive possibilities in the consumer product industry with consumers being able to experience products with their real-life uses. Example: Trying on clothes, Glasses and many more. Augmented Reality can be used in concerts to experience somethings better, for example, some attractive treasure hunt rounds or other means of additional entertainment can be kept to keep the concert users active and excited throughout the concert. AR can also be used to stream concerts into a normal wall to watch Television. Virtual reality takes us into a completely new world whereas Augmented Reality just elevates our existing reality.

With the present trends, people are preferring online streaming rather than real-life content. The present generation prefers doing things online from the comfort of their homes with platforms like Amazon for shopping, Netflix for movies, and Slack for offices. The authors aim to create a trend for users to experience live music from the comfort of their homes. The present methods are artists performing live from their homes on social media channels like Instagram, Facebook and, YouTube. Festivals are using platforms like Billboard and Sound kick to connect with their fans and host virtual concerts too. They are presently streaming themselves playing music which is in 2D without any special effects or realism. The authors' approach to this problem certainly adds a new dimension by letting the user experience the concert in 3D. It also enables the user to interact with the elements on the screen thereby providing a realistic experience compared to the present conventional methods.

The proposed platform is a 3D computer-generated environment that holds a live music arena consisting of a 3D stage, speakers, lights, console, and a virtually projected artist. We used traditional building information modeling software to create 3D structures of the stage, speakers, the console, and the whole arena which were then exported in the required graphic formats to the rendering engine. The rendering engine is where all the components came to life to generate a VR based application.

The music generated by the artist was fed as an mp3 input to the speakers which would react accordingly with the user, it also had a 3D surround sound module implemented to give the user a complete experience of hearing the music at the highest quality. The lighting for the system was controlled through a third-party lighting software which used Artnet UDP to communicate with the rendering engine and provide the lighting data at the exact times. The 3D stage had certain portions that were converted into LED screens to display the background visuals for the performance. The visuals were fed in as an mp4 input and programmed to play along with the music. The most challenging and exciting part was the projection of the artist in this 3D environment. We recorded a 2D video of the artist in a green screen studio, which was then programmed to be projected in a small holographic section on the stage, to convert it into a 3D projection. We also included other special effects like firecrackers, CO_2 jets, Smoke, lasers, and pyro jets to simulate the whole experience of a real-life EDM concert. After developing the whole concert arena, we had to program some other light components like enabling it to interact along with the VR headset to give the user the complete experience.

RELATED WORK

Tomasz Mazuryk and Michael Gervutz (1999) (Mazuryk & Gervautz, 1996) introduced the concept and history of Virtual Reality and how it has been gaining popularity in the past few years then. In the work carried out, the authors speak about the advantages, drawbacks, the positive and negative impact of VR and the problems that virtual reality faces in the coming years. Pietrzak, E., Pullman, S., & McGuire, A. (2014) (Pietrzak et al., 2014) conducted a literature study on how virtual reality and games can be used to improve traumatic brain injury rehabilitation. They researched about the different studies conducted to improve recovery of brain injuries through VR. Aufegger et. Al., (2016) (Aufegger et al., 2017) explain how simulation training can be used to understand musician's perception in a live show and be used to train and enhance their performance skills. Antonio Maffei and Mauro Onori (2019) (Maffei & Onori, 2019) evaluate how VR can be used to increase efficiency in Production Engineering. The authors make a study on how a fully immersive VR environment can impact the production engineering curricula. Simon Ruber and Miquel Bosch Brugera (2019) (Bruguera et al., 2019) implemented an interactive cockpit panel of a spaceship through VR which simulated a spaceship launch and control for PTK-Federatsiya. Aufegger et. Al., (2020) (Aufegger & Wasley, 2020) explain how Virtual Reality can be used to influence musicians and train them to face the audience. In their work, they simulated positive and negative feedback generated by the audience and studied the physical and mental response of the musicians.

Stefania Serafin et. al. (Serafin et al., 2017) outlined a series of different possibilities on how Virtual Reality and Augmented Reality can be used in music education. This work discusses the various applications of Virtual Reality and Augmented Reality in training rhythmical skills, play together when users are apart, stage fear removal, composing and music production and training acoustics. Inwook Hwang et. al. (Hwang et al., 2017) proposed AirPiano music system to provide virtual touchable experience in Head Mounted Display (HMD) based virtual reality with mid-air haptic feedback. The drawback of this system is to track multiple figures to play more complicated musical notes. It also lags in precise timing. Hong-Zuan Bian (Bian, 2016) proposed Virtual Reality based visual reality thinking technique to reform the traditional music teaching method. The results were analyzed by considering the variable values of skewness and kurtosis. Abel Vargas et. al. (Vargas et al., 2020) proposed usage of Virtual Reality based music in cognitive disability therapy. The proposed work proved the improvement in rehabilitation process. Emily Honzel et. al. (Honzel et al., 2019) discusses a detailed review on how Virtual Reality and Music Therapy can be combined to heal the pain of patients. This paper also discusses the technical applications and audio-based interventions in Virtual Reality and Music Therapy field. Evelyn K. Orman et. al. (Orman et al., 2017) discusses the feasibility of using Virtual Reality learning environment to improve the music skills. Experiments were conducted on ten undergraduate music students at a University which included 9 male and 1 female student. The results were promising. Liang Men and Nick Bryan-Kinns (Men & Bryan-Kinns, 2018) proposed a collaborative musical making system in Virtual Reality. It discusses the 3D annotations used in the system, namely, LeMo. Raul Altosaar et. al. (Altosaar et al., 2019) proposed an audio-only Virtual Reality system which provides a high reconfigurable musical performance environment. It is used to develop a relationship to the audience to enable expressive and embodied musical interaction.

Mishra Sra et. al. (Sra et al., 2017) proposed mood-based Virtual Reality technique to generate images. It involves the various phases, namely, fetching the song lyrics, phase extraction, mood classification. Then followed by Virtual Reality generation. This gives a pleasant mental relaxation for the users. YanXiang Zhang et. al. (Zhang et al., 2019) developed a Virtual Reality interactive orchestral music concert using 3D audio technology. Authors have used standard MIDI files and imported into a Digital Audio Workstation program for the better experience. Edoardo Degli Innocenti et. al. (Innocenti et al., 2019) discusses the problem of enhancing music study using Mobile Virtual Reality. The proposed techniques were tested on the kids of age group of 10 years. The results show that the musical learning increases with the use of Virtual Reality technology. Thomas Deacon et. al. (Deacon et al., 2016) discusses an exploratory study on interactive Music Virtual Reality system. Authors have presented the design implications for Novice Virtual Reality interactive systems. Josiane Bissonnette et. al. (Bissonnette et al., 2016) discussed the exploratory knowledge in the music field concerning Virtual Reality exposure training. This paper gives a detailed study on the sequences of the Virtual Reality environments.

To conclude, there are various works related to musical Virtual Reality concepts. Based on the literature review, we have designed an efficient Virtual Reality based platform for virtual concerts. The term efficient, here in the proposed title, refers to the minimal hardware overhead support and with minimum processing time.

IMPLEMENTATION DETAILS

The proposed platform is a 3D computer-generated environment that holds a live music arena consisting of a 3D stage, speakers, lights, console, and a virtually projected artist. We used traditional building information modeling software to create 3D structures of the stage, speakers, the console, and the whole arena which were then exported in the required graphic formats to the rendering engine. The rendering engine is where all the components came to life to generate a VR based application.

The music generated by the artist was fed as an mp3 input to the speakers which would react accordingly with the user, it also had a 3D surround sound module implemented to give the user a complete experience of hearing the music at the highest quality. The lighting for the system was controlled through a third-party lighting software which used Art net UDP to communicate with the rendering engine and provide the lighting data at the exact times. The 3D stage had certain portions that were converted into LED screens to display the background visuals for the performance. The visuals were fed in as an mp4 input and programmed to play along with the music. The most challenging and exciting part was the projection of the artist in this 3D environment. We recorded a 2D video of the artist in a green screen studio, which was then programmed to be projected in a small holographic section on the stage, to convert it into a 3D projection. We also included other special effects like firecrackers, CO_2 jets, Smoke, lasers, and pyro jets to simulate the whole experience of a real-life EDM concert. After developing the whole concert arena, we had to program some other light components like enabling it to interact along with the VR headset to give the user the complete experience.

3D Model of the Stage

The concert arena was designed to represent the stage of ULTRA Miami 2018, an international music festival held in Miami. The concert arena was built using a Building Information modelling software, where we created the Arena, the stage, Led screen for the visuals, speakers, lighting systems and SFX assets. The whole model was built in different layers and realistic materials were added to it. The different 3D assets built were integrated together in a game engine called Unity. The design of the different elements was done with a top-down approach, which started from designing the major elements like the stage, the LED screens, the trusses to hold the lights and speakers, moving on to the tiny elements like speakers, lights, lasers, CO_2 emission jets, Pyro emission cylinders and finally the deck of the artist. Figure 1 shows the concert arena of Ultra Miami 2018. Figure 2 shows Concert arena built using BIM.

Figure 1. Concert arena of Ultra Miami 2018.

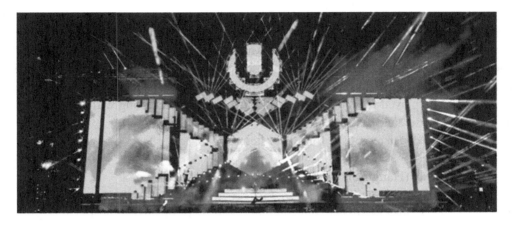

Figure 2. Concert arena built using BIM.

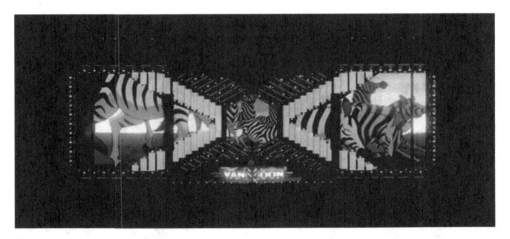

Development of the Concert

The concert was bought together in a cross-platform game engine called Unity. This is a software used by major game companies to create PC and VR games. Some of the major games that were built on this engine are Assassins Creed Identity, Pokémon Go, Temple Run and Subway surfers. Unity provides a 3D space to develop realistic environments and enables us to create a timeline of events along the gameplay. We utilized this to place the different 3D assets and to combine it into one working module. The different elements were made into different modules to act independently. The models developed in the BIM software's were exported into a 3D file like fbx or obj and imported into unity along with their respective textures and materials. The main elements that constituted the concert were audio, visuals, lights, SFX, the artist and the cameras.

Audio

The concert was created along with Raghav Sehej Paul aka DJ Van Moon, a music producer based in Delhi, India. Due to the covid-19 pandemic, it was impossible to get a live recording of the music, visuals and the DJ. Hence, we had to record the 3 separately. The music was produced by Raghav, at his residence in Delhi using production software's and was exported as an mp3 audio file. The file was then programmed to be played from the speakers in the concert arena along with some features like 3D surround sound and noise cancellation.

The speaker system consisted of the following items.

1. PA system, in array (Hanging)
2. Amplifiers (on the ground)
3. Sub woofers (on the ground) to give the complete experience of a bass-boosted 3D surround sound.

Figure 3 shows the speaker setup in the concert arena.

Figure 3. The speaker setup in the concert arena.

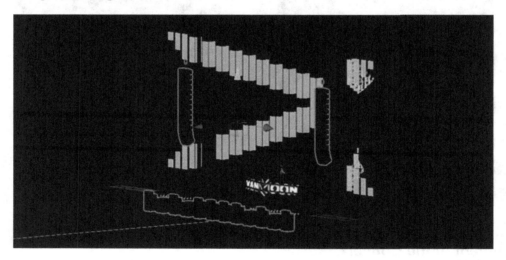

Visuals

The visuals or the background video played on the led screens help bring another dimension into the concert experience. The visuals for the concert were curated to match the beats of the audio, to enhance the experience. The visuals were rendered as an mp4 file on video editing software's and fed into the LED screen using Emissive shader materials. The visuals had other post processing techniques used to make it look realistic. Figure 4 shows the LED screen after using emissive shaders for video display.

Figure 4. LED screen after using emissive shaders for video display.

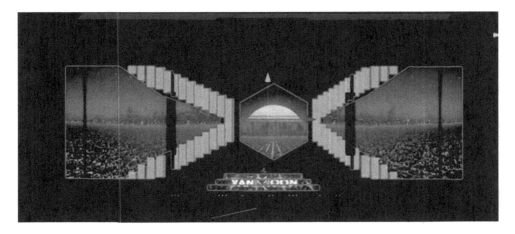

The Post-processing Techniques Used

Ambient occlusion was used to determine automatically how much light can hit a point on a surface at any given time, this helps give different light feels at different locations of the arena. Depth of Field was used to automatically adjust the depth of focus of the camera lens depending on the location of the user to always give maximum quality visuals. Bloom was used to reproduce the imaging artifact of real-life cameras which contributed to that bright light hitting the eye effect at certain locations. Color Grading was used to alter and correct the color and luminance of the final image.

Lights

The lights are the backbone of a concert, complementing the music to give an amazing experience of the concert show. Some festivals have light shows alone, which gather in a huge amount of crowd.

The lighting devices used for the concert were

1. Sharpies
2. Spotlights
3. Strip lights
4. Lasers

The different lights have different functions based on hue, saturation, intensity, physical movements, light diameters and the type of use. The authors simulated the exact real-life working of the lights by programming their functionalities accordingly. Figure 5 shows the lights used in the Unity.

Figure 5. Lights used in the Unity.

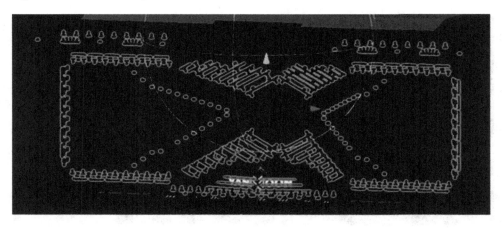

Figure 6. Light Jams.

The whole arena had more than 300 light devices. Hard coding each of the light would be a hectic task and hence the authors decided to use a third-party software called Light jams as a power source to the lighting module. Light jam is a software used by Light Engineers throughout the world to control the lights at a concert through their laptop. It can also be connected externally to a lighting control console like DMX to control the lights in a concert arena. Fig. 6 shows the Light Jams.

Light jams and unity connected with each other through an Art-net UDP to exchange the data and power the lights. With this, we were able to control most of the functions in the lighting system like the hue, saturation and intensity of the lights along with the physical movements of the lighting.

Art net is an ethernet protocol based on the TCP/IP suite used to transfer huge amounts of DMX512 data over a wide area. In the project, the authors used it to send back and forth the data required to power the lighting devices in the concert arena. The lights could be controlled in Real-time to give out different patterns, colors and shapes.

Special Effects (SFX)

Special effects help give an energy into a concert by the mind-blowing effects that they create. SFX systems generally consist of a lot of fireworks, pyro jets, flame throwers, cO2 emission jets and many more. In our project, we have recreated the functionalities into unity and programed the module to be accessed at the right time. It gives the light engineer complete freedom to program the SFX along with the beats of the music. The SFX was generated with a feature called as Particle system inside Unity. It is a programmable module that enables us to re-create real-life particles like water, smoke, fire, sparks and many such features. With this, we can control the many dimensions of the particles like Duration, Looping, Pre-warm, Start Delay, Start lifetime, Start speed, 3D start size, Start size, 3D start rotation, Start rotation, Start color, Gravity modifier, Simulation Space, Simulation Speed, Delta time, Scaling mode and many other features. Fig. 7 shows the special effects used. (Fog, Smoke, CO2 jets, flames, fireworks).

Figure 7. The special effects used. (Fog, Smoke, CO2 jets, flames, fireworks)

The Artist/Performer

To simulate the concert performance, it needed an artist to be present behind the deck of the stage. The authors had to simulate a 2D video of file of the artist performance, which was recorded earlier into a 3D environment. This was achieved with the help of Chromakey shaders.

Chroma key is a technique used by media channels around the world to simulate artificial environments on to the screen. The original video is shot in a studio with a green screen behind the actors, which is then eliminated using the chromakey shader. The shader identifies the background depending on the user specification and can be replaced accordingly with another set of images or videos in the background, if required. News channels, TV series and huge production houses use Chroma key to render realistic background in their content.

The artist Mr. Raghav, recorded a set of his performance on a dark background at his home in Delhi and had sent the 2D mp4 file across to us, which was then processed used a chromakey shader in Unity to project an image of the DJ on the deck in our 3D environment. Fig. 8 shows the DJ recording on a green screen. Fig. 9 shows the artist after Chroma key compositing in our 3D environment.

The created environment is also capable to take in multiple artists as a team or as individuals. The artists just have to make sure that the recording is being done in a Standard procedure to be able to attain maximum quality on the stage. The artists, take a band, must be present together in the same room under a green screen or can also be at their houses in front of a dark background or a green screen to attain maximum quality. However, there might be quality issues or lag in the music created if in case there are any problems internet. Hence, it is suggested that the artists of the band be present in the same room at their convenience, under a green screen.

Figure 8. The DJ recording on a green screen.

Camera

The cameras play a huge role in any virtual reality application as it is the main component which enables you to view the whole environment in a First-person view. The cameras in Unity behave like digital cameras and can be configured to capture images or videos in High Definition. The authors also used some post processing techniques to enhance the render quality. Post processing filters like Bloom, Ambient

Occlusion, Chromatic Aberration, Grain, Color grading and Motion Blur were used which come in as standard post processing effects in Unity.

Figure 9. The artist after chroma key compositing in our 3D environment.

The cameras can also be given different animations to move around the arena in the gameplay, if incase a 360° video needs to be recorded. Fig. 10 shows the Before Post Processing snapshot and Fig. 11 shows after post processing effect. However, the processing power of the camera depends on the GPU of the developer/user. As the GPU renders the whole scene. The dynamic range of Unity lies between 8-10 f-stops and hence postprocessing techniques need to be used to get a higher resolution renders of the scene.

Figure 10. Before Post Processing.

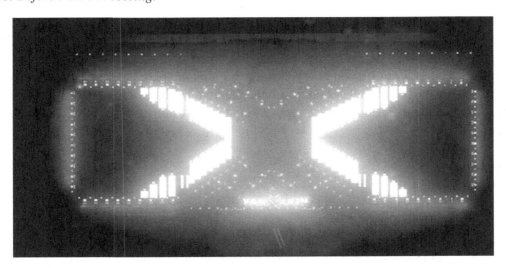

The Console

After all the individual components were programmed to function like real life entities, the authors created a console, which was able to control all the systems from one control section. The authors scripted down the functions of each component created and were able to define the parameters such as start time, stop time, delay, intensity, duration, etc. Once the console was scripted, the authors controlled the modules at the specific time of the gameplay to match with the music. The console made it easier to mix and match the different lighting and special effects to put together a virtual concert.

Figure 11. After Post Processing.

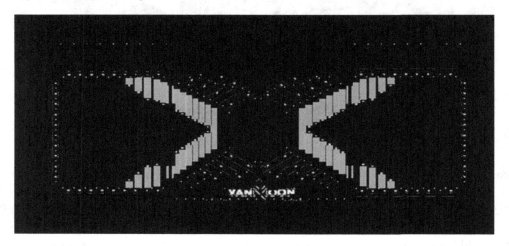

Steam VR

Virtual Reality is updating at a rapid rate and with so many VR headsets coming up, it is very difficult to create the adaption algorithm of the application to the different models. STEAM VR removes the need to code the adaptation of the application to different devices through the STEAM VR plugin. Instead of writing a code for the whole action in specific, the developer needs to just write a code for the action. For example: Instead of writing a code for the trigger button long press=push the box. We just have to focus on pushing the box with trigger button and the plugin takes care of the coding part on its own.

The plugin has separated actions into 6 types of inputs and 1 output to simplify the development of VR applications.

1.   Boolean (true or false)
2.   Single (an analog value)
3.   Vector 2 (2 analog values)
4.   Vector 3 (3 analog values)
5.   Pose (rotation, position, velocity and angular velocity)
6.   Skeleton (uses the VR skeleton to recognize movement in each bone of your hand)

Once we have defined and created the actions required (grab, pull, push, etc.) we can import these in our own scripts by calling them. SteamVR_Behaviour_Boolean, SteamVR_Behaviour_Single, etc. are some of the unity components which pre-exist in the plugin.

The plugin also automatically converts the gameplay into a VR ready build .exe file ready to be played along with a VR headset in the market.

RESULTS

After the creation of the whole gameplay of the concert, the authors had to build it into a virtual reality application. For this, they used STEAM VR, a gaming platform that hosts Virtual Reality games and applications, Unity has a plugin which allows steam to access the application built and convert it into a Virtual Reality application.

Steam VR plugin in Unity makes it possible to create any normal 3D game built in Unity into a Virtual Reality Application and enables the camera to rotate along with the headset of the end user. Before building the application, some factors must be pre-defined to give maximum quality in the user experience. The controls and their functions must be defined and assigned accordingly to the different VR headsets that are in the market, which are all possible with this plugin.

Figure 12. Snapshot of Unity Package

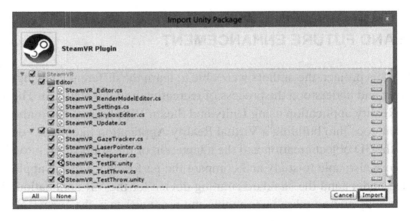

Finally, the product was built and accessed to stream the virtual concert of DJ Van Moon online.

The VR application is only designed to run on a Personal Computer with a graphics card and the authors conducted a small survey on how it ran on computers with different GPUs ranging from Nvidia GTX 1050 to Nvidia RTX 2070. Fig. 13 shows GPU vs Fps rates.

Figure 13. GPU vs Fps rates

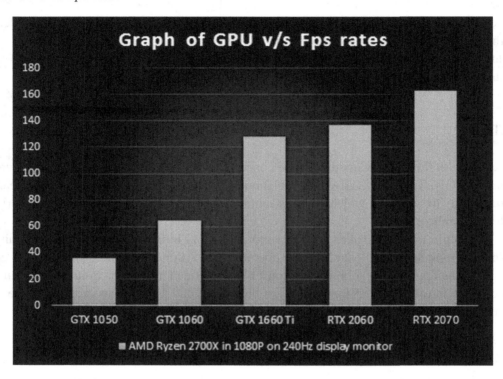

CONCLUSION AND FUTURE ENHANCEMENT

During the work on this project, the authors were able to learn the different challenges faced in producing a musical concert and understood the process of recreating it in the platform. The authors were able to create a Virtual Reality application using Unity and Steam VR plugins. The authors learnt about the in-depth features that goes into building a Virtual Reality Application like the 3D environment design, material texturing, the 3D object creation and the adaptation of the application into different VR headsets. The authors were also able to study and compare the performance of the application on different GPUs which helped understand the standard running device for the VR application. This work can be enhanced in the future by adding more instruments and more artists in the Virtual Reality concert. The sound quality and the visual quality may be improved.

REFERENCES

Altosaar, R., Tindale, A., & Doyle, J. (2019). Physically Colliding with Music: Full-body Interactions with an Audio-only Virtual Reality Interface. *Proceedings of the Thirteenth International Conference on Tangible, Embedded, and Embodied Interaction.* 10.1145/3294109.3301256

Aufegger & Wasley. (2020). *Virtual reality feedback influences musicians' physical responses and mental attitude towards performing.* Academic Press.

Aufegger, L., Perkins, R., Wasley, D., & Williamon, A. (2017). Musicians' perceptions and experiences of using simulation training to develop performance skills. *Psychology of Music*, *45*(3), 417–431. doi:10.1177/0305735616666940

Bian, H. (2016). Application of virtual reality in music teaching system. *International Journal of Emerging Technologies in Learning*, *11*(11), 21–25. doi:10.3991/ijet.v11i11.6247

Bissonnette, J., Dubé, F., Provencher, M. D., & Moreno Sala, M. T. (2016). Evolution of music performance anxiety and quality of performance during virtual reality exposure training. *Virtual Reality (Waltham Cross)*, *20*(1), 71–81. doi:10.100710055-016-0283-y

Bruguera, M. B., Ilk, V., Ruber, S., & Ewald, R. (2019). *Use of Virtual Reality for astronaut training in future space missions-Spacecraft piloting for the Lunar Orbital Platform-Gateway*. LOP-G.

Deacon, T., Stockman, T., & Barthet, M. (2016). User experience in an interactive music virtual reality system: an exploratory study. In *International symposium on computer music multidisciplinary research*. Springer.

Honzel, E., Murthi, S., Brawn-Cinani, B., Colloca, G., Kier, C., Varshney, A., & Colloca, L. (2019). Virtual reality, music, and pain: Developing the premise for an interdisciplinary approach to pain management. *Pain*, *160*(9), 1909–1919. doi:10.1097/j.pain.0000000000001539 PMID:30817437

Hwang, I., Son, H., & Kim, J. R. (2017). AirPiano: Enhancing music playing experience in virtual reality with mid-air haptic feedback. In *2017 IEEE World Haptics Conference (WHC)*. IEEE. 10.1109/WHC.2017.7989903

Innocenti, D., Edoardo, M. G., Vescovi, D., Nordahl, R., Serafin, S., Ludovico, L. A., & Avanzini, F. (2019). Mobile virtual reality for musical genre learning in primary education. *Computers & Education*, *139*, 102–117. doi:10.1016/j.compedu.2019.04.010

Maffei, A., & Onori, M. (2019). Evaluation of the potential impact of fully-immersive virtual reality on production engineering curricula. In *2019 IEEE AFRICON* (pp. 1–5). IEEE. doi:10.1109/AFRICON46755.2019.9133929

Mazuryk & Gervautz. (1996). *Virtual reality-history, applications, technology and future*. Academic Press.

Men, L., & Bryan-Kinns, N. (2018). LeMo: supporting collaborative music making in virtual reality. In *2018 IEEE 4th VR workshop on sonic interactions for virtual environments (SIVE)*. IEEE. 10.1109/SIVE.2018.8577094

Orman, E. K., Price, H. E., & Russell, C. R. (2017). Feasibility of using an augmented immersive virtual reality learning environment to enhance music conducting skills. *Journal of Music Teacher Education*, *27*(1), 24–35. doi:10.1177/1057083717697962

Pietrzak, E., Pullman, S., & McGuire, A. (2014). Using virtual reality and videogames for traumatic brain injury rehabilitation: A structured literature review. *Games for Health*, *3*(4), 202–214. doi:10.1089/g4h.2014.0013 PMID:26192369

Serafin, S., Adjorlu, A., Nilsson, N., Thomsen, L., & Nordahl, R. (2017). Considerations on the use of virtual and augmented reality technologies in music education. In *2017 IEEE Virtual Reality Workshop on K-12 Embodied Learning through Virtual & Augmented Reality (KELVAR),* (pp. 1-4). IEEE. 10.1109/KELVAR.2017.7961562

Sra, M., Vijayaraghavan, P., Maes, P., & Roy, D. (2017). Deepspace: Mood-based image texture generation for virtual reality from music. *Proceedings of the IEEE Conference on Computer Vision and Pattern Recognition Workshops*, 41-50. 10.1109/CVPRW.2017.283

Valve Software. (2020). https://valvesoftware.github.io/steamvr_unity_plugin/articles/intro.html

Vargas, A., Díaz, P., & Zarraonandia, T. (2020). Using Virtual Reality and Music in Cognitive Disability Therapy. *Proceedings of the International Conference on Advanced Visual Interfaces*. 10.1145/3399715.3399916

Zhang, Tao, Shen, Clayton, & Abassin. (2019). Interactive virtual reality orchestral music. *ACM SIGGRAPH 2019 Posters*, 1-2.

Chapter 9

Increasing Participation in Large–Scale Virtual Environments:
Rethinking the Ecological Cognition Frameworks for the Augmented, Mixed, and Virtual Reality

Jonathan Bishop
ⓘ https://orcid.org/0000-0002-9919-7602
Crocels Community Media Group, UK

ABSTRACT

The proliferation of media-rich social networking services has changed the way people use information society and audio-visual media services. Existing theories of cognition in human-computer interaction have limitations in dealing with the unique problems that exist in contemporary virtual environments. The presence of significant numbers of people using these at the same time causes behavioural issues not previously envisaged at the time of multi-user domains (MUDs) or the first massively-multiplayer online role-playing games. To understand such large-scale virtual environments, this chapter makes use of data generated from questionnaires, usability testing, and social and web metrics to assess the relevance of ecological cognition theory for the current age. Through making use of a biometric measure called 'knol', the chapter suggests a new framework for measuring emotion and cognition in these and future environments.

INTRODUCTION

The term large-scale virtual environment (LSVE) can be seen to encompass many forms of computer-mediated communication platforms where more than one user participates. Online communities have been large-scale virtual environments insofar as many users contribute to the platform, but social networking

DOI: 10.4018/978-1-7998-4703-8.ch009

Copyright © 2021, IGI Global. Copying or distributing in print or electronic forms without written permission of IGI Global is prohibited.

services like Twitter and Facebook have increased users of online communities from tens of people to thousands of people. These social networking services are thus truly large-scale virtual environments, where many people take part in a virtually synchronous manner. Even if the technologies would have at one point been considered asynchronous, such as bulletin board systems, social networking services have due to the volume of people using them made such technologies virtually asynchronous. For instance, Twitter was once seen as a micro-blogging platform, but because users 'tweet' each other synchronously, it is more like a chat group than a weblog platform due to its LSVE structure. Naturally, in any communication platform where there is a human element, there is a strong potential for conflict in LSVEs, especially as the number of users is far more than prior to social networking services being adopted by the masses. The aim of this paper is therefore to refute the ecological cognition framework that was first created prior to the existence of Facebook and Twitter and to make it more relevant to a time when the complexities of LSVEs is not accounted for in other models or frameworks.

Conflict Management in Large-scale Virtual Environments

Conflict in computer mediated communication environments, including large-scale virtual environments, has been explored in detail since the dawn of the World Wide Web (Campbell, Fletcher, & Greenhill, 2009; Hardaker, 2013a; Hardaker, 2013b; Smith, 1999). There have been many attempts to find ways to increase participation and sense of community in these environments, especially where there is community dimension to them (Bishop, 2007b; de Souza & Preece, 2004; Nonnecke, Andrews, & Preece, 2006). Factors affecting the level of conflict in a LSVE are strongly linked to the behaviour and attitudes of those that use in them (Hardaker, 2013a; Hardaker, 2010). In particular, this paper argues that lurking, flaming and defriending are behaviours that need to be managed to increase participation so that their opposites of delurking, kudos and befriending can be encouraged so as to increase sense of community (Kommers, 2014; McMillan & Chavis, 1986; Peterson, Speer, & McMillan, 2008).

Lurking and Delurking

Lurking is a behaviour attributed to "lurkers." A lurker has been conceived as a "*visitor to a newsgroup or chatroom who simply views activity without taking part or subscribing, and therefore remains anonymous*" (Cowpertwait & Flynn, 2002). It has been argued that lurking is "*generally regarded as harmless pastime, especially among newbies and the terminally shy*" and that the "*process of breaking silence and contributing to a discussion for the first time is called delurking*" (Geer, 2003). Others have described lurking as reading "*through mailing lists or newsgroups and get the feel for a topic before posting your own messages,*" arguing that it is "considered good netiquette to 'lurk' a while before joining in the discussion" (Marcus & Watters, 2002). In this paper, lurking is generally seen as a form of retreat, where someone who feels the loss of a sense of community in a LSVE ceases to take as active a part in it. Equally, delurking is seen as something that happens when a sense of community is created to the point a person feels able to participate (Kommers, 2014; Nonnecke & Preece, 2003; Nonnecke et al., 2006; Preece, 2008). The paper therefore shows how it is possible to model LSVEs in relation to the mental states of the actors who use them to encourage delurking and help prevent lurking.

Flaming and Kudos

Flaming has been defined as an *"abusive communication from a fellow Internet user, usually in a newsgroup but sometimes by e-mail or in a chat forum,"* where common causes are *"failure to observe netiquette, ignorance of a FAQ and simple stupidity, or intemperance on either side"* (Geer, 2003). In this paper, flaming is seen as a behaviour that is likely to lead someone to defriend the person who is flaming them, to lurk due to feeling a lack of sense of community, or even to themselves flame the person who is flaming them. The paper shows how it is possible to model participation in LSVEs in order to reduce lurking and encourage kudos.

Defriending and Befriending

Defriending is argued to the act of ceasing to be associated with someone who is already on one's buddylist (Neff, 2013). On social networking service platforms, defriending can be as easily done as befriending (Gashi & Knautz, 2016). It is known as a means of effectively resolving disputes between people in conflict (Tsai, Shen, & Chiang, 2015). In this paper, defriending is seen as one of the consequences of adverse behaviours like flaming. Through defriending, a person will unfriend someone from their buddylist, unfollow them, or similar, in order that they are not re-exposed to the abuse that might come from that person's behaviour towards them. The paper shows how LSVEs can be understood in order to encourage befriending and discourage defriending.

BACKGROUND

For some the term large-scale virtual environment (LSVE) is synonymous with 3D Virtual Worlds (Feng & Song, 2011; Tseng, Tsai, & Chao, 2013). However, from the point of view of this paper the term is used to refer to virtual environments that are multi-user, as they have been traditionally seen as in human-computer interaction (Mantovani, 1996a; Mantovani, 1996b; Suchman, 1987; Suchman, 2007). An important aspect of LSVEs, however, is that they are collaborative in the manner in which they are used, rather than being systems which have many actors who never interact (Clarke & Dede, 2007). This means that when seeking to understand how to increase participation in LSVEs, it should be assumed from the outset that the problems and opportunities that arise are no different from any other environment that is dependent on humans working together. Figure 1 presents different forms of post-cognitivist psychology, including the one discussed in detail in this article, namely ecological cognition.

Figure 1. Forms of post-cognitive psychology for information systems in the information society

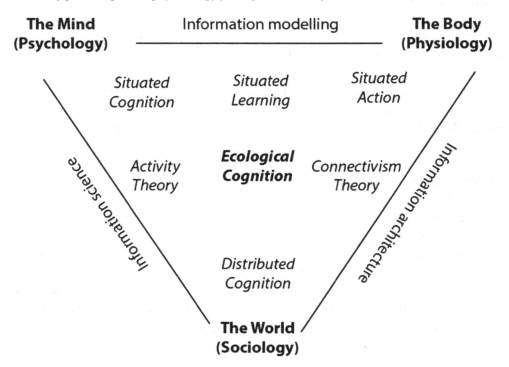

Figure 1 sets out the various approaches to understanding large-scale virtual environments, along with the established disciplines they fall between. It can be seen that ecological cognition is in the middle of all the other paradigms.

Cognitive Dimensions

An important consideration in the design of Large-scale virtual environments (LSVEs) is the concept of cognitive presence, namely the "the ability of learners to construct meaning making through communication" (Garrison, Anderson, & Archer, 2001; Ortiz, 2012). Knowing how it is possible to construct cognitive presence in LSVEs is therefore an important part of understanding how actors can increase their participation within. The concept measuring the likelihood of someone to continue participation in LSVEs is called stickiness. Stickiness refers to the information of features of an information system that gives its users a reason to use it frequently (Jansen & James, 1995; Jansen, 2002){Jansen}. An attempt to understand this stickiness was systematically engineering seductive hypermedia (Mbakwe & Cunliffe, 2002; Mbakwe & Cunliffe, 2007; Mbakwe & Cunliffe, September 26 2003). A model demonstrating this approach is in Figure 2.

Figure 2. Systematically engineering seductive hypermedia

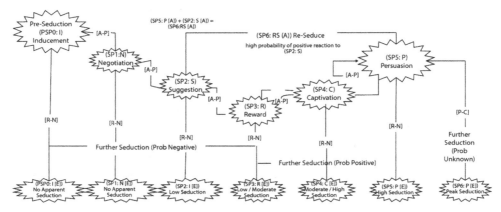

Figure 3. The Base-3 ecological cognition framework (2002)

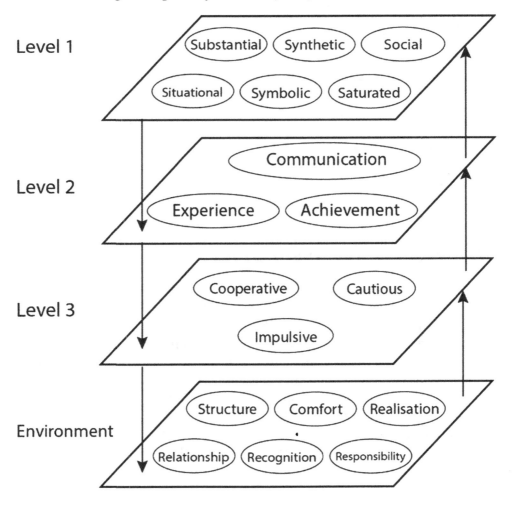

Figure 4. The Base-4 ecological cognition framework (2004)

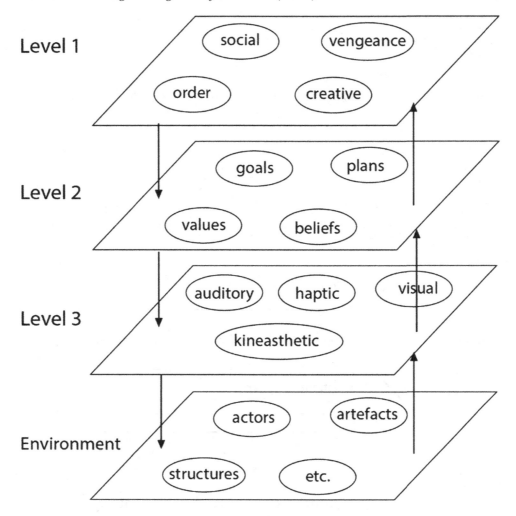

The Ecological Cognition Framework

A further attempt to understand stickiness in the case of online communities was the ecological cognition framework, which has undergone several iterations to date. Base-3 from 2002 is presented in Figure 3, Base 4 from 2004 is presented in Figure 4 and Base-5 from 2005 and 2007 is presented in Figure 5.

The ecological cognition framework (ECF) has presented a purpose-built alternative to Abraham Maslow's hierarchy of needs theory in terms of understanding of virtual environments (Bishop, 2007b), which has been especially online communities and other large-scale virtual environments (LSVEs). Maslow's model has been referred to by a number of scholars in the area of online communities (Del Grosso, 2001; Kim, 2000; Shneiderman, 2002), but equally the ecological cognition framework has become adopted widely to understand online communities (Bougrine, Ouchraa, Ahiod, & El Imrani, 2014; Cheng & Chen, 2014; Kutay, 2014; Stutsky, 2009). Unlike Maslow's hierarchy of needs, however, the ECF has a theoretical basis in cognitive neurobiology as many of the elements that form part of it are verifiable through forms of neuro-imaging (Bishop, 2011c; Bishop, 2012). It is therefore essential for any enhancement of the ECF to account for these advances, such as accounting for the role of the role of the inferior-parietal lobule (Bishop, 2007b) and prefrontal cortex (Bishop, 2011c) in understanding participation in online environments, such as large-scale virtual environments. The fact that Maslow's hierarchy has not been replicated by research studies since its creation means its use for online communities should also be seen as limited (Bishop, 2016a).

Figure 5. The Base-5 ecological cognition framework (2005-2007)

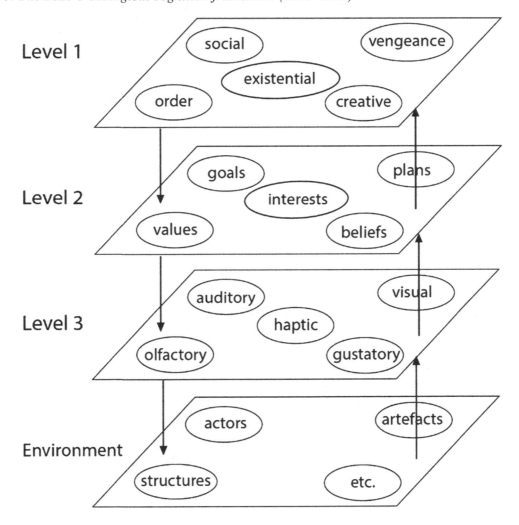

Personality Traits Dimensions

There have been several attempts to capture the differences in personality among those who participate in online communities and other forms of Large-scale virtual environment. Some have suggested

Abraham Maslow's hierarchy of needs (Figure 6) as a suitable approach (Del Grosso, 2001; Kim, 2000; Shneiderman, 2002).

Figure 6. Maslow's hierarchy of needs

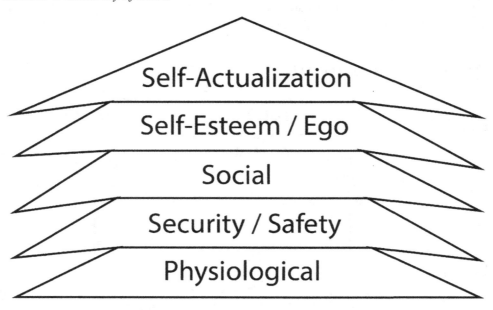

Some have suggested character theories (Bartle, 1996; Bishop, 2008; Campbell et al., 2009), and others have tried to identify the behaviours specific to such environments (Hardaker, 2013a; Powazek, 2002; Preece, Nonnecke, & Andrews, 2004; Wallace, 1999). On their own, these offer little value, but this study seeks to make use of a way of understanding personality that conceptualises behaviour by people focuses on friendship and socialising as empathic and behaviour focused around individuality and ideas as autistic (Bishop, 2013; Bishop, 2015b; Bolognini, 1997). Online communities have on the one hand been seen as empathic communities (Preece, 1998) and by others as communities of practice (Johnson, 2001; Preece, 2003). It is therefore clear that there is a divide that exists between users that can be considered empathic and those that can be considered autistic, which can help explain in terms of different types of users who take part in LSVEs and the problems they are likely to encounter due to others with different personalities.

Equatricism

Since the creation of the ecological cognition framework (Bishop, 2007a; Bishop, 2007b; Bishop, 2009), the a set of principles in Table 1 have been created and called equatricism (Bishop, 2011b). Equatricism refers to 'the study of economics through three dimensions.' Those three dimensions are based on the 'learn, create, communicate' model.

Table 1. The elements of 'equatricism'

Concept	Learn	Create	Communicate
Socio-legal: There has been a breakdown of traditional community structures and an emergence of a network society.	**Acquisition:** Actors should not be subject to autocratic and broadcasted information sources but should have their individual Identities recognised when they learn.	**Application:** Information providers should facilitate actors in creating new knowledge through combining theory with practice.	**Articulation:** Information providers should respect communities and seek to add value to them through facilitating actors in communicating their knowledge.
Economic: There has been a breakdown of traditional economic structures and an emergence of a digital economy.	**Boundlessness:** Actors do not have a hierarchy of needs or necessarily know what they are looking for during an activity but will seek to minimise discomfort and maximise gratification.	**Bestowal:** The exchange and use of artefacts and not capital is the driver in an economy.	**Breath:** Actors will continually be seeking to increase the extent to which they have access to the things they enjoy.
Info-scientific: There has been a breakdown of traditional educational structures and an emergence of a globalised virtual community.	**Consciousness:** Actors are not usually aware of the reason for their actions until after the event.	**Context:** Actors have individual interpretations of an event that is often different from others.	**Consideration:** Actors do not usually have full access to all their cognitions to facilitate an informed bargaining position.
Techno-cultural: There has been a breakdown in traditional power-structures and communication channels and the emergence of a public square of uncontrolled expression.	**Determination:** Actors will be continually seeking to realise their goals and other cognitions and will be inventive and reflective in their use of artefacts in order to do so.	**Didactic:** Actors will look for meaning in their experiences, even where there is none, and will seek to document such memories and experiences.	**Decoration:** Actors will make use of artefacts in order to express their identity and personality and seek approval from others relating to their use of those artefacts.

Neuroeconomic Dimensions and Parametric User Modelling

Neuroeconomics is a way of quantifying the way the brain engages with the environments in which is constructs a social reality (Berger & Luckmann, 1991). Equation 1 shows a parametric user model for explaining how an actor will develop an attitude towards an artefact or other representation within their environment (Fishbein, 1967a; Fishbein, 1967b; Fishbein, 1967c; Fishbein & Ajzen, 1980; Mowen & Minor, 2001)

$$A_O = \sum_{i=0}^{N} b_i e_i$$

Equation 1 Fishbein and Ajzen's parametric user model for understanding attitude towards the object (artefact)

The links between the ecological cognition framework (ECF) and neurobiology has been effectively expressed through the discipline of neuroeconomics (Bishop, 2011b; Bishop, 2014). The role of the inferior parietal lobule and the prefrontal cortex have been important in the role the ECF has played in understanding LSVEs (Bishop, 2007b; Bishop, 2011c). Neuroeconomics as a discipline seeks to link an actor's internal mental states with external behaviours that are quantifiable, especially in terms of money and other actors (Kugler & Zak, 2017). The main purpose of neuroeconomics is to understand decision-making from the point of view of the neurological bases to them (Reuter & Montag, 2016). As embodied in Equation 3, the creation of an equation for computing brain productivity in the form of a unit called knol (Bishop, 2011c; Bishop, 2012) refers to a means of assessing the combined impact of an actor's external environmental and their internal mental state on them neurobiologically. A knol (represented in Equation 2) can theoretically run from 0 to an infinite value with the former reflecting someone who is braindead, which should not be considered the same as suffering from locked-in syndrome where knol operates no differently. When knol is 1 or above an actor's brain is operating at its highest capacity and fastest speed, which is commonly referred to as flow (Csikszentmihalyi, 1975; Csikszentmihalyi, 2000; Csikszentmihalyi, 2009). It is important to note that in the case of knol, flow is linked to dopamine and involvement is linked to serotonin to reflect that the more effort an actor has to put into a task the higher their involvement and serotonin levels, whereas if they need to put in less effort their flow and dopamine levels are high (Bishop, 2012). This might seem counter-intuitive to those that define flow as an actor 'acting with total involvement' (Csikszentmihalyi, 1974; Csikszentmihalyi, 1992; Csikszentmihalyi, 1997; Csikszentmihalyi, 2000; Csikszentmihalyi, 2002; Csikszentmihalyi, 2009; Csikszentmihalyi, 2013; Csikszentmihihalyi, 1997), but in terms of knol it is understood that an actor that is consciously involved in a task has high involvement, and those who are not consciously involved in a task have low involvement. When a person has equilibrium of flow and involvement, they are still considered 'acting with total involvement' in old school language (Csikszentmihalyi, 1974; Csikszentmihalyi, 1992; Csikszentmihalyi, 1997; Csikszentmihalyi, 2000; Csikszentmihalyi, 2002; Csikszentmihalyi, 2009; Csikszentmihalyi, 2013; Csikszentmihihalyi, 1997) or 'in the zone' in new school language (Brolin, 2017; Craig, 2001; Craig, 2013; Douglas, 2000; Kuypers, 2011; Sears, 2020), whereas if either flow or involvement are lack equilibrium they are not 'in the zone' nor 'acting with total involvement'. Equation 2 provides a simple model for measuring the extent to which someone's flow and involvement levels are in equilibrium through a proposed unit of measurement called knol (Bishop, July 19 2012; Bishop, September 10 2011)

$$k = \frac{P}{H}.$$

Equation 2 A simple equation for modelling knol

Table 2. Table for calculating knol using the interest cognition from the Base-5 and Base-6 ecological cognition frameworks

Signifier Representation	Reducer	Signification Internal Representation	Reducer	Signified External Representation	Reducer	Shifter	Transformer	Phantasy	Fantasy	Brain function (Pre-frontal cortex)
x / x_{4S}	$x_1 / \emptyset$ Ca_{eS}	y / y_{2a}	$y_1 / \emptyset$ Cb_{eS}	z / z_{3S}	$z_2 / \emptyset$ Cb_{dS}	$\check{z} / \emptyset$ Cc_{eS}	$c / c_{1eS} /$ $2c_{1dS}$	p_e	f_d	g
Interest	0	Goal	0	Strategy	0	45.5	8.9	Devoted	Persistent	Problem-solving
Interest	0	Plan	3	Method	3	25.5	4.9	Loving	Caring	Self-control
Interest	0	Value	0	Rule	0	20.5	3.9	Respectful	Reverential	Conscience
Interest	0	Belief	4	Meme	4	35.5	6.	Trusting	Expectant	Working memory
Interest	0	Interest	0	Amity	0	50.5	9.9	Cherishing	Relishing	Empathy
Interest	0	Detachment	1	Enmity	1	35.5	6.9	Affinity	Attracted	Deception
Interest	0	Faith	1	Illusion	1	10.5	1.9	Interested	Attentive	Attention
Interest	0	Ardour	2	Delusion	2	10.5	1.9	Delight	Elation	Speech

$$k = \frac{\left(\dfrac{\sum_{e=0}^{M} \left(\dfrac{\left((x+x_1)*(y+y_1) - \overset{\emptyset}{z} \right) / (i+j))_e}{c} \right)}{5} \right) + F}{\left(\dfrac{\sum_{d=0}^{D} \left(\dfrac{\left((x+x_1)*(z+z_1) - \overset{\emptyset}{z} \right) / 2n)_d}{2c} \right)}{2.5} \right) + Ob}.$$

Equation 3 A complex equation for modelling knol

Table 2 presents the values required to use Equation 2 and Equation 3 to transfer how an actor interprets elements of the external environment (measured through x) in reference to their internal cognitions (measured through y). When the external representation (x) is combined with the internal cognition (y) it produces a phantasy (p_e). A phantasy, which is named from the Freudian concept, can be seen in the same light as a schema, but an important difference in ecological cognition phantasies always produce emotions and so impact an actor's resulting behaviour significantly. Phantasies are always valued between -5 and +5, which is why the additional elements in the equation (i.e. x_1, y_1, z, c) are needed to transform the cognitions measured through x and y into phantasies. Each phantasy represents and emotion that impacts on the functioning of the prefrontal cortex. The functions of the prefrontal cortex include problem-solving (Mushiake et al., 2009), self-control (Figner et al., 2010), conscience (Blair, 2007; Moll, Eslinger, & Oliveira-Souza, 2001), working-memory (Canuet et al., 2011; Meyer, Qi, Stanford, & Constantinidis, 2011; Zanto, Rubens, Thangavel, & Gazzaley, 2011), empathy (Seitz, Nickel, & Azari, 2006; Shamay-Tsoory, Tomer, Berger, & Aharon-Peretz, 2003) and deception (Christ, Van Essen, Watson, Brubaker, & McDermott, 2009; Ito et al., 2010; Priori et al., 2008). The links between these functions and the phantasies that affect them are in Table 2, which is for converting interests and other cognitions into phantasies and fantasies. Interests run from 1 to 10, phantasies from -5 to +5 and fantasies from -2.5 to 2.5, meaning the conversion variable for a phantasy is half that for a fantasy. An interest that is perceived as external to an actor is called an amity in the Base-6 ecological cognition framework, an actor in the Base-4 to Base-5 ecological cognition frameworks.

When the knol (k) is computed using Equation 3 there are a number of thresholds that can be used to assess the impact of the value computed. One will find that if knol is at the deindividuation threshold (k=0.5) then a person is at risk of lurking, trolling or defriending. An actor whose knol is at the optimal threshold (k=0.81) can easily change their behaviour to fit the situation to avoid being forced to lurk, flame or defriend. An actor whose knol is at the serendipity threshold (k=0.98) will either operate at their modus operandi and perform the behaviours they would without thinking about the consequences of their actions, or those behaviours will be totally out of character for them. These behaviours are as likely to be lurking or delurking, kudos or flaming, or befriending or defriending, depending on what is normal for the actor concerned. An actor who is most likely to feel the need to lurk would be at the deindividuation threshold, but if that actor wants to post and their knol hits the serendipity threshold there is a high chance they will delurk and start posting at the same time as enjoying the experience. Conversely, an actor who begrudgingly lurks and doesn't feel like posting in any case stands the chance of flaming when the serendipity threshold is past, such as following reading a piece of persuasive or provocative text. Table 3 shows the thresholds for knol.

Table 3. Thresholds for knol

Knol	Threshold	Description
0.5	Deindividuation	The deindividuation threshold is where an actor has such high serotonin levels and dopamine levels that they detach from the external environment to concentrate solely on their internal thought processes.
0.81	Optimal	The optimal threshold is where an actor's dopamine and serotonin levels are in equilibrium to the point that they can optimally engage with their external environment at the same time as being able engage with their own internal needs and wants.
0.98	Serendipity	The serendipity threshold is where an actor's dopamine levels are so high and their serotonin levels so low that they engage with their internal and mental states with so little effort that they have reached their optimal experience.

Rethinking the Ecological Cognition Framework Through Equatricism

The ecological cognition framework (Figure 5) is over 15 years old at the time of writing (Bishop, 2007a; Bishop, 2007b). It was created before the advent of massively multi-user social networking services like Facebook, where there has been a lot of change in the geo-demographics of who uses the Internet. When the ECF was created, older generations did not use the Internet for surveillance and escapism in the way that younger generations typically do (Leung, 2003). Since that time, older generations use Facebook as much for surveillance and escapism as newer generations and so the ECF needs to be updated to accommodate this, such as through the introduction of a sixth binary-opposition force, namely surveillance-escape. Equally, the theory of 'equatrics' (Table 1) is now 6 years old (Bishop, 2011a; Bishop, 2011b) and whilst its principles are as relevant now as then, as a stand-alone theory it is not as useful as it could otherwise be if integrated with other theories. The ecological cognition framework has for instance been used to understand lurking in online communities (Chen, 2013), but through blended it with equatrics, it should be possible to apply it to further contexts using neuroeconomics.

This following section presents several t-tests that have sought to show how the ecological cognition framework needs to change now that social networking services exist as massively large-scale virtual environments. The outcome that it is compared against is what is called the Base-6 ecological cognition framework. This proposed 6-Base ecological cognition framework (Figure 7) accounts for equatricism (Bishop, 2011a; Bishop, 2011b).

Figure 7. The 6-Base ecological cognition Framework (2011-2013)

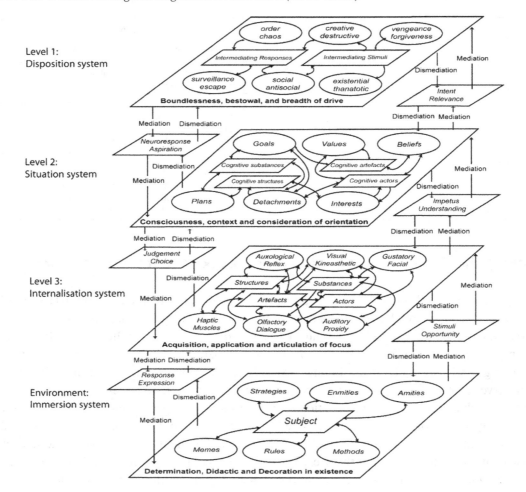

Participants and Data Cleaning

Table 4. Data sources selected and created

Dataset	Autistic (M k)	Empathic (M k)	Primary	Secondary	Computed
Concept-mapping	1.00911262018	1.02080942295	22	0	22
Questionnaire	0.837611750	0.865500000	8	0	8
Location Metrics	0.96572379	0.98758705	18	30	0

The study involved the collecting of primary data from a dyad of participants – one autistic person and one empathic person. In this context, 'autistic' refers to someone who is ideas driven and prefers working on their own and 'empathic' refers to people who prefer being around those whose beliefs are hyper-concordant with their own (Bishop, 2013; Bolognini, 1997). It also involved the use of data that was triangulated from secondary sources and the computation of data from combining the primary and secondary sources where details on the participants are not known. In terms of this secondary data, it had to be encoded to account for the use of 'empathic' and 'autistic' as a basis for differentiating the other variables.

Table 5. Online behaviours selected for analysis

Behaviour	Autistic (M k)	Empathic (M k)	Primary
Delurking	0.799169860	0.788117284	8
Kudos	0.784163474	0.783740741	8
Befriending	0.909450830	0.893641975	8

Table 4 sets out each of the datasets created and how many of the observations recorded in the datasets were primary data, secondary data or a computation of data from making use of the data collected to create new observations suitable for analysis with traditional statistical software. The concept-mapping study involved the autistic and empathic participants creating a collage from various forms of available media and those they created themselves, such as photographs. The autistic participant focussed on places and objects, whereas the empathic participant focussed on people. The questionnaire was administered to the autistic and empathic participant after they had taken part in five types of virtual and physical environment. Namely, a community venue without computers, a community venue with computers, a virtual reality engagement, a computer lab and a community venue with all of these. The location metrics were generated from using the United Kingdom Government's census data from 2011. In terms of the computed column in Table 4, this is to indicate that the items were based on encoding visual data in the case of the concept-mapping and in terms of turning the data on its side so that participants become what is measured and not the questions, in a similar way to what happens with Q-methodology. The benefit of this is that it assumes the questions are what is homogeneous and not the participants, meaning a normal distribution is not required to make the data statistically valid.

Table 6. Cognitions selected for analysis

Cognition	Autistic M k	Empathic M k	Computed
Plan	0.82403416	0.79851466	8
Belief	0.82215837	0.79796759	8
Interest	0.83781928	0.81170525	8

Table 4 also shows the Mean knol for the autistic and empathic participants in each dataset. As can be seen, the serendipity threshold has been met in both cases in terms of the concept-mapping data, but only in terms of the empathic when it comes to the location metrics.

Table 5 sets out the Mean knol for autistics and empathics in reference to their responses to the elements of the questionnaire administered to measure delurking, kudos and befriending, which are respectively the positive opposites of lurking, flaming and defriending. As can be seen from this table, the autistics have a greater flow in relation to all of these, with the empathics being around 0.1 knol adrift. None of the Means meet the serendipity threshold of 0.98, but in terms of the optimal threshold these are met in terms of befriending for both the autistics and empathics. This shows that autistics have a higher degree of flow than empathics when it comes to these online behaviours, which might be to do with the fact the imagination of people with autism is better suited to systems, including virtual environments, whereas people with empathism are better suited to hyper-concordant environments where the opportunities to delurk towards, show kudos to or befriend new people and new ideas is limited (Bolognini, 1997; Golan & Baron-Cohen, 2006; Overskeid, 2016; Wheelwright et al., 2006).

Table 6 presents the Mean knol for autistics and empathics in reference to computed variables representing the cognitions of the ecological cognition framework. The flow for the autistic participant was again greater than the empathic, with the latter being around 0.3 knol adrift. The autistic passed the

Table 7. Creation of dummy variables based on external representations (signifiers)

Base-6 Element	Original Variable	High	Low	Reasoning
Methods	Minutes of Exercise	280	0	Methods refer to the conduct of activities, so minutes of exercise captures this.
Rules	Class Size	90	0	Rules refers to imposed or accepted values such as division of labour.. The higher the class size the more difficult it is for an educator to impose rules.
Enmities	Learner-Teacher Ratio	38	0	Enmities refers to those actors who inhibit ones aims. The fewer the number of learners that an educator must teach then the more autocratic they will become.
Amities	Detachment	6	0	Amities refer to those actors who help an actor meet their aims. The more an actor feels detached the fewer amities they have.
Memes	NVQ Level	4	1	Memes are the beliefs and other knowledge an actor holds. The higher their NVQ Level the more information in the environment they should be able to process.
Strategies	Performance	100%	19%	Strategies are the goals of others than an actor likely must accommodate. The higher an actor's performance the more Strategies they can navigate.

optimal threshold of 0.81 in all cases, whereas the empathic did not in the case of plan and belief. The serendipity threshold of 0.98 was not passed in any of the cases. This again suggests that those with autism have greater flow in making use of their cognitions for imagining systems and ideas than those with empathism are.

Table 7 presents the dummy variables that were created from the primary and secondary data in order to investigate Levels 3 and E in terms of signifiers – those observable and understandable parts of the external environment. These signifiers, namely Methods, Enmities, Amities, Memes and Strategies were identified in previous research (Bishop, 2011b; Bishop, 2015a; Bishop, 2016b).

Methods, which refer to the behaviour of others towards the actor that either help or hinder them in achieving their goals, were based on minutes of exercise, with the highest value being 280 and the lowest value being 0. Rules are those impositions on an actor that can either aide them in achieving their goals or make them more difficult to achieve. Class size was chosen in this context because it was assumed that the higher a class's size the more difficult it is for an individual actor to achieve their goals. Enmities, which refer to the persons in an environment that inhibit the actor's abilities to achieve their goals, were based on the learner-teacher ratio. The assumption on this being that the smaller number of learners to each educator then the fewer people the actor must compete with. Amities, which refers to those persons in an environment who can help the actor in achieving their goals, was measured through Detachment. That is, the less sense of community an actor has with one or more people in their environment, the less they are willing to see them as a friend or ally. Memes, which refer to the beliefs in an environment a person is expected to adopt to succeed within it, was measured through NVQ Level. The assumption being that the higher a person's NVQ level, the more they had been exposed to alternative or necessary belief systems and worldviews. Strategies, which refers to the goals of others than an actor has to manage, are reflected in the Performance variable, because the better an actor is doing across all subjects the more they are likely having to accommodate different worldview from different persons, such as educators.

In terms of Table 8, this refers to the senses of a person that interface between their external environment and their internal one. Auxological / Reflex refers to how those unseen aspects of the environment, such as air quality and heat, interact with actor's wellbeing, such as whether they feel tense. The Child-Adult Ratio was used to reflect this because the more adults present in a learning environment the less

Table 8. Creation of dummy variables based on internal/external senses

Base-6 Element	Original Variable	High	Low	Reasoning
Auxological / Reflex	Child-Adult Ratio	0	9	Auxological/Reflex refers to the interaction between an actor's physical and mental being. The more an adult is present in a child's space the more restricted they feel.
Visual / Kinaesthetic	Learner-Visitor Ratio	4	0	Visual/Kinaesthetic refers to an actor's ability to see what they want in their environment and access it. The more unnecessary 'visitors' in an environment the more restricted an actor feels.
Gustatory / Facial	Teacher-Parent Ratio	0.2	0	Gustatory/Facial refers to the effect emotions – such as from perceiving substances – have on an actor's face to be picked up by others. The more parents to a teacher, the more likely their shared emotions will show.
Haptic / Muscles	Enjoys PE	87%	0%	Haptic/Muscles refers to an actor's ability to sense through motion and touch. Those who take part in PE (Physical Education) require these senses more.
Olfactory / Dialogue	Maths	100%	0%	Olfactory/Dialogue refers to the cognitive impact being in an environment has on an actor, such as from the extent to which optimal oxygen input affects through and speech. Mathematical ability is linked to cognition which is also linked to olfactory perception.
Auditory / Prosody	English	100%	0%	Auditory/Prosody refers to an actor's ability to listen to and convey emotion though speech. Performance at English, or other first languages, impacts on ability to combine words with emotional intonations.

Figure 8. Level 1 of the ecological cognition framework at Base 3 (a), Base 4 (b), Base-5 (c) and Base-6 (d)

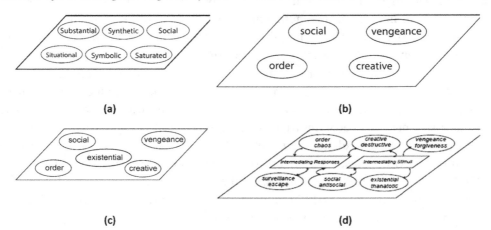

Figure 9. Level 2 of the Base-5 ECF (a) and Level 2 of the Base-6 ECF (b)

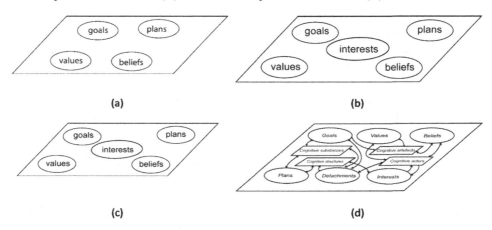

comfortable the children are likely to feel. "Visual / Kinaesthetic" refers to the aspects of an environment that an actor must monitor and physically respond to. The Learner-Visitor Ratio was used because the more unnecessary people within the environment the more of an obstruction they are, both visually and physically. "Gustatory / Facial" refers to the aspects of an environment that impact on the function of an actor's head, including those that produce facial expressions and salivation. Teacher-Parent Ratio was used in this context, because having two authority figures present in an environment can increase anxiety and therefore impact on these aspects of a person's affect. "Haptic / Muscles" refers to how an actor must physically interact with an environment, including using their body to shape it to achieve their goals. In the case, the "Enjoys Physical Education" the more flexibility they have in their muscles and thus capabilities to express themselves in a haptic fashion. "Olfactory / Dialogue" refers to the ability of an actor to take in enough oxygen at the opportune moment to generate thoughts and produce speech that achieves that actor's goals. The performance in the subject of Mathematics was used in this context because cognition and olfactory perception are linked (Westervelt, Ruffolo, & Tremont, 2005).

"Auditory / Prosody" refers to the ability of an actor to hear and express emotion through soundwaves in order to encourage behaviours to achieve their goals and detect risk of those goals being at risk of being inhibited. The variable of performance at English was chosen because it is through words that such emotion is conveyed.

Methodology

The methodology for this paper makes use of established statistical techniques to analyse data which whilst not quasi-experimental, can be best understood using a comparison of means via the t-test statisti-

Table 9. Data for reviewing 'Level 2'

Cognition	High Mean k (N)	Low Mean k (N)	t-score	p-score
Plan	.824034163 (8)	.798514660 (8)	11.562	0.083
Belief	.822158365 (8)	.797967593 (8)	14.673	0.000
Interest	.834560185 (8)	.811705247 (8)	6.912	0.000

Figure 10. Level 3 of the Base-5 ECF (a) and Base-6 ECF (b)

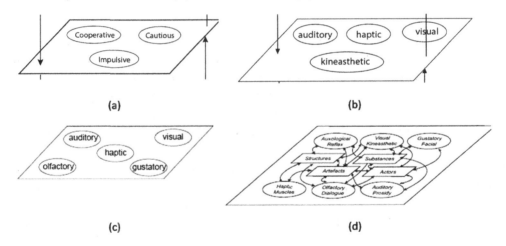

(a)   (b)

(c)   (d)

cal approach. Unlike in traditional uses of the t-test, the aim is not simply to show that the two groups (i.e. autistic and empathics) are significantly different in order to generalise that these groups can be generalised to a wider population, the aim is to show that knol is an effective neuroeconomic measure to carry out such quasi-experimental testing in future studies where two groups are being studied so as to determining the differences in neuro-biological functioning between them.

Results

The results show that overall, the data collected and analysed showed that the changes to the ecological cognition framework to make it the Base-6 ecological cognition framework are supported. This was especially the case when the primary data was used, but not always the case when secondary or computed data was used in place of original empirical observations.

Reviewing Level 1

In terms of reviewing level 1 of the ecological cognition framework, this would be outside the scope of this paper as it depends on the analysis of video observations of the affect the two participants present, as well as the use of biometric data in the form of EEG, eye-movement and heart rate measurements. It would in other words require a research paper in its own right. However, it is possible to discuss how a new level 1 would work in practice by discussing it in the subsequence analyses of the other levels.

In the 3-Base ecological cognition framework (Figure 9 (a)) the drivers were structure, comfort, realisation, relationship, recognition and responsibility. In the Base 4 to base 5 ecological cognition framework (Figure 9 (b)-(c)) they included social, vengeance, existential, order and creative. However, in the Base-6 ecological cognition framework they have been adapted to be order-chaos, creative-destructive, vengeance-forgiveness, social-antisocial, existential-thanatotic, as well as including surveillance-escape.

Reviewing Level 2

Level 2 of the ecological cognition framework conveyed the internal cognitions that are brought into working memory when an actor is engaging with their environment. The cognitions to be found in Base 4 to Base 6 (Figure 9 (a)-(d)) were goals, plans, values, beliefs, interests and detachments.

The changes needed in the Base-6 ecological cognition framework not only include this additional cognition, but elements once thought to be external representations, namely actors, artefacts, structured and substances are now thought to be cognitive manifestations of stimuli which interact with these, as can be seen in Figure 9 (d).

The three cognitions explored in Table 11 show that this approach can be effective at conceptualising the internal mental processes that result in the calculation of knol as a unit of brain use. In terms of Plan, the highest Mean knol ($k<0.8241$) exceeds the optimal threshold of 0.81 and the lowest Mean knol ($k<0.7852$) does not reach it. The fact that the t-score is very high ($t=11.56$) and the p-score is somewhat significant ($p<0.084$) suggests it is an effective measure. In terms of Belief, the highest Mean knol ($k<0.8222$) exceeds the optimal threshold of 0.81 and the lowest Mean knol ($k<0.7980$) does not reach it. The fact that the t-score is very high ($t=<14.674$) and is very significant ($k<0.001$) suggests it is also an effective measure. In terms of Interest, it was not as effective an output as the other two tested variables. Whilst the highest Mean knol ($k<0.8346$) exceeded the threshold of 0.81, so did the lowest Mean knol ($k<0.8118$). Whilst the t-score was good ($t=<6.913$) and highly significant ($p<0.001$), this would suggest that in order to properly use knol, the t-scores need to be in double figures when it comes to Level 2 (see Table 9).

Reviewing Level 3

As can be seen from Figure 8(a), Level 3 of the ecological cognition framework is intended to reflect the sensory inputs that interface between an actor's external environment and their internal interpretations of it. The proposed revision in the Base-6 ecological cognition framework in Figure 8(b) extends this to include an auxological sense and for the external signifiers in Level E of the ecological cognition framework to be placed here to reflect the view that these are socially constructed.

The data in Table 10 shows quote clearly that the functioning of knol at Level 3 is very much close to the originally calculated serendipity threshold of 0.98. The lowest value was very close to 0.98 ($k<0.976$) and so was the highest value ($k<0.998$). What is interesting to note, however, the t-scores were all below 6 and the least significant values corresponded with the lowest Mean knol scores. Namely, the lowest Mean knol of 'Auxological/Reflex' ($k<0.972$) corresponded with low significance ($p<0.651$) and the lowest Mean knol of 'Gustatory/Facial' ($k<0.968$) corresponded with low significance also ($p<0.903$).

Table 10. Data for reviewing 'Level 3'

Senses	High Mean k (N)	Low Mean k (N)	t-score	p-score
Auxological/Reflex	0.98720222 (22)	0.97193720 (26)	1.712	0.650
Visual/Kinaesthetic	0.99165233 (18)	0.97130247 (30)	2.267	0.028
Gustatory/Facial	0.98752596 (27)	0.96788643 (21)	2.239	0.902
Haptic/Muscles	0.94992984 (15)	0.99211723 (33)	5.492	0.000
Olfactory/Dialogue	0.96027894 (23)	0.99609601 (25)	4.777	0.000
Auditory/Prosody	0.97570272 (41)	0.99785778 (7)	1.763	0.008

Whilst it might be possible to conclude from this that the model is ineffective at using knol, it is worth noting that the data used to analyse Level 3 was computed from existing variables, suggesting it was not the most reliable in any case. To properly test knol at Level 3 would require the use of biometrics linked to each of the sensory inputs and cognitive elements.

Table 11. External representations featured in the concept-mapping study

Cognition	Count	Percent
Actor	8	19.0
Artefact	10	23.8
Structure	22	52.4
Substance	2	4.8
Total	42	100.0

Reviewing Level E

The environmental level of the ecological cognition framework (Level E) was initially thought of in terms of the representations that exist within it, namely actors, artefacts and structures (Bishop, 2007a; Bishop, 2007b). However, as can be seen from Table 11, which was drawn from the concept mapping study referred to in the methodology section, it can be seen that perceiving the environment in this way is ineffective because it disproportionately focusses on structures and artefacts to the exclusion of other stimuli, such as those now called substances (like food, drinks, natural elements), which are not considered, suggesting that these representations manifest internally more so than externally.

Figure *11* shows the 3-base ecological cognition framework's Level E (a), the 4-base framework (b), the 5-bae framework (c) and the 6-base framework (d). One can see that the main difference between base 3 to 5 (a-c) and base 6 (d) is that the actor is at the centre of their embodiment in the world (as subject) in Base-6 and they interpret their environment as external signifiers that reflect the internal cognitions at Level 2.

Figure 11. Level E of the Base-5 ECF (a) and Level E of the Base-6 ECF (b)

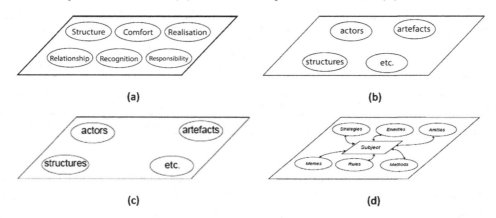

The data presented in Table 12 was also computed, but in this case the results were much more reliable. All the lowest Mean knol calculations were below the forecasted serendipity threshold of 0.98 (from k<0.947 to k<0.973) and all the highest Mean knol calculations were above the serendipity threshold of 0.98 (from k<0.993 to k<1.014). All results were highly significant with the highest t-score being for Methods (t=14.8, p<0.001) and lowest being for Enmities (t=2.542, p<0.003). This might strongly suggest that the knol required to perceive the environment at Level E is much higher than is required to understand it once it is internalised.

Table 12. Data for reviewing 'Level E'

External Representations	Low Mean k (N)	High Mean k (N)	t-score	p-score
Methods	0.94690217 (21)	1.00384705 (27)	14.800	0.000
Rules	0.95219918 (16)	0.99230091 (32)	5.199	0.000
Enmities	0.97263726 (36)	0.99782289 (12)	2.542	0.002
Amities	0.96584786 (32)	1.00510527 (16)	5.028	0.000
Memes	0.95684197 (21)	0.99611610 (27)	5.459	0.000
Strategies	0.96749623 (36)	1.01324598 (12)	5.612	0.000

DISCUSSION

This paper has attempted to provide verification of a way of measuring participation in Large-scale virtual environments (LSVEs), especially those that can be considered online communities. It has done this through reviewing the ecological cognition framework, which has been used for studying online communities for 10 years, by refuting it through statistical analysis. The result has been to create a more complex framework suited for the current age, where participating in online environments often depends on engaging with masses of people that was not the case when the original model was conceived in 2007, prior to the roll out of broadband Internet and the mass uptake of social networking services like Facebook and Twitter.

To refute the original model and devise a newer one based on it, the biometric measure of 'knol' was used to compute how the various aspects of the original framework was suitable or otherwise. The study found that whilst many of the original elements of the framework are verifiable, the complexity of it was not at a level suitable for understanding LSVEs and those who take part in them. Additional complexities were therefore added to the framework, which importantly included moving the model from being based around 5 dimensions to being based around 6, including to account for the fact that there is more detachment and escapism present in online communities since the mass adoption of social networking services that was the case when such environments were islands and non-integrated with other online communities. In other words, Facebook has become like any other form of mass media in the way it is consumed, yet at the same time the existence of others within it that challenge the worldview of the person consuming it adds a dimension that was once easy to avoid when consuming traditional mass media and contribution to traditional online communities such as Usenet, BBSs, among others.

LIMITATIONS AND FUTURE RESEARCH DIRECTIONS

This paper has gone a significant way to reconceptualising personality, cognition and economics where these apply to Large-scale virtual environments (LSVEs) such as online communities. It's limitations including that whilst the data was collected from primary sources – a learner who was empathic and a learner who was autistic – the amalgamation of this with secondary data and the transformation of it into differently structured data meant that the outcomes are not as valid as they otherwise would be if the data had been collected in a different way. Indeed, so that it is possible to fully validate the new framework presented in this paper, a significant amount of data will need to be collected from a larger population than the dyad used in this study. However, this paper has importantly refuted and extended a framework that has been used to understanding online communities for more than a decade, making it ideally suited to understanding the LSVEs that exist today, which are denser in terms of numbers of participants, meaning a framework of the complexity of the one presented in this paper is needed. Future research will therefore not only have to refute this new framework but make use of it to understanding participation in online communities at a time when the number of people using the Internet is growing.

REFERENCES

Bartle, R. A. (1996). Players who suit MUDs. *Journal of MUD Research*, *1*(1).

Bishop, J. (2007a). Ecological cognition: A new dynamic for human-computer interaction. In B. Wallace, A. Ross, J. Davies & T. Anderson (Eds.), The mind, the body and the world: Psychology after cognitivism (pp. 327-345). Exeter, UK: Imprint Academic.

Bishop, J. (2007b). Increasing participation in online communities: A framework for human–computer interaction. *Computers in Human Behavior*, *23*(4), 1881–1893. doi:10.1016/j.chb.2005.11.004

Bishop, J. (2008). Increasing capital revenue in social networking communities: Building social and economic relationships through avatars and characters. In C. Romm-Livermore & K. Setzekorn (Eds.), *Social networking communities and eDating services: Concepts and implications* (pp. 60–77). IGI Global.

Bishop, J. (2009). Enhancing the understanding of genres of web-based communities: The role of the ecological cognition framework. *International Journal of Web Based Communities*, *5*(1), 4–17. doi:10.1504/IJWBC.2009.021558

Bishop, J. (2011a). *Equatricism: A new paradigm for research and practice in information technology, the arts, law and sciences. Cardiff Metropolitan University's Annual Poster Symposium*.

Bishop, J. (2011b). *The equatrics of intergenerational knowledge transformation in techno-cultures: Towards a model for enhancing information management in virtual worlds (Unpublished MScEcon)*. Aberystwyth, UK: Aberystwyth University.

Bishop, J. (2011c). *The role of the prefrontal cortex in social orientation construction: A pilot study*. Poster Presented to the BPS Welsh Conference on Wellbeing, Wrexham, UK.

Bishop, J. (2012). Taming the chatroom bob: The role of brain-computer interfaces that manipulate prefrontal cortex optimization for increasing participation of victims of traumatic sex and other abuse online. *Proceedings of the 13th International Conference on Bioinformatics and Computational Biology (BIOCOMP'12)*.

Bishop, J. (2013). The empathic psychopathy in public life: Towards an understanding of 'autism' and 'empathism' and 'dopaminergic-serotonergic asynchronicity. *Conference on the Implications of Research on the Neuroscience of Affect, Attachment, and Social Cognition*.

Bishop, J. (2014). Reducing corruption and protecting privacy in emerging economies: The potential of neuroeconomic gamification and western media regulation in trust building and economic growth. In B. Christiansen (Ed.), *Economic behavior, game theory, and technology in emerging markets* (pp. 237–249). IGI Global. doi:10.4018/978-1-4666-4745-9.ch013

Bishop, J. (2015a). An investigation into the extent and limitations of the GROW model for coaching and mentoring online: Towards 'prosthetic learning. *The 14th International Conference on E-Learning, E-Business, Enterprise Information Systems, and E-Government (EEE'15)*.

Bishop, J. (2015b). Supporting communication between people with social orientation impairments using affective computing technologies: Rethinking the autism spectrum. In L. Bee Theng (Ed.), *Assistive technologies for physical and cognitive disabilities* (pp. 42–55). IGI Global. doi:10.4018/978-1-4666-7373-1.ch003

Bishop, J. (2016a). An analysis of the implications of maslow's hierarchy of needs for networked learning design and delivery. *International Conference on Information and Knowledge Engineering (IKE'16)*.

Bishop, J. (2016b). Enhancing the performance of human resources through E-mentoring: The role of an adaptive hypermedia system called "AVEUGLE". *International Management Review*, *12*(1), 11–23.

Blair, R. J. R. (2007). The amygdala and ventromedial prefrontal cortex in morality and psychopathy. *Trends in Cognitive Sciences*, *11*(9), 387–392. doi:10.1016/j.tics.2007.07.003 PMID:17707682

Bolognini, S. (1997). Empathy and 'empathism'. *The International Journal of Psycho-Analysis*, *78*(2), 279–293. PMID:9152755

Bougrine, S., Ouchraa, S., Ahiod, B., & El Imrani, A. A. (2014). Ant system with acoustic communication. *World Academy of Science, Engineering and Technology, International Journal of Computer, Electrical, Automation. Control and Information Engineering*, *8*(4), 578–582.

Campbell, J., Fletcher, G., & Greenhill, A. (2009). Conflict and identity shape shifting in an online financial community. *Information Systems Journal*, *19*(5), 461–478. doi:10.1111/j.1365-2575.2008.00301.x

Canuet, L., Ishii, R., Iwase, M., Ikezawa, K., Kurimoto, R., Takahashi, H., Currais, A., Azechi, M., Aoki, Y., Nakahachi, T., Soriano, S., & Takeda, M. (2011). Psychopathology and working memory-induced activation of the prefrontal cortex in schizophrenia-like psychosis of epilepsy: Evidence from magnetoencephalography. *Psychiatry and Clinical Neurosciences*, *65*(2), 183–190. doi:10.1111/j.1440-1819.2010.02179.x PMID:21414092

Chen, C. (2013). Exploring antecedents of lurking behavior: A perspective from ecological cognition framework (Master). Chaoyang Institute of Technology.

Cheng, H., & Chen, C. (2014). A study of lurking behavior: The desire perspective. *International Journal of Social, Education. Economics and Management Engineering*, *8*(4), 905–908.

Christ, S. E., Van Essen, D. C., Watson, J. M., Brubaker, L. E., & McDermott, K. B. (2009). The contributions of prefrontal cortex and executive control to deception: Evidence from activation likelihood estimate meta-analyses. *Cerebral Cortex (New York, N.Y.)*, *19*(7), 1557–1566. doi:10.1093/cercor/bhn189 PMID:18980948

Clarke, J., & Dede, C. (2007). LSVEs as a powerful means to study situated learning. *Proceedings of the 8th Iternational Conference on Computer Supported Collaborative Learning*, 144-147.

Cowpertwait, J., & Flynn, S. (2002). The internet from A to Z. Cambridge, UK: Icon Books Ltd.

Csikszentmihalyi, M. (1975). *Beyond boredom and anxiety*. Jossey Bass Wiley.

Csikszentmihalyi, M. (2000). Beyond boredom and anxiety: Experiencing flow in work and play (25th Anniversary ed.). San Francisco CA: Jossey Bass Wiley.

Csikszentmihalyi, M. (2009). *Flow: The psychology of optimal experience* (2nd ed.). HarperCollins.

de Souza, C. S., & Preece, J. (2004). A framework for analyzing and understanding online communities. *Interacting with Computers*, *16*(3), 579–610. doi:10.1016/j.intcom.2003.12.006

Del Grosso, M. (2001). Design and implementation of online communities (Unpublished Master of Science). Naval Postgraduate School, Monterey, CA.

Feng, J., & Song, L. (2011). *Teaching and learning in second life: A case study. In Large-scale virtual environments for the classroom: Practical approaches to teaching in virtual worlds*. IGI Global.

Figner, B., Knoch, D., Johnson, E. J., Krosch, A. R., Lisanby, S. H., Fehr, E., & Weber, E. U. (2010). Lateral prefrontal cortex and self-control in intertemporal choice. *Nature Neuroscience*, *13*(5), 538–539. doi:10.1038/nn.2516 PMID:20348919

Garrison, D. R., Anderson, T., & Archer, W. (2001). Critical thinking, cognitive presence, and computer conferencing in distance education. *American Journal of Distance Education*, *15*(1), 7–23. doi:10.1080/08923640109527071

Gashi, L., & Knautz, K. (2016). *Unfriending, hiding and blocking on facebook*. Paper presented at the 3rd European Conference on Social Media Research, Normandy, France.

Geer, S. (Ed.). (2003). *Essential internet: The essence of the internet from A to Z* (5th ed.). Profile Books Ltd.

Golan, O., & Baron-Cohen, S. (2006). Systemizing empathy: Teaching adults with asperger syndrome or high-functioning autism to recognize complex emotions using interactive multimedia. *Development and Psychopathology*, *18*(2), 591–617. doi:10.1017/S0954579406060305 PMID:16600069

Hardaker, C. (2010). Trolling in asynchronous computer-mediated communication: From user discussions to academic definitions. *Journal of Politeness Research.Language, Behaviour, Culture (Québec)*, *6*(2), 215–242.

Hardaker, C. (2013a). Uh.... not to be nitpicky, but... the past tense of drag is dragged, not drug.": An overview of trolling strategies. *Journal of Language Aggression and Conflict*, *1*(1), 57–85. doi:10.1075/jlac.1.1.04har

Hardaker, C. (2013b). "Obvious trolls will just get you banned": Trolling versus corpus linguistics. In A. Hardie & R. Love (Eds.), *Corpus linguistics 2013* (pp. 112–114). UCREL.

Ito, A., Abe, N., Fujii, T., Ueno, A., Koseki, Y., & Hashimoto, R. (2010). The role of the dorsolateral prefrontal cortex in deception when remembering neutral and emotional events. *Neuroscience Research*.

Johnson, C. M. (2001). A survey of current research on online communities of practice. *The Internet and Higher Education*, *4*(1), 45–60.

Kim, A. J. (2000). *Community building on the web: Secret strategies for successful online communities*. Peachpit Press.

Kommers, P. A. M. (2014). Sense of community: Perceptions of individual and group members of online communities. In J. Bishop (Ed.), *Transforming politics and policy in the digital age* (pp. 1–5). IGI Global. doi:10.4018/978-1-4666-6038-0.ch001

Kugler, J., & Zak, P. J. (2017). *Trust, cooperation, and conflict: Neuropolitics and international relations. In Advancing interdisciplinary approaches to international relations*. Springer.

Kutay, C. (2014). *HCI model for culturally useful knowledge sharing. In New horizons in web based learning*. Springer.

Leung, L. (2003). Impacts of net-generation attributes, seductive properties of the internet, and gratifications-obtained on internet use. *Telematics and Informatics*, *20*(2), 107–129. doi:10.1016/S0736-5853(02)00019-9

Mantovani, G. (1996a). Social context in HCI: A new framework for mental models, cooperation, and communication. *Cognitive Science*, *20*(2), 237–269. doi:10.120715516709cog2002_3

Mantovani, G. (1996b). *New communication environments: From everyday to virtual*. Taylor & Francis.

Marcus, R., & Watters, B. (2002). *Collective knowledge*. Microsoft Press.

McMillan, D. W., & Chavis, D. M. (1986). Sense of community: A definition and theory. *Journal of Community Psychology*, *14*(1), 6–23. doi:10.1002/1520-6629(198601)14:1<6::AID-JCOP2290140103>3.0.CO;2-I

Meyer, T., Qi, X. L., Stanford, T. R., & Constantinidis, C. (2011). Stimulus selectivity in dorsal and ventral prefrontal cortex after training in working memory tasks. *The Journal of Neuroscience: The Official Journal of the Society for Neuroscience*, *31*(17), 6266–6276. doi:10.1523/JNEUROSCI.6798-10.2011 PMID:21525266

Moll, J., Eslinger, P. J., & Oliveira-Souza, R. (2001). Frontopolar and anterior temporal cortex activation in a moral judgment task: Preliminary functional MRI results in normal subjects. *Arquivos de Neuro-Psiquiatria*, *59*(3B), 657–664. doi:10.1590/S0004-282X2001000500001 PMID:11593260

Mushiake, H., Sakamoto, K., Saito, N., Inui, T., Aihara, K., & Tanji, J. (2009). Involvement of the prefrontal cortex in problem solving. *International Review of Neurobiology*, *85*, 1–11. doi:10.1016/S0074-7742(09)85001-0 PMID:19607957

Neff, A. (2013). Cyberbullying on facebook: Group composition and effects of content exposure on bystander state hostility (Master of Arts in Psychology). University of Canterbury.

Nonnecke, B., Andrews, D., & Preece, J. (2006). Non-public and public online community participation: Needs, attitudes and behavior. *Electronic Commerce Research*, *6*(1), 7–20. doi:10.100710660-006-5985-x

Nonnecke, B., & Preece, J. (2003). Silent participants: Getting to know lurkers better. *From Usenet to CoWebs: Interacting with Social Information Spaces,* 110-132.

Ortiz, B. I. L. (2012). *Issues in problem-based learning in online teacher education. In The role of criticism in understanding problem solving.* Springer.

Overskeid, G. (2016). Systemizing in autism: The case for an emotional mechanism. *New Ideas in Psychology, 41,* 18–22. doi:10.1016/j.newideapsych.2016.01.001

Peterson, N. A., Speer, P. W., & McMillan, D. W. (2008). Validation of a brief sense of community scale: Confirmation of the principal theory of sense of community. *Journal of Community Psychology, 36*(1), 61–73. doi:10.1002/jcop.20217

Powazek, D. M. (2002). *Design for community: The art of connecting real people in virtual places.* New Riders.

Preece, J. (1998). Empathic communities: Reaching out across the web. *Interaction, 5*(2), 43. doi:10.1145/274430.274435

Preece, J. (2003). Tacit knowledge and social capital: Supporting sociability in online communities of practice. *Proceedings of I-KNOW,* 3, 2-4.

Preece, J. (2008). An event-driven community in washington, DC: Forces that influence participation. In M. Foth (Ed.), *Handbook of research on urban informatics: The practice and promise of the real-time city.* IGI Global.

Preece, J., Nonnecke, B., & Andrews, D. (2004). The top 5 reasons for lurking: Improving community experiences for everyone. *Computers in Human Behavior, 2*(1), 42. doi:10.1016/j.chb.2003.10.015

Priori, A., Mameli, F., Cogiamanian, F., Marceglia, S., Tiriticco, M., Mrakic-Sposta, S., Ferrucci, R., Zago, S., Polezzi, D., & Sartori, G. (2008). Lie-specific involvement of dorsolateral prefrontal cortex in deception. *Cerebral Cortex (New York, N.Y.), 18*(2), 451–455. doi:10.1093/cercor/bhm088 PMID:17584853

Reuter, M., & Montag, C. (2016). *Neuroeconomics—An introduction. In Neuroeconomics.* Springer. doi:10.1007/978-3-642-35923-1

Seitz, R. J., Nickel, J., & Azari, N. P. (2006). Functional modularity of the medial prefrontal cortex: Involvement in human empathy. *Neuropsychology, 20*(6), 743–751. doi:10.1037/0894-4105.20.6.743 PMID:17100519

Shamay-Tsoory, S. G., Tomer, R., Berger, B. D., & Aharon-Peretz, J. (2003). Characterization of empathy deficits following prefrontal brain damage: The role of the right ventromedial prefrontal cortex. *Journal of Cognitive Neuroscience, 15*(3), 324–337. doi:10.1162/089892903321593063 PMID:12729486

Shneiderman, B. (2002). *Leonardo's laptop: Human needs and the new computing technologies.* MIT Press.

Smith, A. D. (1999). Problems of conflict management in virtual communities. In M. A. Smith & P. Kollock (Eds.), *Communities in cyberspace* (pp. 134–163). Routledge. doi:10.5117/9789056290818

Stutsky, B. J. (2009). *Empowerment and Leadership Development in an Online Story-Based Learning Community*. Academic Press.

Suchman, L. A. (1987). *Plans and situated actions: The problem of human-machine communication*. Cambridge, UK: Cambridge University Press.

Suchman, L. A. (2007). *Human-machine reconfigurations: Plans and situated actions*. Cambridge University Press.

Tsai, C., Shen, P., & Chiang, Y. (2015). Meeting ex-partners on facebook: Users' anxiety and severity of depression. *Behaviour & Information Technology, 34*(7), 668–677. doi:10.1080/0144929X.2014.981585

Tseng, J., Tsai, Y., & Chao, R. (2013). Enhancing L2 interaction in avatar-based virtual worlds: Student teachers' perceptions. *Australasian Journal of Educational Technology, 29*(3). Advance online publication. doi:10.14742/ajet.283

Wallace, P. M. (1999). *The psychology of the internet*. Cambridge University Press. doi:10.1017/CBO9780511581670

Westervelt, H. J., Ruffolo, J. S., & Tremont, G. (2005). Assessing olfaction in the neuropsychological exam: The relationship between odor identification and cognition in older adults. *Archives of Clinical Neuropsychology: The Official Journal of the National Academy of Neuropsychologists, 20*(6), 761–769. doi:10.1016/j.acn.2005.04.010 PMID:15951153

Wheelwright, S., Baron-Cohen, S., Goldenfeld, N., Delaney, J., Fine, D., Smith, R., Weil, L., & Wakabayashi, A. (2006). Predicting autism spectrum quotient (AQ) from the systemizing quotient-revised (SQ-R) and empathy quotient (EQ). *Brain Research, 1079*(1), 47–56. doi:10.1016/j.brainres.2006.01.012 PMID:16473340

Zanto, T. P., Rubens, M. T., Thangavel, A., & Gazzaley, A. (2011). Causal role of the prefrontal cortex in top-down modulation of visual processing and working memory. *Nature Neuroscience, 14*(5), 656–661. doi:10.1038/nn.2773 PMID:21441920

KEY TERMS AND DEFINITIONS

Artefact: An internal or external representation of or a tool, sign, symbol, word or similar that allows an actor to interact with the world whether virtual. mixed or organic.

Ecological Cognition: A research paradigm for understanding information systems, especially online communities

Ecological Cognition Framework: A conceptual framework that represents some of the ontological entities of ecological cognition.

Hypermedia Seduction: A process of using information systems and mediating artefacts to persuade users to perform specific actions.

Parametric User Model: An equation or algorithm for understanding users of information systems, especially from a cyberpsychology perspective.

Structure: An internal or external representation of a plant, building, or other space.

Substance: An internally or externally available source of nutrition or intervention such as food or biochemistry produced by neurotransmitters, respectively.

Chapter 10
LIFI–Based Radiation–Free Monitoring and Transmission Device for Hospitals/Public Places

T. Ananth kumar

(iD) https://orcid.org/0000-0002-0494-7803

IFET College of Engineering, India

T. S. Arun Samuel

National Engineering College, Kovilpatti, India

P. Praveen kumar

IFET College of Engineering, India

M. Pavithra

IFET College of Engineering, India

R. Raj Mohan

IFET College of Engineering, India

ABSTRACT

A wireless patient monitoring system involves remote supervision of sensitive patients by wirelessly transmitting patient information to distant locations, especially in pandemic situations like COVID-19. Li-fi-based communication protocol is used in healthcare which helps in reducing the challenges faced by medical professionals in effectively monitoring multiple patients as well as average persons in public places. Due to COVID-19, doctors/healthcare workers are compelled to work with infected patients. This proposed technique lets them observe patients without being on their bedside, whether in the hospital or at home. This device can also be installed in public places to detect the abnormal and symptomatic persons who are affected by COVID-19. It is used to monitor patient health, ranging from heart rate, body temperature, ECG, breathing, non-invasive blood pressure, oxygen saturation, etc. Wireless patient monitoring using li-fi eliminates national therapy barriers. Thus, a li-fi-based patient monitoring system will lead to a significant role in Healthcare services. The radiation-free device shall be implemented in all the industries to find the COVID-19-affected persons easily.

DOI: 10.4018/978-1-7998-4703-8.ch010

Copyright © 2021, IGI Global. Copying or distributing in print or electronic forms without written permission of IGI Global is prohibited.

1. INTRODUCTION:

In recent times, disease like Covid-19 has been a significant challenge to the medical field all over the globe. Ohannessian (2020) stated that many kinds of research are still working out to get rid of it with a vaccination, but the issues are more dangerous in spreading very fast than expected. As the saying goes like this "prevention is better than cure", It is necessary to follow some essential steps to get through the diseases. Especially public places have to be monitored as they are the most crucial cause for the rapid spread. People can't be quarantined for days as they built up more pressures and depression. The serious of test cases are dealt with this issue.

Figure 1. Advanced Li-Fi Infrastructure

A satisfactory solution of installing a pre-support detection device in all hospitals and public places to detect the primary symptoms, which may lead to any infection to others are only focused instead of dealing with hundreds. This is not a usual testing place with human interference and disturbance. Fig. 1 shows the LiFi based infrastructure which is designed using Femto cells. They are embedded with the sensitive sensors required to analyze the person entering into the centre. These sensors do not disturb the person in anyways. Mongwewarona (2020) discussed in his survey that, it is more important to observe patients remotely using the wireless sensor network. It is also useful for home patients aged or affected by chronic diseases. The healthcare tracking device can benefit patients by delivering resources such as patient surveillance and access to medical data. System aim is to provide early warning of physiological dysfunction to increase patient outcomes. It is used for people living in remote or urban areas. Using RF waves, Wi-Fi transmits data. Wi-Fi networks' EMF emissions will significantly impact health. Long-term use leads to sleep-related disorders, including obesity and depression. To securely communicate health issues information, hospital/public places needs a full green protocol for data transmission. Patient's health details like temperature, ECG, and heart rate, Temperature sensor and few parameters are monitored while entering the room. The most common wireless systems use the lowest portion of the 3KHz-300GHz electromagnetic spectrum, including radio waves. The obtained details were transmitted to the receiver using Wi-Fi technology using electromagnetic spectrum radio frequency band.

The Wi-Fi receiver will receive this radio signal sent as a Wi-Fi antenna, including smartphones and Wi-Fi-equipped computers. It causes health problems like insomnia development, affects cell growth, heart stress, and reduces brain activity. Because of the radiation effects, it was not allowed in Operation Theater because Wi-Fi blocks the signal from monitoring equipment and affects the medical Equipment. Li-Fi, a wireless system that uses visible light or infrared and near-UV frequency waves to overcome the issues in radio waves. Home LED bulbs have used 224 gigabits per second for data transmission. Li-Fi was permitted to use the internet to monitor medical devices in operation theatres rather than Wi-Fi. The proposed system uses Li-Fi to transmit data using visible light communication, requiring sight condition line. It is an optical communication device that uses visible light rays from 400-800 THz frequency range as an optical carrier for data transmission for a small wireless communication network.

Researchers installed several Li-Fi transmitters and receivers in an operating room at Motol University Hospital in Prague. The Li-Fi network managed to transmit data efficiently and without total signal loss in a series of tests. They reached data speeds up to 600 megabits per second — better than other Wi-Fi and cellular networks. "There was no scientific test in a Li-Fi medical case," says Sreelal Maravanchery Mana (2020), a lead author and researcher at HHI. "It's the first time we 're doing practical (medical) tests." Data is transmitted to a transmitter — an LED — in a simple Li-Fi system, which transforms it into light that flashes far too quickly to meet the human eye. A receiver detects the LED light pulses pattern and changes the pulse pattern back into data. Since Li-Fi uses low-frequency light than Wi-Fi, it may, in principle, have higher bandwidth and hence transfer data faster.

Wi-Fi was key to handling the flood of mobile gadgets currently in hospitals and operating rooms. Any equipment restricting wires that can pose a health threat in hospitals is encouraged. However, devices that use Wi-Fi will interfere, causing a lack of communication. "Wireless systems that relay medical data must be extremely secure," says Heikki Karvonen(2020), a Finnish researcher at Oulu University who was not interested in the study. It is essential to "coexist" with each other, says Karvonen. Not everyone is convinced that this crowding is a significant problem for hospitals: one study recommends keeping smartphones running on Wi-Fi networks away from medical devices, using Wi-Fi to prevent interference. Li-Fi is not exceptional. While not facing interference from other medical devices, it can still be interrupted. Unlike Wi-Fi's radio waves that can travel through walls, person or objects effectively block optical light. The HHI researchers used four transmitters and six receivers around the operating room for a total of 24 channels between transmitters and receivers. "Even if 23 of those channels are blocked, you still have one and you can communicate very robustly," says HHI researcher Dominic Schulz. During an operation, doctors or nurses may block some of the links between transmitters and receivers by walking between them. The team plans to continue testing various Li-Fi setups in hospitals and ultimately use the technology to transmit data to medical devices used during the actual surgery. U.S. Now Food and Drug Administration (FDA) has no official Li-Fi status. "When preparing to use Li-Fi — or any other wireless technology — in medical equipment, caution should be taken to align system wireless functions with the strengths and planned efficiency of wireless technology," says FDA electrical engineer Mohamad Omar Al Kalaa (2020).

2. LITERATURE REVIEW

This literature survey describes different methods used to transmit a patient's health status data to the physician. It also demonstrates that each technology has its advantages and drawbacks of the data transmission system.

Wireless Health Monitoring using Passive Wi-Fi Sensing provided a 2D step extraction method to track three necessary activities for the elderly, including breathing rate, critical tremor and falling. Traditional methods of controlling breathing, tremor, and dropping are invasive and inconvenient. Roopa Jayaysingh (2020) discussed about constant monitoring of patient health, which is a vital thing in the medical industry. But it is hard to monitor the patient's constantly, so an Internet based monitoring system has been used to monitor the health of the patient remotely through the cloud. NodeMCU is a microcontroller integrated with Wi-Fi transceiver can be used to monitor the patient's heart rate and record the results periodically in the cloud.

Srimathi (2020). described about the patient monitoring system using Light Fidelity (Li-Fi), it uses block cipher encryption technique to encrypt the transferred data. Arduino devices can be used to obtain the data from the patients in case of emergency alert deep learning algorithms send an alert to the doctors. Authors proposed single light waves to transfer the data using Li-Fi, but multi light waves Li-Fi transfer gives better results compared to the single light waves Li-Fi.

HS. Harshitha. (2020) outlined the patient monitoring system using Li-Fi technology. Li-Fi technology, proposed by German physicist Harold Haas, provides light-borne information transmission by sending information at varying intensities more quickly than the natural eye can travel. Li-Fi is an optical network communication with a two-way connexion, fast and fully connected, and a visible light communication type. The proposed model helps patient checks in clinics and should be possible by using Li-fi as opposed to Wi-Fi innovation to avoid recurring obstruction in the human body. The model uses sensors such as temperature, heartbeat, and movement to perform its own functions. These sensors collect human body data and convert it from analogue to digital converter into a computerised structure. This results in the microcontroller. The AVR microcontroller is the microcontroller used. The microcontroller 's output is managed by the Li-Fi module, which communicates the information as light and collects the data from the receiver, which is to be portable. However, this system will monitor only the small number of patients.

HT Yew (2020) discussed the real time remote monitoring of patients in rural areas. Message Queuing Telemetry Transport (MQTT) was utilized in this paper to transmit the real time ECG (Electrocardiogram) datas of the patients through Wide Area Network (WAN), the doctors access the data remotely through web server and monitor the health of the patients periodically. This system is not able to collect the various health parameters of the patients and in case of any abnormal waves in ECG this system is not able to alert the patients. It simply records and transmits the datas to the doctors. Pirbhulal (2020) stated that wearable health sensors not only transmit critical clinical signs to medical staff but also automate diagnosis and enhance patient results. These event decreases assessment time and allows golden timing in conditions that can contribute to better patient outcomes. Continuous patient safety monitoring is essential during treatment. The cellular health management system also plays a significant role in providing quality medical care, particularly in remote areas.

Dinh-Le's(2020) wearable health management program provides useful real-time data with a user-centred healthcare app that allows you to closely monitor highly vulnerable patients, such as post-operative patients, rehabilitated and rehabilitated patients. This program seeks to improve education and management at a reasonable price. Bewer (2020) enlightened in his paper that Luxel 's popular dosimeter uses luminescence stimulation technology (OSL). Radiologists and factory staff usually use OSL which contains a radiation-prone aluminium oxide layer screened in a dry, humid enclosure. Modak S (2020) stated that Once radioactive compounds are radiated in the aluminium oxide layer, electrons are trapped in an excited state until irradiated with a particular laser light wavelength. Lin, A. J (2020) discussed that the energy released as visible light is assessed to determine the radiation dose. The package contains several filters to determine radiation frequency and intensity. For measuring the radiation level and power, the dosimeter must be used such that it is placed in front of the radiation source faces. Luxury body dosimeters are among the most versatile dosimeters. Selvi, S. A(2020) used Wi-LiFi module to transmit the patient's calculated health parameters. The purpose of the current system was to provide early notice of physiological deterioration to improve patient health. This monitoring system minimized human errors because, without human interference, health parameters were tracked and assessed. It was used by a wider variety of patients, medical practitioners and people living in rural or remote areas. In this process, the measured health parameters were fed to the Arduino ATmega328 micro-controller and then forwarded to doctors or nurses for detection of anomalies and stored data in the database via Wi-Fi module.

3. PROPOSED SYSTEM

Li-FI needs only a few different pieces of equipment, which are not overly costly and are easy to purchase. Today, Li-Fi uses amplitude modulation to reach a respectable 4 Gbps. In the future, if a new data stream could be transmitted through nearly any colour (specifically any 10 nanometers of optical wavelengths, accessible from today's 360 nm to 780 nm optical filters), then each light will have over 100 Gbps of wireless bandwidth. Use ultraviolet wavelengths as well as narrower optical filters, potential data levels of 1,000 Gbps per light can be obtained.

Fig.2. shows the proposed Wireless Patient Monitoring system. The person entering into the room will be shot with a photo if any symptoms are detected. Only those people can be moves to the regular health care detection centre for the complete checkup if needed. In future, all places will be adopted with such health care support centre to avoid infection. For the prevention of congestion, people in the walk can be easily picked up and further supported. This will be radiation-free, as the technology embedded with is Li-Fi. Light Fidelity is an emerging technology to transmit data through light, especially, LED bulbs. Light is used as the transmission medium for quick transfer of data. The information of any detected person can be easily transferred from the room to the support centre outside.

Regarding the scenario, the person carrying the symptoms can be easily found out while getting out of place. The device is a hazardous free environment to simplify the task of the medical health centre. This approach is not specific to one particular type of diseases, based upon the spread, the symptoms can be modified, and the sensor can be fixed accordingly to detect. This idea can ease the job of handling hundreds of people to catch too few members.

Figure 2. Wireless Patient Monitoring system for Pandemic situations

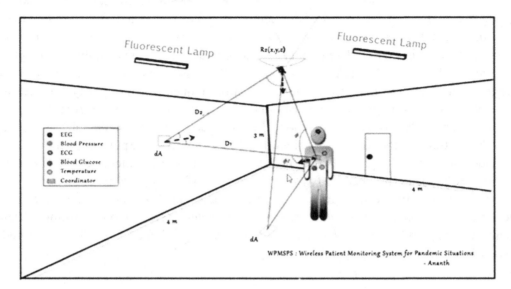

Figure 3. Block diagram of patient monitoring using Li-Fi

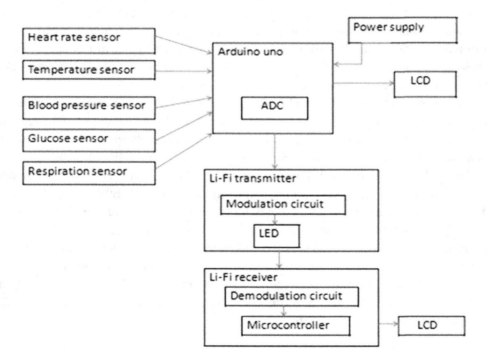

Figure 4. Throughput Graph – Li-Fi vs Other Communication standards

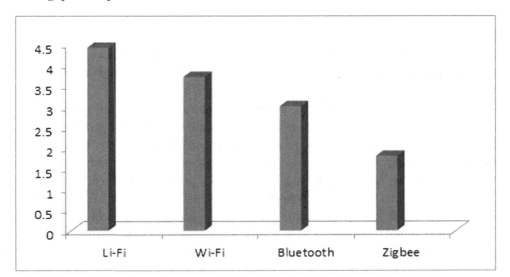

Because of this pandemic situation, in existing infrastructure in world countries like cell towers and existing wireless transmitters, Li-Fi could be equipped. It means that if the world moved to Li-Fi, there wouldn't be a big oil surge, which wouldn't increase the nation's energy consumption and wouldn't affect the environment. Dubai plans to be one of the world's first Li-Fi cities to become a smart city. This will mean that street lights can be set up to transmit product information directly to shoppers' phones, or that Li-Fi enabled street lights to provide internet connectivity to cell phones. Fig. 3 shows the block diagram of patient monitoring using Li-Fi. In this system, the vital signs and health parameters are assessed using sensors and recorded by a device called a medical monitor. The parameters for health monitoring include a patient's hemodynamic, blood glucose, temperature, cardiac and pulse oximetry. The calculated data is fed to the Arduino UNO and then converted to the digital form using the Arduino UNO analogue-to-digital converter. Then the information is transmitted via the Li-Fi module using the light source as binary codes. Here via LED, binary code is shared by on-off keying modulation technique. If the LED is on, the data will be transmitted as a binary one, and the data will be communicated as binary 0. Photodiode segment receives the transmitted data in the Li-Fi receiver module that transforms the digital signal into an electrical signal. Electrical signal noise is eliminated and then amplified. The generated electrical signal can be interpreted as a graph to evaluate the health of patients by connecting the receiver to the computer. Respiration sensor measures a human's respiration rate per minute. Breathing is not the same as breathing. The adult's average breathing rate is 12-25 breaths per minute. If the ratio is above 25 or below 12, an abnormal breathing rate is considered. A temperature sensor is a body temperature measuring thermocouple or resistance detector. Temperature measurement is necessary because it reveals the metabolic rate of hormonal health and body. Glucose sensor finds the blood sugar level. Our body regulates blood glucose levels as part of homeostasis. Glucose is stored at standard 5.5mmol / L as glycogen. ECG sensor measures the bio-potential generated by electrical signals that control cardiac expansion and contraction.

4. RESULTS AND DISCUSSION

The wireless communication standards throughput analysis is shown below, which confirms that Li-Fi with Elliptic Curve Cryptography works better than other technologies. In Li-Fi patient healthcare monitoring system, the use of Elliptic Curve Cryptography, which produces high throughput with secure data transmission, is proposed.

Fig. 4. shows comparison of Li-Fi with Other Communication Standards. Li-Fi has high data throughput rates than Wi-Fi, Bluetooth, and ZigBee. In Li-Fi, LED bulb transmitted data through an LED driver circuit that controls LED on and off. If the LED is on, the binary value one is sent, and if out, binary value 0 is transmitted. LED can flicker on and off quickly, providing an excellent chance to share data. Encoding data is possible by changing the rate of LEDs flicker to give different strings of 0's and 1's. Therefore, the intensity of LED was regulated rapidly, on and off condition of LED cannot be noticed by the human eye, so the output appears constant. The receiver photodetector receives the light signal and returns to an electrical signal, then fed to a Li-Fi receiver where it decodes and decrypts the password and removes the signal noise. This signal then provided and viewed Arduino UNO on the LCD.

Figure 5. Patient Monitoring System- Transmitter section

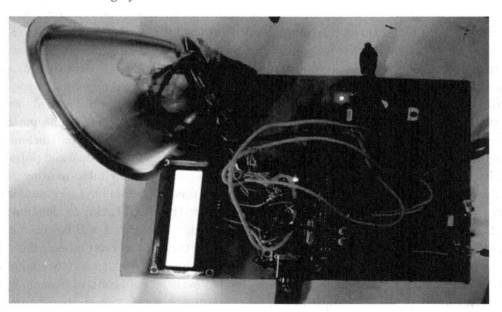

In Li-Fi, LED bulb transmitted data through an LED driver circuit that controls LED on and off. If the LED is on, the binary value one is shared, and if out, binary value 0 is transmitted. LEDs can be flickers on and off quickly, providing an excellent chance to transmit data. Fig. 5 shows the transmitter section in patient monitoring section. Encoding data is possible by changing the rate of LEDs flicker to give different strings of 0s and 1s. Therefore, the intensity of LED was regulated quickly, on and off condition of LED cannot be noticed by the human eye, so the output appears constant. The transmitter module has two sections: the modulation circuit and the white LED. On-off keying does not return to the zero modulation scheme. The LED operates on-off keying (LED transmits health data by switching on and off-state). Then the data will be sent to the receiver using white LED pulses (data rate is 500mbps).

Figure 6. Patient Monitoring System- Receiver section

Figure 7. Patient Monitoring System- LCD display

Fig. 7. Shows the output of patient monitoring system. The receiver photodetector receives the light signal and returns to an electrical signal, then fed to a Li-Fi receiver where it decodes and decrypts the password and removes the noise in the movement. This signal was then fed to Arduino UNO and displayed in the LCD. The receiver module has two sections: demodulation and amplification circuit. The transmitted optical pulse is recovered back into the electrical signal using a photodiode in the demodula-

tion circuit. The converted signal is weak and plagued by noise, so signals must be conditioned before processing. It undergoes amplification and passes through envelope detection to demodulate the carrier signal data. Then voltage comparator transforms the signal into a digital format before being fed to a microcontroller that serially transmits data to another device. Thus, the detailed information obtained from the human in public places is transferred through Li-Fi based system. It is also displayed in the LCD screen of the patient monitoring system.

5. CONCLUSION

Whenever the human entering into public places, the human's mandatory physiological signs must be monitored, especially during this pandemic situation. Therefore, a patient monitoring system has always played an essential role in maintain safety measures. According to this, A prototype is designed for acquiring the values from the human in public places. Improved technologies not only help transmit the mandatory physiological sign to medical staff but also help simplify the measurement and then increase the monitoring system efficiency to notify abnormal conditions via messages, email or alarm signal. Using Li-Fi technology, the health parameters are measured and transmitted faster and secured to the physician. Li-Fi-based healthcare monitoring system with Elliptic Curve Cryptography algorithm has advantages over Wi-Fi and GSM technology. Li-Fi technology provides faster and secure data transmission with low power consumption compared to Wi-Fi and GSM, without harmful effects on the human body. Thus, Li-Fi data transmission is therefore suitable for high speed and secure data transmission in patient/human monitoring in the public places.

REFERENCES

Ohannessian, R., Duong, T. A., & Odone, A. (2020). Global telemedicine implementation and integration within health systems to fight the COVID-19 pandemic: A call to action. *JMIR Public Health and Surveillance*, *6*(2), e18810. doi:10.2196/18810 PMID:32238336

Mongwewarona, W., Sheikh, S. M., & Molefhi, B. C. (2020). Survey on Li-Fi communication networks and deployment. *African Journal of Engineering Research*, *8*(1), 1–9. doi:10.30918/AJER.81.19.036

Mana, S. M., Hellwig, P., Hilt, J., Bober, K. L., Hirmanova, V. J., Chvojka, P., ... Zvanovec, S. (2020, March). LiFi Experiments in a Hospital. In *Optical Fiber Communication Conference* (pp. M3I-2). Optical Society of America.

Ahmed, I., Karvonen, H., Kumpuniemi, T., & Katz, M. (2020). Wireless Communications for the Hospital of the Future: Requirements, Challenges and Solutions. *International Journal of Wireless Information Networks*, *27*(1), 4–17. doi:10.100710776-019-00468-1

Al Kalaa, M. O., Balid, W., Refai, H. H., LaSorte, N. J., Seidman, S. J., Bassen, H. I., Silberberg, J. L., & Witters, D. (2016). Characterizing the 2.4 GHz spectrum in a hospital environment: Modeling and applicability to coexistence testing of medical devices. *IEEE Transactions on Electromagnetic Compatibility*, *59*(1), 58–66. doi:10.1109/TEMC.2016.2602083

Jayaysingh, R., David, J., Raaj, M. J. M., Daniel, D., & BlessyTelagathoti, D. (2020, March). IoT Based Patient Monitoring System Using NodeMCU. In *2020 5th International Conference on Devices, Circuits and Systems (ICDCS)* (pp. 240-243). IEEE.

Srimathi, B., & Ananthkumar, T. (2020). Li-Fi Based Automated Patient Healthcare Monitoring System. *Indian Journal of Public Health Research & Development, 11*(2), 387–392. doi:10.37506/v11/i2/2020/ijphrd/194832

Harshita, H., Mithum, P., Geetha, M., Krutika, M., Sufiyan, K., & Shyma, Z. (2018). Patient Monitoring System using Li-Fi. *International Journal of Engineering Research & Technology (Ahmedabad)*, 6.

Yew, H. T., Ng, M. F., Ping, S. Z., Chung, S. K., Chekima, A., & Dargham, J. A. (2020, February). IoT Based Real-Time Remote Patient Monitoring System. In *2020 16th IEEE International Colloquium on Signal Processing & Its Applications (CSPA)* (pp. 176-179). IEEE.

Pirbhulal, S., Samuel, O. W., Wu, W., Sangaiah, A. K., & Li, G. (2019). A joint resource-aware and medical data security framework for wearable healthcare systems. *Future Generation Computer Systems, 95*, 382–391. doi:10.1016/j.future.2019.01.008

Dinh-Le, C., Chuang, R., Chokshi, S., & Mann, D. (2019). Wearable health technology and electronic health record integration: Scoping review and future directions. *JMIR mHealth and uHealth, 7*(9), e12861. doi:10.2196/12861 PMID:31512582

Bewer, B. (2020). Comparison of dose values predicted by FLUKA to measured values using Luxel+ Ta type dosimeters. *Nuclear Instruments & Methods in Physics Research. Section B, Beam Interactions with Materials and Atoms, 464*, 12–18. doi:10.1016/j.nimb.2019.11.042

Modak, S., Chernyak, L., Lubomirsky, I., & Khodorov, S. (2020). Continuous and Time-Resolved Cathodoluminescence Studies of Electron Injection Induced Effects in Gallium Nitride. In *Advanced Technologies for Security Applications* (pp. 109–117). Springer. doi:10.1007/978-94-024-2021-0_11

Lin, A. J., Kidd, E., Dehdashti, F., Siegel, B. A., Mutic, S., Thaker, P. H., ... Schwarz, J. (2019). Intensity modulated radiation therapy and image-guided adapted brachytherapy for cervix cancer. *International Journal of Radiation Oncology* Biology* Physics, 103*(5), 1088-1097.

Selvi, S. A., Rajesh, R. S., & Ajisha, M. A. T. (2019, December). An Efficient Communication Scheme for Wi-Li-Fi Network Framework. In *2019 Third International conference on I-SMAC (IoT in Social, Mobile, Analytics and Cloud)(I-SMAC)* (pp. 697-701). IEEE.

Chapter 11
The Gamification in Education, Healthcare, and Industry

Puvvadi Baby Maruthi
https://orcid.org/0000-0003-0338-0726
Sri Venkateswara College of Engineering, Tirupathi, India

ABSTRACT

Wireless sensor networks (WSN) consist of large numbers of sensor nodes, which are limited in battery power and communication range and have multi-modal sensing capabilities. In this chapter, energy-efficient data aggregation technique is proposed to improve the lifetime of the sensor. Here, the author has used three layer architecture by deploying mobile element/node, which can periodically visit cluster heads (CHs) at which first level data aggregation has been applied to eliminate redundancy. After collecting data from all CHs, mobile element itself will perform second level of data aggregation to eliminate further redundancy. After collecting data from CHs, mobile element will move towards base station/ sink and transmits data to base station/sink in order to save energy of entire network. Here, the author has made an attempt to prove that in WSN during data gathering if mobile elements are used to collect the aggregated data from CHs, energy consumption of the entire network will be reduced. The proposed data aggregation with mobile node helps in improving the lifetime of the WSN.

1. INTRODUCTION

Gamification is the process of emerging gaming elements into non-gaming applications. It is a way of finding out the solution to a problem or task-based with the predefined gaming constraints.

Augmented Reality (AR) is an interaction between the user's real-time environment with the digital technology where the objects produced in the virtual world generated by the AR hardware like headsets, handheld displays, sunglasses, etc. Virtual Reality (VR) is an interaction of three dimensional environments in which the user experiences the real world simulation.

Computer generated Virtual Reality (VR) and Augmented Reality (AR) is the key advances of Virtual Prototyping. They are straightforward User interfaces to a virtual plan space and encourage an intuitive investigation of the usefulness of another item. VR implies a completely PC produced, three-dimensional

DOI: 10.4018/978-1-7998-4703-8.ch011

Copyright © 2021, IGI Global. Copying or distributing in print or electronic forms without written permission of IGI Global is prohibited.

condition, in which the specialist can associate with and control a practical portrayal of the item continuously. AR goes one stage past: rather than VR, AR advances the client's view on this present reality with virtual items, which are put at perfect time and position with respect to client's point of view.

The transition from real environment to virtual environment describing about Milgram and Kishino (1994) based on different combinations of real and virtual objects. Fig1.1. Illustrating about augmented reality is the next step of the real environment. Mixed reality is also called as hybrid reality which is the combination of augmented reality, augmented virtual reality and other mixed configurations. Augmented Virtuality is capable to comprise interpersonal tangible gestures, drawing and verbal expression, colored by means of every interactor's special persona of look and reactive conduct that is paramount in gaining a honest and trusting relationship inside the touchy nature of innovative exchange.

Figure 1. Transition from Real Environment to Virtual Environment.

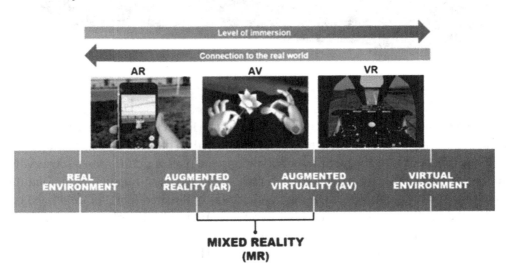

2. AUGMENTED REALITY DEVICES

Although the time period Augmented truth is surprisingly new, early traits in the technological know-how can be traced as a long way as 1900s. Howard Grub, an Irish telescope maker patented a gadget referred to as the collimating reflector. Its principal motive was once to allow larger accuracy when capturing firearms via augmenting the crosshair view precisely at the user's goal vision. It tried to clear up a pertinent undertaking of the human eye of being in a position to center of attention solely at one object at a time. Grubb's invention stimulated the improvement of a variety of army gun sights.

There are four different types of augmented reality devices are available now.

1. Heads up displays
2. Holographic displays
3. Smart glasses
4. Handheld devices

Heads up Displays(HUD): Toshiba developed AR head mounted display which is called as Toshiba Dyan Edge AR100 Viewer composed of noise removal microphones and programmable buttons which is shown in the following fig 2.1. It was easily fitted in traditional sun glasses.

Figure 2. Toshiba Dhyan Edge head mount Display

Heads up displays have been ordinarily invented for mission imperative functions like flight controllers and weapons device dashboards. Critical records are projected on obvious displays set up in the front of the pilot. This permits pilots to appear ahead backyard instead than searching down internal the cockpit. Like Grub's collimating reflector, HUDs tried to resolve the hassle of moving focal point through the use of a kind of collimating projector. The data projected is collimated (parallel mild rays) centered on infinity so that the pilot's eyes do now not want to refocus to view backyard the cockpit.

An ordinary HUD consists of three important components; a projector unit, a viewing glass (combiner) and a pc (symbol generator) and it is shown in the fig 2.2. HUDs assist expand situational recognition by means of lowering the shift of center of attention for pilots. Increasingly heads up displays have been discovering methods into new car designs.

Microsoft Hololens

In the starwar series, minority record and the Iron man collection in the latest times, these kinds of shows use mild diffraction to generate three dimensional varieties of objects in actual space. The truth that holographic shows do no longer require customers to put on any equipment to view them is one of their best advantages and it is shown in the fig 2.3.

These shows have continually been in the realm of science fiction and have currently started out gaining traction with merchandise like Looking Glass and Holovect.

Figure 3. Head up Display

Figure 4. a and Fig 4b: Microsoft Hololens

Magic Leap One

Magic Leap used to be 2018's most trending startup elevating about three billion USD from a couple of large companies. In 2018, they launched Magic Leap One, a modern AR device shown in the fig 2.4. Though the fee is roughly $2295, Magic soar one approves you to see AR photos in the actual world. In a world dominated by using technology, a gadget that doesn't take away you absolutely from the actual world appear like a correct option.

Figure 5. Magic Leap One

Optical see Through

In Optical see via glasses, the person views truth at once thru optical factors such as holographic wave publications and different structures that allow graphical overlay on the actual world. Microsoft's Hololens, Magic Leap One and the Google Glass are current examples of optical see thru clever glasses.

Video see Through

With these varieties of clever glasses, the consumer views truth that is first captured by means of one or two cameras set up on the display. These digital camera views are then blended with laptop generated imagery for the consumer to see. The HTC Vive VR headset has built in digicam which is frequently used for growing AR experiences on the device shown in the following figure.

Figure 6. Optical see through Displays and Video see through Displays

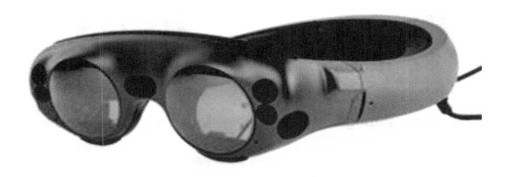

Handheld Devices

Although handheld AR is a kind of video see through, it deserves different mention. The upward push of handheld AR is the tipping factor for the science being in reality pervasive. Augmented truth libraries like ARKit, ARCore, MRKit, have enabled state-of-the-art pc imaginative and prescient algorithms to be reachable for everybody to use. In handheld or cell AR, all you want is a smartphone to have get right of entry to a host of AR experiences.

Google Glass Enterprise Edition

Google Glass was once a failure when it used to be first introduced. With elements like recording video or taking pictures snap shots barring even notifying human beings round made the gadget disagreeable to users shown in the following figure 2.6. However, Google determined a way to get better from it. Using Google's Artificial Intelligence, and aspects like customizing glass as needed, it is now ideal healthy for doctors, mechanics, or entrepreneurs and others alike. It lets in them to use each palms to work whilst staying related with the digital world to make matters extra productive and efficient.

Figure 7. Google Glass Enterprise Edition

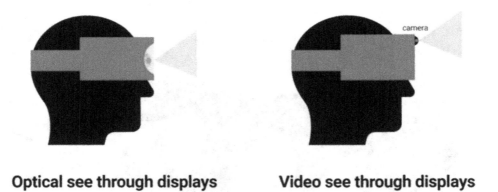

Optical see through displays   **Video see through displays**

3. VIRTUAL REALITY DEVICES

In the present digital world, virtual technology is one of the advanced technologies applicable in the Architecture Engineering and Construction (AEC) in the market. The most common widely used VR devices are now listed below.

Figure 8. a) Inside view of Occulus rift and b) Outside view of Occulus rift.

Occulus Rift

Oculus nowadays introduced the new Rift S headset which ditches exterior monitoring sensors in view of a five-camera inside-out monitoring system. The headset additionally receives a moderate bump in decision over the authentic Rift whilst transferring from OLED to LCD displays. A manufacturer new head mount layout revamps the headsets ergonomics with a 'halo' fashion strap and pinnacle strap.

Rift S is Oculus' first new PC VR headset launched in 2016. It's an absolutely new headset, and in reality Oculus says they tapped Lenovo to assist in sketch and manufacturing.

Rift S brings a bump in decision over the original, now the use of a single show which quantities to 1,280 × 1,440 per eye, up from the 1,080 × 1,200 shows in the authentic Rift, which offers Rift S 1.4instances the complete range of pixels of the unique Rift shown in the figure 3.1(a) and figure 3.1(b) . This is additionally the equal decision located in Oculus Go, and a decrease decision than Oculus Quest (1,440 × 1,600). Rift S lacks the hardware IPD adjustment discovered on Quest, however helps software program adjustments. It is commonly used for VR gaming purpose.

Prio VR

PrioVR Dev Kit's sensors are position based on key factors of full body capture the movements and translate them on-screen in real-time. The machine consists of two movement monitoring hand controllers with motion buttons, triggers, and joysticks. Each of the nineteen sensors in the PrioVR Dev Kit performs the complex mission of fusing the uncooked sensor outputs into a highly accurate orientation estimate and it is shown in the figure 3.2. The sensors themselves are true 9DOF (nine ranges of freedom) movement sensors and therefore show off no orientation flow as do structures that are based solely upon gyros. Thus, the sensors can usually report an correct orientation no be counted the length of use. Prio VR suit has been used for demo games and experience with full body capture freedom from the starting stage to ending stage.

4. APPLICATIONS OF AR AND VR

Medical Education

Numerous surgical treatment trainers and simulators appoint virtual reality, such as laparoscopy (Huber et al., 2015), temporal bone surgical operation (Fang et al., 2014), and even dental training (Steinberg et al., 2007). Some of these VR applications supply haptic (i.e. tactile) feedback and they all allow students to exercise their skills in a secure environment and without the price of practicing on human or animal cadavers. Furthermore, virtual reality has been used to help medical college students visualize anatomy in 3D, supplying a much larger feel of context and scale than the cutaway diagrams and images common to anatomy textbooks (Satava, 1995; Falah et al., 2014).

Augmented fact has additionally been used to help visualize anatomy, lung dynamics, andlaparoscopy (Kamphuis et al., 2014). For example, "Mirracle" is a gadget that uses a digicam to mimic a reflect view of the user, but superimposes pictures from a CT scan giving the consumer a view of "their" anatomy. This determines the place to show the image through developing an infrared-based depth image with a Microsoft Kinect sensor (Blum et al., 2012). ProMIS is an augmented reality laparoscopy simulator that uses a surgical procedure dummy and superimposes labels and interior organs on the digicam feed to both train and evaluate college students (Botden, 2009).

Figure 9. Prio VR Suit

Science

Early uses of virtual reality in science education centered on visualizing chemical reactions (Bell and Fogler, 1998) or learning about molecules via assembling them in a virtual environment (Byrne, 1996). More current makes use of include marker-based augmented fact to visualize the manner of respiration and human meiosis (Weng, 2016) and an astronomy application the usage of a head-mounted display to discover the photo voltaic machine and supply students a grasp for its scale (Hussein and Nätterdal, 2015). Virtual actuality and augmented truth make it possible to visualize concepts that are abstract or difficult to relate to real-world experiences, such as a marker-based augmented fact utility that helps educate electromagnetism and the interaction between special circuit factors (Ibáñez, 2014).

Engineering

A range augmented reality apps have been developed and examined in introductory electrical engineering courses (Martín-Gutiérrez et al., 2014). ElectARManual displays animations and directions over electrical machines used in the lab to assist students research how to use the machines safely. ELECT3D is a marker less machine that reads and interprets electrical diagrams. A third application is known as ElectAR_notes, which is a study assistant that recognizes markers positioned on the route find out about notes and illustrates the principles with video, animations, and more distinct information. Another learn about developed a digital actuality application to teach micro-controllers and Arduino boards with Google Cardboard headsets (Ray and Deb, 2016).

A university in Brazil modeled a whole charcoal mini-blast furnace with all of its subsystems. Their application covered extra information, videos, and 360-degree photos from real blast furnaces and was used to train engineering students how the process works and how the various subsystems engage (Vieira et al., 2017).

History and Social Sciences

One of the best makes use of for digital reality in the realm of history is to take virtual field trips to historical sites or witness historic events "first-hand" (Choi, 2006). The Google Expeditions Pioneer Program does exactly that: the college students use Google Cardboard and their smart phones to experience to their digital destination and explore. The trainer serves as the tour guide for the field outing and their app has the capacity to spotlight areas on their students' views to help direct their interest and includes more records to give an explanation for positive landmarks in more detail (Ray and Deb, 2016). On stay subject trips to historical sites, augmented reality tour guides exist for mobile structures to enrich the journey of the college students and allow them to discover on their own (Olsson et al., 2013).

Behavioral studies have additionally been performed the usage of virtual truth to recreate scenarios that would otherwise be problematical or dangerous. For example, hearth evacuation lookup used virtual actuality simulations to report how human beings would react in a fire, supplying greater accurate results than ordinary techniques (Kinateder et al., 2014).

Foreign Languages

Virtual truth in foreign language training has been targeted on permitting college students to have interactions with native speakers through 3D virtual worlds the usage of Desktop VR. A common 3D virtual world used as an educational device is Second Life due to the fact that it is free to access, permits voice and textual content interaction with different users, and is an open-ended world that any user can create content for (Baker et al., 2009). This bridges the hole of distance, permitting foreign language college students to talk with native audio system from anywhere in the world (Jauregi et al., 2011; Ibáñez et al., 2011; Blasing, 2010).

Distance Learning

The Internet has made distance mastering a ways more available and wealthy in content than ever before, however in many cases the only forum for dialogue and interplay with classmates is through online message boards or e-mail. Virtual actuality can enhance distance learning by allowing simpler and greater natural category discussions in the distance gaining knowledge of setting. The simplest examples are giving lectures in a digital classroom, such as in Second Life (Jarmon, 2009).

Since members are in the equal digital house as the instructor and their classmates, they can ask questions if a idea isn't clear, the trainer can hire study room discussion techniques to foster crucial thinking, and talk or coordinate with their classmates earlier than and after class.

Greater challenges exist in distance learning for instructions that require hands-on application in labs, such as science, engineering, or technology. One answer is to create a 3D virtual lab environment that the college students can perform their activities in. Although digital labs cannot completely substitute the need for hands-on experience, virtual labs can be used to teach simple skills which ought to reduce the frequency and amount of time wished in a physical lab (Potkonjak et al., 2016).

5. ADVANTAGES OF VIRTUAL REALITY

Over the previous two decades, several researches have proven the strengths of virtual and augmented actuality use in the classroom. One of the most massive strengths is that they change the role of the trainer from the deliverer of information into a facilitator who helps the students explore and analyze (Yougnblut, 1998). This strongly complements the constructivist learning theory due to the fact the college students sense empowered and engaged because they have manipulate over the learning process (Dede, 2005; Antonietti et al., 2001). Students can learn experientially and proceed at their very own tempo considering they are exploring a virtual environment, preventing situations where college students are left at the back of all through the lecture and spend the relaxation of the classification making an attempt to capture up (Jonassen et al., 1999).

Furthermore, digital fact can assist students study summary principles because they can experience and visualize these ideas in the virtual surroundings (Sala 2013; Rosenblum, 1997). In distinction with the typical gaining knowledge of process which is generally language-based, conceptual, and abstract, a virtual fact learning surroundings fosters energetic getting to know and helps students grasp summary information (Ray and Deb, 2016). Low-spatial capacities novices particularly benefit from virtual truth because the visualizations assist decrease the extraneous cognitive load of the learning goals (Lee and Wong, 2014).

Virtual fact approves the person to understand structures or objects that are of widely different scales. For example, the charcoal mini-blast furnace digital truth utility (Vieira et al., 2017) permits college students to look at the big picture of how the entire device works and to explore the character components of the system, all in a single, fluid experience. Studying human anatomy with digital truth offers students a better grasp of the relative measurement of the different organs and parts. Furthermore, the additional context of visualizing where the organs are in the body and the surrounding parts makes it less complicated for students to commit the information to memory in contrast to rote memorization of names and phrases (Falah et al., 2014).

Dangerous and rare situations can be simulated in virtual fact enabling students to learn in safety. Some examples encompass training surgery strategies (Ota et al., 1995) or learning how to use machine tools safely (Antonietti et al., 2001). Furthermore, in a simulated environment college students can analyze about the potentially unsafe consequences of failure from failing to follow strategies or exceeding design specifications besides physical damage to equipment or loss of life (Potkonjak et al., 2016).

The ability to effortlessly exchange the digital world opens new possibilities in the realm of testing and design. For instance, digital prototypes can be copied, modified, and examined without the rate and time required to construct and take a look at bodily prototypes. This permits the students to refine and test their plan shortly and inexpensively before creating a bodily version (Sala, 2013). Virtual fact additionally makes it less complicated to check exceptional eventualities and hypotheses due to the fact the environment can be designed to stop extraneous variables from disrupting the take a look at results and the experimental variables can be precisely controlled (Kinateder et al., 2014).

Finally, the immersive nature of digital fact can assist block out different distractions so the students can center of attention on the studying objectives. Several virtual actuality studies have revealed that students are extra targeted and exhibit better attention when the use of immersive virtual reality (Hussein and Nätterdal, 2015; Ibáñez, 2014). The interactive nature of virtual actuality transforms students from passive freshmen into energetic learners, improving pupil motivation and their sense of manipulate over their personal getting to know (Pantelidis, 2010).

6. AUGMENTED REALITY AND VIRTUAL REALITY IN HEALTH CARE

Learning health-related subjects throughout medical, nursing or the other allied health profession coaching involves the study of in depth material and therefore the acquisition. Over the years, academics have tried to include new technologies as tools into the information, to create the additional attention-grabbing into the knowledge. The presence of videogame play nowadays has seen a recent push towards serious games, that is, the appliance of videogame-based technologies to teaching and learning. A study over two hundred medical students in 2010 indicated that ninety eight medical trainees supported technology to boost tending education and ninety five to think about new media technology (i.e., game play) can be higher by incorporating "serious games" into the surgical curriculum might enhance surgical the power of laptop games to bewitch and interact players/learners for a specific purpose like to develop new data or skills and it is shown in the figure 6.1. With regard to students, study engagement has been related to tutorial accomplishment.

Once, serious games have been introduced in the field of nursing, healthcare training, medical students. Role playing is one of the serious activity that has to be done by the nurse with the patient interaction are some of the serious games which were introduced in their nursing education. There are some studies proved that the participation and motivation kind of TV shows like "Game Jeopardy " based on TV show jeopardy. A vast number of topics have been covered with the medical trainees to learn about cardiovascular drugs, microbiology, neonatal care, cancer genetics, clinical practice guidelines and how to do medical practice, etc.

Figure 10. Health care Training through virtual reality games

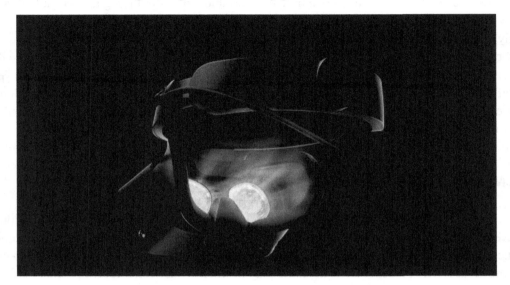

6.1 Ambient Information System for Well-being

Ambient systems believe lights, projections, sounds or objects moving at the peripherals of the user. The following are the characteristics to represent ambient information system.

(1)   Displaying information which is utmost important but not critical
(2)   They can move around and get the focus of the user.
(3)   These systems focus on the visual environment and tangible things.

Stress and Arousal

Several ambient lighting systems are designed to display biosensor data such as the levels of arousal or stress (Roseway et al. 2015; Snyder et al. 2015; Yu et al. 2018a, b).

The DeLight system (Yu et al. 2018a, b) is analogous, but additionally to providing users with feedback about their level of stress, it also offers tools for relaxation assistance. Unlike previous prototypes, DeLight was composed of 1 central light and several ambient lights installed on the ceiling or projected on the wall (see Fig. 6.2). The authors investigated the planning of warm-toned versus cold-toned colour mappings. Results showed that both conditions enable users to regulate their response to stress, although participants "were more likely to associate a warm-toned light with their increased stress when it turned to orange".

Dišimo (Mladenovi´c et al. 2018b) may be a physical artefact that relies on multimodal feedback to encourage users to breathe more regularly and deeply. When the system detects a decrease in pulse variability, it emits a sound to subtlety alert the user, who can plan to take the device in his/her hands (see Fig. 6.2). Audio sounds are played as a breathing guide and physical particles flutter inside the device when heart rate variability increases. Several Dišimo are often used simultaneously, for collaborative relaxation sessions. There in case, light colour and brightness provide information about the opposite participants' activity.

Figure 11. The DeLight system provides biofeedback through ambient light for stress intervention. Light colors change according to the user's level of stress. a Low-stress; b high-stress (warm-toned mapping); c high-stress (cool-tone mapping). Illustration courtesy of the authors (Yu et al. 2018a,

Figure 12. Dišimo provides multimodal biofeedback about heart rate variability in order to encourage and help users focusing on their breath. Illustration courtesy of Jérémy Frey (Mladenovi´c et al. 2018b)

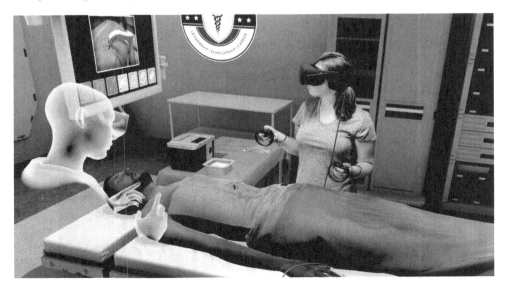

6.2 Pokemon Go

Augmented reality game Pokemon Go is developed by Niantic. Pokémon GO is not only in a one-to-one dialogue and dependence on the local time zones it is also in a one-to-one relationship spatially. The game draws on Google maps. The translation between game and reality is simply: when you walk 100 m down the street in real life, your game character walks 100 m in the game. This design highlights correspondence between the games temporal and spatial structure and reality as such Pokémon GO to one of the two archetypical ways in which augmented reality games can manifest themselves. They can be picture-based and the location-driven (the last possibility with different time structures).

From the perspective of the magic circle transforms such a design the entire planet into a 'consecrated spot' or playing field, see Fig. 6.4. There is no exclusive playing field since it is everywhere. Pokémon GO spatial and temporally expand the magic circle. It extends and encapsulates everywhere and anywhere and align itself time duration and zones. In other words, it is impossible to escape the temporal and spatial boundaries of Pokémon GO except when we fly above the mobile data grid. It should be pointed out that Pokémon GO's world is 2D. It doesn't account for the height of buildings or sea levels. In that sense, it is flat which means you can catch a Pokémon next to your location whether you are on the ground floor or standing at the top of Empire State Building.

The 'traditional' and 'meta-games' mentioned earlier was limited temporally and spatially. In Pokémon GO is the play experience is not confined to a limited 'consecrated spot' neither in front of a screen nor on a geographical playing field. Players can engage in Pokémon GO on street sidewalks or in the middle of traffic. Engaged players regularly trespass to catch Pokémons transgressing real-world social aspects such as what is allowed or prohibited either by common sense or sanctioned by law. Here players display being "grabbed" by play from something (a game) outside themselves. Still the magic circle can be challenged by non-playing people outside (Walther 2011) the game world who are either bypassing, looking at players or accidentally bumping into them. On the other side can the magic circle be reinforced by fellow players creating temporal and spatial pockets of interaction between strangers (McGonigal 2011; Montola 2009). Not only do the player have a shared interest in catching Pokémons, they also help and inspire each other (Majgaard and Larsen 2017). All in all, do interruptions in the real world influence the play experience as well as impacting in the game world.

Figure 13. Virtual pokemons in the physical environment from left and right pictures.

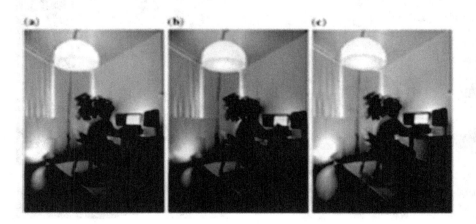

We have investigated the magic circle and located not one but three different interpretations, each with its own implication for how we understand playing and gaming. The primary understanding of the magic circle placed emphasis on a physical place different from lifestyle where play unfolds. The second understanding of the magic circle draw attention to the magic of the magic circle and therefore the mix between play experience and a more or less static simulated space with no significant reference to physical reality. The third understanding of the magic circle blended the two conceptions exemplified by the Augmented Reality game case, Pokémon GO. Here the one-to-one relationship between game time and real time and simulated and real space acted as a guide for understanding the magic circle.

Pokémon GO serves an emblematic and special case via its one-to-one temporal and spatial correspondence with reality along with side design decisions that meet explorative, socializing and archiver influenced player types and play styles. It demands rethinking the various frame layers and elasticity of the magic circle. It now includes in-game player to player interactions trading Pokémons with friends and strangers sleep in the playing field and out-of-game discussions during a host of various virtual environments. As such serves provokes and expand Pokémon GO the bounds and elasticity of the concept of the magic circle, but also play as a phenomenon in itself.

7. AUGMENTED REALITY AND VIRTUAL REALITY GAMIFICATION IN EDUCATION

The education industry has normally been sluggish in embracing new technologies. However, in this ever-changing world, it's indispensable that the industry enforce new technologies such as AR and VR to stay relevant. By developing an immersive and interactive studying trip except the use of textbooks, AR and VR science empowers newcomers to discover and examine at their personal pace, as a consequence stimulating studying and comprehension and enhances necessary retention. VR and AR-based apps for education, that mix digital technologies and learning, enhance the educational procedure and permit college students to collect records visually. These applied sciences grant a solid base to enhance the schooling process. For example, a learner can study about jungle animals with the aid of taking a day trip through a digital jungle the usage of a smartphone app, simple cardboard VR glasses and earphones. Without having to step out of the classroom or their home, students are uncovered to completely new and active gaining knowledge of environments. Teachers should instruct subjects such as Physics, Chemistry, and Biology thru digital labs that now not simply continues students engaged however additionally permits them to exercise before they can test the experiments in real laboratories. Students of remedy can study the precision of anatomy, analyze the intricacies of surgical treatment and simulate medical conditions for practice.

Here are some of the key advantages of the use of AR and VR technology in schooling and learning.

- Facilitates scholar studying thru gamification and interactivity
- Keeps students engaged even while studying hard topics
- Enhances innovative thinking
- Fewer distractions

Figure 14. Reasons to use Virtual Reality in Education
Source – https://www.teachthought.com/

- Can be used for sensible training
- Expanded teaching chances with 3D design, modeling, and presentations

While VR can supply the healthful experience, AR in training can be used as a supplementary tool to textbook learning. No wonder, from giants like Google and Microsoft to start-ups such as EON Reality, Nearpod and Unimersiv, have been targeted on presenting tailored VR experiences. In India, corporations are integrating AR/VR technologies for nursery to eighth-grade curriculums for teenagers mapping the AR/VR journeys with course content material for quite a number subjects.

7.1 Creating Virtual and reading fun experiences with Augmented Imagination

Augmented Reading

Reading is the process of acquiring language, communication and sharing ideas. It decodes the symbols by receiving it through eyes and use brain to derive the words into meaning. In fact, it's possible to differentiate between a minimum of two sorts of reading, namely: active and ludic reading. Active reading is practiced by people who read because they need to (e.g. to review and acquire new knowledge) and requires that readers have critical thinking abilities, are ready to construct new meanings, and are capable of applying acquired information and a selected aiming to a specific context. Active reading is especially useful for learning purposes (Schilit et al. 1998) and relies on different techniques, like underlining important notions or writing marginal notes. Active learning also can be facilitated by the utilization of illustrations or highlighted sections, which may trigger complementary research. On the opposite hand, reading for entertainment, also mentioned as "ludic reading", are often considered as a "play activity" of which the most goal is to immerse the reader into the story or into a pleasurable, fun experience (Nell 1988; Hupfeld et al. 2013). Emotions, imagination and narrative play a crucial role on the reader's experience of immersion.

Imagination is often seen as a process that's fed through information obtained by our senses (Pelaprat and Cole 2011). More precisely, in reading, imagination "involves the facility of reproducing images stored in memory under the suggestion of associated language or of recombining former experiences to make new images that vitalize and animate the text" (Sadoski et al. 1990). In other words, during reading, the visual stimuli (i.e. the text) is converted into streams of data and meaning that end in "new concepts, realities and generate ideas" (Vygotsky 2004; Marzo 2016). The reading experience is therefore influenced by our language, our knowledge and our previous experiences.

Augmented Books

The goal is to spot the missing gaps in knowledge and examine the planning space of hybrid reading experience to offer ideas for future developments. The commonest sort of augmented books are books that embed buttons which gaps in knowledge and examine the planning space of hybrid reading experience to offer ideas for future developments. Some even allow users to record their own voices. For instance, Hallmark Cards Inc. released the Recordable StoryBook2, which may be a storybook that permits users to record voices over a printed-paper book with an integrated sound recorder. This technique supports two main interactions: the recording of reading the story and playing the recording of the story. To record the story, the user simply reads aloud while pressing the record button; to play the story, the user must flip pages. The thought aims to strengthen relationships between relations by integrating an "emotional" value into the reading experience (e.g. a grandparent's voice recorded for grandchildren to concentrate to while flipping the pages of the book).

Instead of that specialize in the book only; several projects investigated the utilization of external devices and stimuli to reinforce the reading experience. For instance, Listen Reader (Back et al. 2001) combines music, sounds and projected graphics to make a special and multimodal atmosphere round the reader, who is sitting on a sofa The system combines RFID technology and field Sensing so as to spot the page that's being read and continually measures the space between the hand and therefore the book. This permits the system to reinforce printed text and pictures with sounds that are associated with the content of the page being read which are continuously played within the background. Whenever the user's fingers touch a special a part of the page, a replacement sound is played in a loop until the user turns the page or touches another element. The sounds are mixed via fade-in and fade-out effects so as to avoid silence and to take care of the reading flow. This technique was one among the primary to implement page tagging, therefore enabling the direct mapping of feedback with the user's action without requiring an interactive pen or an external tracking system. The system was presented during a museum as a part of a 6-months exhibit that was attended by quite 350,000 visitors.

Blink (Kelaidis 2008) stands for book and link. this technique places an external device next to the book. Each page of the book is pre-programmed with conductive ink circuits connected to key words, text or images. Once the user presses a printed hyperlink, the integrated wireless module sends a Bluetooth signal to a computer or a mobile device and shows the content associated with the integrated hyperlink.

Marker-based Augmented Reality is one of the foremost common approaches in integrating digital content in printed books with a variety of examples: World of Fairy Tales (Edgar Arts 2016) Penguin books (The Drum 2012) some Marvel Comics (Hutchings 2012), and therefore the Finnish Disney comic book as seen in Fig. 7.2.

Figure 15. Augmented Reality Book

Magic Tree is a printed book that gives instructions which guide the reader through different steps. The reader must follow these instructions within the appropriate order to finish the story. The instructions include touching, shaking or jiggling the book. Each action enables the reader to reveal the content of the subsequent page. For instance, the reader is asked to the touch each bud of the tree before turning the page. On the subsequent page there was an image of the tree with flowers rather than buds show in the following figure.

Figure 16. Augmented physical books. Top left: a magnet-based dress-up book where the reader dresses up the book characters based on the context. Top right: a pop-up book with characters and additional objects on the side, which the reader can move within the pop-up scene and from page to page. Bottom left: a book with figurines and a playing mat representing the living areas of the main character's house. Bottom right: a sound book where the reader presses buttons on the right edge of the book and plays sounds based on the page

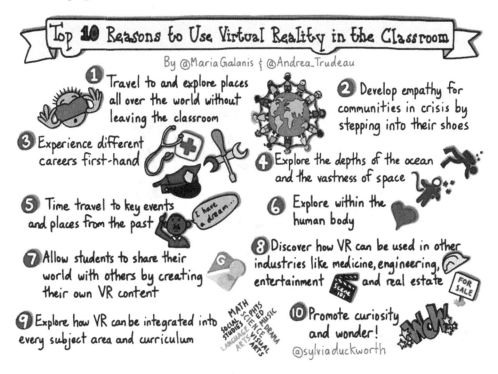

8. AUGMENTED REALITY AND VIRTUAL REALITY GAMIFICATION IN INDUSTRY

Now, gamification is a billion-dollar industry. In 2019, the enterprise used to be reportedly well worth $7.17 billion. It is now being more and more used in a range of industries and many pinnacle and small corporations have embraced it with open hands, to enhance their businesses.

The concept of gamification has emerged as a modernized fashion in latest years and the advantages of gamification apps in business, advertising are massive. It has drawn activity each from teachers and practitioners, due to the fact of digitalization of our daily lives. Now, video games are a quintessential section of our life, and anybody performs them whether or not these are console or mobile, or in the offline world. For many adults, gaming is an entertainment activity. Research says world video games market grew in 2019 to a remarkable one hundred twenty billion USD.

Gamification has been with us for some time now, however it's so versatile that it applies to each type of business. The splendor of gamification is that it can lend itself to many one of the major functions like marketing, agency way of life building, undertaking management, recruitment.

Figure 17. Juego Studio assists Real Estate Industry

How Gamification Works

Gamification makes use of the contemporary lookup findings in behavioral psychology to foster effective human behaviour. It frees the resource-intensive rational section of our thought from having to make selections all the time and as an alternative makes use of a few cutting-edge strategies to have an effect on a lots primitive section of the Genius that has a massive impact on our choice making.

The following are the list of common methodologies for gamification in business industry.

Points: Points act as advantageous remarks to the users. In each video games and gamified applications, the participant receives factors when they utilize proper action. This receiving of factors in addition motivates the participant to repeat these actions.

Badges: Badges are testaments of a user's achievements. Usually, players receive badges once they complete a specific challenge or accumulate a set of points. Once a badge is won, the user can show it off to others. This provides both a personal and social motivation.

Progress Graphs: As the name indicates, it is a marks progress. They exhibit customers how lots they have elevated their work over time and how a long way they have come on account that they at the beginning started. This feeling of growth is a very properly way to inspire people.

Leaderboards: Leaderboards pit users' achievements inside a sport or app in opposition to every other. It compares the achievements of all the customers and ranks them in accordance to positive metrics.

By the use of leaderboards gamified utility builders can foster healthful opposition amongst their users, which is a excellent supply of motivation.

Teams: Teams introduce a non-competitive social thing to gamified applications. Instead of being competitive, it makes customers cooperative with every other. Members of a crew can assist and assist every different whilst every of them pursues their personal goals.

There are several scenarios to implement the principles of gamification in industry level.

8.1 Real Estate industry

Technology is appearing as a catalyst in each enterprise and the actual property enterprise is no exception. Technology has modified the way is delivered to renters and buyers. Virtual Reality actual property and Augmented Reality actual property are amongst such applied sciences that are bringing alternate in the way actual property tasks are experienced. VR permits lenders to go to the plot or condo from anywhere, whenever with VR headset whilst AR provides more layers of records in bodily plane. At Juego Studios provide infinite chances in reworking actual property enterprise thru use of such technologies. People who are searching for flats or locations for lease can now down load exceptional apps to take a look out residences in accordance to their requirements. We work on exterior, interior, 360 degree panoramic tour, ground planning and video manufacturing to provide our consumers a great in type experience.

Customer Engagement:

One of the principal challenges in actual property enterprise is to furnish engagement, main to sales. By developing appealing apps which can be skilled on smartphones, tablets, VR & AR enabled devices, Juego Studios helps actual property agencies to appeal to extra customers. Using VR and AR technologies, businesses can provide client visits or excursions of actual property properties, every time and from anywhere, as in contrast to real deliberate property visits.

Realistic Rendering:

Virtual Reality is mainly used for demo version of apartments, villas includes visualization techniques for the allocation of rooms, floor planning environment created virtually. The overall visualization of customers experience to imagine dream home virtually so that very easy for the customer to understand the requirements for their dream home and also saves cost and time.

8.2 Gaming & Entertainment

Gaming enterprise has developed over the years as new applied sciences and more modern systems and gadgets have come to foray. The gaming leisure enterprise has additionally considered a massive shift the way it presents content material or engages users, with the creation of the new generation of gaming enterprise trends.

Figure 18. AR & VR in Gaming & Entertainment

Fig. 7.5 shows Augmented and Virtual Reality in gaming industry.Game development services such as AR and VR includes Unity3D, OpenGL, WebGL,etc.

8.3 Automotive Industry

Recent developments in digital applied sciences have superior the tempo of operations in the automobile industry.

Today in a world linked with clever devices, more than a few tactics in the car industry, from manufacturing to meeting and from grant chain administration to sales, have been revamped with the aid of use of applied sciences and options like simulation, visualization, gamification & IoT.

9. CHALLENGES OF AUGMENTED REALITY AND VIRTUAL REALITY

Some of the frequent challenges of the usage of augmented reality technological know-how are that there's warfare to use the new applied sciences via teachers. Moreover, not all college students have the smartphones successful of aiding AR content. Virtual Reality, on the different hand, faces absolutely distinctive challenges. High prices of hardware, accessibility and lack of nice content material are some of the constraints that have stored VR from being the breakthrough technology in education.

CONCLUSION

Augmented and Virtual reality gamification highlighted how to utilize and needs and deeds of AR and VR games in education, healthcare and industry. In education field, the teaching and learning practices with the implementation of AR and VR is revealing with suitable applications. The implementation of Augmented and Virtual Reality is more prominent in the field of healthcare in which describing the nursing training practices and also providing prospective applications like Ambient Information Systems and PokemonGo. In the field of industry, manufacturing and assembling areas, augmented and virtual reality play a prominent role which increases industry growth. This chapter concludes with a summary of specified and most vital applications in AR and VR gamification.

REFERENCES

Rossmann, J., & Sommer, B. (2008). The Virtual Testbed: Latest Virtual Reality Technologies for Space Robotic Applications. *CDROM-Proceedings of 9th International Symposium on Artificial Intelligence, Robotics and Automation in Space (i-SAIRAS 2008)*.

Rossmann, J. (1999). Projective Virtual Reality: Bridging the Gap between Virtual Reality and Robotics. *IEEE Transactions on Robotics and Automation, 15*(3), 411–422. doi:10.1109/70.768175

Pretzsch, H., Biber, P., & Dursky, J. (2002). The single tree based stand simulator SILVA. Construction, lication and evaluation. *Forest Ecology and Management, 162*(1), 3–21. doi:10.1016/S0378-1127(02)00047-6

Wokke, F. J. P., & Pronk, Z. (2000) Mission Validation and Training Facility for the European Robotic Arm (ERA). *Proceedings of SESP 2000, 6th International Workshop on Simulation for European Space Programmes*. https://www.accenture.com/gb-en/blogs/blogs-long-time-no-speak

Milgram, P., & Kishino, F. (1994). A taxonomy of mixed reality visual displays. *IEICE Transactions on Information and Systems, 12*, 1321–1329.

Hughes & Stapleton. (n.d.). *The Shared Imagination: Creative Collaboration in Augmented Virtuality*. Academic Press.

Papasin, R., Betts, B. J., Del Mundo, R., Guerrero, M., Mah, R. W., McIntosh, D. M., & Wilson, E. (2003). Intelligent Virtual Station. *Proceedings of 7th International Symposium on Artificial Intelligence, Robotics and Automation in Space*.

Ma, Gausemeier, Fan, & Grafe. (n.d.). Virtual Reality & Augmented Reality in Industry. *The 2nd Sino-German Workshop.*

Kron, F. W., Gjerde, C. L., Sen, A., & Fetters, M. D. (2010). Medical student attitudes toward video games and related new media Technologies in medical education. *BMC Medical Education, 10*(1), 50. doi:10.1186/1472-6920-10-50 PMID:20576125

Graafland, M., Schraagen, J. M., & Schijven, M. P. (2012). Systematic review of serious games for medical education and surgical skills training. *British Journal of Surgery, 99*(10), 1322–1330. doi:10.1002/bjs.8819 PMID:22961509

Corti, K. (2006). Game-based Learning; A Serious Business Application. PIXELearning, Coventry.

Shute, V. J. (2009). Melding the power of serious games and embedded assessment to monitor and foster learning. In U. Ritterfeld, M. Cody, & P. Vorderer (Eds.), *Serious Games Mechanisms and Effects*. Routledge Publishers.

Ericsson, K. A. (2004). Deliberate practice and the acquisition and maintenance of expert performance in medicine and related domains. *Academic Medicine, 79*(10, SUPPL.), S70–S81. doi:10.1097/00001888-200410001-00022 PMID:15383395

Stapleton, A. J. (2004). Serious games: serious opportunities. *Proceedings of Australian*Game Developers' Conference.

Becker, K., & Parker, J. R. (2012). *The Guide to Computer Simulations and Games*. Wiley.

Kanthan, R., & Senger, J. L. (2011). The impact of specially designed digital games-based learning in undergraduate pathology and medical education. *Archives of Pathology & Laboratory Medicine, 135*(1), 135–142. PMID:21204720

Johnston, B., Boyle, L., MacArthur, E., & Manion, B. F. (2013). The role of technology and digital gaming in nurse education. *Nursing Standard, 27*(28), 35–38. doi:10.7748/ns2013.03.27.28.35.s9612 PMID:23556215

Bellotti, F. (2013). Assessment in and of serious games: an overview. *Adv. Human Comput. Inter., 1.*

Rottet, S. M. (1974). Gaming as a learning strategy. *Journal of Continuing Education in Nursing, 5*(6), 22–25. PMID:4497850

Davidhizar, R. E. (1982). Simulation games as a teaching technique in psychiatric nursing. *Perspectives in Psychiatric Care, 20*(1), 8–12. doi:10.1111/j.1744-6163.1982.tb00142.x PMID:6921627

Smoyak, S. A. (1977). Use of gaming simulation by health care professionals. *Health Education Monographs, 5*(1_suppl), 11–17. doi:10.1177/10901981770050S103 PMID:870454

Greenblat, C.S. (1977). Gaming-simulation and health education an overview. *Health Educ. Monogr., 5*(suppl 1), 5-10.

Corbett, N. A., & Beveridge, P. (1982). Simulation as a tool for learning. *Topics in Clinical Nursing, 4*(3), 58–67. PMID:6922661

Martin, R., & Coleman, S. (1994). Playing games with cardiopulmonary resuscitation. *J. Nurs. Staff Dev.: JNSD*, *10*(1), 31–34. PMID:8120644

D'Alessandro, D. M., Ellsbury, D. L., Kreiter, C. D., & Starner, T. (2002). Pediatric jeopardy may increase residents' medical reading. *Ambulatory Pediatrics*, *2*(1), 1–3. doi:10.1367/1539-4409(2002)002<0001:PJ MIRM>2.0.CO;2 PMID:11888428

Gordon, D. W., & Brown, H. N. (1995). Fun and games in reviewing neonatal emergency care. *Neonatal Network*, *14*(3), 45–49. PMID:7603420

Wargo, C. A. (2000). Blood clot: Gaming to reinforce learning about disseminated intravascular coagulation. *Journal of Continuing Education in Nursing*, *31*(4), 149–151. doi:10.3928/0022-0124-20000701-04 PMID:11261156

Schuh, L., Burdette, D. E., Schultz, L., & Silver, B. (2008). Learning clinical neurophysiology: Gaming is better than lectures. *Journal of Clinical Neurophysiology*, *25*(3), 167–169. doi:10.1097/WNP.0b013e31817759b3 PMID:18469726

Beylefeld, A. A., & Struwig, M. C. (2007). A gaming approach to learning medical microbiology: Students' experiences of flow. *Medical Teacher*, *29*(9), 933–940. doi:10.1080/01421590701601550 PMID:18158668

Nosek, T. M. (2007). A serious gaming/immersion environment to teach clinical cancer genetics. *Studies in Health Technology and Informatics*, *125*, 355–360. PMID:17377303

Jirasevijinda, T., & Brown, L. C. (2010). Jeopardy! An innovative approach to teach psychosocial aspects of pediatrics. *Patient Education and Counseling*, *80*(3), 333–336. doi:10.1016/j.pec.2010.06.002 PMID:20619997

Duque, G., Fung, S., Mallet, L., Posel, N., & Fleiszer, D. (2008). Learning while having fun: The use of video gaming to teach geriatric house calls to medical students. *Journal of the American Geriatrics Society*, *56*(7), 1328–1332. doi:10.1111/j.1532-5415.2008.01759.x PMID:18482292

Akl, E. A., Mustafa, R., Slomka, T., Alawneh, A., Vedavalli, A., & Schünemann, H. J. (2008). An educational game for teaching clinical practice guidelines to internal medicine residents: Development, feasibility and acceptability. *BMC Medical Education*, *8*(1), 50. doi:10.1186/1472-6920-8-50 PMID:19017400

Hannig, A., Kuth, N., Özman, M., Jonas, S., & Spreckelsen, C. (2012). EMedOffice: A web-based collaborative serious game for teaching optimal design of a medical practice. *BMC Medical Education*, *12*(1), 104. doi:10.1186/1472-6920-12-104 PMID:23110606

Diehl, L. A., Souza, R. M., Alves, J. B., Gordan, P. A., Esteves, R. Z., Jorge, M. L. S. G., & Coelho, I. C. M. (2013). InsuOnline, a serious game to teach insulin therapy to primary care physicians: Design of the game and a randomized controlled trial for educational validation. *JMIR Research Protocols*, *2*(1), e5. doi:10.2196/resprot.2431 PMID:23612462

Telner, D. (2010). Game-based versus traditional case-based learning: Comparing effectiveness in stroke continuing medical education. *Can. Fam. Phys.*, *56*(9), e345–e351. PMID:20841574

Roth, M., Rieß, P., & Reiners, D. (2006). Load Balancing on Cluster-Based Multi Projector Display Systems. *Proceedings of the International Conference in Central Europe on Computer Graphics WSCG.*

Berndt, R., Havemann, S., Settgast, V., & Fellner, D. (2008). Sustainable Markup and Annotation of 3D Geometry. *Proceedings of the 14th International Conference on Virtual Systems and Multimedia.*

Jung, Y., Keil, J., Behr, J., Webel, S., Zöllner, M., Engelke, T., Wuest, H., & Becker, M. (2008). Adapting X3D for Multi-touch Environments. *Proceedings of the 13th International Symposium on 3D Web Technology.* 10.1145/1394209.1394218

Chapter 12
Multimedia Data Transmission:
Algorithm to Improve Reliability in Multimedia Data Transmission

Deepalakshmi Rajendran

Velammal College of Engineering and Technology, India

Vijayalakshmi R.

Velammal College of Engineering and Technology, India

ABSTRACT

Investigating multimedia traffic over optical networks that provide extremely high data rates makes it a very attractive medium for multiservice transmission in building networks at low cost. Recently, there has been active research going on congestion control in optical networks to provide the communication reliability and bandwidth efficiency. The authors investigate the mutual diversity technique as a candidate solution for congestion control over multimedia traffic in optical network. This chapter proposes a new robust medium access control (MAC) protocol, called mutual diversity MAC (MD-MAC), where each terminal proactively selects a consort for mutual operation and lets it pass on concurrently so that this mitigates interference from nearby terminals and thus improves the reliability of network and its bandwidth efficiency. For meticulous evaluation, this study presents and uses a realistic reception by taking bit error rate (BER) and the corresponding frame error rate (FER) into consideration.

1. INTRODUCTION

Optical communication networks play a vital role in today's internet world as they offer huge competence in utilization of large bandwidth available on the optical channel. Wavelength Division Multiplexing (WDM) technology epitomized the optical communication by increasing the capacity in by several orders of magnitude. Signal attenuations in static and fixed network and interference are the two major obstacles reduce the potential in delivering signals through optical networks. Conventional routing layer solutions support the mutual delivery of information by selecting intermediate routing nodes for a given source destination pair. But, it may be difficult to maximize the performance till all the routing nodes

DOI: 10.4018/978-1-7998-4703-8.ch012

Copyright © 2021, IGI Global. Copying or distributing in print or electronic forms without written permission of IGI Global is prohibited.

are coordinated to cooperate at lower levels. Because the network capacity is always determined by the fundamental MAC and PHY layer protocols. For example, consider a *carrier sense* (CS)-based *medium access control* (MAC) protocol. A routing node is regarded as a greedy challenger to other nodes as they compete with each other to grab the shared medium, interfere in each other's communication and cause collisions. Also incurs energy wastage by rendering them to overhear.

According to Amin, O et al., Mutual MAC algorithms are the hotspurs in active research in the field of the data transfer. For example, in *Mutual - MAC*, cooperating routing nodes are determined in a pro-active manner and are used to forward frames at higher bit rates. The endeavor is to deliver frames at a faster rate by utilizing multi-rate capability at the same instant, improve the communication reliability in interference-rich environment (S. Krco & M. Dupcinov, 2003) *Mutual communication* at the PHY layer (Castillo-Vazquez et al.,2009) directly enhances the link reliability; mutual communication exploits miscellany offered by multiple users, known as *multiuser* or *mutual diversity*. It results a dramatic improvement in *bit error rate* (BER), which leads to improve the link reliability, the primary incentive of mutual diversity as mentioned in this paper.

The proposed MD-MAC maneuvers on a single channel and uses a single consort. Each transmitter sends its signal along with its consort in a mutual manner to improve the communication reliability. The important aspect of MD- MAC is the selection of *consort, as* each routing node monitors its neighbors and dynamically determines a single consort as that one exhibits the best link quality.

The proposed MD-MAC maneuvers on a single channel and uses a single consort. Each transmitter sends its signal along with its consort in a mutual manner to improve the communication reliability. The important aspect of MD-MAC is the selection of *consort, as* each routing node monitors its neighbors and dynamically determines a single consort as that one exhibits the best link quality.

This paper enhances the MD-MAC algorithm in two ways.

(i)   In the MD-MAC algorithm, a sender and its consort mutually transmit a frame whenever the sender experiences a transmission failure (T. D. Shahida, 2007). If it is due to the interference, it assists as the communication becomes more robust in the presence of channel error. This is incorporated in the enhanced MD-MAC protocol presented in this paper.

(ii)   The MD-MAC assumes to exchange two short control frames (RTS and CTS) before transmitting a data frame, which is not usually the case. However this paper employs the two control frames optionally in order to increase performance.

The proposed MD-MAC algorithm has been evaluated via simulation using ns-2 (T. D. Shahida et al.,2007). Most of previous researches only concentrated on evaluating BER, but this paper evaluates system-level performance such as packet delivery capability. BER and Frame Error Rate (FER) statistics are used as an evaluative parameter. This is the first kind of study on mutual communication that offers elemental system-level comparisons with the BER and FER in optical networks as per the knowledge of the author. The End-to-end packet delay is evaluated for MDMAC. Performance variation due to the changes in fiber noise level has been observed to analyze the MD-MAC. It shows a best performance consistently regardless of the fiber noise level. Effect of network traffic in terms of varying number of communication sessions and varying packet rate has been measured in order to understand the scalability of MD-MAC in optical network.

The rest of the paper is organized as: Background and system model are summarized in Section II. Section III presents the proposed MD-MAC protocol; the four-way handshaking algorithm and the consort selection mechanism. Performance study and evaluation results are discussed in Section IV. Finally, conclusions are drafted in Section V.

2. BACKGROUND AND SYSTEM MODEL

One of the efficient MAC schemes is MD-MAC which makes use of PHY layer allying for reliable communication. The system model assumed throughout this paper is explained in this section

2.1. Mutual Diversity

Diversity techniques such as co-located optical routing nodes can mitigate the interference problem by transmitting redundant signals over essentially independent channels. However, due to the physical size and hardware complexity, it may not be always feasible in practice for each node to have multiple transmitting light sources. Recently, a new class of diversity techniques called *mutual diversity* has been proposed, in which the routing nodes interact with each other to jointly transmit information exploiting diversity offered by multiple users (S. Krco & M. Dupcinov, 2003).

There are two types of mutual diversity algorithms: *repetition-based* and *mutual operation based* algorithms *(Abou-Rjeily,2011)*. The transmission of multiple copies of a data stream is disseminated among the cooperating routing nodes. Consider a simple three routing node example with a sender, a consort and a receiver device as in Fig. 1. In time slot 1, the sender device transmits two symbol blocks, D(x) and D(x+1), to the consort. The sender and its consort mutually transmit the blocks in time slot 2 as in the figure. It is not only possible for both the sender and the consort to transmit concurrently on the same channel but also improves the reliability of the communication.

2.2. Mutual Diversity in Optical Networks

The communication link reliability is the very important factor in optical networks at noisy and unstable environments. In case of disseminat*ed automatic repeat request* mechanism, a source and distributed repeater nodes concurrently transmit the same data frame repeatedly till the source correctly receives an acknowledgement from the destination (S. Krco & M. Dupcinov, 2013).This mechanism enhances the communication reliability at the cost of more power dissipation, more routing overhead, and more network traffic, and consequently results in the reduction of network throughput.

In the research of *Mutual MAC* (M-MAC), four control frames such as *Relaying Start* (RS), *Relay Acknowledgement* (RA), *Relay Broadcasting* (RB) and *Transmission Start* (TS) are defined in addition to conventional *Request-To-Send* (RTS), *Clear-To-Send* (CTS), and ACK. When a DATA frame is transmitted using mutual diversity, all control frames are transmitted through the conventional *Single-Input-Single-Output* (SISO) link. This results in unreliable delivery of control frames, limit the applicability of this protocol. Directional knowledge of consorts is required for routing in this method.

According to the concept of Virtual *Multiple-Input-Single-Output* and multiple consorts supported MAC protocol, a *Single-Input-Single-Output* path between a source and a destination is exposed using an routing protocol like *Dynamic Source Routing* (DSR) (R. Deepalakshmi et al.,2010) and multiple consorts are selected by exchanging periodic *one-hop hello* packets. The source and its consorts mutually transmit to an intermediate node which is several-hop away on the routing path. The drawback of this algorithm is, for successful cooperation, the receiver must have at least *k* consorts when the sender uses *k* consorts. All the concepts mentioned above are different from the proposed MD-MAC like they use multiple channels (S. Moh,2017;R. Deepalakshmi et al.,2010) in the paper proposed where as MD-MAC operates on a single channel and is consistent with the standard routing layer protocols.

Figure 1.

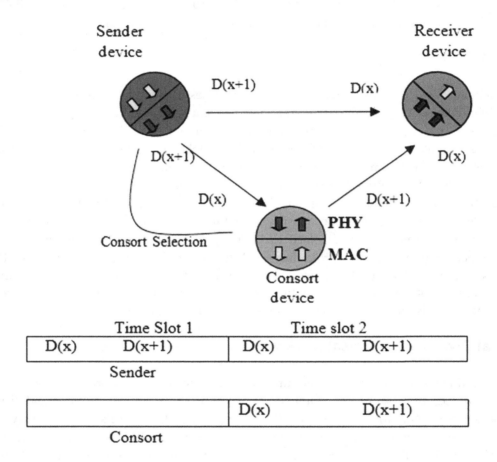

2.3. Signal Propagation and Reception Model

Data stream propagation within a optical fiber channel is characterized by means of three effects: *attenuation* due to distance between the sender and the receiver, *dispersion* due to the manufacturing defects of the fiber and *scattering* due to collision of photons in a multipath propagation Tao Luo . To successfully receive a transmitted data stream two conditions have to be satisfied. First, the receiver must be within the periphery of the sender, that is the received signal power must be equal or larger than the *receive threshold*. Second, the received signal power must be strong enough to overcome the influence of the noise and interference. This condition is described by the following *Signal-Interference-Noise Ratio* (SINR) model.

$$SINR = \frac{P_r}{N + \sum_{i \neq r} P_i} \geq Z_0.$$

Where, P_r is the received signal power, P_i denotes the received power of other signals arrived at the receiver, N is the effective noise at the receiver, and Z_0 is the minimum required SINR, commonly called *Capture Threshold*. As signal reception in real-life environment is not deterministic, a smaller SINR increases *Bit Error Rate* (BER) and thus a communication could fail with a higher probability.

3. MUTUAL DIVERSITY MAC (MD-MAC)

In an optical network, many nodes are spread over a network area and communicate with each other using multi hop pathway rather than direct communication in the mutual communication to increase the reliability as well bandwidth efficiency.

3.1. Consort Selection and Its Propagation

Technological advancement in the field of optical communication has unearthed the solutions for the above mentioned problems. The following operation decorum has been employed in the proposed MD-MAC:

- The RTS/CTS exchange is normally disabled.
- Each node (A) maintains $n_{A,B}$ for each possible neighbor, which is the number of consecutive communication failures. It is incremented when A's transmission to B fails and is reset to zero when it is successful.
- On the other hand, the RTS/CTS exchange is used only when a sender (A) experiences transmission failures at least once with a consort neighbor (B) in the recent past. It can also be explained as, it is enabled when $n_{A,B}$ is larger than a certain threshold (n_{th}), which is called *RTS probing*, commonly used in multi rate adaptation protocols (T. D. Shahida et al.,2007 ; R. Deepalakshmi et al.,2011). Fig. 3(a) shows the four-way handshaking in the MD-MAC protocol.
- No mutual communication is rendered for RTS and CTS control frames as in Fig. 3(a) because transmission failures of those short control frames are usually due to collisions. This should be contrasted with the simple scheme in Fig. 2(a), where the mutual communication is applied to every frame including RTS and CTS.
- Mutual communication is used for DATA and ACK frames in case data transmission failed, but subsequently the RTS/CTS exchange was successful.
- Transmission of symbol blocks in MD-MAC is projected in Fig. 3(b). Comparing to the transmission scenario shown in Fig. 2(b), time slot 1 for the symbol blocks of M-DATA (M-ACK) is skipped and thus, the frame transmission time is not larger than the original DATA (ACK). This is possible because frame from node A doesn't have to repeat the original symbol blocks unlike in Fig. 1 and Fig. 2(b). However, the first two symbol blocks can optionally be transmitted for the synchronization purpose between A and D_A. Regarding the ACK frame, D_B as well as B receives M-DATA and thus D_B can generate M-ACK as well.

Figure 2.

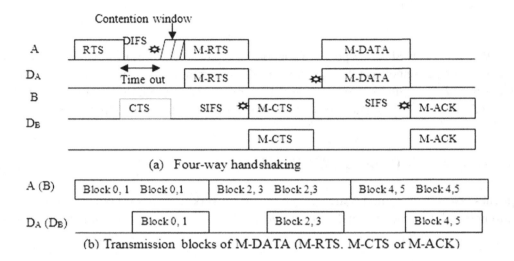

(a) Four-way handshaking

(b) Transmission blocks of M-DATA (M-RTS. M-CTS or M-ACK)

Figure 3.

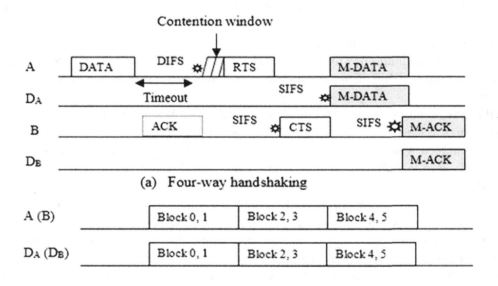

(a) Four-way handshaking

Fig. 4(a), 4(b) and 4(c) illustrates the state transition diagram for the sender, the receiver and the consort, respectively. In Fig. 4(a), if n is smaller than n_{th}, the RTS/CTS exchange is skipped because the prior communication is successful and the communication environment is free from channel errors. No mutual communication of DATA will be initiated. In other hand, the RTS/CTS exchange will perform the data communication and DATA transmission occurs concurrently with its consort. Fig. 4(b) shows the state transition diagram of a receiver. Fig. 4(c) explicit the state transition of a consort of node A. Since node A can be either a sender or a receiver, the figure includes both state transitions. As a transmit consort (*i.e.*, node A is a sender), it will mutually send M-DATA when it hears RTS from A as well as

CTS to A. As a receive consort (*i.e.*, node A is a receiver), it will mutually send M-ACK when it hears RTS to B, CTS from A and M-DATA from A. It is shown on the right hand side in Fig. 4(c).

Figure 4.

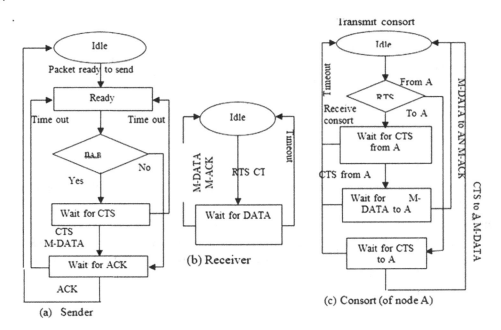

(a) Sender

(b) Receiver

(c) Consort (of node A)

3.2. Consort Selection and Its Propagation

In order to perform the mutual transmission in MD-MAC, each and every node should opt for its consort by monitoring or overhearing its neighbors with respect to *link quality*. Among all neighbors, the neighbor with the best link quality is chosen as its consort. There are three reasons behind this choice: (i) Communication between a node and its consort must be highly reliable. (ii) A consort with the best link quality is most probably the closest node. (iii) It ensures that the sender and the consort share the same communication environment so that they can make a consistent decision on cooperation. The mutual diversity can be effective when a node and its consort are spaced at least $\lambda/4$ apart, where λ is the wavelength.

SINR, distance, load, interference level and *Signal Strength* are some factors used to indicate link quality. Here, SINR is preferred as it takes noise and interference into account and is measurable with no additional support. When a sender does not hear any further frames from the chosen consort, the corresponding binding expires. In addition to this, when a sender hears a frame from a different node that exhibits a better link quality, it employs this node as a new consort.

Once a consort is determined, each node must inform to the chosen consort with all the frames it transmits. For this purpose, it uses an address field (Addr4) in MAC frame as in Fig. 5 so that its neighbors as well as the selected consort become to know about the selection. MD-MAC does not require any data format changes. A sender and a consort transmit the exactly same copy at the MAC layer while they are different at the physical layer. When the node does not have a frame to transmit for an extended period of time, it will broadcast a hello frame, the format follows M-DATA, with the destination (Addr1) and the source (Addr2) to be the transmitter itself.

Figure 5.

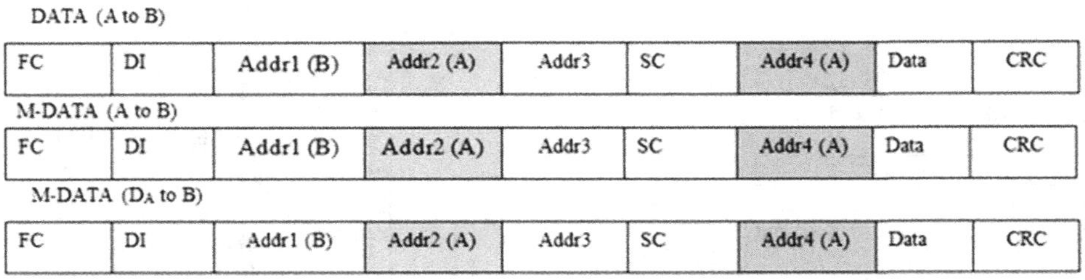

DATA (A to B)

FC	DI	Addr1 (B)	Addr2 (A)	Addr3	SC	Addr4 (A)	Data	CRC

M-DATA (A to B)

FC	DI	Addr1 (B)	Addr2 (A)	Addr3	SC	Addr4 (A)	Data	CRC

M-DATA (D_A to B)

FC	DI	Addr1 (B)	Addr2 (A)	Addr3	SC	Addr4 (A)	Data	CRC

Mutual communication may face three important situations. They are: (i) What if the consort does not cooperate when it should? (ii) What if the consort cooperates when it shouldn't? and (iii) what if two different senders select the same consort? Consider the example, where D_A and D_B are the consorts of node A and B, respectively. When $n_{A,B} \geq n_{th}$ and the RTS/CTS exchange is successful, node A will send M-DATA. When node D_A does not receive either the RTS or the CTS, it does not attempt to send M-DATA together with node A. But, this situation does not do any harm and does not violate the semantic of MAC protocol and there is no algorithmic ambiguity.

The second case happens when node A sends an RTS and node B replies with a CTS, which is successfully received by node D_A but not by node A. It may cause confusion because node D_A transmits M-DATA but node A doesn't. Any way, it doesn't do any harm. Node A will retransmit the same frame, which is a duplicate frame for node B. Such duplicate frames can be filtered out within B's MAC based on the original functionality, called *duplicate packet filtering*. This algorithm matches the sender address (Addr2 in Fig. 5) and the sender-generated sequence control number (SC) of a new frame against those of previously received ones. If there is a match, the receiver transmits ACK but ignores the duplicate frame.

Consort conflict is the third case. When two senders select the same consort and transmit concurrently, what should the consort do? In this situation mutual communication is attempted only after the successful exchange of RTS/CTS in MD-MAC. Hence, when both senders wish to transmit data frames mutually, they already have exchanged RTS and CTS successfully with their corresponding receivers concurrently. Consort is in proximity to both senders and will participate in the mutual transmission of one of the two senders but will not be able to participate on behalf of the other sender. This is the case where the consort does not participate when it should. This does not make trouble as explained above.

4. PERFORMANCE EVALUATION

The performance of the proposed MD-MAC protocol is evaluated in comparison to the conventional method using ns-2 T. D. Shahida. Section IV-A introduces the realistic reception model we have proposed in this paper and Section IV-B explains the simulation parameters. Simulation results are presented in Section IV-C.

4.1. Signal Reception in the Modified Ns-2

The signal reception model implemented in ns-2 is based on three fixed PHY parameters, *i.e.*, *carrier sense threshold* (CSThresh), *receive threshold* (RxThresh) and *capture threshold* (CPThresh). They were introduced in Sections II. When a frame is received, each node compares the received signal power against CSThresh and RxThresh as explained in Section II-C. If it is smaller than CSThresh, the receiver ignores the signal. If it is in between the two thresholds, the receiver considers the medium busy as but does not receive the signal (frame in error). While it is higher than RXThresh, the receiver receives the frame. However, when the node receives another signal during receiving the first signal, their ratio is compared against CPThresh. If the ratio is larger than CPThresh, the stronger signal survives (if it is the first one) and the weaker signal is dropped; otherwise, both frames are considered failed. This deterministic reception model based on the three thresholds serves reasonably well when evaluating high level protocols such as network and transport layer algorithms. However, when evaluating lower layer protocols, it is important to simulate a more realistic reception model. We modified ns-2 network simulator (T. D. Shahida et al.,2007) to take *bit error rate* (BER) into consideration when determining the success or failure of a received signal. It is based on the following 3-step process: (i) Compute SINR, (ii) look up the BER-SINR curve to obtain BER, and (iii) calculate *Frame Error Rate* (FER) and determine whether to receive or drop the frame.

First, SINR is calculated based on the equation introduced in Section II-C. According to that equation, the effective noise N is one of key parameters that determine SINR. In this paper, we first compute the thermal noise level within the channel bandwidth. According to the well known noise density of -174 dBm/Hz, it is -101 dBm. Assuming a system noise figure of 6 dB, the effective noise at the receiver is -95 dBm. It is assumed that the environment noise is fixed to be -83 or -90 dBm in this paper and that fading is contained in the noise.

Figure 6.

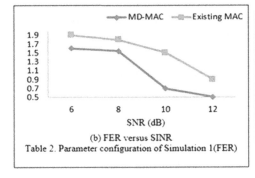

SNR(dB)	FER of existing MAC	FER of MD-MAC
6	1.89	1.6
8	1.8	1.53
10	1.5	0.7
12	0.9	0.4

(b) FER versus SINR
Table 2. Parameter configuration of Simulation 1(FER)

Second, the BER-SINR curve used in our simulation study is obtained. The BER-E_b / N_0 curve is converted to the BER-SINR curve based on the relationship SINR=E_b / N_0 × R/B_r, where E_b is energy required per bit of information, N_0 is noise (plus interference) in 1 Hz of bandwidth, R is system data rate, and B_r is system bandwidth that is given by B_r = R Cooperation reduces the required SNR by about 5 dB for the same BER. A frame consists of *physical layer convergence protocol* (PLCP) *preamble*, PLCP header and payload (data), and they may be transmitted at different rate. Hence, since BER is a function of SINR and modulation method as well as the mutual diversity, it should be calculated separately for the three parts of a frame.

Third, once BER is obtained, FER can be calculated, which determines the percentage that a frame is received correctly. For example, given α-bit preamble, β-bit PLCP header and γ-bit payload with BER of p_a, p_b, p_c respectively, FER is obtained by $1-(1-p_a)^\alpha(1-p_b)^\beta(1-p_c)^\gamma$. FER without cooperation is much higher than that with mutual diversity and that's how mutual communication improves the reliability of an optical link. In summary, FER is not deterministically but probabilistically determined based on SINR in our simulation, making our evaluation more realistic and meaningful.

4.2. Simulation Environment

It is assumed that 50 nodes located over a square area of $300 \times 1500m^2$. Each simulation has been run for 900 seconds of simulation time. The propagation channel of *optical fiber* is assumed with a data rate of 1 Mbps. The environment noise level of -83 or -90 dBm is modeled as a Gaussian random variable with the standard deviation of 1 dB. Noise level of -90 dBm is considered ignorable and interference from other transmitters dominates. On the other hand, noise level of -83 dBm is used to simulate a harsh communication environment.

Four constant bit rate (CBR) sources transmit UDP-based traffic at 2 packets per second and the data payload of each packet is 512 bytes long. Source-destination pairs are randomly selected. Routing protocol is used to discover a routing path for a given source-destination pair. Performance metrics are *packet delivery ratio, average end-to-end delay, route discovery frequency* and *cooperation ratio*. (i) The packet delivery ratio is the ratio of the number of data packets successfully delivered to the destination over the number of data packets sent by the source. (ii) The average end-to-end delay is the averaged end-to-end data packet delay including all possible delays caused by buffering during route discovery, queuing delay at the interface, retransmission delays at MAC, propagation and transfer times. (iii) The route discovery frequency indirectly refers to the number of route failures because a source node is supposed to discover a new routing path if an existing one does not work. This happens when any one of the links of a multi-hop path breaks. Link breaks caused by unavoidable due to unreliable communication environment and it can be overcome, which is in fact the main theme of this paper. (iv) Finally, the cooperation ratio refers to how often nodes mutually transmit frames in MD-MAC. Since MD-MAC attempts to use the existing method whenever possible, it is interesting to know how often it succeeds and how often it resorts to mutual communication.

4.3. Simulation Results and Discussion

The simulation results of MD-MAC are shown and discussed in this session. Fig.7 shows the *packet delivery ratio* (PDR) of existing technique and MD-MAC with two environment noise levels of -90 and -83dBm. As shown in the figure, MD-MAC consistently outperforms existing technique but the gap becomes more significant (53~73% increases) when the environment noise is high (-83 dBm). This is because noisy environment makes optical link less reliable and mutual diversity is usefully exploited in MD-MAC in this case. However, the same trend has been consistently observed in other simulation-based studies including R. Deepalakshmi et al., This is due to the complex interplay among MAC and routing layer protocols.

Figure 7.

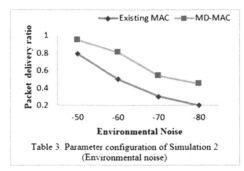

Environmental Noise (dbm)	Packet Delivery Ratio of Existing MAC	Packet Delivery Ratio of MD-MAC
-50	0.79	0.95
-60	0.50	0.81
-70	0.32	0.54
-80	0.21	0.45

Table 3. Parameter configuration of Simulation 2 (Environmental noise)

Less route discoveries in MD-MAC have been observed in comparison to existing technique, it is reduced by 22~50% and 35~69% with the noise level of -90 and -83 dBm, respectively. This clearly tells that the path or link reliability is improved significantly with MD-MAC. MD-MAC eliminates around half of the *false alarms* caused by link breaks due to collisions and thus helps reduce the control overhead for finding new routing paths.

Nodes in MD-MAC cooperate only when a primary link does not work. When the environment noise level is high (-83 dBm), the cooperation happens more frequently to survive the harsh communication environment. It is easy to understand that the cooperation ratio is about 20% (or 40%) when the environment noise is -90 dBm (or -83 dBm). Because still there are number of unreliable links exist in the network for example due to inter-node interference.

To see the impact of noise in more detail, the packet delivery ratio with the different environment noise levels of -90~ -74 dBm is shown in Fig. 7. While the performance decreases sharply in a noisier environment, MD-MAC consistently performs better than existing technique and the gap widens as the noise increases. Network traffic is one of the most important system parameter. Fig. 8 shows the effect of network traffic in terms of the number of sessions and the packet rate. During the simulation, two network traffic factors of 4 sessions and 2 packets per second are applied as default values. It is clear that, the performance is degraded with the increased network traffic. In particular, the performance quickly drops when the traffic increases beyond a certain threshold i.e. 14 sessions and 8 packets/sec in the simulation as shown in Fig. 8(a) and 8(b) respectively. This is because the network overhead is rapidly increased beyond the threshold and becomes congested. However, MD-MAC still outperforms and this effect is more significant in the harsh environment of -83 dBm.

Figure 8.

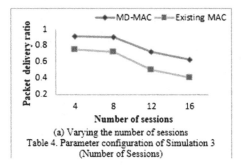

(a) Varying the number of sessions
Table 4. Parameter configuration of Simulation 3
(Number of Sessions)

Number of Sessions	Packet Delivery Ratio of Existing MAC	Packet Delivery Ratio of MD-MAC
4	0.75	0.91
8	0.72	0.90
12	0.50	0.72
16	0.41	0.63

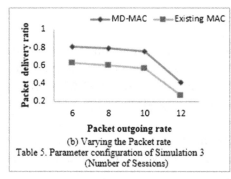

(b) Varying the Packet rate
Table 5. Parameter configuration of Simulation 3
(Number of Sessions)

Packet Outgoing Rate	Packet Delivery Ratio of Existing MAC	Packet Delivery Ratio of MD-MAC
6	0.63	0.81
8	0.60	0.79
10	0.57	0.76
12	0.27	0.41

5. CONCLUSIONS AND FUTURE WORK

This paper proposes a solution through *mutual diversity MAC* (MD-MAC) protocol and discusses design issues and performance benefits in optical networks. When a communication link is unreliable, a sender transmits its signal together with its consort delivering the signal with greater reliability. In order to select a consort, each node sleuths its neighbors with respect to link quality by receiving periodic hello packets and overhearing ongoing communications. The proposed MD-MAC is designed based on the IEEE 802.3 network architecture without requiring any changes in frame formats. According to the system-level simulation results, MD-MAC significantly outperforms the conventional IEEE 802.3 standards, particularly in a harsh environment.

As a future work, exploiting mutual diversity based on multi-channel interfaces will be investigated. Development a mutual diversity-aware routing algorithm is a forthcoming attainment. Cross-layer approach is expected to dramatically boost the network performance because it gives a progression to exploit other advantages of mutual communication such as lengthening the transmission range in addition to improving the link reliability. More efficient consort node selection is yet another important future prospective.

REFERENCES

Abou-Rjeily & Slim. (2011). Cooperative Diversity for Free-Space Optical Communications: Transceiver Design and Performance Analysis. *IEEE Transactions on Communications, 59,* 345–356.

Amin, O., Ikki, S. S., & Uysal, M. (2011). On the Performance Analysis of Multirelay Cooperative Diversity Systems with Channel Estimation Errors. *IEEE Transactions on Vehicular Technology*, *60*(5), 490–501. doi:10.1109/TVT.2011.2121926

Karimi, M., & Nasiri-Kenari, M. (2009). BER Analysis of Cooperative Systems in Free-Space Optical Networks. *Journal of Lightwave Technology*, *27*(24), 5639–5647. doi:10.1109/JLT.2009.2032789

Luo, T., Lin, F., Jiang, T., Guizani, M., & Chen, W. (2011). Multicarrier Modulation And Cooperative Communication In Multihop Cognitive Radio Networks. *IEEE Wireless Communications*, *18*(1), 1536–1284. doi:10.1109/MWC.2011.5714024

Castillo-Vazquez, Garcia-Zambrana, & Castillo-Vazquez. (2009). Closed-form BER expression for FSO links with transmit laser selection over exponential atmospheric turbulence channels. IEEE Electronics Letters. *Transactions on Communications*, *45*, 1098–1110.

Tsiftsis, T., Sandalidis, H., Karagiannidis, G., & Uysal, M. (2009). Optical wireless links with spatial diversity over strong atmospheric turbulence channels. *IEEE Transactions on Wireless Communications*, *8*(2), 951–957. doi:10.1109/TWC.2009.071318

Abou-Rjeily. (2011). On the Optimality of the Selection Transmit Diversity for MIMO-FSO Links with Feedback. *IEEE Communications Letters*, 15.

Liu, Tao, Narayanan, Korakis, & Panwar. (2007). CoopMAC: A Cooperative MAC protocol for Wireless LANs. *IEEE Journal on Selected Areas in Communications, 25*.

Moh, S., Yu, C., Park, S.-M., Kim, H.-N., & Kim, J. (2007). CDMAC: Cooperative Diversity MAC for Robust Communication in Wireless Ad Hoc Networks. *Proc. of IEEE ICC*.

Shahida, T. D., Othman, M., & Khazani, M. (2007). Routing algorithms in optical multistage interconnection networks. *World Engineering Congress*.

Krco, S., & Dupcinov, M. (2003). Improved Neighbor Detection Algorithm for AODV Routing Protocol. *IEEE Communications Letters*, *7*(12), 584–586. doi:10.1109/LCOMM.2003.821317

Navidpour, S., Uysal, M., & Kavehrad, M. (2007). BER performance of freespace optical transmission with spatial diversity. *IEEE Transactions on Wireless Communications*, *6*(8), 2813–2819. doi:10.1109/TWC.2007.06109

Garfield, M., Liang, C., Kurzweg, T. P., & Dandekar, K. R. (2006). MIMO space-time coding for diffuse optical communication. *Microwave and Optical Technology Letters*, *48*(6), 48. doi:10.1002/mop.21558

Li, Y., Cao, B., Wang, C., You, X., Daneshmand, H. Z., & Jiang, T. (2009). Dynamical Cooperative MAC Based on Optimal Selection of Multiple Helpers. *IEEE Global Telecommunications Conference*. 10.1109/GLOCOM.2009.5425531

Liu, Fei, & Zhang. (2009). Classification Research on Power Allocation Schemes in Cooperative Communication System. *Journal of Shandong Institute of Light Industry*.

Zhenzhen, Zhu, & Jing. (2009). Differential SpaceTime-Frequency Transmission for Amplify-and-Forward Asynchronous Cooperative Communications. *Journal of Xi'an Jiaotong University*.

Deepalakshmi & Rajaram. (2011a). New MAC Protocol for Traffic Routing in Optical Networks by exploiting Delays in Dynamic Bandwidth Allocation. *International Conference on Computer Applications & Industrial Electronics*, 307-312. 10.1109/ICCAIE.2011.6162154

Deepalakshmi & Rajaram. (2011b). A Novel Medium Access Control Protocol for Routing Multimedia Traffic in Optical Networks by exploiting Delays with improved Dynamic Bandwidth Allocation. *ARPN Journal of Systems and Software, 1.*

Deepalakshmi & Rajaram (2010a). Multimedia Traffic Routing Algorithm for Optical Networks with Enhanced Performance Characteristics. *International Conference on Internet Multimedia Systems Architecture and Applications.* 10.1109/IMSAA.2010.5729406

Deepalakshmi & Rajaram. (2010b). A Dynamic Cost Optimized Provisioning Algorithm- (DCOPA) for Optical Networks with less Rejection Ratio. *Proceedings of the International Conference on Communication and Computational Intelligence.*

Zhao, L., Zhang, X., & Zhang, X. (2017). Intelligent analysis oriented surveillance video coding. *IEEE International Conference on Multimedia and Expo (ICME),* 37-42. 10.1109/ICME.2017.8019429

Wang, Wang, & Sohraby. (2016). Multimedia sensing as a service (MSaaS): exploring resource saving potentials of at cloud edge IoTs and Fogs. *IEEE Internet of Things Journal, 4,* 487-495.

Othman, H. R., Ali, D. M., Yusof, N. A. M., Noh, K. S. S. K. M., & Idris, A. (2014, August). Performance analysis of VoIP over mobile WiMAX (IEEE 802.16 e) best-effort class. In *Control and System Graduate Research Colloquium (ICSGRC), 2014 IEEE 5th* (pp. 130-135). IEEE.

Chapter 13
Optimal Camera Placement in a Virtual Environment

Hocine Chebi
Université Sidi Bel Abbes, Algeria

ABSTRACT

Camera placement in a virtual environment consists of positioning and orienting a 3D virtual camera so as to respect a set of visual or cinematographic properties defined by the user. Carrying out this task is difficult in practice. Indeed, the user has a clear vision of the result he wants to obtain in terms of the arrangement of the objects in the image. In this chapter, the authors identify three areas of research that are relatively little covered by the literature dedicated to camera placement and which nevertheless appear essential. On the one hand, existing approaches offer little flexibility in both solving and describing a problem in terms of visual properties, especially when it has no solution. They propose a flexible solution method which computes the set of solutions, maximizing the satisfaction of the properties of the problem, whether it is over constrained or not. On the other hand, the existing methods calculate only one solution, even when the problem has several classes of equivalent solutions in terms of satisfaction of properties. They introduce the method of semantic volumes which computes the set of classes of semantically equivalent solutions and proposes a representative of each of them to the user. Finally, the problem of occlusion, although essential in the transmission of information, is little addressed by the community. Consequently, they present a new method of taking into account occlusion in dynamic real-time environments.

INTRODUCTION

However, the classic camera placement process is particularly counterintuitive. The user must perform a mental inversion in order to infer the position and orientation of the camera in the 3D environment leading to the desired result (Kritter 2019; Chebi 2015; Chebi 2018; Chebi 2018b; Chebi 2017;Chebi 2020; Chebi 2017b). Methods of assisting with camera placement therefore appear particularly beneficial for users. In this thesis, we identify three areas of research relatively little covered by the literature dedicated to camera placement and which nevertheless appear essential to us. On the one hand, existing

DOI: 10.4018/978-1-7998-4703-8.ch013

Copyright © 2021, IGI Global. Copying or distributing in print or electronic forms without written permission of IGI Global is prohibited.

approaches offer little flexibility in both solving and describing a problem in terms of visual proper-ties, especially when it has no solution. We propose a flexible solution method that computes the set of solutions, maximizing the satisfaction of the properties of the problem, whether it is over constrained or not. On the other hand, the existing methods calculate only one solution, even when the problem has several classes of equivalent solutions in terms of satisfaction of properties. We introduce the method of semantic volumes which computes the set of classes of semantically equivalent solutions and proposes a representative of each of them to the user. Finally, the problem of occlusion, although essential in the transmission of information, is little addressed by the community. Consequently, we present a new method of taking into account occlusion in dynamic real-time environments.

Visual perception brings together all the optical, chemical and nervous phenomena involved in the human eye's discrimination of shape, size, color, luminosity and their variations over time (AN-GLADA et all, 2004; ALEFELD et all, 1983;AKENINE-MÖLLER et all, 2002;BECKHAUS et all, 2001;CHRISTIE et all, 2005). Jacques Aumont (AUMONT, 1990), University Professor in Cinema and Audiovisual, specifies that the study of visual perception began in the 19th century with the work of Fechner (FECHNER et all, 1860) and von Helmholtz (VON HELMHOLTZ, 1995), then evolved to be today a scientific field studied by psychophysical laboratories. Visual perception helps to understand the physiological phenomena involved in the transformation of the image perceived by the eye into nerve impulses transmitted to the brain.

However, this notion is only the first step in understanding the complex relationship between images and humans, in particular (the power of images to contain and transport us) (VON HELMHOLTZ, 1995). Serge Tisseron, psychiatrist and psychoanalyst, studied the evolution of devices created by humans to produce images, from the use of hands, then pencils, brushes, cameras, cameras, to computers. Accord-ing to him, the desire to create images stems from the fact that Man constitutes the first device capable of creating his own images (psychic images: dreams, imagination, metaphors, mental representations, etc.). This is to be compared with the capacity to produce more and more (real) images, which invite the viewer to no longer stay (in front of) the images, but to (enter) them. The desire to create virtual, interactive worlds in which we can meet other humans through virtual avatars is the culmination of Man's desire to create images. The containing power of image gives way to the transformative power of images.

Unlike psychoanalysts, semiologists tend to restrict the image to the signs it expresses. Semiology (or semiotics) is based on the concept of sign, formed by the relationship between a perceptible ele-ment, the signifier (e.g. an image) and the associated concept: the signified (wikipedia). However, the theory of semiology of images, or visual semiology, shows limits. Indeed, semiology, an instrument thought up by Peirce (PEIRCE, 1978) and Saussure (DE SAUSSURE, 1916), concerns only the internal relations between the signifier of the image and its referent, forgetting the main problem posed by any image concerning the relation that its spectator tied with it (S. Tisseron (TISSERON, 1996)). The im-age should no longer be thought of as a set of signs but as a set of relationships. Indeed, the image first had the value of (sign) for the development of thought in the West, allowing it to rely on images that it was constantly called upon to transcend. Image thus ensured Western civilization mastery of symbolic thought, first theological and religious, then scientific and technical in a form of symbolic representation of the surrounding world, then of imaginary and virtual worlds.

This paper to solve an optimal camera placement problem as MAX-NCSP, we need to instantiate the algorithm presented in this article, as well as the local search framework introduced in order to take into account the specifics related to camera control. We therefore proposed an implementation of the local search framework extended to the intervals presented in the camera placement. For more information on this implementation. We do not detail the algorithms further in this paper and we just specify a camera placement problem in the form of MAX-NCSP, and then solve it.

This article is organized as follows: before presenting our contribution to the problem of camera placement in virtual environments using the MAX-NCSP approach. Our contribution concerning a digital approach for camera placement in a virtual environment is developed in section 2. Then presented the results of our work concerning the management of the occlusion of objects of interest in dynamic real-time environments is described in section. 3. Finally, we end with a conclusion in section 4.

MAX-NCSP APPROACH FOR THE PROBLEM OF CAMERA PLACEMENT IN 3D ENVIRONMENT

In order to solve a problem of camera placement as MAX-NCSP, we must instantiate the algorithms presented below, as well as the local search framework introduced in algorithm 1 in order to take into account the specificities related to camera control. . We therefore proposed an implementation of the local search framework extended to the intervals presented in the previous section. We do not detail in this section the algorithms presented previously and we just specify a camera placement problem in the form of MAX-NCSP, and then solve it.

To do this, first, we present the expression of cinematographic properties used for modeling a camera placement problem as numerical constraints. These expressions allow the resolution of a camera placement problem by our MAX-NCSP algorithm.

Then, we present a set of test sets having appeal to camera control, present the results obtained and analyze them. In conclusion of this paper, we offer avenues of explanation concerning the results as well as avenues for improvements to be made to our approach.

Algorithm 1: Naive internal approximation calculation algorithm for a MAX-NCSP problem by evaluation-bisection.

```
AIBissectionMaxCSP(in: C,B ∈ In; ε ∈ R
out: ResultL: liste < boîtes CPN >)
begin
ResultL ← ∅
L ← {hB,CS(C,B),PS(C,B),NS(C,B)i}
while (non estVide(L))
hB,cs,ps,nsi ← récupèreBoîte(L)
 if (|ps| = 0) then
ResultL ← ResultL ∪ hB,cs,ps,nsi
else
% partially satisfied constraints remain in B
hB',B''i ← bissection(hB,cs,ps,nsi)
 if (plusPetiteDimension(B') > ε) then
 L ← L ∪ hB',CS(C,B'),PS(C,B'),NS(C,B')i
if (plusPetiteDimension(B'') > ε) then
L ← L ∪ hB'',CS(C,B''),PS(C,B''),NS(C,B'')i
end
```

```
endwhile
return meilleuresBoîtes(ResultL)
 end
```

Algorithm 1 uses a box cutting method, as well as an operator to realize the difference between two blocks. The bisection method corresponds to a classic cutting of pavers on each of their dimensions. The algorithm therefore needs precision, allowing it to reject boxes that are too small. The difference operation between two blocks is described after the presentation of algorithm 1.

The principle of the naive MAX-NCSP resolution algorithm by evaluation-bisection is presented in Figure 1. The latter presents a screenshot of the USV software allowing to visualize the obtained result. The studied problem consists of a problem similar to the problem presented in and consists of determining the zones belonging to the intersections of three circles C1, C2, C3 representing three real relations. A color code has been implemented to represent the CPN characterizations of the boxes in the search space. The characteristic of this naive evaluation-bisection algorithm is that it produces regular tiles, resulting from the bisection of the domains of the variables at each iteration.

The problem consists in determining the zones belonging to the intersections of three circles representing three real relations. This problem is a MAX-NCSP since the three circles do not intersect, so the algorithm must determine the maximum areas belonging to the circles. Figure 2 shows a screenshot of the USV software where the three circles C1, C2 and C3 are superimposed. The tiles represent the boxes of the search space and the color code allows visualizing their CPN characterization, that is to say the number of constraints certainly satisfied, possibly satisfied and not satisfied. Note the presence of extended boxes in the area of maximum blocks (red) located at the intersection of circles C1 and C2. We recognize them by their more elongated shape than the boxes resulting from the bisection process.

Figure 1. Application of the inner extension algorithm presented in Table 3.6 to an intersection problem of three circles C1, C2, C3. The method retrieves Configuration is instantiated by a choice of midpoint. The resolution time is 0.87 seconds. The algorithm performed 4261 iterations and a maximal box (i.e. satisfying 2 constraints) was found after 3 iterations. The search domain is {[−3, 3], [−3, 3]} for the variables X and Y involved; the bisection precision is 0.01.

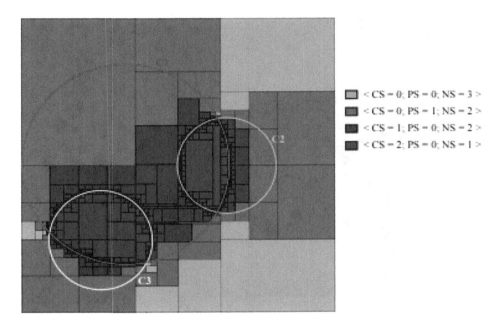

Once we have presented the general algorithm used to solve a MAX-NCSP problem, let's look at its instantiation for solving camera placement problems in virtual environments. The following subsection is devoted to the presentation of the adaptation of cinematographic properties to numerical constraints.

FROM PROPERTIES TO CONSTRAINTS

The formalization of a camera placement problem as a MAX-NCSP requires the translation of the visual properties specified on the desired result on the screen or the properties defined directly on the parameters of the camera into a set of exploitable constraints by the algorithm presented previously. This section is therefore devoted to the presentation of the translation into constraints of a certain number of cinematographic properties. In this next chapter is dedicated to the detailed presentation of a certain number of cinematographic properties, the reader is invited to refer to this section for more details on this type of properties. For each of the constraints specified in the rest of this section, the representations of the camera and of the objects are those presented.

1)   The framing property

Figure 2. Application of the presented inner extension algorithm to an intersection problem of three circles C1, C2, C3. The resolution time is 1.19 seconds. The algorithm performed 5431 iterations and a maximal box (i.e. satisfying 2 constraints) was found after 41 iterations. The search domain is {[−3, 3], [−3, 3]} for the variables X and Y involved; the bisection precision is 0.01.

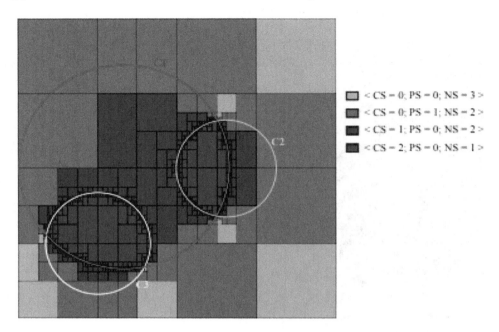

The framing property of an object consists of constraining its projection in a rectangle to the image. The representation of an object consists of an enclosing sphere, that is, a 3D position P and a radius r. The frame C is defined as a rectangle in the image by four components (Xmin, Xmax, Ymin, Ymax).

The framing property is verified if the projection of the bounding sphere of the object of interest is contained in C. Let Pcam (xcam, ycam, zcam) be the transform of P (x, y, z) in the frame of reference of the camera (the calculations for change of coordinate system and projection of a 3D point), the framing constraint is then defined as follows (where γC represents the focal length of the camera):

$$
\begin{cases}
Xmin \le \left(x_{cam} - r \right) / \left(\dfrac{z_{cam}}{\text{ãC}} \right) \\[2em]
Xmax \ge \left(x_{cam} + r \right) / \left(\dfrac{z_{cam}}{\text{ãC}} \right) \\[2em]
Ymin \le \left(y_{cam} - r \right) / \left(\dfrac{z_{cam}}{\text{ãC}} \right) \\[2em]
Ymax \ge \left(y_{cam} + r \right) / \left(\dfrac{z_{cam}}{\text{ãC}} \right)
\end{cases}
\qquad (1)
$$

2) Orientation property

From the representations of the camera and the objects taken into account, the orientation constraint of an object on the screen is based on the dot product between the vision vector of the camera and the orientation vector of the object. The goal is to minimize the gap between the desired orientation of the object and the vector connecting the camera and the object in question. In order not to be too restrictive, we add a parameter to define an angle between the ideal difference between the orientation of the object and the object-camera vector. This parameter α thus represents an interval of values accepted as satisfying the orientation property. Let C (xC, yC, zC) be the position of the camera, O (xO, yO, zO) the position of the object and $\vec{V}(xV, yV, zV)$ .the unit vector representing the orientation of the latter, the constraint c associated with the orientation property is as follows:

$$
\begin{cases}
x_T = x_C - x_O \\
y_T = y_C - y_O \\
z_T = z_C - z_O \\
n_T = \sqrt{x_T{}^2 + y_T{}^2 + z_T{}^2} , c = \left(\vec{T}, \vec{N} \le á\right) \\
\vec{T} = \left(\dfrac{x_T}{n_T}, \dfrac{y_T}{n_T}, \dfrac{z_T}{n_T}\right)
\end{cases}
\tag{2}
$$

The principle is to calculate the unit vector $\vec{T}$. connecting the camera to the object of interest, then to calculate its dot product with the intrinsic orientation of the object. Finally, as we presented above, an angle α allows to add flexibility to the satisfaction of the property.

3) The distance property between the camera and the object

This property allows to constrain the distance between the camera and an object of interest in the 3D scene, ensuring that this distance is greater than a value defined by the user. The associated constraint is specified based on the position of the object of interest O (xO, yO, zO), that of the camera C (xC, yC, zC) and a user-defined distance d:

$$
\sqrt{(x_C - x_O)^2 + \left(y_C - y_O\right)^2 + \left(z_C - z_O\right)^2}
\tag{3}
$$

RESULTS

The results presented in this section are obtained first of all from a problem having appeal to the placement of camera in a virtual environment, then to a problem aiming to discriminate the performances of the different proposed versions of algorithm 1 of problem solving MAXNCSP. We propose two different sets of tests to illustrate the relevance of our approach: the first consists of a typical application of visual composition, while the second consists of a generation of 2D circles of random centers and radii in a search space of size given. The tests are carried out on the following set of algorithms:

- The naive evaluation-bisection algorithm (EvalBissect),
- The improved naive algorithm which studies only promising boxes, that is to say with updating of an optimal value of constraints certainly satisfied (EvalBissectOpt),
- The improved algorithm with evaluation of the current block by generating the central point and updating the current optimum (EvalBissectOptMidPoint),
- The improved algorithm with evaluation by central point and interior extension (which we refer to as EvalBissectOptMidPointInner),
- The improved algorithm with evaluation by central point, interior extension and propagation of constraints possibly satisfied (EvalBissectOptMidPointInnerPropag),
- The improved algorithm with evaluation of the current block by applying a continuous local search procedure (EvalBissectOptLS),
- The improved algorithm with evaluation by continuous local search and interior extension (noted EvalBissectOptLSInner),
- The improved algorithm with evaluation by continuous local search, interior extension and propagation of possibly satisfied constraints (EvalBissectOptLSInnerPropag).

Each algorithm was applied to the test sets for three different precisions (0.5, 0.1 and 0.01) defining the minimum bisection size of the search space boxes. In addition, the algorithms based on local search adapted to the intervals with floating limits are parameterized by three additional variables (maxEssais, maxEtapes and nbVois) representing respectively the number of random restarts of the algorithm, the number of steps for each of these random restarts and the number of neighbors generated at each step. Each of the algorithms using the local search procedure is indexed by the values of these three parameters. For example, the EvalBissectOptLS555 algorithm corresponds to an instantiation of the three parameters to the value 5, i.e. maxEssais = maxEtapes = nbVois = 5. In order to compare the performance of the algorithms, we propose the following evaluation criteria:

- The total execution time of the algorithm (Ttot),
- The maximum number of constraints certainly satisfied (MaxSat),
- The number of iterations performed by the algorithm (#It),
- The iteration in which the first MaxSat box was identified (1 reMaxSat).

1) Test set: visual composition

Visual composition consists of specifying the placement of objects within the resulting image. The user can thus characterize the layout of the resulting image without having to directly manipulate the camera. The example presented here will lead to the construction of two distinct classes of solutions, in order to highlight the specificities of our method. The 3D scene taken into account comprises three distinct objects A, B and C aligned, as illustrated in FIG. 3, which represents a top view of the 3D scene studied. The description of the problem is based on the use of two types of properties:

Figure 3. Top view of the search space associated with the visual composition problem. The blue and green areas correspond to the camera positions that can lead to view objects A and C from the front. The represented search space has a size of [−3, 3] on the two dimensions X and Z.

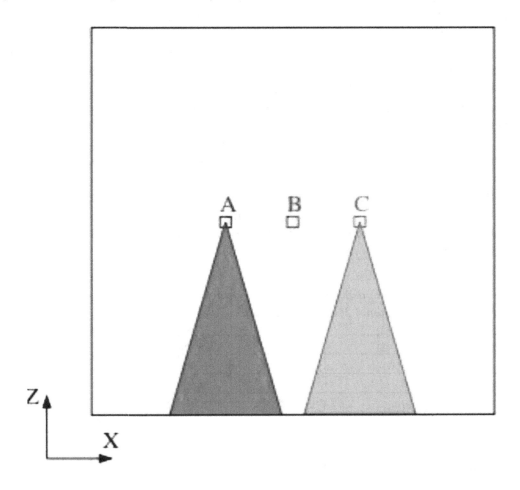

- The framing property: which allows you to specify the membership of an object inside a 2D rectangle in the final image,
- The orientation property: which allows you to specify from which angle of view (face, profile, etc.) an object should be filmed. The problem is composed of five distinct properties defined on the three objects A, B and C:
- Frame object A to the left of the result image, in frame F1,
- Frame object B to the right of the result image, in frame F2,
- Frame object C to the right of the result image, in the same frame as object B (ie F2),
- See object A from the front,
- See object C from the front.

The problem is specified in such a way that it is over-constrained, that is, satisfying all five properties at once is impossible. In fact, a camera cannot both respect the framing of the objects specified in the description and see A and C from the front. It is, however, possible to satisfy four of the five properties, choosing to see either object A or object C frontally. Figure 3.18 illustrates a top view of the search space associated with the visual composition problem. The blue and green zones correspond to the camera positions that can lead to a front view of objects A and C. We can notice that the satisfaction of all the constraints is impossible since the intersection of these two zones is empty. Thus, the number of properties that can be satisfied in this test set is 4. We also see that we can limit the domain of definition of the variable Z of the camera to the values $[-1.5, 0]$ since values greater than 0 would position the camera behind the objects A and C. Tables 1, 2 and 3 present the results obtained for each of the algorithms applied to the visual composition problem for each of the precisions studied. The problem is composed of five properties, involves seven variables whose domains of definition are as follows: $DX = [-3.3]$, $DY = [0,0]$, $DZ = [-1.5,0]$, $D\varphi = [0, 0]$, $D\theta = [-\pi, \pi]$, $D\psi = [-\pi, \pi]$, $D\gamma = [1,1]$.

The results presented in table 1 clearly show the superiority of approaches based on interior extensions coupled with an evaluation of the current block by selecting a central point. Indeed, the EvalBissectMidPointInner and EvalBissectMidPointInnerPropag algorithms find the areas maximizing the set of constraints even for the coarsest precision (0.5). The inner extension procedure and, to a lesser extent, the constraint propagation procedure offer much better results in terms of satisfied constraints but incur an overhead compared to basic algorithms.

Table 1. Results of the visual composition test set with cutting precision of 0.5 (Times expressed in seconds with a Linux system, Pentium 4 2GHz, 1GB RAM).

Algorithm	T_{tot}	MaxSat	#It	1st MaxSat
EvalBissect	0.64	1	255	48
EvalBissectOpt	0.64	1	255	48
EvalBissectOptMidPoint	0.52	1	165	29
EvalBissectMidPointInner	1.47	4	245	11
EvalBissectMidPointInnerPropag	1.9	4	262	11
EvalBissectOptLS$_{555}$	0.65	1	203	50
EvalBissectOptLSInner$_{555}$	9.23	2	264	28
EvalBissectOptLSInnerPropag$_{555}$	8.7	2	201	157
EvalBissectOptLS$_{101010}$	0.65	1	203	50
EvalBissectOptLSInner$_{101010}$	9.13	2	264	28
EvalBissectOptLSInnerPropag$_{101010}$	8.57	2	201	157

The approaches based on local search adapted to the intervals prove to be more efficient in terms of quality of solutions (i.e. in number of constraints satisfied) than the basic algorithms which generally characterize the current block, but the generation procedures point by local search induces a significant additional cost at each iteration. Additionally, we notice that adding constraint propagation does not improve the results since the first maximum iteration is found later. However, this propagation makes it possible to reduce the number of iterations and therefore the total time of the algorithm. We can assume that local search does not provide a satisfactory result, possibly due to inefficient aggregation of cost functions associated with constraints. Remember that the evaluation method chosen for all our test sets consists of a sum of the constraints that are certainly and possibly satisfied. Likewise, the dimension of the neighborhood generated at each local search step depends directly on the size of the boxes studied and therefore on the precision of the problem. The greater the precision, the larger the neighborhood generated for each of the configurations. Thus, for each iteration of the local search procedure, the neighborhood is only very partially explored, which may explain the poor quality of the solutions provided by the local search.

The results obtained with a precision of 0.1 and presented in table 2 show an overall increase in the results of the algorithms. For less precision, we observe that the results obtained by local search-based methods rise to the level of the EvalBissectMidPointInner and EvalBissectMidPointInnerPropag algorithms. These results tend to confirm the hypothesis made previously regarding the direct influence of neighborhood size on local search performance. Note also here that only the approaches based on the interior extension succeed in isolating the MAXSAT zones. Contrary to table 1, the addition of the procedure of propagation of the constraints possibly satisfied involves here an algorithmic overhead due to an increase in the number of boxes to be processed and therefore a degradation of performance. Moreover, even if the local search methods provide satisfactory results in terms of satisfaction of constraints, they remain by far the least efficient in terms of execution time.

Table 2. Results of the visual composition test set with cutting precision of 0.1 (Times expressed in seconds with a Linux system, Pentium 4 2GHz, 1GB RAM).

Algorithm	T_{tot}	MaxSat	#It	1st MaxSat
EvalBissect	8.64	3	4379	277
EvalBissectOpt	8.64	3	4379	277
EvalBissectOptMidPoint	4.37	3	2101	29
EvalBissectMidPointInner	8.1	4	2705	11
EvalBissectMidPointInnerPropag	8.85	4	2696	11
EvalBissectOptLS$_{555}$	4.7	3	2155	377
EvalBissectOptLSInner$_{555}$	23.28	4	2576	81
EvalBissectOptLSInnerPropag$_{555}$	26.21	4	2635	81
EvalBissectOptLS$_{101010}$	5.2	3	2155	377
EvalBissectOptLSInner$_{101010}$	23.32	4	2576	81
EvalBissectOptLSInnerPropag$_{101010}$	27.67	4	2635	81

Table 3 shows the results obtained for a very fine cutting precision of the search space, namely 0.01. Unsurprisingly, the EvalBissectMidPointInner algorithms, based on inner extension, and EvalBissectMidPointInnerPropag (inner extension and constraint propagation) are once again the most efficient. However, for this fineness of bisection, all the algorithms manage to isolate the MAXSAT zones (except the naive evaluation-bisection algorithm). We can notice that the local search algorithms significantly reduce the performance gap in terms of execution time, but that they perform less in terms of solution quality. Indeed, the best solution is obtained later in the algorithm. This is probably explained, once again, by the size of the neighborhood generated with each local search step. Indeed, for a low precision, the studied boxes are of reduced size, so the generated neighborhood remains very close to the current configuration. Thus the search space is only little explored around the current configuration, which is detrimental for the discovery of interesting configurations.

Table 3. Results of the visual composition test set with cutting precision of 0.01 (Times expressed in seconds with a Linux system, Pentium 4 2GHz, 1GB RAM).

Algorithm	T_{tot}	MaxSat	#It	1st MaxSat
EvalBissect	¥	-	-	-
EvalBissectOpt	687.23	4	374019	3364
EvalBissectOptMidPoint	639.13	4	372665	29
EvalBissectMidPointInner	455.03	4	254425	11
EvalBissectMidPointInnerPropag	474.81	4	253660	11
EvalBissectOptLS$_{555}$	716.72	4	372719	377
EvalBissectOptLSInner$_{555}$	492.5	4	259515	97
EvalBissectOptLSInnerPropag$_{555}$	534.72	4	260572	97
EvalBissectOptLS$_{101010}$	682.39	4	372719	377
EvalBissectOptLSInner$_{101010}$	494.99	4	259515	97
EvalBissectOptLSInnerPropag$_{101010}$	548.12	4	260572	97

Together, these three results allow us to observe the relevance of the inner extension approach for solving MAX-NCSP problems. Indeed, for the three precisions studied, the algorithms implementing the internal extension procedure (Inner) are the most efficient. The advantage of a local search procedure at each iteration of the algorithm in order to evaluate the current tiles should be qualified. This is because algorithms based on local search procedures are significantly less efficient in terms of execution time than box evaluation methods by generating a central point. The performance gap is reduced for low precision; however these methods are generally less attractive. Finally, the addition of a constraint propagation procedure possibly satisfied, in addition to the interior extension procedure, does not prove to be convincing for this example. One possible explanation for this observation lies in the very limited number of properties (5) making up the problem of visual composition.

CONCLUSION

We have proposed in this paper a generic algorithm for solving numerical equation satisfaction maximization problems. Our MAX-NCSP approach can equally well solve over-constrained, under-constrained or well-constrained problems composed of numerical inequalities. Indeed, our method consists in calculating the cobblestones inside the constraint store maximizing the number of satisfied constraints and providing the list of satisfied constraints to the user in the case of solving an over-constrained problem. We also ensure the completeness property by characterizing all the boxes of the initial search space with respect to a triplet of values hcs, ps, nsi representing respectively the sets of certainly satisfied, possibly satisfied, and unsatisfied constraints of the constraint store. This CPN characterization of all tiles in the search space quickly eliminates uninteresting boxes during the resolution process. Indeed, by keeping throughout the resolution a value m representing the current optimum of the number of constraints certainly satisfied, we can devote ourselves to the study of the blocks which can lead to an improvement of the value m, that is - ie when the sets C and P of the studied box contain more constraints than the current optimum, ie: $| C | + | P |^3$ m. The basic algorithm consists of three successively woven steps:

- The search for an internal starting point (ie solution to a subset of the inequalities of the constraint system).
- An interior extension step to maximize the area of the search space located in the vicinity of the starting point obtained in the previous step.
- A stress propagation step applied to the interior extension obtained previously. The propagation concerns only the set of Possibly satisfied constraints, in order to restrict the search space to potentially interesting areas for the next step of the algorithm. Indeed, taking into account only the possibly satisfied constraints makes it possible to favor the characterization of the constraints of the problem between Certainly and N we satisfy, thus the algorithm converges more quickly.

REFERENCES

Akenine-Möller, T., & Haines, E. (2002). Real-Time Rendering (2nd ed.). A. K. Peters, Ltd.

Alefeld, G., & Herzberger, J. (1983). Introduction to Interval Computations. Academic Press Inc.

Anglada, A., Codognet, P., & Zimmer, L. (2004). An adaptive search for the NSCSPs. *Proceedings of the 8th ERCIM/CoLogNet workshop on Constraint Solving and Constraint Logic Programming (CSCLP 2004)*.

Aumont, J. (1990). *L'image* (2nd ed.). Nathan.

Beckhaus, S., Ritter, F., & Strothotte, T. (2001). Guided exploration with dynamic potential fields: The cubicalpath system. *Computer Graphics Forum*, 20(4), 201–210. doi:10.1111/1467-8659.00549

Chebi, H., & Acheli, D. (2015, December). Dynamic detection of anomalies in crowd's behavior analysis. In *2015 4th International Conference on Electrical Engineering (ICEE)* (pp. 1-5). IEEE. 10.1109/INTEE.2015.7416735

Chebi, H., Acheli, D., & Kesraoui, M. (2017, April). Strategy of detecting abnormal behaviors by fuzzy logic. In *2017 Intelligent Systems and Computer Vision (ISCV)* (pp. 1-5). IEEE.

Chebi, H., Acheli, D., & Kesraoui, M. (2017, October). Intelligent Detection Without Modeling of Behavior Unusual by Fuzzy Logic. In *International Conference on Model and Data Engineering* (pp. 300-307). Springer. 10.1007/978-3-319-66854-3_23

Chebi, H., Acheli, D., & Kesraoui, M. (2018). Automatic shadow elimination in a high-density scene. *International Journal of Intelligent Systems Design and Computing*, 2(3-4), 224–237. doi:10.1504/IJISDC.2018.097468

Chebi, H., Acheli, D., & Kesraoui, M. (2018). Crowd events recognition in a video without threshold value setting. *International Journal of Applied Pattern Recognition, 5*(2), 101–118. doi:10.1504/IJAPR.2018.092518

Chebi, H., Tabet-Derraz, H., Sayah, R., Meroufel, A., Acheli, D., Benaissa, A., & Meraihi, Y. (2020). Intelligence and Adaptive Global Algorithm Detection of Crowd Behavior. *International Journal of Computer Vision and Image Processing, 10*(1), 24–41. doi:10.4018/IJCVIP.2020010102

Christie, M., & Normand, J.-M. (2005). A semantic space partitioning approach to virtual camera composition. *Computer Graphics Forum, Eurographics 2005 Conference Proceedings, 24*(3), 247–256.

De Saussure, F. (1916). *Cours de linguistique générale*. Bayot.

Fechner, G. T. (1860). *Elemente der Psychophysik*. Breitkof und Hartel. https://fr.wikipedia.org/wiki/Sémiotique

Kritter, J., Brévilliers, M., Lepagnot, J., & Idoumghar, L. (2019). On the optimal placement of cameras for surveillance and the underlying set cover problem. *Applied Soft Computing, 74*, 133–153. doi:10.1016/j.asoc.2018.10.025

Peirce, C. S. (1978). *Écrits sur le signe*. Seuil.

Tisseron, S. (1995). *Psychanalyse de l'image – Des premiers traits au virtuel* (2nd ed.). Dunod.

Tisseron, S. (1996). *Le bonheur dans l'image*. Les empêcheurs de penser en rond.

Von Helmholtz, H. (1867). Handbuch der physiologischen Optik. Academic Press.

Chapter 14
Scalable Data Analysis Application to Web Usage Data

Hocine Chebi

Faculty of Electrical Engineering, Djillali Liabes University, Sidi Bel Abbes. Algeria

ABSTRACT

The number of hits to web pages continues to grow. The web has become one of the most popular platforms for disseminating and retrieving information. Consequently, many website operators are encouraged to analyze the use of their sites in order to improve their response to the expectations of internet users. However, the way a website is visited can change depending on a variety of factors. Usage models must therefore be continuously updated in order to accurately reflect visitor behavior. This remains difficult when the time dimension is neglected or simply introduced as an additional numeric attribute in the description of the data. Data mining is defined as the application of data analysis and discovery algorithms on large databases with the goal of discovering non-trivial models. Several algorithms have been proposed in order to formalize the new models discovered, to build more efficient models, to process new types of data, and to measure the differences between the data sets. However, the most traditional algorithms of data mining assume that the models are static and do not take into account the possible evolution of these models over time. These considerations have motivated significant efforts in the analysis of temporal data as well as the adaptation of static data mining methods to data that evolves over time. The review of the main aspects of data mining dealt with in this thesis constitutes the body of this chapter, followed by a state of the art of current work in this field as well as a discussion of the major issues that exist there. Interest in temporal databases has increased considerably in recent years, for example in the fields of finance, telecommunications, surveillance, etc. A growing number of prototypes and systems are being implemented to take into account the time dimension of data explicitly, for example to study the variability over time of analysis results. To model an application, it is necessary to choose a common language, precise and known by all members of a team. UML (unified modeling language, in English, or unified modeling language, in French) is an object-oriented modeling language standardized by the OMG. This chapter aims to present the modeling with the diagrams of packages and classes built using UML. This chapter presents the conceptual model of the data, and finally, the authors specify the SQL queries used for the extraction of descriptive statistical variables of the navigations from a warehouse containing the preprocessed usage data.

DOI: 10.4018/978-1-7998-4703-8.ch014

Copyright © 2021, IGI Global. Copying or distributing in print or electronic forms without written permission of IGI Global is prohibited.

INTRODUCTION

Access profiles to a website can be influenced by certain parameters of a temporal nature, such as for example: the time and day of the week, seasonal events, external events in the world (wars, economic crises), etc. In this context, most of the methods devoted to Web Usage Mining (Cooley et al., 1999) take into account in their analysis the entire period that records traces of use: The results obtained are therefore naturally those which predominate over the entire period. Thus, certain types of behavior, which take place during short sub-periods are not taken into account, and therefore remain ignored by conventional methods. It is, however, important to study these behaviors and therefore to carry out an analysis covering significant sub-periods. As the volume of data considered is very high, it is also important to use summaries to represent the profiles considered.

To overcome the problem of acquiring real usage data, we propose a methodology for the automatic generation of artificial data allowing the simulation of changes. Guided by the avenues arising from exploratory analyzes, we propose a new approach based on non-overlapping windows for the detection and monitoring of changes on evolving data. This approach characterizes the type of change undergone by the behavior groups (appearance, disappearance, merger, split) and applies two validation indices based on the extension of the classification to measure the level of changes identified at each time step. Our approach is completely independent of the classification method and can be applied to different types of data other than usage data. Experiments on artificial data as well as on real data from different fields (academic, tourism and marketing) were carried out to assess the effectiveness of the proposed approach.

Relatively recently, usage analysis began to take into account the time dependence of behavior patterns. In (Roddick and Spiliopoulou, 2002), the authors review previous work. They summarize the proposed solutions and the outstanding problems in the exploitation of temporal data, through a discussion on temporal rules and their semantics, but also by the investigation of the convergence between data mining and temporal semantics. . Most recently, in (Laxman and Sastry, 2006) the authors discuss in a few lines methods to discover sequential patterns, frequent patterns and partial periodic patterns in data streams.

When it comes to big and dynamic data sources, the web has become the most relevant example with the colossal increase in the number of documents uploaded and new information added every day. From the perspective of attracting new customers and meeting the expectations of existing customers, a knowledgeable website manager should always keep in mind that offering more information is not always a good solution. In fact, users of a website will appreciate more the way this information is presented within the site. The analysis of usage traces (recorded in log type files by the server that hosts the website) is proving to be an increasingly necessary practice to better understand the practices of Internet users. In this context, the time dimension plays a very important role because the underlying distribution of usage data can change over time. This change can be caused by updating the content and / or structure of the website or by the natural change in interest of users of a website.

The change in individual behavior has also caught the attention of professionals in the humanities. Indeed, we are currently in the decade of behavior (2000-2010) established by the American Psychological Association (APA) and whose goal is to promote meetings for raising awareness on the importance of research in the field of science social and behavioral. Website access patterns are dynamic in nature and can be influenced by certain temporal factors, for example: the time and day of the week a website visit takes place, seasonal events (summer, winter, Christmas holidays), one-off events around the world (economic crises, sports competitions, epidemics, etc.). It is therefore necessary to take the temporal dimension into account for the analysis of this type of data.

In recent years, all these considerations have motivated significant efforts in the analysis of Internet user traces as well as the adaptation of classification methods to data on the Web. However, most of the methods devoted to the analysis of usage data take into account the entire period that records the usage traces. Consequently, the behavioral models emerging by these methods are those which predominate over the entire period of time analyzed. Minority behaviors that can occur for short periods of time thus remain unnoticed by conventional methods. In the context of the Web, when a webmaster queries the logs of his site, he wants the results proposed in response to his query to be faithful to the period of time analyzed and not to the general behavior observed throughout the entire period analyzed. In addition, if an analysis of the behavior of Internet users does not follow up on these behaviors over time, it would be impossible for the webmaster to identify the period of time when the possible change (s) of behavior. of use have taken place. To deal with this problem, a possible solution would be to define a strategy capable of providing the necessary means so that those responsible for a website can be notified when the appearance, disappearance or change of behavior profiles of their users. It would also be possible for the site administrator to be able to measure the impact of a new online strategy as well as the popularity of the pages using the analysis of traces left by Internet users during visits.

This article proposes to follow the change of behavior using the summaries obtained by an evolutionary approach of the classification applied over sub-periods of time. The article is organized as follows: the next section presents the usage analysis approach based on time sub-periods. We also present in this section the experiments carried out, analyzing the results and comparing them with those of the classical methods. The final section presents the conclusions and the future work envisaged.

TEMPORAL DATA MINING

Interest in temporal databases has increased considerably in recent years, for example in the fields of finance, telecommunications, surveillance, etc. A growing number of prototypes and systems are being implemented to take into account the time dimension of data explicitly, for example to study the variability over time of analysis results.

Temporal Data Mining (TDM) [62] is an important extension of classical data mining because it focuses more on the analysis of activities than of states. As a result, it makes it possible to search for cause and effect associations by jointly exploiting contextual and temporal proximities. It is about exploiting the fact that causes precede effects, which is difficult when the time dimension is neglected or simply introduced as an additional numerical attribute in the description of the data.

In addition, temporal data mining is directly linked to data mining on large sequential files. By sequential data is meant data that is ordered according to the sequence index. Temporal data is a special case of sequential data in which time plays the role of indexing. Other examples of sequential data are gene (DNA) sequences and movement sequences in a game of chess. Here, although there is no notion of time as such, the order of observations is very important and even essential for the description and analysis of such data.

Historically, the problem of time series forecasting has been one of the most studied [19] in meteorology, finance, and the stock market. The main difference between time data mining and time series analysis concerns the nature of the information you want to estimate or highlight. The framework of time data mining extends beyond standard forecasting applications or control applications for time series analysis. In the analysis of time series forecasting plays a central role, while in time data mining it is rather the evolution that we try to model.

In [83], the authors summarize the proposed solutions and the outstanding problems in the exploitation of temporal data, through a discussion on the temporal rules and their semantics, but also by the investigation of the convergence between the excavation data and temporal semantics.

Figure 1. Classic diagram of web data mining.

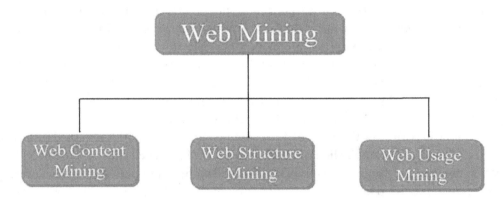

CLASSIFICATION APPROACHES FOR DETECTING CHANGES

The DEMON system (Ganti et al., 2000) advocates the distinction between systematic and non-systematic changes in data. The system searches the time dimension for data blocks that must be processed in order to extract new patterns. The incremental classification algorithm used comes from DBSCAN (Density-Based Spatial Clustering of Applications with Noise) (Ester et al., 1996). The system examines which parts of the current clusters are affected by a database update over a time window and adjusts the groups accordingly. The main goal is to update a knowledge base by integrating the identified changes.

The FOCUS system (Yang et al., 2005) compares two datasets using a measure of deviation based on the data-induced patterns. For comparison, the authors assume that a model is formed by a structure component and a measurement component. For example, the structure component of a decision tree is a representation of its nodes, while the measurement component captures the distribution of classes in each node. To compare two patterns, they are broken down and interesting regions are identified. These are regions where two patterns are at odds in the distribution of classes. The subset of data belonging to each region is then summarized by the measurement component. Clusters are considered as non-overlapping regions described by a set of attributes (structure component) and corresponding to a set of data (measurement component). In this system, the emphasis is on comparing sets of data.

The PANDA system (PAtterns for Next-generation DAtabase systems) (Bartolini et al. 2004) provides methods based on aggregation logic for the comparison of simple patterns, defined on raw data, for example a cluster, and complex patterns, defined on other models, for example a score. The distance between two complex patterns is calculated in an ascending way based on the distances between the simple patterns that compose them. In the PANDA system, emphasis is given to the generic and efficient comparison between any complex patterns.

The MONIC (Modeling and Monitoring Cluster) system (Spiliopoulou et al, 2006) is inspired by the PANDA and PAM systems. In this system, an age function is applied for weighting the data over time. The MONIC system assumes a cumulative database to which a clustering method is reapplied when new data arrives, which demands a lot of physical resources when the database assumes large dimensions. In this system, no reduction strategy or data summary is applied.

The authors of (Neill et al, 2005) studied the stability of clusters from the observation of spatial regions. In their approach, no clustering method is applied, a cluster then corresponds to the negation of the homogeneity hypothesis. The cluster detection procedure consists of identifying spatial regions which present, for a certain property, values greater than expected. The set of regions is static and known in advance. Predicted values are calculated from time series analysis of past values. A window of sliding time is adopted for the detection of emerging, persistent and evolving clusters.

The authors of (Yang et al., 2005) proposed a method for the detection of changes on clusters generated from scientific data. They studied the Spatial Object Association Patterns (SOAP). SOAP is characterized by the number of 'snapshots' of the data, where it occurs and the number of instances in a snapshot. With this information, the algorithm detects cluster formation, dissipation and continuation events. Their method is not necessarily devoted to the analysis of clusters, it relates rather to patterns in general.

For (Aggarwal et al., 2005), a cluster corresponds to the densification of data in a multidimensional space, where each dimension corresponds to an attribute. Intuitive examples for this type of cluster definition are easily found in Geographic Information Systems (GIS). For example, a city can be seen as an area where the concentration of houses is more dense than in its surroundings. The evolution of the city (for example, its growth or shrinkage) can be modeled as a change in density. The author matches clusters with kernel functions and calculates changes in density of the nucleus at each spatial point. Density changes at neighboring spatial points are aggregated, so that sectors that change at different speeds can be detected from their neighborhoods.

For each point at time t, the future density corresponds to the change in density of the nucleus after time t, while the past density corresponds to the change in density of the nucleus before time t. The difference between these two calculated densities constitutes the rate of change (Aggarwal et al., 2005). The author distinguishes between different types of change and the emphasis is on (i) the speed of change and (ii) the points with the highest speed - the epicenters. A particular feature of his method is the identification of the properties of the data that contribute the most to the changes.

All the approaches in this category operate on a trajectory and assume that this does not change. Therefore, these methods cannot be combined with all types of clustering algorithms, for example hierarchical algorithms or density-based algorithms. Hierarchical clustering algorithms employ ultrametric, so their clusters cannot be studied outside the metric space that produced them. In addition, these methods juxtapose each cluster to the trajectory and cannot trace interferences among clusters, for example the absorption (merger) of one cluster by another.

CLASSIFICATION APPROACH BY SUB-PERIODS OF TIME

The characterization of user groups consists of identifying usage traits shared by a sufficient number of website users and thus providing clues allowing inference of the profile of each group (Da Silva et al., 2006a, b). The approach proposed in this article consists first of all in dividing the period analyzed into more significant sub-periods (month of the year). Then, a classification is made on the data for each sub-period, as well as on the entire period. The results provided are therefore compared with each other.

In this context, we have made four classifications as follows:

- Global classification: this classification is obtained on all the individuals;
- Independent local classification: for each a priori time zone, a classification is made of all the navigations concerned. As each zone is distinct, each classification is therefore independent of the others;
- Previous: local classification: here, the classificatory structure of the previous time period is used to obtain a partition of the current period;
- Local dependent classification: here, we initialize the algorithm for a period of time with the results of this algorithm applied over the previous period.

The conceptual data model (CDM) aims to formally describe the data that will be used by the information system. It is thus an easily understandable representation of the data, making it possible to define the dependencies or relationships between these different data. Figure 3 shows the diagram of the data warehouse produced by our scalable data classification approach. This diagram contains a total of 12 tables, detailed in the following paragraphs.

The tb_stat_navigation table records the descriptive variables of the navigations. The filling of this table is done automatically. The SQL queries used to do this are presented in the section of this chapter.

The tb_couting table stores the data of the analyzed contingency table. In this table, fields of the type ci specify the page themes analyzed. In this example, the pages are distributed among 5 themes. If necessary, more fields can be added to this table in order to process clicks on new page themes.

In the two tables cited above, the individuals are recorded in chronological order. The navigation_id field assumes positive integer values and represents the order in which individuals appear in the table in question. The IDNavigation field represents the original navigation identifier assigned during the preprocessing process. The value of these two fields may be different depending on the application of navigation selection filters (for example, minimum number of clicks, minimum duration, etc.).

The tb_experiment table stores the parameters to be used during the experiments. The fields in this table are described in Table 1. It is important to note that a single table of data (either described by statistical variables or by the count of clicks on page themes) can be subject to several experiments. Therefore, it is possible to apply our classification approach to the same data set while keeping the target data table (table field of the tb_experiment table) and varying the parameters of experiments (for example the type of windowing, the size of the data window, etc.). Once the data table has been chosen and the parameters of the experiment defined, our classification approach can be applied.

ALGORITHM AND EVALUATION CRITERIA

For the classification of navigations, we use a dynamic cloud type algorithm (see Celeux et al. (1989)) applicable on a data table (see table 1). In particular, the algorithm must: (1) be able to assign new observations to an existing classification, and (2) be able to initialize the algorithm with the results of another realization of itself. For all classification procedures, we requested 10 classes with a number of random initializations equal to 100, except in the case of the local dependent classification.

Figure 2. Diagram of classes contained in the application package.

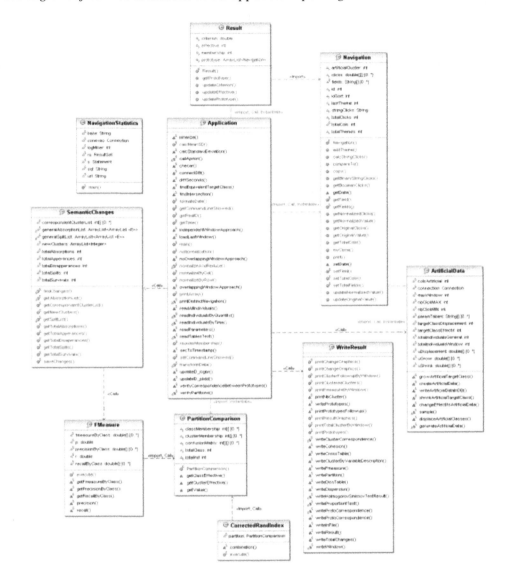

To analyze the results, we use two criteria. For a class-by-class analysis, we consider van Rijsbergen's F-measure (1979). For a more global analysis, we use the corrected Rand index (see Hubert and Arabia (1985)). For the two indices, the value 0 corresponds to a total absence of link between the partitions considered, while the value 1 indicates a perfect link.

While browsing a website, the user may face error messages on the requested page (when the page was not found), redirect (when the requested page has been physically moved), d 'error on the web server (when the server in question is busy or down), etc. The return code of a request is identified in the web log files by the status field. Request return codes assume values standardized by the W3C. A request is said to be successful when its return code is equal to 200. In all other cases, the request is considered failed. In order to discriminate the number of successful and failed requests during a navigation, we respectively use the variables NbRequests_OK and NbRequests_Bad. The NbRequests variable represents the total number of clicks made during navigation, all statuses combined.

Figure 3. Schematic of the data warehouse produced by our scalable data classification approach.

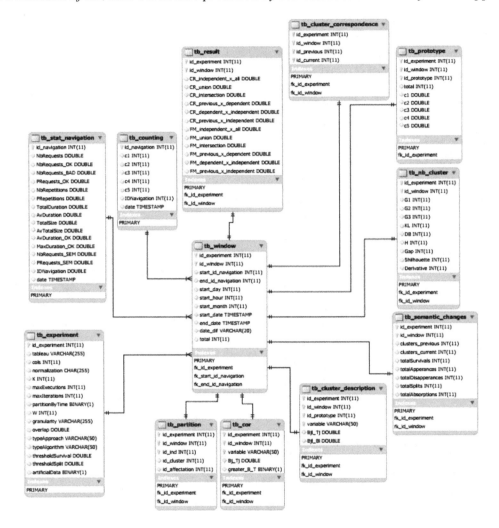

While browsing, a user can, for any reason, return to a page already visited. The pages revisited during a navigation are often those which attract the most attention of the Internet user. The NbRepetitions and PRepetitions variables respectively contain the number and percentage of pages revisited in a navigation.

The Total DureeT variable represents the time (in seconds) spent by the Internet user visiting the website in question. The MDuree variable represents the average time spent on the pages visited during navigation. The MDuree_OK variable keeps the average visit time among the successful requests.

Table 1. Descriptive attributes of navigation.

N°	Field	Meaning
1	IDNavigation	Code of navigation
2	NbRequests_OK	Number of successful requests (status = 200) in navigation
3	NbRequests_bad	Number of failed requests (status < > 200) in the navigation
4	PRequests_OK	Percentage of successful requests (= NbRequests_OK / NbRequests)
5	NbRepetitions	Percentage of repeated requests in the navigation
6	PRepetitions	Percentage of repetitions (= NbRepetitions / NbRequests)
7	Total Duration	Total navigation time (in seconds)
8	MDuree	Average duration of requests (= TotalDuration / NbRequests)
9	MDuree_OK	Average duration of successful requests (= DureeTotale_OK / NbRequests_OK)
10	NbRequests_Sem	Number of requests reported to dynamic pages which form the semantic structure of the site
11	PRequests_Sem	Percentage of semantic requests (= NbRequests_Sem / NbRequests) in the navigation
12	TotalSize	Sum of bytes transferred in the navigation
13	MSize	Average bytes transferred (= TotalSize / NbRequests_OK)
14	DureeMax_OK	Maximum duration among successful requests

If the main pages of the site in question are organized under a pre-established semantic structure, variables 10 and 11 are provided to discriminate clicks on the pages of this structure. The NbRequests_Sem variable counts the number of clicks made by the Internet user on the pages present in the semantic structure. The PRequests_Sem variable represents the percentage of clicks devoted to the pages of the semantic structure among all the clicks made during navigation.

The TotalSize variable counts the number of bytes transmitted by the Web server to the Internet user's machine during their entire navigation. The MSize variable represents the average of these values. The DureeMax_OK variable continues the maximum time (in seconds) spent by the user for viewing a page.

The variables presented in this section are intended to describe the navigation of Internet users of any website using data extracted from the log files of the web server that hosts the site in question. They can thus contribute to a more detailed analysis of the browsing habits presented by the audience of the website auditioned.

APPLICATION AND RESULTS

The usage data for a website comes mainly from the log files of the affected servers. Various preprocessing techniques can be used to extract navigations from these files, for example those of Tanasa and Trousse (2004), used in this article. Navigation is a series of requests from the same user and separated by no more than 30 minutes.

We use as a reference site that of the Computer Center of Recife-Brazil. This site is made up of a set of static pages and dynamic pages, the latter being managed by servlets programmed in Java (see Rossi

Figure 4. Local classifications: independent (left) and dependent (right).

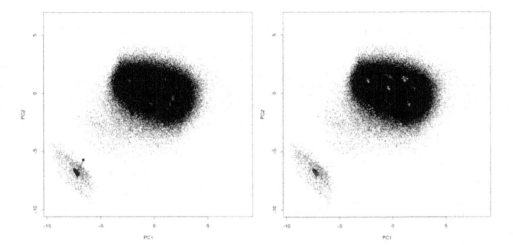

et al. (2006a, b) for an analysis of this part of the site). We studied the accesses to the site from July 1, 2002 to May 31, 2003. After filtering and eliminating outliers, we obtained a total of 138,536 navigations.

We carried out a follow-up of the prototypes of the classes (month by month) for the local independent and dependent classifications, then we projected these prototypes in the factorial plane (see figure 4). In this representation, each circle represents a prototype. In the dependent classification, the ten classes are represented by different colors. There is some stability despite the diversity of months analyzed. In the case of independent classification, the temporal trajectory is simply materialized by the lines which join a prototype to its nearest neighbor in the previous time period. This does not give perfectly identified trajectories because some prototypes share the same predecessor at one point. We note in fact that only four classes are perfectly identified and stable, the others undergoing mergers and separations over time. By analyzing the intra-class variance, we can see that the classes obtained by the independent local classification present more cohesion within the meaning of this criterion (see Figure 5).

From the values of the corrected Rand index (see figure 6), in the case of an independent versus global comparison of classifications there are almost systematically low values, i.e. some classes of the independent classification are not found in the global classification. We also see that the "previous" classification does not give results very different from those obtained by the dependent classification, which confirms the intuition acquired by the observation of the prototypes in the factorial plane: the latter move "little" during the course. time.

These differences are confirmed by the F-measurement (see figure 7). What emerges clearly is that the classes are very stable over time when using the dependent classification method. In fact, no index goes below 0.877, which is a very good value. On the other hand, in the case of the independent classification, one obtains on the contrary very different classes from those obtained overall (with values lower than 0.5).

Figure 5. Within-class variance of classifications: independent (black line), dependent (red line) and global (blue line).

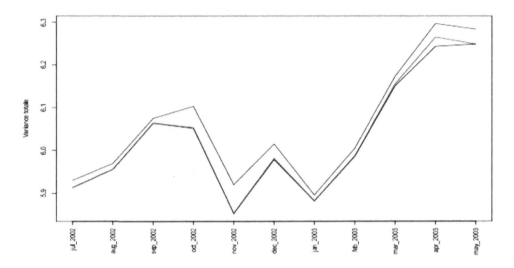

Figure 6. Rand index corrected class by class.

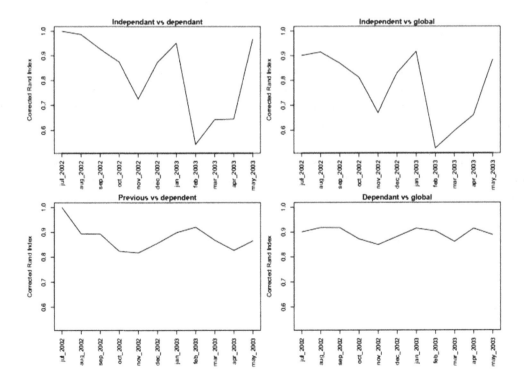

CONCLUSIONS AND FUTURE PERSPECTIVES

Figure 7. Boxplots corresponding to F-measures class by class.

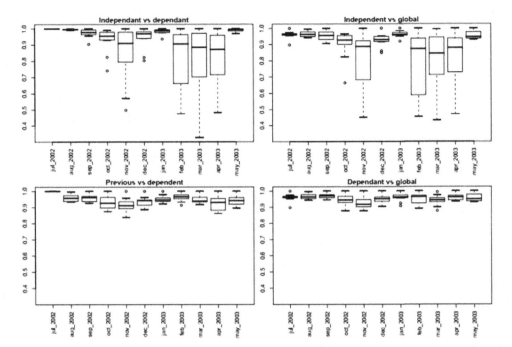

In this article, we have addressed the issue of dynamic data processing in the context of web usage analysis. Through our experiments, we can say that the local dependent classification method shows that the classifications obtained do not change or change little over time, while the independent local classification method is more sensitive to changes that can occur without a sub-period to another. In a secondary plan, the independent local classification approach also makes it possible to overcome the difficulties linked to the limits of the machines (such as the size of the memory, the speed of the processor, etc.) because we focus the analysis on a part of available data. As a possibility for future work we can point out the application of other classification methods and the implementation of techniques allowing automatic discovery of the number of classes, as well as the introduction of the process of merging or splitting of classes.

REFERENCES

Celeux, G., Diday, E., Govaert, G., Lechevallier, Y., & Ralambondrainy, H. (1989). *Classification Automatique des Données*. Bordas.

Cooley, R., Mobasher, B., & Srivastava, J. (1999). Data preparation for mining world wide web browsing patterns. *Journal of Knowledge and Information Systems*, *1*(1), 5–32. doi:10.1007/BF03325089

Da Silva, A., Carvalho, F. D., Lechevallier, Y., & Trousse, B. (2006a). Mining web usage data for discovering navigation clusters. *ISCC*, *2006*, 910–915. doi:10.1109/ISCC.2006.102

Da Silva, A., De Carvalho, F., Lechevallier, Y., & Trousse, B. (2006b). Characterizing visitor groups from web data streams. *GrC*, *2006*, 389–392. doi:10.1109/GRC.2006.1635822

Hubert, L., & Arabie, P. (1985). Comparing partitions. *Journal of Classification*, *2*(1), 193–218. doi:10.1007/BF01908075

Laxman, S., & Sastry, P. S. (2006). A survey of temporal data mining. SADHANA - Academy Proceedings in Engineering Sciences. *Indian Academy of Sciences*, *31*(2), 173–198.

Roddick, J. F., & Spiliopoulou, M. (2002). A survey of temporal knowledge discovery paradigms and methods. *IEEE Transactions on KDE*, *14*(4), 750–767. doi:10.1109/TKDE.2002.1019212

Rossi, F., De Carvalho, F., Lechevallier, Y., & Da Silva, A. (2006a). Comparaison de dissimilarités pour l'analyse de l'usage d'un site web. EGC 2006. *RNTI-E*, *6*(II), 409–414.

Rossi, F., De Carvalho, F., Lechevallier, Y., & Da Silva, A. (2006b). Dissimilarities for web usage mining. *IFCS*, *2006*, 39–46.

Tanasa, D., & Trousse, B. (2004). Advanced data preprocessing for intersites web usage mining. *IEEE Intelligent Systems*, *19*(2), 59–65. doi:10.1109/MIS.2004.1274912

van Rijsbergen, C. J. (1979). *Information Retrieval* (2nd ed.). Butterworths.

Aggarwal, C. C. (2005). *On change diagnosis in evolving data streams*. IEEE Transactions on. doi:10.1109/TKDE.2005.78

Aggarwal, C. C. (2005). On change diagnosis in evolving data streams. *Knowledge and Data Engineering*, *17*(5), 587–600. doi:10.1109/TKDE.2005.78

Bartolini, I., Ciaccia, P., Ntoutsi, I., Patella, M., & Theodoridis, Y. (2004). A unified and flexible framework for comparing simple and complex patterns. *PKDD '04: Proceedings of the 8th European Conference on Principles and Practice of Knowledge Discovery in Databases*.

Ester, M. Kriegel, H.P. Sander, J., & Xu, X. (1996). A density-based algorithm for discovering clusters in large spatial databases with noise. *2nd International Conference on Knowledge Discovery and Data Mining (KDD-96)*.

Ganti, V., Gehrke, J., & Ramakrishnan, R. (2000). Demon: Mining and monitoring evolving data. *IEEE Transactions on Knowledge and Data Engineering*, *2000*, 439–448.

Ganti, V., Gehrke, J., Ramakrishnan, R., & Loh, W.Y. (1999). A framework for measuring changes in data characteristics. In *PODS*. ACM Press.

Neill, D., Moore, B. A. W., Sabhnani, M., & Daniel, K. (2005). Detection of emerging space-time clusters. *Proceedings of the Eleventh ACM SIGKDD International Conference on Knowledge Discovery and Data Mining*, 218–227. 10.1145/1081870.1081897

Spiliopoulou, M., Ntoutsi, I., Theodoridis, Y., & Schult, R. (2006). Monic: modeling and monitoring cluster transitions. *Proceedings of the Twelfth ACM SIGKDD International Conference on Knowledge Discovery and Data Mining*.

Yang, H., Parthasarathy, S., & Mehta, S. (2005). A generalized framework for mining spatiotemporal patterns in scientific data. *KDD '05: Proceedings of the eleventh ACM SIGKDD international conference on Knowledge discovery in data mining*, 716–721. 10.1145/1081870.1081962

Chapter 15
Current Trends, Challenges, and Future Prospects for Augmented Reality and Virtual Reality

Sathiya Narayanan
School of Electronics Engineering, Vellore Institute of Technology, Chennai, India

Nikshith Narayan Ramesh
School of Electronics Engineering, Vellore Institute of Technology, Chennai, India

Amit Kumar Tyagi
Research Division of Advanced Data Science, Vellore Institute of Technology, Chennai, India

L. Jani Anbarasi
School of Computer Science and Engineering, Vellore Institute of Technology, Chennai, India

Benson Edwin Raj
Higher Colleges of Technology, Fujairah, UAE

ABSTRACT

In the recent years, innovations such as Augmented Reality (AR), Virtual Reality (VR), and internet of things have enhanced user experience dramatically. In general, AR is completely different from VR and provides real-time solutions to users by projecting layers of information on real-world environments. Advancements in computer-generated sensory have made the concept of believable virtual environments a reality. With the availability of such technologies, one can investigate "how these technologies can be applied beyond gaming or other useful applications" and "how further improvements can be made to allow for full digital immersion." This chapter provides a detailed description about AR and VR, followed by interesting real-world examples of AR applications. In addition, this chapter discusses the issues and challenges faced with AR/VR with a motivation of exploring the options for improvement.

DOI: 10.4018/978-1-7998-4703-8.ch015

Copyright © 2021, IGI Global. Copying or distributing in print or electronic forms without written permission of IGI Global is prohibited.

1. INTRODUCTION

In the last 6-7 years, several product developers have started focusing on Virtual Reality (VR), Augmented Reality (AR) and Mixed Reality (MR) (Lengthy History of Augmented Reality, 2016)-(Schueffel, 2017). VR has been a topic in technology circles for decades and it depends a lot on the virtual information. Since 1990s, the concept of MR and AR started gaining more attention. AR depends on computer generated information whereas MR attempts to produce new environments and visualizations by merging real and virtual information (Augmented Reality, n.d.). Until early 1990s, AR/VR/MR is used in game development only but later it was adapted by various sectors: entertainment, military and healthcare (Robotics Business Review, n.d.). The advancements in VR, AR and MR are key factors for the growth of technology industry. Therefore, this article will present the history of AR/VR/MR and explain their applications in detail. More importantly, this article will discuss the issues and challenges faced while implementing these technologies.

In this article, we present the history of AR/VR/MR in section 2. Details of the AR/VR/MR enabled technologies will be discussed along with their features and timelines. In section 3, various applications of AR/VR/MR will be discussed in detail. In section 4, the dos and don'ts are presented and discussed. The issues and challenges faced by AR/VR/MR are given in section 5. Section 6 concludes the paper.

2. HISTORY OF USING AR AND VR

In the middle of the 20th century, VR products were modelled in the form of glasses, masks (Robotics Business Review, n.d.). The reality was built using 3D imaging, widescreen vision and stereo sound. In 1970s and 1980s, the focus was on developing gloves. The first wired glove was built in 1977 and then it was improved in 1980s. The gloves used optic flex sensors for sensing and magnetic and ultrasonic waves for hand position tracking. The first functional AR system, the virtual fixtures, was built by the US Air Force in 1992 (Rosenberg, 1992)-(Rosenberg, 1993). In 1990s, the commercial AR systems were built for gaming businesses only. Later the AR/VR experience was extended to others fields: education, entertainment, communication and healthcare. In the beginning of 21st century, advanced AR/VR systems were built utilizing computer vision techniques. In smart phones, AR/VR was used for object recognition tasks. Interactive AR systems were shown to provide realistic experience for the users through digitally manipulated information. Table 1 shows the details of AR/VR systems along with the timeline.

Table 1. Details of AR/VR systems

S. No	AR/VR/MR system	Features	Year/Timeline
1	Telesphere Mask	The first ever Head-Mounted Display (HMD) VR developed by Morton Heilg	1960
2	Sayre Glove	The first wired glove with AR/VR technology invented by scientists at the University of Illinois - Electronic Visualization laboratory	1977
3	Power Glove and Dataglove	Renovated glove-modelled sensor that used optical sensor for hand position tracking. Developed by Thomas G. Zimmerman and Jaron Lanier	1982
4.	Virtual Fixtures	First functional AR system developed by U.S. Air Force to provide mixed reality experience	1992
5.	Arcade machines and video games	Video game consoles and full body suit simulations created jointly by NASA and Nintendo	1990s
6.	Smart Phones with AR cameras	Used for object recognition applications	21st Century
7.	HoloLens headset (Dupzyk, 2016)	Mixed reality headset introduced by Microsoft	2013
8.	VR headset	Introduced by Oculus	2013
9.	Google Cardboard	An eyewear virtual reality simulation available for $15	2014
9.	Apple's AR Kit	Paved way for several iPhone and iPad Apps	2016
10.	Sony Playstation VR add-on	Virtual reality headset for gamers (Samsung and HTC also have this option)	2016

3. APPLICATIONS USING AUGMENTED REALITY, VIRTUAL REALITY, AND MIXED REALITY

Technology has changed every aspect of our lives, from how we communicate with each other to the way we interact with our environment (Augmented Reality, n.d.). This has allowed humans to have more realistic and engaging experiences in all forms of entertainment and communication. We have always wanted to have an immersive experience – whether be it playing video games or watching a movie. The introduction of the first 3D game allowed its players to have a fully interactive experience and we have exponentially improved our ability to have an extra dimension to our experience. This has about us to the advent of Extended Reality (XR) technology - VR, AR and MR.

The XR technology has applications in all domains ranging from entertainment to communication and medical sciences. The entertainment industry has bought virtual reality handset to the consumer market. Gadgets like Facebook's Oculus and Microsoft's HoloLens provide complete immersion of the user in the computer world.

The pandemic has disrupted economies all around the world and its effect can be seen largely in the education, tourism, and entertainment industry. With schools, colleges, theatres, and tourism places closed for over 6 months now, we are dependent on technology now, more than ever. The AR, VR, and MR industry has come to the rescue.

The entertainment industry uses XR technology as a means to cater to its consumers. There have been many virtual concerts, allowing music lovers to avoid long travel and overcrowded venues to listen to their favourite music while being safe in their homes. Another entertainment sector gaining huge popularity is the concept of virtual live concepts and film viewing, allowing a user to watch live events and giving them an interactive experience.

Virtual and Augmented reality is increasingly being used in the education sector to actively engage young school students to learn their lessons (How to Transform Your Classroom with Augmented Reality, 2015)-(van der Crabben, 2018). An example of this, the Google Lens which allows students to visualize flora and fauna and various scientific and natural processes like the eruption of volcanoes, insects pollinating on flowers, in their environment. Teachers and Professors are able to interactively take classes to students and find it effective in grabbing student's attention. Educational Institutions around the globe are conducting virtual graduation ceremonies for its graduating batch of students to mark an important milestone in their lives, and that they don't miss out on the experience due to COVID-19.

Augmented and Mixed Reality has also been proven to be effective in the treatment of various behavioural anxieties and cure them through rehabilitation. Patients suffering from various phobias and eating disorders can now use augmented reality to overcome them. The use of this technology can be used to treat children with social disorders, by allowing them to discover the interaction with people in a safe stimulation.

Doctors use augmented reality to assist them in complicated surgeries. MEVIS is a project initiated the Fraunhofer Research Institute, which involves the use of an iPad-based AR application to support liver operations. As doctors need to know as accurately as possible before and during an operation where blood vessels are located inside the organ, this AR application supports the surgeon by comparing the actual operation with the planned visual data collected from 3D X-ray images.

There are several defense applications of MR which allows a pilot to use a drone for surveillance and monitor its video output in a virtual environment for better reconnaissance. The XR technology has its application for every domain, and it is need of the hour that will allow us to use it effectively.

4. DOS AND DON'TS OF AUGMENTED REALITY, VIRTUAL REALITY AND MIXED REALITY

The augmented reality, when done correctly, will transform a task/campaign to a great extent. On the other hand, if it is not done correctly, the campaign will fall flat. Figure 1 shows the dos and don'ts of augmented reality.

To motivate and inspire the audience, a strong 'call-to-act' is required (Adsreality, n.d.). This will ensure the active engagement of the end user. Next, it is necessary that the audience should know that the task uses augmented reality. If they don't know, then the technology will remain unused. In any task, the AR should add value. In other words, it should be beneficial, informative or fun. Such experience will motivate the audience towards using the technology. This will also prevent them from rolling back to standard technologies. The technology should use the right tool, and more often than not, the tool should be generic. Consider for example, while developing/improving an application for handphone users, the solution should work in both Android and iOS platforms. Otherwise, one group of users will not use the technology.

Having said that AR should add value to a task, it is important that one should use AR only when it adds value. If it doesn't add any value, then AR might just result in increased complexity. A descriptive and diagnostic analysis should be carried out throughout the process, to verify whether the objectives are met. Therefore, one should not forget to analyse. It is important to provide a briefing of task in the campaign. This might increase the engagement level in users. AR is powerful but it cannot perform wonders. It is capable of doing what it can. Therefore, one should not expect the AR to perform beyond its capability. At the same time, one should not be scared to use AR when it is feasible. All the above mentioned guidelines are applicable for virtual reality and mixed reality as well.

Figure 1. Dos and don'ts of augmented reality.

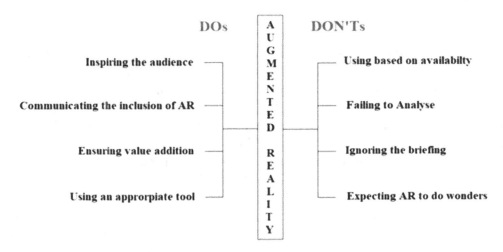

5. ISSUES, CHALLENGES AND POSSIBLE PROSPECTS WITH AUGMENTED REALITY, VIRTUAL REALITY AND MIXED REALITY (IN NEAR FUTURE)

The advent of Augmented Reality, Virtual Reality, and Mixed Reality technology is bridging the gap in the existing system and the steady increase in the demand for better technology, as a result of the insufficiency in the current system or the new obstacles due to the COVID-19 pandemic. Though these technologies have shown their capability in better performance and their use in a range of volatile applications, there exist some challenges that come with it.

To analyze the issues, challenges, and prospects, we must understand what virtual reality, augmented reality and mixed reality mean. Virtual Reality is where we visualize the contents in a new digital environment. An example of this is Facebook's Oculus, which delivers a virtual environment to users through its handset. Augmented Reality overlaps the digital content on top of the real environment. Google's in-built feature to view flora and fauna, and creative augmented filters in Snapchat and Instagram are some examples of AR. Mixed Reality is a combination of virtual and augmented reality where digital content is superimposed partially in virtual as well as a real environment. A famous example is the EDITH glasses from the Spider-Man and Iron-Man movies.

The XR uses three components to deliver an immersive experience – visual quality, sound quality, and intuitive interactions. The visual quality is always correlated with image quality. Ultimately, a good visual quality corresponds to pixel quality and quantity. We have come up with various algorithms to increase the pixel quantity. The obstacle is to provide a seamless pixel quality to improve the overall quality. This is one of the primary issues in the effective implementation of the XR technology.

The sound quality is attributed to a good hardware design that provides high-resolution audio and sound integrity with the visual content. The key issue is to make the hardware smaller and lighter. This allows the user to use the headset without any difficulties. There is ongoing research to make the hardware compatible with the user expectation.

The third component – intuitive interactions – is related to the good connectivity of the handset to the internet. 3G internet connectivity that is used all over India is not capable of delivering this experience to the desired expectation. The increase in the 4G internet connectivity and promising research in the field of 5G has been associated with new digital applications that come with the hyper-connectivity and edge computing.

The technological issues and challenges can be overcome with cutting- edge research and development carried out by the industry. With any technology, there is some extent of social issues that come with it and a clear boundary has to be established with the use of the technology.

The use of XR has been associated with the possibility of causing physical harm to its users. We have seen many cases throughout this decade, one such example id the rise of the augmented mobile game, Pokémon Go. It uses the mobile's GPS to locate, capture, battle, and train virtual creatures, called Pokémon, which appear as if they are in the player's real-world location.

Multilevel research has concluded that more than a quarter of the players are likely to play the game while driving, walking, and spending more hours playing the game and sacrificing their sleep time. This has significantly contributed to increased mental and physical stress among the players. One such incident is the increase in the number of traffic accidents and caused by either distracted pedestrians or drivers. The players tend to neglect the rules to go behind their Pokémon in the player's real world.

This technology may seem popular among tech enthusiasts but has not received the same reception among the public and consumer markets. This is due to the expensive gadget that comes with technology. The headsets are generally priced on the high of the price scale, making them a part of the luxury category. Another influencing factor is the lack of proper content and its availability. Only a handful of companies and organizations have designed digital content compatible with this technology and are not popular among the general public.

Technological advances have led to the rise in its application among various industrial areas, which may lead to successful opportunities. The use of augmented reality and virtual reality are increasingly used in the automotive industry for vehicle design, assembly, and maintenance. Some of the features include safe distance tracking with nearby vehicles, a safe car parking system, and adaptive cruise control. These have proved to be successful prospects of the technology in the near future. There has been an exponential use of virtual and augmented reality in the health sector among developed countries. The applications included medical training and education, surgical preparation and assistance, improved patient care and treatment. Developing countries have started using these technologies, following the developed, in the view of better growth and opportunity in the healthcare industry. The extended technology (XR) has shown promising prospected and can outweigh the negative aspects.

6. CONCLUSION

In this article, we have presented the history of AR/VR/MR and explained their applications in detail. In addition, we have discussed the issues and challenges faced while embedding AR/VR/MR experience. The progress in AR/VR/MR experience is the key to the growth of technology industry. Though AR/VR/MR was used for gaming in the early days, they started finding their applications in diverse field owing to the value they add to the technology. Currently, two sectors are largely making use of AR/VR/MR: education and healthcare. Among these two, the healthcare sector will depend on AR a lot whereas the education sector will make use of all three.

REFERENCES

Adsreality. (n.d.). http://adsreality.com/dos-donts-augmented-reality/

Augmented Reality. (n.d.). In *Wikipedia*. https://en.wikipedia.org/wiki/Augmented_reality

Dupzyk, K. (2016). I Saw the Future Through Microsoft's Hololens. *Popular Mechanics*.

How to Transform Your Classroom with Augmented Reality. (2015, Nov. 2). *EdSurge News*.

Lengthy History of Augmented Reality. (2016, May 15). *Huffington Post*.

Robotics Business Review. (n.d.). https://www.roboticsbusinessreview.com/news/infographic-the-history-and-future-of-augmented-virtual-reality/

Rosenberg, L. B. (1992). *The Use of Virtual Fixtures as Perceptual Overlays to Enhance Operator Performance in Remote Environments*. Academic Press.

Rosenberg, L. B. (1993). Virtual fixtures: Perceptual tools for telerobotic manipulation. *Proceedings of IEEE Virtual Reality Annual International Symposium*, 76–82. 10.1109/VRAIS.1993.380795

Schueffel, P. (2017). *The Concise Fintech Compendium*. Fribourg: School of Management Fribourg/Switzerland.

van der Crabben, J. (2018). *Why We Need More Tech in History Education*. ancient.eu

Compilation of References

Abou-Rjeily & Slim. (2011). Cooperative Diversity for Free-Space Optical Communications: Transceiver Design and Performance Analysis. *IEEE Transactions on Communications, 59*, 345–356.

Abou-Rjeily. (2011). On the Optimality of the Selection Transmit Diversity for MIMO-FSO Links with Feedback. *IEEE Communications Letters, 15.*

Acevedo, D., Vote, E., Laidlaw, D. H., & Joukowsky, M. S. (2001). Archaeological data visualization in vr: Analysis of lamp finds at the great temple of petra, a case study. *Proceedings of the conference on Visualization'01*, 493–496. 10.1109/VISUAL.2001.964560

Adak, C., Chaudhuri, B. B., & Blumenstein, M. J. I. A. (2019). *An empirical study on writer identification and verification from intra-variable individual handwriting.* Academic Press.

Adobe Photoshop. (n.d.). Retrieved from https://en.wikipedia.org/wiki/Adobe_Photoshop

Aggarwal, C. C. (2005). *On change diagnosis in evolving data streams.* IEEE Transactions on. doi:10.1109/TKDE.2005.78

Ahmed, S. B., Hameed, I. A., Naz, S., Razzak, M. I., & Yusof, R. J. I. a. (2019). *Evaluation of handwritten Urdu text by integration of MNIST dataset learning experience.* Academic Press.

Ahmed, I., Karvonen, H., Kumpuniemi, T., & Katz, M. (2020). Wireless Communications for the Hospital of the Future: Requirements, Challenges and Solutions. *International Journal of Wireless Information Networks, 27*(1), 4–17. doi:10.100710776-019-00468-1

Ahn, B., Ryu, J., Koo, H. I., Cho, N. I. J. E. J. o. I., & Processing, V. (2017). *Textline detection in degraded historical document images.* Academic Press.

Akçayır, M., Akçayır, G., Pektaş, H. M., & Ocak, M. A. (2016). AR in science laboratories: The effects of AR on university students' laboratory skills and attitudes toward science laboratories. *Computers in Human Behavior, 57*, 334–342. doi:10.1016/j.chb.2015.12.054

Akenine-Möller, T., & Haines, E. (2002). Real-Time Rendering (2nd ed.). A. K. Peters, Ltd.

Akl, E. A., Mustafa, R., Slomka, T., Alawneh, A., Vedavalli, A., & Schünemann, H. J. (2008). An educational game for teaching clinical practice guidelines to internal medicine residents: Development, feasibility and acceptability. *BMC Medical Education, 8*(1), 50. doi:10.1186/1472-6920-8-50 PMID:19017400

Al Kalaa, M. O., Balid, W., Refai, H. H., LaSorte, N. J., Seidman, S. J., Bassen, H. I., Silberberg, J. L., & Witters, D. (2016). Characterizing the 2.4 GHz spectrum in a hospital environment: Modeling and applicability to coexistence testing of medical devices. *IEEE Transactions on Electromagnetic Compatibility, 59*(1), 58–66. doi:10.1109/TEMC.2016.2602083

Alefeld, G., & Herzberger, J. (1983). Introduction to Interval Computations. Academic Press Inc.

Alotaibi, F., Abdullah, M. T., Abdullah, R. B. H., Rahmat, R. W. B. O., Hashem, I. A. T., & Sangaiah, A. K. J. I. A. (2017). *Optical character recognition for quranic image similarity matching.* Academic Press.

Aly, S., & Mohamed, A. J. I. A. (2019). *Unknown-length handwritten numeral string recognition using cascade of PCA-SVMNet classifiers.* Academic Press.

Amin, O., Ikki, S. S., & Uysal, M. (2011). On the Performance Analysis of Multirelay Cooperative Diversity Systems with Channel Estimation Errors. *IEEE Transactions on Vehicular Technology, 60*(5), 490–501. doi:10.1109/TVT.2011.2121926

Andreoli, R., De Chiara, R., Erra, U., Scarano, V., Pontrandolfo, A., Rizzo, L., & Santoriello, A. (2005). An interactive 3d reconstruction of a funeral in andriuolos necropolis in paestum. CAA 2005-Computer Applications and Quantitative Methods in Archaeology, 1.

Anglada, A., Codognet, P., & Zimmer, L. (2004). An adaptive search for the NSCSPs. *Proceedings of the 8th ERCIM/ CoLogNet workshop on Constraint Solving and Constraint Logic Programming (CSCLP 2004).*

Antonik, P., Marsal, N., & Rontani, D. J. I. J. o. S. T. i. Q. E. (2019). *Large-scale spatiotemporal photonic reservoir computer for image classification.* Academic Press.

Apollonio, F. I., Gaiani, M., & Benedetti, B. (2012). 3d realitybased artefact models for the management of archaeological sites using 3d gis: A framework starting from the case study of the pompeii archaeological area. *Journal of Archaeological Science, 39*(5), 1271–1287. doi:10.1016/j.jas.2011.12.034

Appinventiv. (n.d.a). https://appinventiv.com/blog/augmented-reality-in-retail/

Appinventiv. (n.d.b). https://appinventiv.com/blog/augmented-reality-benefits-for-businesses/

Arsalan, M., & Santra, A. J. I. S. J. (2019). *Character recognition in air-writing based on network of radars for human-machine interface.* Academic Press.

Atzeni, S. P. P. (2007). Interoperability for Semantic Annotations. *18th International Workshop on Database and Expert Systems Applications (DEXA).* 10.1109/DEXA.2007.52

Aumont, J. (1990). *L'image* (2nd ed.). Nathan.

Ayzeren, Y. B., Erbilek, M., & Çelebi, E. J. I. A. (2019). *Emotional state prediction from online handwriting and signature biometrics.* Academic Press.

Azuma, R. T. (1997). A survey of augmented reality. *Presence (Cambridge, Mass.), 6*(4), 355–385. doi:10.1162/pres.1997.6.4.355

Bacca, J., Baldiris, S., Fabregat, R., Kinshuk, & Graf, S. (2015). Mobile AR in vocational education and training. *Procedia Computer Science, 75*, 49–58. doi:10.1016/j.procs.2015.12.203

Bai, K., An, Q., Liu, L., & Yi, Y. J. I. T. o. V. L. S. I. S. (2019). *A training-efficient hybrid-structured deep neural network with reconfigurable memristive synapses.* Academic Press.

Bai, X., Yao, C., & Liu, W. J. I. T. o. I. P. (2016). *Strokelets: A learned multi-scale mid-level representation for scene text recognition.* Academic Press.

Bartle, R. A. (1996). Players who suit MUDs. *Journal of MUD Research, 1*(1).

Bartolini, I., Ciaccia, P., Ntoutsi, I., Patella, M., & Theodoridis, Y. (2004). A unified and flexible framework for comparing simple and complex patterns. *PKDD '04: Proceedings of the 8th European Conference on Principles and Practice of Knowledge Discovery in Databases.*

Bauminger, N. (2007). Brief report: Group social-multimodal intervention for HFASD. *Journal of Autism and Developmental Disorders*, *37*(8), 1605–1615. doi:10.100710803-006-0246-3 PMID:17072752

Bechhofer, S. (2009). *OWL: Web Ontology Language*. Academic Press.

Becker, K., & Parker, J. R. (2012). *The Guide to Computer Simulations and Games*. Wiley.

Beckhaus, S., Ritter, F., & Strothotte, T. (2001). Guided exploration with dynamic potential fields: The cubicalpath system. *Computer Graphics Forum*, *20*(4), 201–210. doi:10.1111/1467-8659.00549

Bekele, M. K., Pierdicca, R., Frontoni, E., Malinverni, E. S., & Gain, J. (2018). A survey of augmented, virtual, and mixed reality for cultural heritage *Journal on Computing and Cultural Heritage*, *11*(2), 7. doi:10.1145/3145534

Bellotti, F. (2013). Assessment in and of serious games: an overview. *Adv. Human Comput. Inter., 1.*

Berndt, R., Havemann, S., Settgast, V., & Fellner, D. (2008). Sustainable Markup and Annotation of 3D Geometry. *Proceedings of the 14th International Conference on Virtual Systems and Multimedia.*

Berners-Lee. (2001). The Semantic Web. *Scientific American*. doi:10.5209/CLAC.59071

Bewer, B. (2020). Comparison of dose values predicted by FLUKA to measured values using Luxel+ Ta type dosimeters. *Nuclear Instruments & Methods in Physics Research. Section B, Beam Interactions with Materials and Atoms*, *464*, 12–18. doi:10.1016/j.nimb.2019.11.042

Beylefeld, A. A., & Struwig, M. C. (2007). A gaming approach to learning medical microbiology: Students' experiences of flow. *Medical Teacher*, *29*(9), 933–940. doi:10.1080/01421590701601550 PMID:18158668

Bharath, A., Madhvanath, S. J. I. t. o. p. a., & Intelligence, m. (2011). *HMM-based lexicon-driven and lexicon-free word recognition for online handwritten Indic scripts*. Academic Press.

Bhushananantramani & Amuthajeyakumar. (2016). Smart Ambulance System. *International Journal of Computer Applications*.

Bhushananantramani & Amuthajeyakumar. (2018). *Smart ambulance guidance system*. Academic Press.

Bi, H., Zhang, J., & Chen, Y. J. I. A. (2020). SmartGe. *Identifying Pen-Holding Gesture With Smartwatch.*, *8*, 28820–28830.

Billinghurst, M. (2002). Augmented reality in education. *New Horizons for Learning*, *12*(5), 1-5.

Bishop, J. (2007a). Ecological cognition: A new dynamic for human-computer interaction. In B. Wallace, A. Ross, J. Davies & T. Anderson (Eds.), The mind, the body and the world: Psychology after cognitivism (pp. 327-345). Exeter, UK: Imprint Academic.

Bishop, J. (2011c). *The role of the prefrontal cortex in social orientation construction: A pilot study*. Poster Presented to the BPS Welsh Conference on Wellbeing, Wrexham, UK.

Bishop, J. (2015a). An investigation into the extent and limitations of the GROW model for coaching and mentoring online: Towards 'prosthetic learning. *The 14th International Conference on E-Learning, E-Business, Enterprise Information Systems, and E-Government (EEE'15).*

Bishop, J. (2007b). Increasing participation in online communities: A framework for human–computer interaction. *Computers in Human Behavior*, *23*(4), 1881–1893. doi:10.1016/j.chb.2005.11.004

Bishop, J. (2008). Increasing capital revenue in social networking communities: Building social and economic relationships through avatars and characters. In C. Romm-Livermore & K. Setzekorn (Eds.), *Social networking communities and eDating services: Concepts and implications* (pp. 60–77). IGI Global.

Bishop, J. (2009). Enhancing the understanding of genres of web-based communities: The role of the ecological cognition framework. *International Journal of Web Based Communities, 5*(1), 4–17. doi:10.1504/IJWBC.2009.021558

Bishop, J. (2011a). *Equatricism: A new paradigm for research and practice in information technology, the arts, law and sciences. Cardiff Metropolitan University's Annual Poster Symposium.*

Bishop, J. (2011b). *The equatrics of intergenerational knowledge transformation in techno-cultures: Towards a model for enhancing information management in virtual worlds (Unpublished MScEcon)*. Aberystwyth, UK: Aberystwyth University.

Bishop, J. (2012). Taming the chatroom bob: The role of brain-computer interfaces that manipulate prefrontal cortex optimization for increasing participation of victims of traumatic sex and other abuse online. *Proceedings of the 13th International Conference on Bioinformatics and Computational Biology (BIOCOMP'12).*

Bishop, J. (2013). The empathic psychopathy in public life: Towards an understanding of 'autism' and 'empathism' and 'dopaminergic-serotonergic asynchronicity. *Conference on the Implications of Research on the Neuroscience of Affect, Attachment, and Social Cognition.*

Bishop, J. (2014). Reducing corruption and protecting privacy in emerging economies: The potential of neuroeconomic gamification and western media regulation in trust building and economic growth. In B. Christiansen (Ed.), *Economic behavior, game theory, and technology in emerging markets* (pp. 237–249). IGI Global. doi:10.4018/978-1-4666-4745-9.ch013

Bishop, J. (2015b). Supporting communication between people with social orientation impairments using affective computing technologies: Rethinking the autism spectrum. In L. Bee Theng (Ed.), *Assistive technologies for physical and cognitive disabilities* (pp. 42–55). IGI Global. doi:10.4018/978-1-4666-7373-1.ch003

Bishop, J. (2016a). An analysis of the implications of maslow's hierarchy of needs for networked learning design and delivery. *International Conference on Information and Knowledge Engineering (IKE'16).*

Bishop, J. (2016b). Enhancing the performance of human resources through E-mentoring: The role of an adaptive hypermedia system called "AVEUGLE". *International Management Review, 12*(1), 11–23.

Blair, R. J. R. (2007). The amygdala and ventromedial prefrontal cortex in morality and psychopathy. *Trends in Cognitive Sciences, 11*(9), 387–392. doi:10.1016/j.tics.2007.07.003 PMID:17707682

Blog, U. (2020). *Add Unity Powered Features To Your App Using Unity As A Library*. Retrieved from https://blogs.unity3d.com/2020/09/16/add-unity-powered-features-to-your-app-using-unity-as-a-library/

Blumrosen, G., Sakuma, K., Rice, J. J., & Knickerbocker, J. J. I. A. (2020). Back to Finger-Writing. *Fingertip Writing Technology Based on Pressure Sensing., 8*, 35455–35468.

Bolognini, S. (1997). Empathy and 'empathism'. *The International Journal of Psycho-Analysis, 78*(2), 279–293. PMID:9152755

Bougrine, S., Ouchraa, S., Ahiod, B., & El Imrani, A. A. (2014). Ant system with acoustic communication. *World Academy of Science, Engineering and Technology, International Journal of Computer, Electrical, Automation. Control and Information Engineering, 8*(4), 578–582.

Building an intelligent transport system using internet of things (IOT). (n.d.). intelligent-transport-systemblueprint.pdf

Bulan, O., Kozitsky, V., Ramesh, P., & Shreve, M. J. I. T. o. I. T. S. (2017). *Segmentation-and annotation-free license plate recognition with deep localization and failure identification*. Academic Press.

Caggianese, G., & Gallo, L. (2016). Smart underground: Enhancing cultural heritage information access and management through proximity-based interaction. *International Conference on P2P, Parallel, Grid, Cloud and Internet Computing*, 105–114.

Caggianese, G., Colonnese, V., & Gallo, L. (2019). Situated Visualization in Augmented Reality: Exploring Information Seeking Strategies. *2019 15th International Conference on Signal-Image Technology & Internet-Based Systems (SITIS)*. 10.1109/SITIS.2019.00069

Caggianese, G., Gallo, L., & Neroni, P. (2018). Exploring the feasibility of diegetic user interfaces in immersive virtual exhibitions within the cultural heritage. *2018 14th International Conference on Signal-Image Technology & Internet-Based Systems (SITIS)*. 10.1109/SITIS.2018.00101

Caggianese, G., De Pietro, G., Esposito, M., Gallo, L., Minutolo, A., & Neroni, P. (2020). Discovering Leonardo with artificial intelligence and holograms: A user study. *Pattern Recognition Letters*, *131*, 361–367. doi:10.1016/j.patrec.2020.01.006

Campbell, J., Fletcher, G., & Greenhill, A. (2009). Conflict and identity shape shifting in an online financial community. *Information Systems Journal*, *19*(5), 461–478. doi:10.1111/j.1365-2575.2008.00301.x

Canuet, L., Ishii, R., Iwase, M., Ikezawa, K., Kurimoto, R., Takahashi, H., Currais, A., Azechi, M., Aoki, Y., Nakahachi, T., Soriano, S., & Takeda, M. (2011). Psychopathology and working memory-induced activation of the prefrontal cortex in schizophrenia-like psychosis of epilepsy: Evidence from magnetoencephalography. *Psychiatry and Clinical Neurosciences*, *65*(2), 183–190. doi:10.1111/j.1440-1819.2010.02179.x PMID:21414092

Cardoso, J. (2007). The Semantic Web Vision : Where are We? *IEEE Intelligent Systems*, *22*(October), 22–26. doi:10.1109/MIS.2007.4338499

Castillo-Vazquez, Garcia-Zambrana, & Castillo-Vazquez. (2009). Closed-form BER expression for FSO links with transmit laser selection over exponential atmospheric turbulence channels. IEEE Electronics Letters. *Transactions on Communications*, *45*, 1098–1110.

Celeux, G., Diday, E., Govaert, G., Lechevallier, Y., & Ralambondrainy, H. (1989). *Classification Automatique des Données*. Bordas.

Celsoazevedo. (n.d.). https://www.celsoazevedo.com/files/android/google-camera/ar/

Chan, C. J. I. A. (2020). *Stroke extraction for offline handwritten mathematical expression recognition*. Academic Press.

Chebi, H., & Acheli, D. (2015, December). Dynamic detection of anomalies in crowd's behavior analysis. In *2015 4th International Conference on Electrical Engineering (ICEE)* (pp. 1-5). IEEE. 10.1109/INTEE.2015.7416735

Chebi, H., Acheli, D., & Kesraoui, M. (2017, April). Strategy of detecting abnormal behaviors by fuzzy logic. In *2017 Intelligent Systems and Computer Vision (ISCV)* (pp. 1-5). IEEE.

Chebi, H., Acheli, D., & Kesraoui, M. (2017, October). Intelligent Detection Without Modeling of Behavior Unusual by Fuzzy Logic. In *International Conference on Model and Data Engineering* (pp. 300-307). Springer. 10.1007/978-3-319-66854-3_23

Chebi, H., Acheli, D., & Kesraoui, M. (2018). Automatic shadow elimination in a high-density scene. *International Journal of Intelligent Systems Design and Computing*, *2*(3-4), 224–237. doi:10.1504/IJISDC.2018.097468

Chebi, H., Acheli, D., & Kesraoui, M. (2018). Crowd events recognition in a video without threshold value setting. *International Journal of Applied Pattern Recognition*, *5*(2), 101–118. doi:10.1504/IJAPR.2018.092518

Chebi, H., Tabet-Derraz, H., Sayah, R., Meroufel, A., Acheli, D., Benaissa, A., & Meraihi, Y. (2020). Intelligence and Adaptive Global Algorithm Detection of Crowd Behavior. *International Journal of Computer Vision and Image Processing, 10*(1), 24–41. doi:10.4018/IJCVIP.2020010102

Chen, C. (2013). Exploring antecedents of lurking behavior: A perspective from ecological cognition framework (Master). Chaoyang Institute of Technology.

Chen, Y.-Y., Lin, Y.-H., Kung, C.-C., Chung, M.-H., & Yen, I. J. S. (2019). *Design and implementation of cloud analytics-assisted smart power meters considering advanced artificial intelligence as edge analytics in demand-side management for smart homes*. Academic Press.

Cheng, H., & Chen, C. (2014). A study of lurking behavior: The desire perspective. *International Journal of Social, Education. Economics and Management Engineering, 8*(4), 905–908.

Chernyshova, Y. S., Sheshkus, A. V., & Arlazarov, V. V. J. I. A. (2020). *Two-Step CNN Framework for Text Line Recognition in Camera-Captured Images*. Academic Press.

Christie, M., & Normand, J.-M. (2005). A semantic space partitioning approach to virtual camera composition. *Computer Graphics Forum, Eurographics 2005 Conference Proceedings, 24*(3), 247–256.

Christ, S. E., Van Essen, D. C., Watson, J. M., Brubaker, L. E., & McDermott, K. B. (2009). The contributions of prefrontal cortex and executive control to deception: Evidence from activation likelihood estimate meta-analyses. *Cerebral Cortex (New York, N.Y.), 19*(7), 1557–1566. doi:10.1093/cercor/bhn189 PMID:18980948

Clarke, J., & Dede, C. (2007). LSVEs as a powerful means to study situated learning. *Proceedings of the 8th Iternational Conference on Computer Supported Collaborative Learning*, 144-147.

Cooley, R., Mobasher, B., & Srivastava, J. (1999). Data preparation for mining world wide web browsing patterns. *Journal of Knowledge and Information Systems, 1*(1), 5–32. doi:10.1007/BF03325089

Corbett, N. A., & Beveridge, P. (1982). Simulation as a tool for learning. *Topics in Clinical Nursing, 4*(3), 58–67. PMID:6922661

Corti, K. (2006). Game-based Learning; A Serious Business Application. PIXELearning, Coventry.

Cowpertwait, J., & Flynn, S. (2002). The internet from A to Z. Cambridge, UK: Icon Books Ltd.

Csikszentmihalyi, M. (2000). Beyond boredom and anxiety: Experiencing flow in work and play (25th Anniversary ed.). San Francisco CA: Jossey Bass Wiley.

Csikszentmihalyi, M. (1975). *Beyond boredom and anxiety*. Jossey Bass Wiley.

Csikszentmihalyi, M. (2009). *Flow: The psychology of optimal experience* (2nd ed.). HarperCollins.

D'Alessandro, D. M., Ellsbury, D. L., Kreiter, C. D., & Starner, T. (2002). Pediatric jeopardy may increase residents' medical reading. *Ambulatory Pediatrics, 2*(1), 1–3. doi:10.1367/1539-4409(2002)002<0001:PJMIRM>2.0.CO;2 PMID:11888428

Da Silva, A., Carvalho, F. D., Lechevallier, Y., & Trousse, B. (2006a). Mining web usage data for discovering navigation clusters. *ISCC, 2006*, 910–915. doi:10.1109/ISCC.2006.102

Da Silva, A., De Carvalho, F., Lechevallier, Y., & Trousse, B. (2006b). Characterizing visitor groups from web data streams. *GrC, 2006*, 389–392. doi:10.1109/GRC.2006.1635822

Das, A., Patra, G. R., & Mohanty, M. N. (2020). *LSTM based Odia Handwritten Numeral Recognition.* Paper presented at the 2020 International Conference on Communication and Signal Processing (ICCSP). 10.1109/ICCSP48568.2020.9182218

Das, D., Nayak, D. R., Dash, R., Majhi, B. J. M. T., & Applications. (2020). *MJCN: Multi-objective Jaya Convolutional Network for handwritten optical character recognition.* Academic Press.

Dash, K. S., Puhan, N. B., & Panda, G. J. a. p. a. (2020). Sparse Concept Coded Tetrolet Transform for Unconstrained Odia Character Recognition. Academic Press.

Dash, K. S., Puhan, N. B., & Panda, G. J. I. I. p. (2015). *Handwritten numeral recognition using non-redundant Stockwell transform and bio-inspired optimal zoning.* Academic Press.

Davidhizar, R. E. (1982). Simulation games as a teaching technique in psychiatric nursing. *Perspectives in Psychiatric Care, 20*(1), 8–12. doi:10.1111/j.1744-6163.1982.tb00142.x PMID:6921627

De Saussure, F. (1916). *Cours de linguistique générale.* Bayot.

de Souza, C. S., & Preece, J. (2004). A framework for analyzing and understanding online communities. *Interacting with Computers, 16*(3), 579–610. doi:10.1016/j.intcom.2003.12.006

Deepalakshmi & Rajaram (2010a). Multimedia Traffic Routing Algorithm for Optical Networks with Enhanced Performance Characteristics. *International Conference on Internet Multimedia Systems Architecture and Applications.* 10.1109/IMSAA.2010.5729406

Deepalakshmi & Rajaram. (2010b). A Dynamic Cost Optimized Provisioning Algorithm- (DCOPA) for Optical Networks with less Rejection Ratio. *Proceedings of the International Conference on Communication and Computational Intelligence.*

Deepalakshmi & Rajaram. (2011a). New MAC Protocol for Traffic Routing in Optical Networks by exploiting Delays in Dynamic Bandwidth Allocation. *International Conference on Computer Applications & Industrial Electronics,* 307-312. 10.1109/ICCAIE.2011.6162154

Deepalakshmi & Rajaram. (2011b). A Novel Medium Access Control Protocol for Routing Multimedia Traffic in Optical Networks by exploiting Delays with improved Dynamic Bandwidth Allocation. *ARPN Journal of Systems and Software, 1.*

Deggim, S., Kersten, T. P., Tschirschwitz, F., & Hinrichsen, N. (2017). Segeberg 1600–reconstructing a historic town for virtual reality visualisation as an immersive experience. *The International Archives of the Photogrammetry, Remote Sensing and Spatial Information Sciences, 42*(W8), 87–94. doi:10.5194/isprs-archives-XLII-2-W8-87-2017

Del Grosso, M. (2001). Design and implementation of online communities (Unpublished Master of Science). Naval Postgraduate School, Monterey, CA.

Deng, L., & Yu, D. (2014). Deep learning: Methods and applications. *Found Trends Signal Process, 7*(3–4), 197–387. doi:10.1561/2000000039

Diaz, M., Ferrer, M. A., Ramalingam, S., Guest, R. J. I. T. o. I. F., & Security. (2019). *Investigating the Common Authorship of Signatures by Off-line Automatic Signature Verification without the Use of Reference Signatures.* Academic Press.

Diehl, L. A., Souza, R. M., Alves, J. B., Gordan, P. A., Esteves, R. Z., Jorge, M. L. S. G., & Coelho, I. C. M. (2013). InsuOnline, a serious game to teach insulin therapy to primary care physicians: Design of the game and a randomized controlled trial for educational validation. *JMIR Research Protocols, 2*(1), e5. doi:10.2196/resprot.2431 PMID:23612462

Din, I. U., Siddiqi, I., Khalid, S., Azam, T. J. E. J. o. I., & Processing, V. (2017). *Segmentation-free optical character recognition for printed Urdu text.* Academic Press.

Ding, L. Z. (2009). Study on Construction of University Course Ontology : *Content. International Conference on Computational Intelligence and Software Engineering.* 10.1109/CISE.2009.5363158

Dinh-Le, C., Chuang, R., Chokshi, S., & Mann, D. (2019). Wearable health technology and electronic health record integration: Scoping review and future directions. *JMIR mHealth and uHealth, 7*(9), e12861. doi:10.2196/12861 PMID:31512582

Dudeja, K., Baidya, S., & Gupta, S. S. (2019). Low-Cost 3DOF Virtual Reality First Aid Training Programs. *International Journal of Engineering and Advanced Technology, 8*(5).

Duque, G., Fung, S., Mallet, L., Posel, N., & Fleiszer, D. (2008). Learning while having fun: The use of video gaming to teach geriatric house calls to medical students. *Journal of the American Geriatrics Society, 56*(7), 1328–1332. doi:10.1111/j.1532-5415.2008.01759.x PMID:18482292

Ebner, T., Feldmann, I., Renault, S., Schreer, O., & Eisert, P. (2017). Multi-view reconstruction of dynamic real-world objects and their integration in augmented and virtual reality applications. *Journal of the Society for Information Display, 25*(3), 151–157. doi:10.1002/jsid.538

Ericsson, K. A. (2004). Deliberate practice and the acquisition and maintenance of expert performance in medicine and related domains. *Academic Medicine, 79*(10, SUPPL.), S70–S81. doi:10.1097/00001888-200410001-00022 PMID:15383395

Ester, M. Kriegel, H.P. Sander, J., & Xu, X. (1996). A density-based algorithm for discovering clusters in large spatial databases with noise. *2nd International Conference on Knowledge* Discovery and Data Mining (KDD-96).

Fang, D., & Zhang, C. J. I. A. (2020). *Multi-Feature Learning by Joint Training for Handwritten Formula Symbol Recognition.* Academic Press.

Farhat, A., Hommos, O., Al-Zawqari, A., Al-Qahtani, A., Bensaali, F., Amira, A., . . . Processing, V. (2018). *Optical character recognition on heterogeneous SoC for HD automatic number plate recognition system.* Academic Press.

Fatta, F. (2015). Communication, technology, and digital culture for the conservation and enhancement of the architectural heritage. In *Handbook of Research on Emerging Digital Tools for Architectural Surveying, Modeling, and Representation* (pp. 446–475). IGI Global. doi:10.4018/978-1-4666-8379-2.ch016

Fechner, G. T. (1860). *Elemente der Psychophysik.* Breitkof und Hartel. https://fr.wikipedia.org/wiki/Sémiotique

Feng, J., & Song, L. (2011). *Teaching and learning in second life: A case study. In Large-scale virtual environments for the classroom: Practical approaches to teaching in virtual worlds.* IGI Global.

Ferndndez, M., Gmez-p, A., & Juristo, N. (1997). Methontology: From Ontological Art Towards Ontological Engineering. *AAAI Technical Report,* 33–40.

Figner, B., Knoch, D., Johnson, E. J., Krosch, A. R., Lisanby, S. H., Fehr, E., & Weber, E. U. (2010). Lateral prefrontal cortex and self-control in intertemporal choice. *Nature Neuroscience, 13*(5), 538–539. doi:10.1038/nn.2516 PMID:20348919

Gaia, G., Boiano, S., & Borda, A. (2019). Engaging museum visitors with ai: the case of chatbots. In *Museums and Digital Culture* (pp. 309–329). Springer. doi:10.1007/978-3-319-97457-6_15

Ganti, V., Gehrke, J., Ramakrishnan, R., & Loh, W.Y. (1999). A framework for measuring changes in data characteristics. In *PODS.* ACM Press.

Ganti, V., Gehrke, J., & Ramakrishnan, R. (2000). Demon: Mining and monitoring evolving data. *IEEE Transactions on Knowledge and Data Engineering, 2000,* 439–448.

Garfield, M., Liang, C., Kurzweg, T. P., & Dandekar, K. R. (2006). MIMO space-time coding for diffuse optical communication. *Microwave and Optical Technology Letters, 48*(6), 48. doi:10.1002/mop.21558

Garrison, D. R., Anderson, T., & Archer, W. (2001). Critical thinking, cognitive presence, and computer conferencing in distance education. *American Journal of Distance Education, 15*(1), 7–23. doi:10.1080/08923640109527071

Gashi, L., & Knautz, K. (2016). *Unfriending, hiding and blocking on facebook.* Paper presented at the 3rd European Conference on Social Media Research, Normandy, France.

Geer, S. (Ed.). (2003). *Essential internet: The essence of the internet from A to Z* (5th ed.). Profile Books Ltd.

Ghanbarian, A., Ghiasi, G., Safabakhsh, R., & Arastouie, N. J. I. I. P. (2019). *Writer identification with n-tuple direction feature from contour.* Academic Press.

Ghosh, S., Shivakumara, P., Roy, P., Pal, U., & Lu, T. J. C. T. o. I. T. (2020). *Graphology based handwritten character analysis for human behaviour identification.* Academic Press.

Golan, O., & Baron-Cohen, S. (2006). Systemizing empathy: Teaching adults with asperger syndrome or high-functioning autism to recognize complex emotions using interactive multimedia. *Development and Psychopathology, 18*(2), 591–617. doi:10.1017/S0954579406060305 PMID:16600069

Gómez-Pérez & Corcho. (2002, February). Ontology languages for the Semantic Web. *IEEE Intelligent Systems.* Advance online publication. doi:10.1109/5254.988453

Gong, C., Shi, H., Yang, J., Yang, J. J. I. T. o. C., & Technology, S. f. V. (2019). *Multi-manifold positive and unlabeled learning for visual analysis.* Academic Press.

Gonizzi Barsanti, S., Caruso, G., Micoli, L., Covarrubias Rodriguez, M., & Guidi, G. (2015a). 3d visualization of cultural heritage artefacts with virtual reality devices. *25th International CIPA Symposium 2015, Copernicus Gesellschaft mbH,* 165–172.

Gonizzi Barsanti, S., Caruso, G., Micoli, L., Covarrubias Rodriguez, M., & Guidi, G. (2015b). 3d visualization of cultural heritage artefacts with virtual reality devices. *The International Archives of the Photogrammetry, Remote Sensing and Spatial Information Sciences, XL-5*(W7), 165–172. doi:10.5194/isprsarchives-XL-5-W7-165-2015

Gopalan, V., Zulkifli, A. N., & Abubakar, J. A. A. (2016). A study of students' motivation using the AR science textbook. *AIP Conference Proceedings, 1761,* 27–35. doi:10.1063/1.4960880

Gordon, D. W., & Brown, H. N. (1995). Fun and games in reviewing neonatal emergency care. *Neonatal Network, 14*(3), 45–49. PMID:7603420

Graafland, M., Schraagen, J. M., & Schijven, M. P. (2012). Systematic review of serious games for medical education and surgical skills training. *British Journal of Surgery, 99*(10), 1322–1330. doi:10.1002/bjs.8819 PMID:22961509

Grasset, R., Langlotz, T., Kalkofen, D., Tatzgern, M., & Schmalstieg, D. (2012). Image-driven view management for augmented reality browsers. *2012 IEEE International Symposium on Mixed and Augmented Reality (ISMAR),* 177–186. 10.1109/ISMAR.2012.6402555

Greenblat, C.S. (1977). Gaming-simulation and health education an overview. *Health Educ. Monogr., 5*(suppl 1), 5-10.

Hannig, A., Kuth, N., Özman, M., Jonas, S., & Spreckelsen, C. (2012). EMedOffice: A web-based collaborative serious game for teaching optimal design of a medical practice. *BMC Medical Education, 12*(1), 104. doi:10.1186/1472-6920-12-104 PMID:23110606

Hardaker, C. (2010). Trolling in asynchronous computer-mediated communication: From user discussions to academic definitions. *Journal of Politeness Research.Language, Behaviour, Culture (Québec), 6*(2), 215–242.

Hardaker, C. (2013a). Uh.... not to be nitpicky, but... the past tense of drag is dragged, not drug.": An overview of trolling strategies. *Journal of Language Aggression and Conflict*, *1*(1), 57–85. doi:10.1075/jlac.1.1.04har

Hardaker, C. (2013b). "Obvious trolls will just get you banned": Trolling versus corpus linguistics. In A. Hardie & R. Love (Eds.), *Corpus linguistics 2013* (pp. 112–114). UCREL.

Harshita, H., Mithum, P., Geetha, M., Krutika, M., Sufiyan, K., & Shyma, Z. (2018). Patient Monitoring System using Li-Fi. *International Journal of Engineering Research & Technology (Ahmedabad)*, 6.

Heflin, J. (2000). *University Ontology* (Vol. 0). Academic Press.

Hong, C., Wei, X., Wang, J., Deng, B., Yu, H., Che, Y. J. I. t. o. n. n., & Systems, L. (2019). *Training spiking neural networks for cognitive tasks: A versatile framework compatible with various temporal codes*. Academic Press.

Horridge, M., Knublauch, H., Rector, A., Stevens, R., & Wroe, C. (2004). A Practical Guide To Building OWL Ontologies Using The Prot'eg'e-OWL Plugin and CO-ODE Tools Edition 1.0 Matthew. World. Academic Press.

How to Improve Medical Diagnosis Using Machine Learning. (2017). Academic Press.

Hubert, L., & Arabie, P. (1985). Comparing partitions. *Journal of Classification*, *2*(1), 193–218. doi:10.1007/BF01908075

Hughes & Stapleton. (n.d.). *The Shared Imagination: Creative Collaboration in Augmented Virtuality*. Academic Press.

Ibáñez, M., & Delgado-kloos, C. (2018). AR for STEM learning: A systematic review. *Computers & Education*, *123*, 109–123. doi:10.1016/j.compedu.2018.05.002

Impedovo, D., & Pirlo, G. J. I. r. i. b. e. (2018). *Dynamic handwriting analysis for the assessment of neurodegenerative diseases: a pattern recognition perspective*. Academic Press.

Ito, A., Abe, N., Fujii, T., Ueno, A., Koseki, Y., & Hashimoto, R. (2010). The role of the dorsolateral prefrontal cortex in deception when remembering neutral and emotional events. *Neuroscience Research*.

Jalali, R., El-Khatib, K., & McGregor, C. (2015). Smart city architecture for community level services through the Internet of Things. *Proc. IEEE 18th Int. Conf. Intell. Next Generat. New. (ICIN)*, 108–113.

Jayaysingh, R., David, J., Raaj, M. J. M., Daniel, D., & BlessyTelagathoti, D. (2020, March). IoT Based Patient Monitoring System Using NodeMCU. In *2020 5th International Conference on Devices, Circuits and Systems (ICDCS)* (pp. 240-243). IEEE.

Jena, O. P., Pradhan, S. K., Biswal, P. K., & Nayak, S. (2020). *Recognition of Printed Odia Characters and Digits using Optimized Self-Organizing Map Network*. Paper presented at the 2020 International Conference on Computer Science, Engineering and Applications (ICCSEA). 10.1109/ICCSEA49143.2020.9132915

Jena, O. P., Pradhan, S. K., Biswal, P. K., Tripathy, A. R. J. I. J. o. R. T., & Engineering. (2019). *Odia Characters and Numerals Recognition using Hopfield Neural Network based on Zoning Features*. Academic Press.

Jiang, Y., Dong, H., & El Saddik, A. J. I. A. (2018). *Baidu Meizu deep learning competition: Arithmetic operation recognition using end-to-end learning OCR technologies*. Academic Press.

Jirasevijinda, T., & Brown, L. C. (2010). Jeopardy! An innovative approach to teach psychosocial aspects of pediatrics. *Patient Education and Counseling*, *80*(3), 333–336. doi:10.1016/j.pec.2010.06.002 PMID:20619997

Johnson, C. M. (2001). A survey of current research on online communities of practice. *The Internet and Higher Education*, *4*(1), 45–60.

Johnston, B., Boyle, L., MacArthur, E., & Manion, B. F. (2013). The role of technology and digital gaming in nurse education. *Nursing Standard*, 27(28), 35–38. doi:10.7748/ns2013.03.27.28.35.s9612 PMID:23556215

Jung, Y., Keil, J., Behr, J., Webel, S., Zöllner, M., Engelke, T., Wuest, H., & Becker, M. (2008). Adapting X3D for Multi-touch Environments. *Proceedings of the 13th International Symposium on 3D Web Technology*. 10.1145/1394209.1394218

Kalfoglou, Y., & Schorlemmer, M. (2003). Ontology mapping: The state of the art. *The Knowledge Engineering Review*, 18(1), 1–31. doi:10.1017/S0269888903000651

Kanthan, R., & Senger, J. L. (2011). The impact of specially designed digital games-based learning in undergraduate pathology and medical education. *Archives of Pathology & Laboratory Medicine*, 135(1), 135–142. PMID:21204720

Karimi, M., & Nasiri-Kenari, M. (2009). BER Analysis of Cooperative Systems in Free-Space Optical Networks. *Journal of Lightwave Technology*, 27(24), 5639–5647. doi:10.1109/JLT.2009.2032789

Katiyar, G., & Mehfuz, S. J. s. (2016). *A hybrid recognition system for off-line handwritten characters*. Academic Press.

Kaufmann & Schmalstieg. (2002). Mathematics and geometry education with collaborative augmented reality. In *ACM SIGGRAPH 2002 conference abstracts and applications (SIGGRAPH '02)* (pp. 37–41). Association for Computing Machinery.

Khan, F. A., Khelifi, F., Tahir, M. A., Bouridane, A. J. I. T. o. I. F., & Security. (2018). *Dissimilarity Gaussian mixture models for efficient offline handwritten text-independent identification using SIFT and RootSIFT descriptors*. Academic Press.

Khan, A., Pohl, M., Bosse, S., Hart, S., & Turowski, K. (2017). A Holistic View of the IoT Process from Sensors to the Business Value. *Proceedings of the 2nd International Conference on IoTBDS*, 392-399. 10.5220/0006362503920399

Kim, A. J. (2000). *Community building on the web: Secret strategies for successful online communities*. Peachpit Press.

Kommers, P. A. M. (2014). Sense of community: Perceptions of individual and group members of online communities. In J. Bishop (Ed.), *Transforming politics and policy in the digital age* (pp. 1–5). IGI Global. doi:10.4018/978-1-4666-6038-0.ch001

Kotronis, C. (2017). *Managing Criticalities of e-Health IoT systems. IEEE Wireless Broadband*.

Krco, S., & Dupcinov, M. (2003). Improved Neighbor Detection Algorithm for AODV Routing Protocol. *IEEE Communications Letters*, 7(12), 584–586. doi:10.1109/LCOMM.2003.821317

Kritter, J., Brévilliers, M., Lepagnot, J., & Idoumghar, L. (2019). On the optimal placement of cameras for surveillance and the underlying set cover problem. *Applied Soft Computing*, 74, 133–153. doi:10.1016/j.asoc.2018.10.025

Kron, F. W., Gjerde, C. L., Sen, A., & Fetters, M. D. (2010). Medical student attitudes toward video games and related new media Technologies in medical education. *BMC Medical Education*, 10(1), 50. doi:10.1186/1472-6920-10-50 PMID:20576125

Kugler, J., & Zak, P. J. (2017). *Trust, cooperation, and conflict: Neuropolitics and international relations. In Advancing interdisciplinary approaches to international relations*. Springer.

Kumar Malik, S., Prakash, N., & Rizvi, S. A. M. (2010). Developing an University Ontology in Education Domain using Protégé for Semantic Web. *International Journal of Engineering Science and Technology*, 2(9), 4673–4681.

Kutay, C. (2014). *HCI model for culturally useful knowledge sharing. In New horizons in web based learning*. Springer.

Laxman, S., & Sastry, P. S. (2006). A survey of temporal data mining. SADHANA - Academy Proceedings in Engineering Sciences. *Indian Academy of Sciences, 31*(2), 173–198.

Le, A. D., Clanuwat, T., & Kitamoto, A. J. I. A. (2019). *A human-inspired recognition system for pre-modern Japanese historical documents.* Academic Press.

Leem, S. K., Khan, F., Cho, S. H. J. I. T. o. I., & Measurement. (2019). *Detecting mid-air gestures for digit writing with radio sensors and a CNN.* Academic Press.

Leung, L. (2003). Impacts of net-generation attributes, seductive properties of the internet, and gratifications-obtained on internet use. *Telematics and Informatics, 20*(2), 107–129. doi:10.1016/S0736-5853(02)00019-9

Li, Z., Xiao, Y., Wu, Q., Jin, M., & Lu, H. J. T. J. o. E. (2020). *Deep template matching for offline handwritten Chinese character recognition.* Academic Press.

Lin, A. J., Kidd, E., Dehdashti, F., Siegel, B. A., Mutic, S., Thaker, P. H., ... Schwarz, J. (2019). Intensity modulated radiation therapy and image-guided adapted brachytherapy for cervix cancer. *International Journal of Radiation Oncology* Biology* Physics, 103*(5), 1088-1097.

Liu, Fei, & Zhang. (2009). Classification Research on Power Allocation Schemes in Cooperative Communication System. *Journal of Shandong Institute of Light Industry.*

Liu, Tao, Narayanan, Korakis, & Panwar. (2007). CoopMAC: A Cooperative MAC protocol for Wireless LANs. *IEEE Journal on Selected Areas in Communications, 25.*

Liu, Y., Qian, K., Hu, S., An, K., Xu, S., Zhan, X., & ... Systems. (2019). *Application of Deep Compression Technique in Spiking Neural Network Chip.* Academic Press.

Li, X., Zhao, Z., Zhu, X., & Wyatt, T. (2011). Covering models and optimization techniques for emergency response facility location and planning: A review. *Mathematical Methods of Operations Research, 74*(3), 281–310. doi:10.100700186-011-0363-4

Li, Y., Cao, B., Wang, C., You, X., Daneshmand, H. Z., & Jiang, T. (2009). Dynamical Cooperative MAC Based on Optimal Selection of Multiple Helpers. *IEEE Global Telecommunications Conference.* 10.1109/GLOCOM.2009.5425531

Lopes, G. S., da Silva, D. C., Rodrigues, A. W. O., & Reboucas Filho, P. P. J. I. L. A. T. (2016). *Recognition of handwritten digits using the signature features and Optimum-Path Forest Classifier.* Academic Press.

Loring, W., & Hamilton, M. (2011). *Visual Supports and Autism Spectrum Disorder.* Academic Press.

Lu, W., Sun, H., Chu, J., Huang, X., & Yu, J. J. I. A. (2018). *A novel approach for video text detection and recognition based on a corner response feature map and transferred deep convolutional neural network.* Academic Press.

Luo, T., Lin, F., Jiang, T., Guizani, M., & Chen, W. (2011). Multicarrier Modulation And Cooperative Communication In Multihop Cognitive Radio Networks. *IEEE Wireless Communications, 18*(1), 1536–1284. doi:10.1109/MWC.2011.5714024

Ma, Gausemeier, Fan, & Grafe. (n.d.). Virtual Reality & Augmented Reality in Industry. *The 2nd Sino-German Workshop.*

Ma, L., Long, C., Duan, L., Zhang, X., Li, Y., & Zhao, Q. J. I. A. (2020). *Segmentation and Recognition for Historical Tibetan Document Images.* Academic Press.

Mana, S. M., Hellwig, P., Hilt, J., Bober, K. L., Hirmanova, V. J., Chvojka, P., ... Zvanovec, S. (2020, March). LiFi Experiments in a Hospital. In *Optical Fiber Communication Conference* (pp. M3I-2). Optical Society of America.

Mantovani, G. (1996a). Social context in HCI: A new framework for mental models, cooperation, and communication. *Cognitive Science*, *20*(2), 237–269. doi:10.120715516709cog2002_3

Mantovani, G. (1996b). *New communication environments: From everyday to virtual.* Taylor & Francis.

Marcus, R., & Watters, B. (2002). *Collective knowledge.* Microsoft Press.

Martin, R., & Coleman, S. (1994). Playing games with cardiopulmonary resuscitation. *J. Nurs. Staff Dev.: JNSD*, *10*(1), 31–34. PMID:8120644

McLean, G., & Wilson, A. (2019). Shopping in the digital world: Examining customer engagement through augmented reality mobile applications. *Computers in Human Behavior*, *101*, 210–224. doi:10.1016/j.chb.2019.07.002

McMillan, D. W., & Chavis, D. M. (1986). Sense of community: A definition and theory. *Journal of Community Psychology*, *14*(1), 6–23. doi:10.1002/1520-6629(198601)14:1<6::AID-JCOP2290140103>3.0.CO;2-I

Mengu, D., Luo, Y., Rivenson, Y., & Ozcan, A. J. I. J. o. S. T. i. Q. E. (2019). *Analysis of diffractive optical neural networks and their integration with electronic neural networks.* Academic Press.

Meyer, T., Qi, X. L., Stanford, T. R., & Constantinidis, C. (2011). Stimulus selectivity in dorsal and ventral prefrontal cortex after training in working memory tasks. *The Journal of Neuroscience: The Official Journal of the Society for Neuroscience*, *31*(17), 6266–6276. doi:10.1523/JNEUROSCI.6798-10.2011 PMID:21525266

Microsoft, microsoft hololens. (n.d.). Available: https://www.microsoft.com/it-it/hololens

Microsoft. (n.d.). https://www.microsoft.com/en-us/hololens

Mike Uschold, M. G. (1996). Ontologies : Principles, Methods and Applications. *The Knowledge Engineering Review*, *11*(February).

Milgram, P., & Kishino, F. (1994). A taxonomy of mixed reality visual displays. *IEICE Transactions on Information and Systems*, *12*, 1321–1329.

Ministry of Education Special Programs Branch. (2000). *Teaching Student with Autism: A Resources Guide for Schools.*

Mizoguchi, R. (2016). Ontology development, tools and languages. *IEEE Intelligent Systems*, *2*, 1–27.

Modak, S., Chernyak, L., Lubomirsky, I., & Khodorov, S. (2020). Continuous and Time-Resolved Cathodoluminescence Studies of Electron Injection Induced Effects in Gallium Nitride. In *Advanced Technologies for Security Applications* (pp. 109–117). Springer. doi:10.1007/978-94-024-2021-0_11

Moh, S., Yu, C., Park, S.-M., Kim, H.-N., & Kim, J. (2007). CDMAC: Cooperative Diversity MAC for Robust Communication in Wireless Ad Hoc Networks. *Proc. of IEEE ICC.*

Moll, J., Eslinger, P. J., & Oliveira-Souza, R. (2001). Frontopolar and anterior temporal cortex activation in a moral judgment task: Preliminary functional MRI results in normal subjects. *Arquivos de Neuro-Psiquiatria*, *59*(3B), 657–664. doi:10.1590/S0004-282X2001000500001 PMID:11593260

Mongwewarona, W., Sheikh, S. M., & Molefhi, B. C. (2020). Survey on Li-Fi communication networks and deployment. *African Journal of Engineering Research*, *8*(1), 1–9. doi:10.30918/AJER.81.19.036

Morán, A., Frasser, C. F., Roca, M., & Rosselló, J. L. J. I. T. C. (2019). *Energy-Efficient Pattern Recognition Hardware With Elementary Cellular Automata.* Academic Press.

Morrison, A. (2009). Like Bees Around the Hive: A Comparative Study of a Mobile Augmented Reality Map, *Proc. 27th Int'l Conf. Human Factors in Computing Systems*, 1889-1898. 10.1145/1518701.1518991

Mushiake, H., Sakamoto, K., Saito, N., Inui, T., Aihara, K., & Tanji, J. (2009). Involvement of the prefrontal cortex in problem solving. *International Review of Neurobiology, 85*, 1–11. doi:10.1016/S0074-7742(09)85001-0 PMID:19607957

Navidpour, S., Uysal, M., & Kavehrad, M. (2007). BER performance of freespace optical transmission with spatial diversity. *IEEE Transactions on Wireless Communications, 6*(8), 2813–2819. doi:10.1109/TWC.2007.06109

Nayak, M., Nayak, A. K. J. I. J. o. C. V., & Robotics. (2017). *Odia character recognition using backpropagation network with binary features.* Academic Press.

Naz, S., Umar, A. I., Ahmed, R., Razzak, M. I., Rashid, S. F., & Shafait, F. J. S. (2016). *Urdu Nasta'liq text recognition using implicit segmentation based on multi-dimensional long short term memory neural networks.* Academic Press.

Neff, A. (2013). Cyberbullying on facebook: Group composition and effects of content exposure on bystander state hostility (Master of Arts in Psychology). University of Canterbury.

Neill, D., Moore, B. A. W., Sabhnani, M., & Daniel, K. (2005). Detection of emerging space-time clusters. *Proceedings of the Eleventh ACM SIGKDD International Conference on Knowledge Discovery and Data Mining*, 218–227. 10.1145/1081870.1081897

Nicola Guarino, P. G. (1995). *Ontologies and knowledge bases : towards a terminological clarification Ontologies and Knowledge Bases.* IOS Press.

Nonnecke, B., & Preece, J. (2003). Silent participants: Getting to know lurkers better. *From Usenet to CoWebs: Interacting with Social Information Spaces,* 110-132.

Nonnecke, B., Andrews, D., & Preece, J. (2006). Non-public and public online community participation: Needs, attitudes and behavior. *Electronic Commerce Research, 6*(1), 7–20. doi:10.100710660-006-5985-x

Nosek, T. M. (2007). A serious gaming/immersion environment to teach clinical cancer genetics. *Studies in Health Technology and Informatics, 125*, 355–360. PMID:17377303

Ohannessian, R., Duong, T. A., & Odone, A. (2020). Global telemedicine implementation and integration within health systems to fight the COVID-19 pandemic: A call to action. *JMIR Public Health and Surveillance, 6*(2), e18810. doi:10.2196/18810 PMID:32238336

Ortiz, B. I. L. (2012). *Issues in problem-based learning in online teacher education. In The role of criticism in understanding problem solving.* Springer.

Othman, H. R., Ali, D. M., Yusof, N. A. M., Noh, K. S. S. K. M., & Idris, A. (2014, August). Performance analysis of VoIP over mobile WiMAX (IEEE 802.16 e) best-effort class. In *Control and System Graduate Research Colloquium (ICSGRC), 2014 IEEE 5th* (pp. 130-135). IEEE.

Ott, M., & Pozzi, F. (2011). Towards a new era for cultural heritage education: Discussing the role of ict. *Computers in Human Behavior, 27*(4), 1365–1371. doi:10.1016/j.chb.2010.07.031

Overskeid, G. (2016). Systemizing in autism: The case for an emotional mechanism. *New Ideas in Psychology, 41*, 18–22. doi:10.1016/j.newideapsych.2016.01.001

Pagliarini, S. N., Bhuin, S., Isgenc, M. M., Biswas, A. K., Pileggi, L. J. I. T. o. N. N., & Systems, L. (2019). *A Probabilistic Synapse With Strained MTJs for Spiking Neural Networks.* Academic Press.

Paint 3D. (n.d.). Retrieved from https://en.wikipedia.org/wiki/Paint_3D

Pan, T.-Y., Kuo, C.-H., Liu, H.-T., & Hu, M.-C. J. I. T. o. E. T. i. C. I. (2018). *Handwriting trajectory reconstruction using low-cost imu.* Academic Press.

Papasin, R., Betts, B. J., Del Mundo, R., Guerrero, M., Mah, R. W., McIntosh, D. M., & Wilson, E. (2003). Intelligent Virtual Station. *Proceedings of 7th International Symposium on Artificial Intelligence, Robotics and Automation in Space.*

Park, J., Lee, J., & Jeon, D. J. I. J. o. S.-S. C. (2019). *A 65-nm Neuromorphic Image Classification Processor With Energy-Efficient Training Through Direct Spike-Only Feedback.* Academic Press.

Pattanayak, S. S., Pradhan, S. K., & Mallik, R. C. (2020). Printed Odia Symbols for Character Recognition: A Database Study. In Advanced Computing and Intelligent Engineering (pp. 297-307). Springer. doi:10.1007/978-981-15-1081-6_25

Peirce, C. S. (1978). *Écrits sur le signe.* Seuil.

Peng, F., & Zhai, J. (2017). A mobile augmented reality system for exhibition hall based on Vuforia. *2nd International Conference on Image, Vision and Computing (ICIVC),* 1049-1052.

Peterson, N. A., Speer, P. W., & McMillan, D. W. (2008). Validation of a brief sense of community scale: Confirmation of the principal theory of sense of community. *Journal of Community Psychology, 36*(1), 61–73. doi:10.1002/jcop.20217

Pilapitiya, S. U. (2017). Appropriate Ontology Matching Algorithm. IEEE.

Pirbhulal, S., Samuel, O. W., Wu, W., Sangaiah, A. K., & Li, G. (2019). A joint resource-aware and medical data security framework for wearable healthcare systems. *Future Generation Computer Systems, 95,* 382–391. doi:10.1016/j.future.2019.01.008

Pirlo, G., & Impedovo, D. J. I. T. o. F. S. (2011). *Fuzzy-zoning-based classification for handwritten characters.* Academic Press.

Ponce-Hernandez, W., Blanco-Gonzalo, R., Liu-Jimenez, J., & Sanchez-Reillo, R. J. I. A. (2020). *Fuzzy Vault Scheme Based on Fixed-Length Templates Applied to Dynamic Signature Verification.* Academic Press.

Powazek, D. M. (2002). *Design for community: The art of connecting real people in virtual places.* New Riders.

Pramanik, R., & Bag, S. J. I. I. P. (2020). *Segmentation-based recognition system for handwritten Bangla and Devanagari words using conventional classification and transfer learning.* Academic Press.

Preece, J. (1998). Empathic communities: Reaching out across the web. *Interaction, 5*(2), 43. doi:10.1145/274430.274435

Preece, J. (2003). Tacit knowledge and social capital: Supporting sociability in online communities of practice. *Proceedings of I-KNOW, 3,* 2-4.

Preece, J. (2008). An event-driven community in washington, DC: Forces that influence participation. In M. Foth (Ed.), *Handbook of research on urban informatics: The practice and promise of the real-time city.* IGI Global.

Preece, J., Nonnecke, B., & Andrews, D. (2004). The top 5 reasons for lurking: Improving community experiences for everyone. *Computers in Human Behavior, 2*(1), 42. doi:10.1016/j.chb.2003.10.015

Pretzsch, H., Biber, P., & Dursky, J. (2002). The single tree based stand simulator SILVA. Construction, lication and evaluation. *Forest Ecology and Management, 162*(1), 3–21. doi:10.1016/S0378-1127(02)00047-6

Priori, A., Mameli, F., Cogiamanian, F., Marceglia, S., Tiriticco, M., Mrakic-Sposta, S., Ferrucci, R., Zago, S., Polezzi, D., & Sartori, G. (2008). Lie-specific involvement of dorsolateral prefrontal cortex in deception. *Cerebral Cortex (New York, N.Y.), 18*(2), 451–455. doi:10.1093/cercor/bhm088 PMID:17584853

Qiu, J., Zhou, Y., Wang, Q., Ruan, T., & Gao, J. J. I. T. o. N. (2019). *Chinese clinical named entity recognition using residual dilated convolutional neural network with conditional random field.* Academic Press.

Reddy & Khare. (2017). *A Smart Ambulance System.* Academic Press.

Rehman, K. U. U., & Khan, Y. D. J. I. A. (2019). *A Scale and Rotation Invariant Urdu Nastalique Ligature Recognition Using Cascade Forward Backpropagation Neural Network*. Academic Press.

Ren, X., Zhou, Y., Huang, Z., Sun, J., Yang, X., & Chen, K. J. I. A. (2017). *A novel text structure feature extractor for Chinese scene text detection and recognition*. Academic Press.

Ren, Y., Wang, C., Chen, Y., Chuah, M. C., & Yang, J. J. I. T. o. M. C. (2019). *Signature verification using critical segments for securing mobile transactions*. Academic Press.

Reuter, M., & Montag, C. (2016). *Neuroeconomics—An introduction. In Neuroeconomics*. Springer. doi:10.1007/978-3-642-35923-1

Richter & Raška. (n.d.). Influence of Augmented Reality on Purchase Intention", Master Thesis in International Marketing, http://hj.diva-portal.org/smash/get/diva2:1115470/FULLTEXT01.pdf

Roddick, J. F., & Spiliopoulou, M. (2002). A survey of temporal knowledge discovery paradigms and methods. *IEEE Transactions on KDE, 14*(4), 750–767. doi:10.1109/TKDE.2002.1019212

Rossi, F., De Carvalho, F., Lechevallier, Y., & Da Silva, A. (2006a). Comparaison de dissimilarités pour l'analyse de l'usage d'un site web. EGC 2006. *RNTI-E, 6*(II), 409–414.

Rossi, F., De Carvalho, F., Lechevallier, Y., & Da Silva, A. (2006b). Dissimilarities for web usage mining. *IFCS, 2006*, 39–46.

Rossmann, J., & Sommer, B. (2008). The Virtual Testbed: Latest Virtual Reality Technologies for Space Robotic Applications. *CDROM-Proceedings of 9th International Symposium on Artificial Intelligence, Robotics and Automation in Space (i-SAIRAS 2008)*.

Rossmann, J. (1999). Projective Virtual Reality: Bridging the Gap between Virtual Reality and Robotics. *IEEE Transactions on Robotics and Automation, 15*(3), 411–422. doi:10.1109/70.768175

Roth, M., Rieß, P., & Reiners, D. (2006). Load Balancing on Cluster-Based Multi Projector Display Systems. *Proceedings of the International Conference in Central Europe on Computer Graphics WSCG*.

Rottet, S. M. (1974). Gaming as a learning strategy. *Journal of Continuing Education in Nursing, 5*(6), 22–25. PMID:4497850

Rua, H., & Alvito, P. (2011). Living the past: 3d models, virtual reality and game engines as tools for supporting archaeology and the reconstruction of cultural heritage–the casestudy of the roman villa of casal de freiria. *Journal of Archaeological Science, 38*(12), 3296–3308. doi:10.1016/j.jas.2011.07.015

Saha Raun, & Saha. (2017). *Monitoring Patient's Health with Smart Ambulance system using Internet of Things (IOTs)*. IEEE.

Saha, Raun, & Saha. (2017). Monitoring Patient"s Health with Smart Ambulance system using Internet of Things (IOTs). *8th Annual Industrial Automation and Electromechanical Engineering Conference (IEMECON)*.

Sahare, P., & Dhok, S. B. J. I. a. (2018). Multilingual character segmentation and recognition schemes for Indian document images. *6*, 10603-10617.

Sahlol, A. T., Abd Elaziz, M., Al-Qaness, M. A., & Kim, S. J. I. A. (2020). *Handwritten Arabic Optical Character Recognition Approach Based on Hybrid Whale Optimization Algorithm With Neighborhood Rough Set*. Academic Press.

Sahoo, S., & Lakshmi, R. (2020). *Offline handwritten character classification of the same scriptural family languages by using transfer learning techniques*. Paper presented at the 2020 3rd International Conference on Emerging Technologies in Computer Engineering: Machine Learning and Internet of Things (ICETCE).

Sahoo, R. C., & Pradhan, S. K. Pattern Storage and Recalling Analysis of Hopfield Network for Handwritten Odia Characters Using HOG. In *Advances in Machine Learning and Computational Intelligence* (pp. 467–476). Springer.

Samani & Zhu. (2016). Robotic Automatetd External Defibrillator Ambulance for Emergency Medical Service in Smart Cities. *IEEE Access, 4*.

Schuh, L., Burdette, D. E., Schultz, L., & Silver, B. (2008). Learning clinical neurophysiology: Gaming is better than lectures. *Journal of Clinical Neurophysiology, 25*(3), 167–169. doi:10.1097/WNP.0b013e31817759b3 PMID:18469726

Seitz, R. J., Nickel, J., & Azari, N. P. (2006). Functional modularity of the medial prefrontal cortex: Involvement in human empathy. *Neuropsychology, 20*(6), 743–751. doi:10.1037/0894-4105.20.6.743 PMID:17100519

Selvi, S. A., Rajesh, R. S., & Ajisha, M. A. T. (2019, December). An Efficient Communication Scheme for Wi-Li-Fi Network Framework. In *2019 Third International conference on I-SMAC (IoT in Social, Mobile, Analytics and Cloud) (I-SMAC)* (pp. 697-701). IEEE.

Sethy, A., & Patra, P. K. (2020). R-HOG Feature-Based Off-Line Odia Handwritten Character Recognition. In *Examining Fractal Image Processing and Analysis* (pp. 196–210). IGI Global. doi:10.4018/978-1-7998-0066-8.ch010

Sethy, A., Patra, P. K., & Nayak, D. R. (2018). Off-line handwritten Odia character recognition using DWT and PCA. In *Progress in Advanced Computing and Intelligent Engineering* (pp. 187–195). Springer. doi:10.1007/978-981-10-6872-0_18

Shahida, T. D., Othman, M., & Khazani, M. (2007). Routing algorithms in optical multistage interconnection networks. *World Engineering Congress*.

Shaik, Bowen, Bole, Kunzi, Bruce, Abdelgawad, & Yelamarthi. (2018). Smart Car: An IoT Based Accident Detection System. *2018 IEEE Global Conference on Internet of Things (GCIoT)*.

Shamay-Tsoory, S. G., Tomer, R., Berger, B. D., & Aharon-Peretz, J. (2003). Characterization of empathy deficits following prefrontal brain damage: The role of the right ventromedial prefrontal cortex. *Journal of Cognitive Neuroscience, 15*(3), 324–337. doi:10.1162/089892903321593063 PMID:12729486

Shao, L., Li, M., Yuan, L., & Gui, G. J. I. A. (2019). *InMAS: Deep learning for designing intelligent making system*. Academic Press.

Shao, L., Liang, C., Wang, K., Cao, W., Zhang, W., Gui, G., & Sari, H. J. I. A. (2019). *Attention GAN-based method for designing intelligent making system*. Academic Press.

Sharma, A. J. V. J. o. C. S. (2015). *A combined static and dynamic feature extraction technique to recognize handwritten digits*. Academic Press.

Shneiderman, B. (2002). *Leonardo's laptop: Human needs and the new computing technologies*. MIT Press.

Shukla, U., Mishra, A., Jasmine, S. G., Vaidehi, V., & Ganesan, S. (2019, January 1). A Deep Neural Network Framework for Road Side Analysis and Lane Detection. *Procedia Computer Science, 165*, 252–258. doi:10.1016/j.procs.2020.01.081

Shute, V. J. (2009). Melding the power of serious games and embedded assessment to monitor and foster learning. In U. Ritterfeld, M. Cody, & P. Vorderer (Eds.), *Serious Games Mechanisms and Effects*. Routledge Publishers.

Singh, A., Bacchuwar, K., Bhasin, A. J. I. J. o. M. L., & Computing. (2012). *A survey of OCR applications*. Academic Press.

Smith, M. K., Systems, E. D., Welty, C., & Mcguinness, D. L. (2009). OWL Web Ontology Language Guide. *W3C Recommendation*, 1–40.

Smith, A. D. (1999). Problems of conflict management in virtual communities. In M. A. Smith & P. Kollock (Eds.), *Communities in cyberspace* (pp. 134–163). Routledge. doi:10.5117/9789056290818

Smoyak, S. A. (1977). Use of gaming simulation by health care professionals. *Health Education Monographs, 5*(1_suppl), 11–17. doi:10.1177/10901981770050S103 PMID:870454

Spiliopoulou, M., Ntoutsi, I., Theodoridis, Y., & Schult, R. (2006). Monic: modeling and monitoring cluster transitions. *Proceedings of the Twelfth ACM SIGKDD International Conference on Knowledge Discovery and Data Mining.*

Sprott, J. C. (2006). *Physics Demonstrations: A sourcebook for teachers of physics.* Univ of Wisconsin Press.

Srihari, S. N., Cha, S.-H., Arora, H., & Lee, S. J. J. o. f. s. (2002). *Individuality of handwriting.* Academic Press.

Srimathi, B., & Ananthkumar, T. (2020). Li-Fi Based Automated Patient Healthcare Monitoring System. *Indian Journal of Public Health Research & Development, 11*(2), 387–392. doi:10.37506/v11/i2/2020/ijphrd/194832

Stapleton, A. J. (2004). Serious games: serious opportunities. *Proceedings of Australian*Game Developers' Conference.

Stutsky, B. J. (2009). *Empowerment and Leadership Development in an Online Story-Based Learning Community.* Academic Press.

Styliani, S., Fotis, L., Kostas, K., & Petros, P. (2009). Virtual museums, a survey and some issues for consideration. *Journal of Cultural Heritage, 10*(4), 520–528. doi:10.1016/j.culher.2009.03.003

Suchman, L. A. (1987). *Plans and situated actions: The problem of human-machine communication.* Cambridge, UK: Cambridge University Press.

Suchman, L. A. (2007). *Human-machine reconfigurations: Plans and situated actions.* Cambridge University Press.

Sulaiman, A., Omar, K., Nasrudin, M. F., & Arram, A. J. I. A. (2019). *Length Independent Writer Identification Based on the Fusion of Deep and Hand-Crafted Descriptors.* Academic Press.

Tanasa, D., & Trousse, B. (2004). Advanced data preprocessing for intersites web usage mining. *IEEE Intelligent Systems, 19*(2), 59–65. doi:10.1109/MIS.2004.1274912

Tang, Y., & Wu, X. J. I. T. o. M. (2018). *Scene text detection using superpixel-based stroke feature transform and deep learning based region classification.* Academic Press.

Tao, D., Lin, X., Jin, L., & Li, X. J. I. t. o. c. (2015). *Principal component 2-D long short-term memory for font recognition on single Chinese characters.* Academic Press.

Tatzgern, M. (2015). *Situated visualization in augmented reality* (Ph.D. dissertation). Graz University of Technology.

Telner, D. (2010). Game-based versus traditional case-based learning: Comparing effectiveness in stroke continuing medical education. *Can. Fam. Phys., 56*(9), e345–e351. PMID:20841574

Terlikkas, C., & Poullis, C. (2014). Towards a more effective way of presenting virtual re- ality museums exhibits. *2014 International Conference on Computer Vision Theory and Applications (VISAPP)*, 237–241.

Tilty, Mary, & Baspin. (2017). Shopping Application using Augmented Reality. *International Journal of Interdisciplinary Research, 3*(3).

Tisseron, S. (1995). *Psychanalyse de l'image – Des premiers traits au virtuel* (2nd ed.). Dunod.

Tisseron, S. (1996). *Le bonheur dans l'image.* Les empêcheurs de penser en rond.

Tobar-Muñoz, H., Fabregat, R., & Baldiris, S. (2014). Using a videogame with AR for an inclusive logical skill learning session. *2014 International Symposium on Computers in Education (SIIE)*, 189–194. 10.1109/SIIE.2014.7017728

Tolosana, R., Vera-Rodriguez, R., Fierrez, J., & Ortega-Garcia, J. J. I. T. o. I. F., & Security. (2020). BioTouchPass2. *Touchscreen Password Biometrics Using Time-Aligned Recurrent Neural Networks*, *15*, 2616–2628.

Toumanidis, L., Karapetros, P., Giannousis, C., Kogias, D. G., & Feidakis, M. (2019). Developing the museum-monumental experience from linear to inter- active using chatbots. In *Strategic Innovative Marketing and Tourism* (pp. 1159–1167). Springer. doi:10.1007/978-3-030-12453-3_133

Tsai, C., Shen, P., & Chiang, Y. (2015). Meeting ex-partners on facebook: Users' anxiety and severity of depression. *Behaviour & Information Technology*, *34*(7), 668–677. doi:10.1080/0144929X.2014.981585

Tseng, J., Tsai, Y., & Chao, R. (2013). Enhancing L2 interaction in avatar-based virtual worlds: Student teachers' perceptions. *Australasian Journal of Educational Technology*, *29*(3). Advance online publication. doi:10.14742/ajet.283

Tsiftsis, T., Sandalidis, H., Karagiannidis, G., & Uysal, M. (2009). Optical wireless links with spatial diversity over strong atmospheric turbulence channels. *IEEE Transactions on Wireless Communications*, *8*(2), 951–957. doi:10.1109/TWC.2009.071318

Udawant, Thombare, Chauhan, Hadke, & Waghole. (2017). Smart Ambulance System using IoT. In *2017 International Conference on Big Data, IoT and Data Science (BID)*. Vishwakarma Institute of Technology.

UNESCO. (2005). *Information and communication technologies in schools - a handbook for teachers*. UNESCO.

van Rijsbergen, C. J. (1979). *Information Retrieval* (2nd ed.). Butterworths.

Vas, G. K. R. (2006). Ontology based adaptive examination system in E-learning environment. *28th International Conference on Information Technology Interfaces*. 10.1109/ITI.2006.1708455

Venugopal, V., & Sundaram, S. J. I. B. (2020). *Online writer identification system using adaptive sparse representation framework*. Academic Press.

Venugopal, D. G. R. A. (2015). A Study On Verbalization Of OWL Axioms Using Controlled Natural Language Cite this Research Publication. *International Journal of Applied Engineering Research*, *10*(7), 16953–16960.

Verge. (n.d.). https://www.theverge.com/2018/2/5/16966530/intel-vaunt-smart-glasses-announced-ar-video

Vishal Jain, M. S. (2013). Ontology Development and Query Retrieval using Protégé Tool. *International Journal of Intelligent Systems and Applications*, *9*(9), 67–75. doi:10.5815/ijisa.2013.09.08

Vive. (n.d.). https://www.vive.com/sea/product/#vive

Von Helmholtz, H. (1867). Handbuch der physiologischen Optik. Academic Press.

Vuforia. (2020). *About Vuforia*. Retrieved from https://developer.vuforia.com/

Wagner, D., Schmalstieg, D., & Billinghurst, M. (2006). Handheld AR for Collaborative Edutainment. *Proc. 16th Int'l Conf. Artificial Reality and Telexistence (ICAT 06)*, 85-96.

Wallace, P. M. (1999). *The psychology of the internet*. Cambridge University Press. doi:10.1017/CBO9780511581670

Wang, F., Guo, Q., Lei, J., & Zhang, J. J. I. C. V. (2017). *Convolutional recurrent neural networks with hidden Markov model bootstrap for scene text recognition*. Academic Press.

Wang, Q.-F., Yin, F., Liu, C.-L. J. I. t. o. p. a., & Intelligence, M. (2011). *Handwritten Chinese text recognition by integrating multiple contexts*. Academic Press.

Wang, Wang, & Sohraby. (2016). Multimedia sensing as a service (MSaaS): exploring resource saving potentials of at cloud edge IoTs and Fogs. *IEEE Internet of Things Journal, 4*, 487-495.

Wargo, C. A. (2000). Blood clot: Gaming to reinforce learning about disseminated intravascular coagulation. *Journal of Continuing Education in Nursing, 31*(4), 149–151. doi:10.3928/0022-0124-20000701-04 PMID:11261156

Warthan, J. G., & McMillan, R. M. (1983). OCR/Variable head slot reader. Google Patents.

Wei, X., Weng, D., Liu, Y., & Wang, Y. (2015). Teaching based on AR for a technical creative design course. *Computers & Education, 81*, 221–234. doi:10.1016/j.compedu.2014.10.017

Weldegebriel, H. T., Liu, H., Haq, A. U., Bugingo, E., & Zhang, D. J. I. A. (2019). *A New Hybrid Convolutional Neural Network and eXtreme Gradient Boosting Classifier for Recognizing Handwritten Ethiopian Characters*. Academic Press.

Westervelt, H. J., Ruffolo, J. S., & Tremont, G. (2005). Assessing olfaction in the neuropsychological exam: The relationship between odor identification and cognition in older adults. *Archives of Clinical Neuropsychology: The Official Journal of the National Academy of Neuropsychologists, 20*(6), 761–769. doi:10.1016/j.acn.2005.04.010 PMID:15951153

Wheelwright, S., Baron-Cohen, S., Goldenfeld, N., Delaney, J., Fine, D., Smith, R., Weil, L., & Wakabayashi, A. (2006). Predicting autism spectrum quotient (AQ) from the systemizing quotient-revised (SQ-R) and empathy quotient (EQ). *Brain Research, 1079*(1), 47–56. doi:10.1016/j.brainres.2006.01.012 PMID:16473340

White, S., & Feiner, S. (2009a). Sitelens: situated visualization techniques for urban site visits. *Proceedings of the SIGCHI conference on human factors in computing systems*, 1117–1120. 10.1145/1518701.1518871

White, S., & Feiner, S. (2009b). *Interaction and presentation techniques for situated visualization*. Columbia University.

Williamson, I. A., Hughes, T. W., Minkov, M., Bartlett, B., Pai, S., & Fan, S. J. I. J. o. S. T. i. Q. E. (2019). *Reprogrammable electro-optic nonlinear activation functions for optical neural networks*. Academic Press.

Wokke, F. J. P., & Pronk, Z. (2000) Mission Validation and Training Facility for the European Robotic Arm (ERA). *Proceedings of SESP 2000, 6th International Workshop on Simulation for European Space Programmes*. https://www.accenture.com/gb-en/blogs/blogs-long-time-no-speak

Wu, Y., Shivakumara, P., Lu, T., Tan, C. L., Blumenstein, M., & Kumar, G. H. J. I. T. o. I. P. (2016). *Contour restoration of text components for recognition in video/scene images*. Academic Press.

Wu, G., Tang, G., Wang, Z., Zhang, Z., & Wang, Z. J. I. A. (2019). *An Attention-Based BiLSTM-CRF Model for Chinese Clinic Named Entity Recognition*. Academic Press.

Wu, H., Lee, S. W., Chang, H., & Liang, J. (2013). Current status, opportunities and challenges of AR in education. *Computers & Education, 62*, 41–49. doi:10.1016/j.compedu.2012.10.024

Wu, X., Chen, Q., You, J., & Xiao, Y. J. I. S. P. L. (2019). *Unconstrained Offline Handwritten Word Recognition by Position Embedding Integrated ResNets Model*. Academic Press.

Xiang, Z., You, Z., Qian, M., Zhang, J., Hu, X. J. E. J. o. I., & Processing, V. (2018). *Metal stamping character recognition algorithm based on multi-directional illumination image fusion enhancement technology*. Academic Press.

Xue, H. G. (2008). Research on the Building and Reasoning of Travel Ontology. In *International Symposium on Intelligent Information Technology Application Workshops* (pp. 1–2). 10.1109/IITA.Workshops.2008.162

Xu, L., Wang, Y., Li, X., & Pan, M. J. I. A. (2019). *Recognition of Handwritten Chinese Characters Based on Concept Learning*. Academic Press.

Yang, F., Jin, L., Lai, S., Gao, X., & Li, Z. J. I. A. (2019). *Fully convolutional sequence recognition network for water meter number reading*. Academic Press.

Yang, Y., Li, D., & Duan, Z. J. I. I. T. S. (2017). *Chinese vehicle license plate recognition using kernel-based extreme learning machine with deep convolutional features*. Academic Press.

Yang, H., Parthasarathy, S., & Mehta, S. (2005). A generalized framework for mining spatiotemporal patterns in scientific data. *KDD '05: Proceedings of the eleventh ACM SIGKDD international conference on Knowledge discovery in data mining*, 716–721. 10.1145/1081870.1081962

Yew, H. T., Ng, M. F., Ping, S. Z., Chung, S. K., Chekima, A., & Dargham, J. A. (2020, February). IoT Based Real-Time Remote Patient Monitoring System. In *2020 16th IEEE International Colloquium on Signal Processing & Its Applications (CSPA)* (pp. 176-179). IEEE.

Zang, Y., Chen, M., Yang, S., & Chen, H. J. I. J. o. S. T. i. Q. E. (2019). *Electro-optical neural networks based on time-stretch method*. Academic Press.

Zanto, T. P., Rubens, M. T., Thangavel, A., & Gazzaley, A. (2011). Causal role of the prefrontal cortex in top-down modulation of visual processing and working memory. *Nature Neuroscience*, *14*(5), 656–661. doi:10.1038/nn.2773 PMID:21441920

Zhang, J., Du, J., & Dai, L. J. I. T. o. M. (2018). *Track, attend, and parse (tap): An end-to-end framework for online handwritten mathematical expression recognition*. Academic Press.

Zhang, J., Li, Y., Li, T., Xun, L., & Shan, C. J. I. S. J. (2019). *License plate localization in unconstrained scenes using a two-stage CNN-RNN*. Academic Press.

Zhang, X.-Y., Yin, F., Zhang, Y.-M., Liu, C.-L., Bengio, Y. J. I. t. o. p. a., & Intelligence, M. (2017). *Drawing and recognizing chinese characters with recurrent neural network*. Academic Press.

Zhang, Y., Lu, J., Wang, K., Zhao, J., Cui, G., & Gao, X. J. I. A. (2020). *Dimensionality Reduction Method for 3D-Handwritten Characters Based on Oriented Bounding Boxes*. Academic Press.

Zhang, J., Bi, H., Chen, Y., Wang, M., Han, L., & Cai, L. J. I. I. T. J. (2019). SmartHandwriting. *Handwritten Chinese Character Recognition With Smartwatch.*, *7*(2), 960–970.

Zhao, L., Zhang, X., & Zhang, X. (2017). Intelligent analysis oriented surveillance video coding. *IEEE International Conference on Multimedia and Expo (ICME)*, 37-42. 10.1109/ICME.2017.8019429

Zhao, H., Chu, H., Zhang, Y., & Jia, Y. J. I. A. (2020). *Improvement of Ancient Shui Character Recognition Model Based on Convolutional Neural Network*. Academic Press.

Zhenzhen, Zhu, & Jing. (2009). Differential SpaceTime-Frequency Transmission for Amplify-and-Forward Asynchronous Cooperative Communications. *Journal of Xi'an Jiaotong University*.

Zhou, X.-D., Wang, D.-H., Tian, F., Liu, C.-L., Nakagawa, M. J. I. T. o. P. A., & Intelligence, M. (2013). *Handwritten Chinese/Japanese text recognition using semi-Markov conditional random fields*. Academic Press.

Zuo, L.-Q., Sun, H.-M., Mao, Q.-C., Qi, R., & Jia, R.-S. J. I. A. (2019). *Natural scene text recognition based on encoder-decoder framework*. Academic Press.

About the Contributors

Amit Kumar Tyagi is Assistant Professor (Senior Grade), and Senior Researcher at Vellore Institute of Technology (VIT), Chennai Campus, India. He received his Ph.D. Degree in 2018 from Pondicherry Central University, India. He joined the Lord Krishna College of Engineering, Ghaziabad (LKCE) for the periods of 2009-2010, and 2012-2013. Also, he was an Assistant Professor and Head- Research, Lingaya's Vidyapeeth (formerly known as Lingaya's University), Faridabad, Haryana, India in 2018-2019. His current research focuses on Machine Learning with Big data, Blockchain Technology, Data Science, Cyber Physical Systems, Smart and Secure Computing and Privacy. He has contributed to several projects such as "AARIN" and "P3- Block" to address some of the open issues related to the privacy breaches in Vehicular Applications (such as Parking) and Medical Cyber Physical Systems (MCPS). Also, he has published more than 8 patents in the area of Deep Learning, Internet of Things, Cyber Physical Systems and Computer Vision. Recently, he has awarded best paper award for paper titled "A Novel Feature Extractor Based on the Modified Approach of Histogram of oriented Gradient", ICCSA 2020, Italy (Europe). He is a regular member of the MIRLabs, ACM and IEEE.

* * *

L. Jani Anbarasi is an Assistant Professor (Senior) in School of Computer Science and Engineering, Vellore Institute of Technology, Chennai, India. She has received B.E., from Manonmanium Sundaranar University, India in 2000 and M.E., and Ph.D. degrees from Anna University, India in 2005 and 2015, respectively. She has published more than 50 papers in reputed International Conferences and refereed Journals. Her research interests include Visual Cryptography, Image Processing and Medical applications. Steganography, Watermarking, Multimedia 3D Model Security, and Artificial Intelligence and Machine Learning. She serves as a Life Member in ISTE, ACM bodies. She has received best paper awards in IEEE International Conference on Computational Intelligence and Computing Research in 2017.

T. S. Arun Samuel received B.E degree in Electronics and Communication Engineering from Syed Ammal Engineering College (2004) and M.E degree in Computer and communication engineering from National Engineering College (2006). He has awarded a Ph.D. on Nanoelectronic Devies (2014) from Thiagarajar College of Engineering, Tamilnadu, India, under Anna University Chennai. He is currently working at National Engineering College, Kovilpatti, India, as Associate Professor. He has authored more than 50 research articles in National & International Journals and Conferences, including SCI and Scopus indexed journals. He is the life member of the Institute of Engineering (IE), India, and a member of IEEE.

Mohan B. A. is an Associate Professor in Dept. of CS&E at NMIT. He has total 15 years of experience both in research and teaching. He has done his B.E in BMS Evening College, M.Tech in SJCE Mysore and Ph.D. in VTU University under the guidance of Dr. Sarojadevi H, (Ph.D. in IISc) currently working as Professor in Dept. CS&E at NMIT. His area of interest are Wireless Sensor Network, Cloud Computing and Blockchain. He has done few certifications like "Linux System Administration" and "Data Centre Technical Specialist" by Novell, Cisco certified Network Associate (CCNA by Cisco), Java J2EE Certification by Wipro. He has been entitled as CCNA trainer by Cisco and certified faculty to teach Java J2EE by Wipro.

Puvvadi Baby Maruthi received Ph.D. degree from Sri Padmavati Mahila Visva Vidyalayam, Tirupati, in 2019. She completed Master of Computer Applications degree from JNTU Ananthapur in 2010. She is currently working as Assistant Professor at Sri Venkateswara College of Engineering, Tirupati. Her research interests include soft computing, information security, digital image processing, and Machine Learning. She got a gold medal in R programming in NPTEL. She has done few certifications in Python, SCILAB, Spatial Informatics by NPTEL.

Jonathan Bishop is an information technology executive, researcher and writer. He founded the newly expanded Centre for Research into Online Communities, E-Learning and Socialnomics in 2005, which is a partnership between members of the Crocels Community Media Group. Jonathan's research and development work generally falls within human-computer interaction. He has over 100 publications in this area, including on Internet trolling, digital addiction, affective computing, gamification; cyber-law, multimedia forensics, cyber-stalking; Classroom 2.0, School 3.0, Digital Teens. In addition to his BSc(Hons) in Multimedia Studies and postgraduate degrees in law, business, economics and e-learning, Jonathan serves in local government as a councillor, and has been a school governor and contested numerous elections, including to the UK Parliament and Welsh Assembly. He is a an FBCS CILIP, FInstAM, FRAI, FRSS, FRSA; SMIEEE, MIET, MACM, MIMarEST MarTech. He has prizes for literary skills and been a finalist in national and local competitions for his environmental, community and equality work, which often form part of action research studies. Jonathan enjoys music, swimming and chess.

Abhishek Das is currently doing his Ph.D. in the Department of Electronics and Communication Engineering, ITER, Siksha 'O' Anushandhan (Deemed to be University), Bhubaneswar, India. He has completed his Master's degree in 2016 from the same institution. His area of research includes Image Processing, Optical character recognition, Signal Processing, Speech synthesis, and Machine Learning.

Ajesh Faizal, Professor, Department of Computer Science and Engineering, Musaliar college of Engineering and Technology, Pathanamthitta, Kerala India (On leave). Received his bachelor degree Computer science and Engineering from Cochin University of science and Technology (CUSAT), Kerala, India in 2006, and obtained Masters in Computer science and Engineering from Anna University Chennai, Tamilnadu, India, in 2011. His research interests include Computer Networks, Medical Image Processing, Machine Learning and Artificial Intelligence. Published various international journals and attended many national and international conferences.

Roshan Fernandes is working as Associate Professor in the Department of Computer Science and Engineering at NMAM Institute of Technology, Nitte, India. His research interests include Natural Language Processing, Machine Learning, and Mobile Web Services.

Arjun Gaonkar is a Bachelor of Engineering Student, Department of Computer Science and Engineering NMAM Institute of Technology, Nitte.

S. Geetha received the B.E., from the Madurai Kamaraj University, M.E., and Ph.D. degrees in Computer Science and Engineering from Anna University, Chennai, in 2000, 2004 and 2011 respectively. She has 14+ years of teaching experience. Currently, she is a professor at School of Computing Science and Engineering at VIT-University, Chennai Campus. She has published more than 50 papers in reputed IEEE International Conferences and refereed Journals. She joins the review committee for IEEE Transactions on Information Forensics and Security and IEEE Transactions on Image Processing, Springer Multimedia Tools and Security, Elsevier – Information Sciences. She was an editor for the Indian Conference proceedings of ICCIIS 2007 and RISES-2013. Her research interests include multimedia security, intrusion detection systems, machine learning paradigms and information forensics. She is a recipient of University Rank and Academic Topper Award in B.E. and M.E. in 2000 and 2004 respectively. She is also a pride recipient of the "Best Academic Researcher Award 2013" of ASDF Global Awards.

Aayush Gupta is currently pursuing Bachelor of Technology in Computer Science and Engineering at Vellore Institute of Technology.

S. Graceline Jasmine has done Ph.D. from VIT University, Chennai. Presently, she is working as Assistant Professor at VIT Chennai. She has published more than 15 research articles in international journal/conferences. Her area of interest includes Remotely Sensed Image processing, Game Development, Artificial Intelligence and Machine Learning.

S. Vinila Jinny is working as an Associate Professor, Department of Computer Science and Engineering, Noorul Islam Centre for Higher Education, Kumaracoil. She received her B.E. degree in Computer Science and Engineering from M.S. University, Tirunelveli in 2004 and M.E degree in Computer Science and Engineering from Anna University, Chennai in 2006. She completed her Doctorate degree in 2016 from Noorul Islam Centre for Higher Education, Kumaracoil, India. She has 12 International publications in Journals and 30 papers in International Conferences to her credit. She is a Member of IEEE. Her field of interest includes data mining, Network Security, image processing. Have teaching experience of 13 years.

Deepak Kumar is presently working as Assistant Professor at AMITY University Uttar Pradesh, Noida, India. He also holds two government-sponsored research project as sole principal investigator namely "Hybrid Urban Landscape Analysis for Green Smart Cities through Geospatial Technology" sponsored from the Science and Engineering Research Board, Department of Science and Technology, Government of India and "Meta-sensing of the urban footprint from airborne synthetic aperture radar (ASAR) data" sponsored from Space Applications Centre (ISRO), Ahmedabad, Gujarat, India. Beyond these, his previous academic background is an amalgamation of computational sciences, geospatial technology, and engineering subjects. He has instructed various courses like Introduction to Geospatial

Technology, Spatial Data Analysis and Modeling, Remote Sensing and GIS Application to Human Settlement and Urban Planning, Thermal and Microwave Remote Sensing, Remote Sensing and GIS Application to Environmental Studies, Satellite-Based Navigation System & Cartography. He has been revisiting a wide range of issues associated with traditional research activities but has own ingest of thinking on other non-traditional/challenging areas/topics for exchange of research activities. More preciously his teaching and research interest lie in the area of Spatial Information Science, Spatial Data modelling and Analysis, Spatio-temporal Data Management & Geovisualization, Spatial and Fractal computing, Spatial Predictive analytics, Spatial cognition, Geoprivacy.

Mihir Narayan Mohanty is currently working as a Professor in the Department of Electronics and Communication Engineering, Institute of Technical Education and Research (FET), Siksha 'O' Anusandhan (Deemed to be University), Bhubaneswar, Odisha. He has received his M. Tech degree in Communication System Engineering from the Sambalpur University, Sambalpur, Odisha and obtained his PhD degree in Applied Signal Processing. He is the fellow of IE (I), and IETE. Also, he is the member of many professional societies including IEEE, IET etc. He has 25 years of teaching and research experience. He has published more than 300 papers in different Journals, Conferences including Book Chapters. He has authored two books. He is the successive reviewer of manuscripts from IEEE, Elsevier, Springer, IGI Global etc. His areas of research interests include Applied Signal and Image Processing, Speech Processing, Antenna, and Intelligent Signal Processing.

Vijaya Padmanabha is working as Assistant Professor in the Department of Mathematics and Computer Science, Modern College of Business and Science, Baushar, Muscat, Sultanate of Oman.

M. Pavithra is working as Assistant Professor in IFET college of Engineering affiliated to Anna University, Chennai.

Felix M. Philip is an Assistant Professor in Computer science and IT department at JAIN (Deemed-to-be University), Kochi. He has more than 9 years of teaching experience. His research interest includes Image Processing, Internet of Things.

Arya Vardhan Prasad is currently pursuing Bachelor of Technology in Computer Science and Engineering at Vellore Institute Of Technology.

P. Praveen Kumar completed his M.E. in Computer science and Engineering in Prist university and B.E. Computer Science and Engineering in Anna University. He is working as Assistant Professor in IFET College of Engineering, India. His area of interests include Networks, Architecture and data mining.

Vijayalakshmi R. received Ph.D (Information and Communication Engineering) degree from Anna University, Chennai in 2018.She Completed her M.E(Computer Science Engineering) degree in 2009 in Anna University, Chennai. She pursued her B.E. (Computer Science Engineering) degree in 1998 from Madras University. Having a rich teaching experience in the field of Computer Science and Engineering for nearly20 years. I currently work as an Associate Professor at Velammal College of Engineering and Technology, Madurai, India. My articles have been published in 23 international journals, 6 national journals. Additionally, I have presented papers in more than 35National and International conferences.

My area of Interests are Data Mining, image processing, pattern recognition, neural network. My research interests include computational model, Data structures, Operating systems and Networking. I am a Reviewer and Editor of many reputed journals. I am also a Life Member of ISTE, CSI, IAENG, IACSIT and UACEE.

Priya R. L. is currently working as an Assistant Professor in V.E.S Institute of Technology, Mumbai having 16 years of teaching experience for undergraduate students of Computer Engineering and Information Technology disciplines in different Engineering Institutes, was obtained her Master degree in Information Technology Engineering from Mumbai University. Also, she had worked as a Software Engineer in different firms in Chennai and Mumbai for 4 years. Her research interest is more into Internet of Things (IoT), Software engineering, Next Generation Networks and Artificial Intelligence.

Rajmohan Rajendirane is pursuing Ph.D at Anna University Working as Associate Professor in the department of CSE at IFET college of engineering Published more than 30 papers in reputed journal Reviewer for Springer journal of Supercomputing Received research fund from TNSCST Government of Tamilnadu Received best Educator Award from I2OR organization Received best project award from IEI chapter Permanent member of ISTE, CSI, IAENG.

Deepalakshmi Rajendran is a Professor at the Department of CSE, Velammal College of Engineering and Technology, Madurai, Tamil Nadu, India. She got a founded project from MNRE worth of 56 lakhs. She has published more than 75 research papers in various SCI and Scopus journals and conferences. She has published a two book entitled Introduction to Grid and Cloud Computing and Algorithm for Improving QoS in Optical Networks and more than 3 book chapters. She has 18 years of teaching experience. Her research interests are networking protocols, data mining and deep learning algorithms. She guided more than 50 UG projects and 20 PG projects and many projects won first prize in project competitions. Delivered more than 20 guest lectures in various government and self-finance institutions. She is Doctorial committee Member for Anna university PhD scholars. She is a reviewer and Editor of many reputed journals and also a Life Member of ISTE, CSI and IAENG.

Anisha Rodrigues is working as Assistant Professor in the Department of Computer Science and Engineering at NMAM Institute of Technology, Nitte, India. Her research interests include Natural Language Processing, Machine Learning, Big Data Analytics.

Aswathy S. U., Associate Professor, Computer Science & Engineering Department, Jyothi Engineering College, Thrissur, Kerala, India. She has received her B.Tech in Electronics and Instrumentation Engineering, M.Tech in Computer and Information Technology and Ph.D in Medical Image Processing during 2005, 2009, 2019 respectively. She is the reviewer of many international journals. She has published 18 articles in various SCI and Scopus indexed journals. Her main area of interest in Medical Image processing, Medical Image analysis, Machine learning, Nano technology and Bio Medical Engineering. She serves as the active member of Editorial board/ reviewer board of various international Journals.

Ananth Kumar T. received his Ph.D. degree in VLSI Design from Manonmaniam Sundaranar University, Tirunelveli. He received his Master's degree in VLSI Design from Anna University, Chennai and Bachelor's degree in Electronics and communication engineering from Anna University, Chennai. He is working as Assistant Professor in IFET college of Engineering afflicted to Anna University, Chennai. He has presented papers in various National and International Conferences and Journals. His fields of interest are Networks on Chips, Computer Architecture and ASIC design. He is the recipient of the Best Paper Award at INCODS 2017. He is the life member of ISTE, and few membership bodies.

Index

A

agent-based modeling 99, 101-103, 105-107, 115, 117
ambulance 42-56, 58-61, 63, 66-67
artefact 83, 173, 193, 218
Asthma 86-88, 94, 96-98
Augmented Reality 68, 71-74, 76, 79, 83-85, 118-121, 132, 149-151, 164, 206-207, 213-215, 217, 220-221, 223-225, 227, 229-230, 275-281

B

bandwidth efficiency 233, 237
bit error rate (BER) 233-234, 237, 241

C

COPD 86-88, 94, 96-97
COVID-19 149, 154, 195-196, 204, 278-279
cyberpsychology 165, 194

D

data analysis 100, 261
deep learning 1, 4, 7, 10, 15, 26, 28, 36-37, 39, 89, 95-96, 198
digital ecology 165
DL query 134, 136, 145-146
dynamic data mining 99-101

E

ecological cognition 165-173, 175-178, 180, 182, 184-189, 193
ecological cognition framework 166, 169-173, 176-178, 180, 182, 184-189, 193
Ecology 165, 229
Ecommerce Application 68
education 68, 83-84, 86, 88-89, 97, 100, 116, 118-120, 123, 129, 132-133, 147, 149, 151, 163-164, 182, 189-192, 198, 206, 213-214, 217, 221-222, 229-231, 276-278, 280-281
e-learning 79, 147, 165, 189
evolving data 261-262, 273

F

Frame Error Rate (FER) 233-234, 241

G

GPS 42, 48-50, 52, 54, 56, 61-63, 66, 72, 280
Growth with AR and VR 275
GSM 42, 48-50, 56, 204

H

handwritten recognition 1, 28
Hypermedia Seduction 193

I

implementation 10-11, 35, 50, 54, 75, 77, 95, 105, 115, 152, 190, 204, 229, 247-249, 272, 280

L

Learning Platform 118, 123
license plate recognition 4, 16, 34-35, 40
Li-Fi 195-205

M

machine learning 1, 15, 38-39, 71, 86-92, 94-98, 136, 147
MAX-NCSP 247-251, 258
media ecology 165
medical applications 9, 27, 68
Medium Access Control protocol 53, 233, 246

microcontroller 42, 44-45, 48, 51, 65, 198, 204
Mixed Reality 68-69, 77, 83, 207, 229, 276-279
Monte-Carlo method 99, 101, 108, 110
Multimedia Traffic 233, 246
mutual diversity 233-235, 237, 239, 242, 244

N

Natural scene text recognition 4, 41
neural network 1, 4, 6, 9-13, 15, 17-20, 22-24, 27, 29-
    31, 33, 35, 37-38, 40, 85-86, 89, 94-96

O

online community 165, 191
ontology 59, 116, 134-142, 145-147
Opportunities in AR and VR 275
optical character recognition 1-5, 12, 15, 17, 20-21,
    24, 34-36, 38
optimal camera placement 247-248
OWL 134-138, 146-147

P

pandemic 149, 154, 195, 200-201, 204, 277, 279
Parametric User Model 173, 194
patient monitoring 56-57, 195, 198-205
pneumonia 86, 88-89, 94, 97-98
Printed Text recognition 1
protégé tool 134-136, 142, 146-147

R

Radiation-less 195

respiratory illness 86-88, 92-94, 96, 98
RFID 42, 48, 51, 57, 62, 223
RNN 1, 15, 21-23, 25, 28, 32-34, 96

S

structure 4, 12-13, 16, 19-21, 38, 49, 57, 63-64, 87,
    89, 99, 102-104, 114, 138, 166, 184, 194, 198,
    220, 262, 264, 266, 269
Substance 194
System stability 99

U

Unity 3D 118, 123, 127

V

virtual 68-69, 71-75, 77-80, 83-85, 102-103, 118-119,
    121, 126-127, 148-152, 158, 160-168, 170-171,
    177, 179-180, 187-188, 190-193, 206-207, 212-
    218, 220-222, 225, 227-230, 232, 235, 247-249,
    251, 253, 260, 275-281
virtual ecology 165
Virtual Reality (VR) 77, 79, 118, 206, 275-276

W

Web Usage Mining (WUM) 261

Purchase Print, E-Book, or Print + E-Book

IGI Global's reference books are available in three unique pricing formats:
Print Only, E-Book Only, or Print + E-Book.
Shipping fees may apply.

www.igi-global.com

Recommended Reference Books

ISBN: 978-1-5225-5912-2
© 2019; 349 pp.
List Price: $215

ISBN: 978-1-5225-8176-5
© 2019; 2,218 pp.
List Price: $2,950

ISBN: 978-1-5225-7811-6
© 2019; 317 pp.
List Price: $225

ISBN: 978-1-5225-7268-8
© 2019; 316 pp.
List Price: $215

ISBN: 978-1-5225-7455-2
© 2019; 288 pp.
List Price: $205

ISBN: 978-1-5225-8973-0
© 2019; 200 pp.
List Price: $195

Do you want to stay current on the latest research trends, product announcements, news and special offers?
Join IGI Global's mailing list today and start enjoying exclusive perks sent only to IGI Global members.
Add your name to the list at **www.igi-global.com/newsletters.**

Publisher of Peer-Reviewed, Timely, and Innovative Academic Research

www.igi-global.com    Sign up at www.igi-global.com/newsletters    facebook.com/igiglobal    twitter.com/igiglobal    linkedin.com/igiglobal

Ensure Quality Research is Introduced to the Academic Community

Become an IGI Global Reviewer for Authored Book Projects

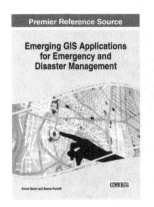
Premier Reference Source
Emerging GIS Applications for Emergency and Disaster Management

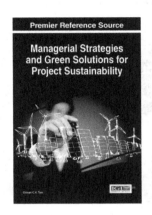
Premier Reference Source
Managerial Strategies and Green Solutions for Project Sustainability

Premier Reference Source
Comparative Approaches to Using R and Python for Statistical Data Analysis

Premier Reference Source
Solutions for High-Touch Communications in a High-Tech World

The overall success of an authored book project is dependent on quality and timely reviews.

In this competitive age of scholarly publishing, constructive and timely feedback significantly expedites the turnaround time of manuscripts from submission to acceptance, allowing the publication and discovery of forward-thinking research at a much more expeditious rate. Several IGI Global authored book projects are currently seeking highly-qualified experts in the field to fill vacancies on their respective editorial review boards:

Applications and Inquiries may be sent to:
development@igi-global.com

Applicants must have a doctorate (or an equivalent degree) as well as publishing and reviewing experience. Reviewers are asked to complete the open-ended evaluation questions with as much detail as possible in a timely, collegial, and constructive manner. All reviewers' tenures run for one-year terms on the editorial review boards and are expected to complete at least three reviews per term. Upon successful completion of this term, reviewers can be considered for an additional term.

If you have a colleague that may be interested in this opportunity, we encourage you to share this information with them.

IGI Global Proudly Partners With eContent Pro International

Receive a 25% Discount on all Editorial Services

Editorial Services

IGI Global expects all final manuscripts submitted for publication to be in their final form. This means they must be reviewed, revised, and professionally copy edited prior to their final submission. Not only does this support with accelerating the publication process, but it also ensures that the highest quality scholarly work can be disseminated.

English Language Copy Editing

Let eContent Pro International's expert copy editors perform edits on your manuscript to resolve spelling, punctuaion, grammar, syntax, flow, formatting issues and more.

Scientific and Scholarly Editing

Allow colleagues in your research area to examine the content of your manuscript and provide you with valuable feedback and suggestions before submission.

Figure, Table, Chart & Equation Conversions

Do you have poor quality figures? Do you need visual elements in your manuscript created or converted? A design expert can help!

Translation

Need your documjent translated into English? eContent Pro International's expert translators are fluent in English and more than 40 different languages.

Hear What Your Colleagues are Saying About Editorial Services Supported by IGI Global

"The service was very fast, very thorough, and very helpful in ensuring our chapter meets the criteria and requirements of the book's editors. I was quite impressed and happy with your service."

– Prof. Tom Brinthaupt,
Middle Tennessee State University, USA

"I found the work actually spectacular. The editing, formatting, and other checks were very thorough. The turnaround time was great as well. I will definitely use eContent Pro in the future."

– Nickanor Amwata, Lecturer,
University of Kurdistan Hawler, Iraq

"I was impressed that it was done timely, and wherever the content was not clear for the reader, the paper was improved with better readability for the audience."

– Prof. James Chilembwe,
Mzuzu University, Malawi

Email: customerservice@econtentpro.com

www.igi-global.com/editorial-service-partners

www.igi-global.com

Celebrating Over 30 Years of Scholarly
Knowledge Creation & Dissemination

InfoSci®-Books

A Database of Over 5,300+ Reference Books Containing Over 100,000+ Chapters Focusing on Emerging Research

GAIN ACCESS TO **THOUSANDS** OF
REFERENCE BOOKS AT **A FRACTION**
OF THEIR INDIVIDUAL LIST **PRICE**.

InfoSci®-Books Database

The **InfoSci®-Books** database is a collection of
over 5,300+ IGI Global single and multi-volume
reference books, handbooks of research, and
encyclopedias, encompassing groundbreaking
research from prominent experts worldwide that
span over 350+ topics in 11 core subject areas
including business, computer science, education,
science and engineering, social sciences and more.

Open Access Fee Waiver (Offset Model) Initiative

For any library that invests in IGI Global's InfoSci-Journals and/
or InfoSci-Books databases, IGI Global will match the library's
investment with a fund of equal value to go toward **subsidizing
the OA article processing charges (APCs) for their students,
faculty, and staff** at that institution when their work is submitted
and accepted under OA into an IGI Global journal.*

INFOSCI® PLATFORM FEATURES

- No DRM
- No Set-Up or Maintenance Fees
- A Guarantee of No More Than a
  5% Annual Increase
- Full-Text HTML and PDF
  Viewing Options
- Downloadable MARC Records
- Unlimited Simultaneous Access
- COUNTER 5 Compliant Reports
- Formatted Citations With Ability to
  Export to RefWorks and EasyBib
- No Embargo of Content (Research
  is Available Months in Advance of
  the Print Release)

*The fund will be offered on an annual basis and expire at the end of
the subscription period. The fund would renew as the subscription is
renewed for each year thereafter. The open access fees will be waived
after the student, faculty, or staff's paper has been vetted and accepted
into an IGI Global journal and the fund can only be used toward
publishing OA in an IGI Global journal. Libraries in developing countries
will have the match on their investment doubled.

To Learn More or To Purchase This Database:
www.igi-global.com/infosci-books

www.igi-global.com

eresources@igi-global.com • Toll Free: 1-866-342-6657 ext. 100 • Phone: 717-533-8845 x100

IGI Global
DISSEMINATOR OF KNOWLEDGE
www.igi-global.com

Publisher of Peer-Reviewed, Timely, and
Innovative Academic Research Since 1988

IGI Global's Transformative Open Access (OA) Model:
How to Turn Your University Library's Database Acquisitions Into a Source of OA Funding

In response to the OA movement and well in advance of Plan S, IGI Global, early last year, unveiled their OA Fee Waiver (Read & Publish) Initiative.

Under this initiative, librarians who invest in IGI Global's InfoSci-Books (5,300+ reference books) and/or InfoSci-Journals (185+ scholarly journals) databases will be able to subsidize their patron's OA article processing charges (APC) when their work is submitted and accepted (after the peer review process) into an IGI Global journal. *See website for details.

How Does it Work?

1. When a library subscribes or perpetually purchases IGI Global's InfoSci-Databases and/or their discipline/subject-focused subsets, IGI Global will match the library's investment with a fund of equal value to go toward subsidizing the OA article processing charges (APCs) for their patrons.

   Researchers: **Be sure to recommend the InfoSci-Books and InfoSci-Journals to take advantage of this initiative.**

2. When a student, faculty, or staff member submits a paper and it is accepted (following the peer review) into one of IGI Global's 185+ scholarly journals, the author will have the option to have their paper published under a traditional publishing model or as OA.

3. When the author chooses to have their paper published under OA, IGI Global will notify them of the OA Fee Waiver (Read and Publish) Initiative. If the author decides they would like to take advantage of this initiative, IGI Global will deduct the US$ 2,000 APC from the created fund.

4. This fund will be offered on an annual basis and will renew as the subscription is renewed for each year thereafter. IGI Global will manage the fund and award the APC waivers unless the librarian has a preference as to how the funds should be managed.

Hear From the Experts on This Initiative:

"I'm very happy to have been able to make one of my recent research contributions, "Visualizing the Social Media Conversations of a National Information Technology Professional Association" featured in the *International Journal of Human Capital and Information Technology Professionals*, freely available along with having access to the valuable resources found within IGI Global's InfoSci-Journals database."

– **Prof. Stuart Palmer**,
Deakin University, Australia

For More Information, Visit: www.igi-global.com/publish/contributor-resources/open-access/read-publish-model
or contact IGI Global's Database Team at eresources@igi-global.com.

Are You Ready to Publish Your Research?

IGI Global offers book authorship and editorship opportunities across 11 subject areas, including business, computer science, education, science and engineering, social sciences, and more!

Benefits of Publishing with IGI Global:

- Free one-on-one editorial and promotional support.

- Expedited publishing timelines that can take your book from start to finish in less than one (1) year.

- Choose from a variety of formats including: Edited and Authored References, Handbooks of Research, Encyclopedias, and Research Insights.

- Utilize IGI Global's eEditorial Discovery® submission system in support of conducting the submission and blind review process.

- IGI Global maintains a strict adherence to ethical practices due in part to our full membership with the Committee on Publication Ethics (COPE).

- Indexing potential in prestigious indices such as Scopus®, Web of Science™, PsycINFO®, and ERIC – Education Resources Information Center.

- Ability to connect your ORCID iD to your IGI Global publications.

- Earn royalties on your publication as well as receive complimentary copies and exclusive discounts.

Get Started Today by Contacting the Acquisitions Department at:

acquisition@igi-global.com

www.igi-global.com/infosci-ondemand

InfoSci®-OnDemand

Continuously updated with new material on a weekly basis, InfoSci®-OnDemand offers the ability to search through thousands of quality full-text research papers. Users can narrow each search by identifying key topic areas of interest, then display a complete listing of relevant papers, and purchase materials specific to their research needs.

Comprehensive Service

- Over 125,000+ journal articles, book chapters, and case studies.
- All content is downloadable in PDF and HTML format and can be stored locally for future use.

No Subscription Fees

- One time fee of $37.50 per PDF download.

Instant Access

- Receive a download link immediately after order completion!

"It really provides an excellent entry into the research literature of the field. It presents a manageable number of highly relevant sources on topics of interest to a wide range of researchers. The sources are scholarly, but also accessible to 'practitioners'."

- Lisa Stimatz, MLS, University of North Carolina at Chapel Hill, USA

"It is an excellent and well designed database which will facilitate research, publication, and teaching. It is a very useful tool to have."

- George Ditsa, PhD, University of Wollongong, Australia

"I have accessed the database and find it to be a valuable tool to the IT/IS community. I found valuable articles meeting my search criteria 95% of the time."

- Prof. Lynda Louis, Xavier University of Louisiana, USA

Recommended for use by researchers who wish to immediately download PDFs of individual chapters or articles.

www.igi-global.com/e-resources/infosci-ondemand

IGI Global
DISSEMINATOR OF KNOWLEDGE

www.igi-global.com

Printed in the United States
By Bookmasters